When We Began
There Were Witchmen

When We Began There Were Witchmen

*An Oral History
from Mount Kenya*

Jeffrey A. Fadiman

UNIVERSITY OF CALIFORNIA PRESS
Berkeley · Los Angeles · London

University of California Press
Berkeley and Los Angeles, California

University of California Press, Ltd.
London, England

© 1993 by
The Regents of the University of California

Library of Congress Cataloging-in-Publication Data

Fadiman, Jeffrey.

   When We Began There Were Witchmen : an oral history from
Mount Kenya / Jeffrey A. Fadiman.
      p. cm.
   Includes bibliographical references and index.
   ISBN 0-520-06507-7 (alk. paper); ISBN 0-520-08615-5 (pbk.: alk. paper)
   1. Meru (African people)—History. 2. Oral tradition—Kenya.
3. Witchcraft—Kenya.   I. Title.
DT433.545.M47F34   1993
967.62'0049639—dc20   92-12639
                                                              CIP

Printed in the United States of America
9   8   7   6   5   4   3   2   1

The paper used in this publication meets the minimum requirements
of American National Standard for Information Sciences—Permanence of Paper for Printed Library Materials, ANSI Z39.48-1984. ∞

To Katarina Yvonne Hollblad-Fadiman,
Closest friend, sharpest critic, dearest wife,
Who opened up so many windows,
And let in so much sunshine,
That the shadows melted
And I could once more see my way.

Contents

List of maps, figures, and tables   ix

Acknowledgments   xi

Introduction:
The Oral Traditions   1

1. Traditions of Origin: 19
   Mysterious Mbwaa
2. Enslavement Traditions: 44
   Persecution and Flight
3. Mount Kenya Traditions: 66
   Fragmentation and War
4. Traditions of Deviance: 94
   Evolution on the Fringes
5. Capitulation Traditions: 121
   The Coming of England
6. The Extortion Traditions: 151
   Dancing Deviants
7. The Colonial Traditions: 175
   Dismantling Elderhood
8. Missionary Traditions: 205
   Spreading God
9. Anti-Christian Traditions: 229
   The War Against Converts
10. Disaster Traditions: 255
    There Were Years When Men Ate Thorns
11. Resistance Traditions: 277
    Kiamas Underground
12. Persecution Traditions: 302
    The Wars to End Witchcraft
13. Reconciliation Traditions: 323
    Meru's Golden Age

Notes   347

Bibliography   367

Glossary-Index   387

Maps, Figures, and Tables

MAPS

Map 1.	Kenya and Meru District	xii
Map 2.	Lamu archipelago	24
Map 3.	Meru migration route: 1700–1730	62
Map 4.	Meru: major subgroups	71

FIGURE

Figure 1.	Ecological zones of Mount Kenya	69

TABLES

Table 1.	Life stages of Meru males	10
Table 2.	Meru history as recalled by Meru age-sets	13
Table 3.	Meru terms and their English equivalents	15
Table 4.	Names of councils	74
Table 5.	Names given Cushitic speakers (precontact)	82
Table 6.	Names given Kalenjin speakers	85
Table 7.	Comparison of Umpua and Ogiek words	88
Table 8.	Language families of Mount Kenya	350
Table 9.	Kiamas of southern Meru, by subtribe	364

Acknowledgments

Whatever this book contains is the result of the knowledge shared with me by the men of Meru, old and young. My thanks and thoughts go out to them, for their wisdom:

To Fabian Njage, Simon P. K. Bengi, Franklin Mugambe, Gerrard Kithinji, and a dozen others, all young men in their early twenties when I began my research in 1969. Their total dedication to the Meru people led to the recovery of this portion of their past.

To M'Thaara M'Mutani, Matiri wa Kirongoro, Hezikiah M'Mukiri, M'Muraa wa Kairanyi, Gituuru wa Gikamata, and more than one hundred others, all men of the Miriti, Murungi, and Kiramana age-sets and thus in their seventies, eighties, and nineties when I collected this data. Their willingness to pass on their wisdom to a stranger will have preserved it for Meru generations yet to come.

To William Henry Laughton, Hugo E. Lambert, Dr. Howard Brassington, Father Bernard Bernardi, Rev. Dr. Clive Irvine, Father B. Airaldi, Capt. Victor McKeag, and J. Gerald H. Hopkins, K. K. Sillitoe, and several others, all of whom had served in Meru long before I began my work there. Their love of this region and its people also makes them "men of Meru."

Men of Meru, thank you for what you have given me. I salute your past.

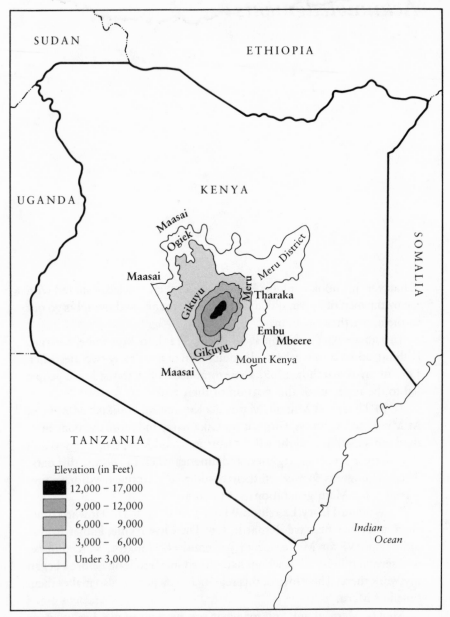

Map 1. Kenya and Meru District, showing peoples of Mount Kenya

Introduction:
The Oral Traditions

"In the beginning, we were not called 'Meru.' In fact, no one now living recalls our tribal name. My grandparents may have known, but I was too young to ask. Now I am too old to remember."[1]

Gituuru wa Gikamata
Kiramana age-set
Age: Early nineties

Sparks snapped away from the flickering cookfire and into an East African night. Rows of seated children, faces momentarily identical in the firelight, grinned for a moment in unison and inched imperceptibly closer to both the speaker and the flames. Behind them ranks of grown men and teenage boys stood quietly in shadow. Beyond them, and farther back in the darkness than I could see, stood groups of girls and women. In theory they were all working, for the air was warm and rich with aromas of millet beer and roasting meat. In practice none were working, for no one laughed. Rather everyone was simply listening. Gituuru wa Gikamata, one of Meru's old, old men and alleged to be the oldest, was beginning to retell one of the people's most beloved oral traditions.

That tale, told around cookfires for more than three hundred years, would last for hours, well into the night. In Meru the phrase "old, old man" implies not a person in decline but one whose age has made him rich in wisdom. To call someone an "old, old man" in Meru is like saying "he who knows the most of all." Gituuru was known for recalling more details of the past, recounted to him by his own grandfathers, than any other elder. He told his stories only rarely, for arthritis had so crippled him that he spent his days in a permanent crouch, unable to stand upright without searing pain.

I recalled a single morning, however, when Gituuru grew so engrossed in retelling a tradition of his warrior years that he forgot his

1

pains. A small circle of us, in those years still in or near warrior age, had asked how men in the old days fought in single combat. Two tattered leather shields and wooden war clubs lay nearby, remnants of Gituuru's own warrior career. I picked up one set, he, the other. First, he squatted, teaching me the basic moves, while pouring scorn on my clumsy efforts. Then, as I assumed a proper fighting pose and faced him, he suddenly forgot that he was old: he rose to his full height, his club and shield in hand, and attacked me in the classic style. The fight was brief. He struck three times, beat down my defense, then dropped back down again—but for that moment he was once again a Meru warrior, and tradition came to life.

Four months later, however, the old voice quavered as he began the night's long tale, and the mind that led it often lost its way, for Gituuru wa Gikamata, perhaps the last surviving member of Meru's oldest generation, was dying. This was the last time he would ever tell the tale in its rich completeness, and his subsequent death impoverished the entire Meru people: in three hundred years of telling the tale had never been written down.

Each time an old man dies in Africa a library is lost to humankind, for within the memories of the old men lies the history of an entire people. It is a complex tale, as rich in drama, incident, and narrative as the far more widely known drama of Homer's Troy, the Viking sagas, or the samurai epics of Japan. Some African traditions take hours to tell, a few take days; those that make up the body of this book stretched over months. Some traditions are fictional, others are based entirely on fact. Some blend fiction and fact, often so artfully that anyone who listens is held spellbound. Some can be retold only in song, often only by tribal troubadours. These traditions are folk art at its finest; they hold Africa's rich past.

COLLECTING THE TRADITIONS

This book contains the traditions of a single tribe, the Meru of Mount Kenya. They were narrated by the "old, old men" (and a few wives) of the age groups known as Kiramana (men in their early nineties), Murungi (late seventies to early eighties), and Miriti (mid-sixties to mid-seventies). In 1969–1970, when many of these traditions were first recorded, these narrators were the oldest living Meru, in the final decades of their lives.

Their narrations touched on every aspect of their tribal past. The most historically significant traditions, however, are those that deal with the system Meru speakers call Urogi, which English speakers translate as *witchcraft*. The system has existed for more than three hundred years. It is composed of continuously evolving tools—verbal formulae (curses, incantations), physical acts (rituals), and herbal, mineral, and animal compounds (potions, medicines)—that are used to invoke specific supernatural powers. The words, actions, or compounds themselves, not the person using them, have the power. Nonetheless, from the perspective of observers, successful users are cloaked in an aura of both respect and fear.

From a historian's perspective the witchcraft traditions provide unexpected windows into the Meru past, windows that permit analysis of smaller segments of the social structure. The Meru have never functioned as a single social unit. Throughout their history smaller segments within the body politic have competed constantly with one another. Often, these segments differentiated themselves from competitors by developing their own specific rituals (incantations, rites, potions). These were intended primarily to invoke a response from the supernatural, but secondarily they were used against rival groups. Thus in the 1700s mainstream Meru cultivators contended with Meru hunter-gatherers while migrating. In the 1800s descendants of both groups competed for the exclusive use of land. In the 1900s their descendants competed, in turn, against one another and the newly arrived British colonialists. In all cases the weapons of choice were invocations, potions, and related ritual. Thus can witchcraft become history.

The Urogi traditions are not quasi-fiction. Their narrators spoke in such detail as only actual practitioners (or their victims) could. The hunting magic of "bite" and "blow," the chanted, clanging curse that tribal smiths banged out on iron, the witchman's curse to stop one's breath: these details did not originate in their imaginations but had been taught them by their grandfathers and practiced throughout their lives. To the people of Meru, the "witchman," "witch doctor," "witch finder," and other supernatural practitioners were real. They were men, now very old, with whom one could visit and from whom one could learn.

But why did the witchmen talk with me? I was young, white, academic, and American. In Meru eyes those traits meant I was also "Christian" and thus implacably hostile—like all earlier Christians—to the so-called pagan portion of their past. Since the British conquest in 1906, these supernatural specialists had been lumped together and denounced as witch doctors by contemptuous whites. They had been publicly opposed, periodically beaten, occasionally arrested, and continually ridiculed by both members of the Christian missions and those government officials that represented British rule. After independence the pagan past fell even farther into disrepute, as Kenya's new African leaders, now either secular or Christian, strove to turn their people toward modern ways. There was no longer room in Meru for traditional religion, and still less for practitioners of the supernatural.

Throughout this century those few who battled to preserve the supernatural traditions had fought back with the only weapon available to the militarily defeated: silence. The Meru supernatural became a tribal secret. To disclose its "secrets" to non-Meru—be they black or white—became a sin against the tribal ancestors. Those who sinned were threatened with illness or death, cursed by the anger of an ancestral spirit who heard every word spoken in the realm of the living.

Thus few spoke. The little that whites learned during the colonial era came primarily from Christian converts, trained to despise and thus distort what they revealed. The identity of Meru's most revered figure, the Mugwe (tribal prophet), for example, remained concealed from the British from 1906 until the 1950s. One man alone could be Mugwe. He was foremost among the ruling elders of his age-set. Nonetheless, whoever served as Mugwe lived wholly unknown among the white Christian colonizers, shielded for decades by a wall of silence. That silence was still largely unbroken on my arrival in 1969. So why did they speak out then? Why speak to me, or to anyone?

The problem posed for me by this reticence was compounded by the lack of written data. The Meru-speaking peoples live on and adjacent to the northeast slope of Mount Kenya, a 17,000-foot-high, long dormant volcano near the center of the modern Kenyan nation. Before the colonial conquest in 1906 the name "Meru" was used by only five of the present nine subgroups that now make up the tribe, the Igoji, Miutini, Imenti, Tigania, and Igembe. Soon after the conquest British administrators decided to include the peoples of Tharaka, who live east of the Meru speakers on the adjacent arid plains. In the 1920s still other British officials added the peoples of Cuka (then spelled "Chuka"), Muthambi, and Mwimbi, whose regions border the five original Meru speakers to the south. Collectively, these nine subtribes now make up both the contemporary Meru administrative unit (Meru Province) and the historical Meru "tribe."

These nine subgroups trace their histories back almost three hundred years, long before any of them were known as "Meru." Unfortunately, existing written records cover only the past ninety of these. Worse, those documents that do exist deal exclusively with the problems encountered by the various whites (English, Scottish, Italian, Dutch, Irish) in imposing colonial rule. Within all of these records, almost without exception, Africans play the role of shadows on the fringes of a European play. They appear either in supporting roles (carriers, servants, unpaid labor) or as comic relief (alchoholics, witch doctors), loyal subordinates (converted Christians, tribal police), noncooperators, and finally Mau Mau rebels, fleeing British imperial justice into the safety of the forests. Such records say too little. What can be learned about any of Mount Kenya's "Africans" (Meru, Maasai, Gikuyu,[2] Ogiek, and so on) during this period, as well in the two preceding centuries, must come not from written documents but from the mouths and memories of the Africans themselves.

Prior to my own arrival on Mount Kenya, however, I did read all the written records I could find. Most complained about the Meru reluctance to conform to British ways. One colonial officer, in particular, complained that he had never had the bad fortune to administer a people so "thoroughly riddled with witchcraft" that "no one could do anything with them because they refused to tell him anything." Both complaints were repeated in reports written throughout much of the British colonial era. I began to realize that there had to be a better way—even a Meru way—to learn about these people.

Fortunately, there was. But the problems facing my potential sources were severe. In 1969, scores of Mount Kenya's oldest men were scattered throughout the nine subtribes but still connected with one another by mutual friends, kinfolk, and reputation. Nevertheless, each had reached the age where he had begun to contemplate the consequences of his impending death. For these dignified old men, death posed a problem that no prior set of elders had faced. Tradition required they pass on the "wisdom of their eldership" to selected members of the younger generations. This wisdom included many long, relatively formalized narrations, passed from grandparent to grandchild for nineteen generations, dealing with the origins and earliest history of each segment of the tribe. There were also scores of shorter, less standardized descriptions, dramatizations, tales, riddles, chants, songs, and verse—a treasure trove of oral literature. To historians these works were important for clues to the Meru past. To the Meru they were the raw materials of their entire heritage and therefore precious beyond price.

By the early 1960s, however, all the elders in Meru had become aware that the younger generations were no longer willing to seek them out, perform the rituals required by traditions, then sit and learn the wisdom that the elders had to teach. The younger age-sets had been either exposed to British schooling or aspired to it, thus forming the first generation of Meru's new literates. More and more of them believed that wisdom lay in books and schoolrooms, not in the old traditions.

In consequence, by the late 1960s the prerequisites for transferring tribal knowledge from the eldest to the young were no longer being met, and thus no transfer could be made. Members of the "warrior" or "apprentice elder" age-sets no longer paid the formal visits that custom demanded. No longer did they appear in respectful bands of learners, bearing the gifts required by tradition: the gourds of milk and beer and the meat and snuff and honey that not only sweetened the lives of many elders but also permitted them to live out their final years in economic dignity.

For every prior generation these formal visits had acted as an informal but effective system of social security. Too old for physical labor, the elders still served the tribe by passing on their knowledge to the young. In exchange they received the gifts of food, drink, and tobacco in quantities sufficient to nourish both body and spirit. It was a system deliberately intended to lighten the burden of aging. The older a man grew, the more he was assumed to know, the more often his juniors would seek him out, and thus the more frequent his gifts became. The old, old men of Meru, unlike those in Western societies, were never seen as useless or left to age and die alone.

But this was the 1960s, and these elders made up the last nonliterate age-sets that the Meru would ever know. Without exception those who formed the oldest living age-sets—the groups that collectively called themselves Kiramana, Murungi, and Miriti—were embittered at those younger than themselves. Most, when asked, felt that the younger age-sets had been "bent by the British as though they were twigs instead of men," and "they scratch in books like foolish guinea hens, seeking seeds [wisdom] from white men while ignoring their own." In consequence all elders feared death in a way unknown to prior generations, less for the loss of their own existence than the loss of the entire Meru past.

My earliest investigation, therefore, was made along lines suggested by those aspects of Meru tradition that I learned from the first Meru elders I met. Their initial lesson covered tribal protocol. It was not enough to talk to any elder; both simple courtesy and respect for age required that I seek out the oldest of them all. Thus I should begin with the acknowledged "oldest man in Meru," then work my way down chronologically into men of middle age. In fact I soon found men in every Meru region who claimed that title. In response I arbitrarily divided the current Meru political province into "interview zones," based on what seemed to be the different historical experiences of the peoples therein.

Thus, because all Meru live along the steep slope of a 17,000-foot volcanic mountain, I assumed that honey hunters in the ice-fogs of the upper rain forests would have different historical experiences from those who cultivated coffee in the temperate midlands. Both those groups probably had different perspectives from those who herded cattle on the arid, baking plains. These three areas thus became the interview zones. I then divided these "forest," "midlands," and "plains" Meru into subtribes (e.g., forest, midlands, and plains Muthambi or Imenti), and subsequently redivided even those into smaller segments.

Within each interview zone I began by asking to meet the oldest living men. Discussions with several of these respected elders generally produced a consensus as to whom within their region was believed most knowledgeable about each aspect of the past. From their perspective such men stood out as "spokesmen" for their age-set and thus for them all. Each spokesman, having shared his knowledge, often suggested other (in theory, still older) individuals, from whom they had sought to learn more of the past.

In time, and within each region, this path always led to one final authority on every issue, a "spokesman of (all other) spokesmen," who was locally believed to know the most of all. After several months of interviewing, I found that a number of unusually aged and knowledgeable elders were considered by their age-mates to be spokesmen-of-spokesmen on almost every aspect of history within their respective regions. These specialists, all far too old to leave their homesteads, lived far apart from one another and were therefore personally unacquainted except by reputation. Nonetheless, because their narrations were frequently comparable, they allowed continuous cross-checks on data collected from earlier informants.

My second tactic was to gather together what in the old days would have been called a "warrior band," in this instance allowed by tradition to seek wisdom instead of war. I selected my research assistants from men of what would have been warrior age had warriorhood survived. Among this group, my foreign background was less conspicuous and intimidating. As long as I was nothing more than one member of a band, Meru elders could still feel that they were teaching Meru youth. My added function was simply to record their words.

By tradition the band was required to present specific gifts to each of the elders we encountered. Once assembled, we visited a selected elder in a "respectful band." Behaving as custom demanded, we presented the traditional gifts of snuff, milk, millet beer, honey wine, or cooked meat to both the informants and their age-mates as symbolic gestures of respect for their years and the traditions they wished so much to keep alive. Only then were we permitted to request the eldest among them to teach us of the past.

The final task required of such a "band" was to listen. That might mean sitting cross-legged and almost motionless, however, until each tradition had been completely told. Often the narrations were brief, but sometimes they flowed for hours. We could never know beforehand. Only after the narrator felt his tale was complete were we allowed to question and probe for details. The final injunction was always to place what we had learned "within our hearts" (i.e., memorize) for that day—still too many years ahead to be imagined—when we too would be old and would begin to transmit the "wisdom" of Kiramana and Murungi and Miriti to a younger generation not yet born.

Here is their wisdom, as passed down word for word by no fewer than nineteen generations of grandfathers to grandsons or as remembered by those personally involved. I recorded it in 1969–1970 during three hundred on-site interviews with more than one hundred of the "wisest" Meru elders. I was thirty-two then and had two infant sons. In Meru eyes I was just beyond the years of warriorhood, when men become "apprentice" (or junior) elders (in Meru, "Aruau"), content to lay aside their spears, seek wives, and father children in the night. Their days, however, were to be spent with "ruling" (or "senior") elders ("Azee"), listening for hours to absorb the wisdom contained in the old, old narrations. Because I wished nothing more than to absorb the elders' wisdom, I was accepted as a pseudo–apprentice elder and allowed to listen as well. But now more than two decades have passed until the tens of thousands of worlds that they taught me have become a book. In Meru terms I am now a senior elder, with two sons of warrior age, and every man who spoke to me has died. It is time to do as I was taught and pass their words on to a younger generation.

AGE-SETS: THE MERU DATING SYSTEM

To be meaningful, the stories recited by Meru informants had to be placed within a chronological system, to provide a framework within which individual events could be carefully reconnected. This task was more difficult than it sounds, for Meru chronology was not calendrical but generational. Like other African peoples, before colonialization imposed a different system, the Meru categorized individuals into age groups marked by biological or social events. A Meru male was a "child" until his second teeth appeared. Thereafter, he became a "boy" until his puberty, and so forth (table 1).

During childhood, membership in each stage was reckoned informally, with entry and exit dictated solely by the appropriate biological change. Passage into the initial stage of adulthood (warriorhood), however, was marked by formal and physical ritual, initially by cutting off the foreskin of the penis and thereafter incorporating those undergoing the operation into a warrior age-set.

Within each region there were always boys who reached puberty in time for "the circumcision season." As soon as sufficient numbers had matured to fill one segment of an existing warrior band (in Meru, a "regiment"), a "circumcision night" (in Meru, "a night of cutting") was formally proclaimed. A "set" then consisted of every male of similar age (literally, age-mates), meaning all those who reached puberty within a single season. Only those circumcised within this period could join the group, and they remained in it throughout their lives.

The proclamation of a circumcision night effectively closed the newly forming age-set to further members. In practice each community proclaimed the period closed as soon as a sufficient number of boys reached puberty, which meant that the timing of the proclamations might vary sharply from group to group. Those who reached the age of circumcision after a proclamation were held back for subsequent inclusion in the following set.

Once the regiment's ranks could be filled, its membership was considered "set." As soon as all regiments were filled in one (or more) of the Meru subtribes, which could take several seasons, every warrior

TABLE I LIFE STAGES OF MERU MALES

Age	Life Stage	Termination	Meru Term for Life Stage	Age-set (1906)
0–7+	Infant/child	Appearance of second teeth	Kiiji	no age-set formed
7–15+	Uncircumcised boy	Puberty	Mwiji; Biiji (pl.)	no age-set formed
15–18+	Elder boy (candidate for circumcision)	Circumcision	Ndinguri (before circumcision); Ntaane (after circumcision)	Miriti (age-set starting to form)
18–29	Warrior (circumcised)	Marriage	Muthaka; Athaka (pl.)	Murungi
29–40+	Family head/apprentice elder	Entry of first son into warriorhood	Muruau; Aruau (pl.)	Kiramana; Kilamunya
40–51+	Ruling elder	Subsequent transfer	Mzee; Azee (pl.)	Kaburia
51–62+	Ritual elder (retired elder)	Subsequent transfer	Mzee; Azee (pl.)	
62–?	The aged	Death	Mzee; Azee (pl.)	Kubai, Nturutimi, Thamburu

regiment would simultaneously assume a single formal name, which its members would retain throughout their lives. Thus Gituuru wa Gikamata joined a regiment whose members, along with similar war bands within both his and adjacent subtribes, assumed the name of Kiramana. (See table 1 for the sequence of age-set names that applied throughout Gituuru's subtribe of Imenti.)

WORKING BACKWARD: AGE-SETS AS GUIDES TO THE PAST

We are fortunate that the African age-set system can act as a guide to the unwritten past. Though precolonial Meru communities planned economic activities according to the seasons, they recalled historic events by reference to whichever warrior age-set was present at the time the events occurred. The British, for example, date their conquest of the entire current Meru region as having occurred in 1906–1907. The Meru date it "soon after the Murungi [age-set] replaced the Kiramana [age-set] as warriors." Both methods work.

This linking of events and warrior age-sets had significant advantages. First, it proved possible to acquire lists of Meru age-sets from large numbers of elders in every region, as well as to secure agreement as to the order in which all of the earliest were formed. I was then able to compare these with similar lists that had been compiled by earlier European investigators as far back as 1912. I was also able to attain a general idea of the time spent by each set in warriorhood by asking elders to recall the number of agricultural cycles that had occurred between successive transfers of power within their lifetimes.

With this information I worked backward from both known events and known dates when new age-sets were formed—such as those occurring after imposition of colonial rule—and estimated the number of years that the sets remained warriors. In Imenti, for example, existing data suggests each set remained warriors for fifteen to sixteen years. In Mwimbi the change is believed to have occurred every twelve to fifteen years. (These intervals, of course, are only elders' estimates.) The actual times of entry into adulthood depended solely on the birth and maturation rates of any given group of Meru males, factors entirely beyond the reach of Western measurements. In addition, either within individual subtribes or throughout the Meru, drought, locusts, war, plague, or fluctuations in the birthrate might reduce the number of males, thereby causing delays in filling the warrior ranks.

Even estimates, however, can illuminate the past. By "working back-ward," researchers can try to correlate these estimated age-set intervals with alleged historic incidents, remembered to have occurred when spe-cific groups were warriors. Thus the precision of historic dating using Arabic numbers in our society is matched with often stunning accuracy by Meru age-sets. When applied to the list of age-sets provided by elders of Imenti and Igoji, for example, this approach reveals almost three hundred years of corresponding historical events (table 2).

DO THESE TRADITIONS REFLECT REALITY?

The mere existence of these oral recollections, however vast and varied, does not suggest that we can accept them entirely as historical records. Rather, we should consider them reflections of past events, as once per-ceived then reorganized over time within the human mind. Such reflec-tions can be subject to considerable distortion. Perhaps the most obvi-ous distorter is the investigator. I found, for instance, that my own background initially imprisoned me, dictating not only what I talked about and with whom, but also which topics, regions, or individuals I ignored. Like many other 1960s investigators of Africa's past, I was not only "young, white, academic, and American" but also "educated and urban." All these factors could have affected the choice of my African assistants and thus everything I learned and recorded.

At first I looked for only those who lived in urban centers and with higher education, primarily because they were more like me and thus seemed easier to talk to. Not surprisingly, they preferred working with educated elders and in cities and simultaneously tried to keep me away from the wilderness and rural regions, which they either looked down on or feared. If as an investigator I had absorbed those feelings (with-out eventually hiring both less urban and less educated staff), I might never have moved far away from city centers, and my results would have been overurbanized and distorted.

Distortion can be compounded by African geography. Rarely do the Gituurus of a region to be researched live conveniently along the major roadsides. My most knowledgeable informants invariably lived in iso-lated rain forest villages best reached on foot. This sounds romantic when the work is being planned in California. It grows less so dur-ing heavy Meru rains at night in the rain forest, or when an icy fog cloaks the volcanic mountains. In consequence the urban, educated in-vestigator may be all too often tempted to restrict inquiries to accessible

TABLE 2   MERU HISTORY AS RECALLED
BY MERU AGE-SETS

Age-Set	Date of Entry into Warriorhood	Remembered Events
Miriti	1916	Served, while warriors, in British East African Campaign, World War I.
Murungi	1904 (estimated)	New warriors at time of subordination to Great Britain (1906).
Kiramana or Kilamunya	1892 (estimated)	Fought several skirmishes with white men. Recorded by European sources, 1890s. Famine, from Igembe to Gikuyu. Recorded in Gikuyu, 1899.
Kaburia	1880	First to see, and fight, white men. First recorded entry into Meru, late 1880s, written sources.
Kubai	1868	Trade with Acomba (men of the coast, i.e., Arabs, Swahili, Somali). Embu traditions record Arabs first entering that area (1860s) and extending trade northward (early 1870s).
Nturutimi	1856	Wars against Maasai. Prophecy: "Last born children of Nturutimi [i.e., Miriti] will walk unarmed" (i.e., because of peace established in their area by Europeans).
Thamburu	1844	One man still living in 1924. (If 90, would have been born in 1834, entered warriorhood in the early 1850s.)
Kiruja Nguthugua Mbaringu Githangaria Ratanya	1826 1813 1800 1787 1774	Made contact with Maa-speaking peoples, either Maasai or (earlier) Maa-speaking Ogiek groups, such as Il Tikirri, Mumunyot. Contact led to decades of warfare, interspersed with periods of peace and intermarriage. Gradual adoption of Maasai methods of war.
Michubu Githarie	1761 1748	First age-sets to make contact with Mt. Kenya's earlier occupants, expelling small bands of Cushitic and Kalenjin-speaking peoples (Galla, Ogiek) from the foothills and slopes of Mt. Kenya.
Mukuruma	1735	Crossed Tana River to reach base of Mt. Kenya. Fragmentation of pre-Meru (then called Ngaa) into small bands, each of which approach Mt. Kenya.

TABLE 2   *(continued)*

Age-Set	Date of Entry into Warriorhood	Remembered Events
		War against Muoko; seized Tigania plains. Other bands advanced up slopes of Mt. Kenya.
Nkuthuku	1722	Fleeing migrants, now known as Ngaa, seek shelter in seasonal papyrus swamps, near the mouth of today's Tana River.
Ntangi	1708	Pre-Meru warrior name; the pre-Meru (earlier name not recalled) lived on Mbwaa, an island location still recalled. Invaded by Arabs (?), enslaved. Fled inland, initially following Tana River. Coastal Arab communities, recovering from recent expulsion of Portuguese, begin to control adjacent tribes. Possible connection to pre-Meru enslavement.

informants while ignoring those in more remote locations. The result may be a "history of the accessible center" of an African tribe, again distorting the past.

More serious distortion may occur for sexual reasons. In Meru the sexes traditionally meet separately in their own Kiamas, or councils, to resolve those matters that concern themselves alone. The other sex is rigidly excluded. As a man I could direct my inquiries into the Meru past primarily toward other, older men. Their replies could deal only with subjects considered "suitable" for men (e.g., war, colonial conquest, or "male" curses). My efforts to inquire among elderly women (about uniquely "female" curses, for example) were usually rebuffed with declarations that I sought to learn things "no man should know." Only rarely did a woman of great age consent to talk to me, and then either in secrecy or with her husband present. Thus my data are both massively incomplete and subject to a masculine distortion.

In at least two areas, however, the investigator *should* distort, if only to enhance the reader's understanding. The first involves reshaping local dialects into the forms required for a book. This becomes particularly important when no exact equivalent exists between the languages. A man of Meru (Mu-Meru), for example, would find himself linguistically unable to translate "nuclear fission" or "genetic splicing" into the

TABLE 3   MERU TERMS AND THEIR ENGLISH EQUIVALENTS

Meru Term	Literal Ki-Meru Meaning	English Equivalent
Kiama	elders' oathing group	elders' council
Mwiriga	cluster of mountain ridges, on which several clans band together for common political administration and military defense	ridgetop community
Murogi	curser, ie., a professional placer of curses that cause victim to sicken	witchman
Muga	curse remover, i.e., professional remover of curses placed by a Murogi	witch doctor
Urogi	a behavior sequence in which a curser (Murogi) places a curse (incantation, verbal malediction) on a victim, causing him or her to sicken	witchcraft

Meru language (Ki-Meru) with precision. Nor would several Meru (Ba-Meru) be able to translate precisely the concept of "corporate merger" into Ki-Meru, though they could achieve one without difficulty. The verbal equivalents simply do not exist within this language. Similarly, American English has no linguistic equivalents for the most common Meru terms. Several of those used early in this book, for instance, are in table 3.

Worse, the plural forms of these common terms have no equivalents in English, because Bantu-speaking peoples (who predominate in much of East, South, and Central Africa) change the initial letters to form plurals. One "Kiama," for instance, becomes two "Biama." One "Mwiriga" can break into several contending "Miiriga." One "Murogi" may meet with other "Arogi," but their combined curse may be lifted by either a single "Muga," or several "Aga" acting in cooperation. In such cases linguistic distortion becomes so inevitable that one must gulp, sigh, and provide approximate (if inaccurate) equivalents.

In addition, the investigator of Africa's "unwritten" past must "distort" the use of footnotes. Academic practice calls for writers to cite their written sources of information, thereby allowing others access to the wellsprings of their thought. This guideline proves difficult when presenting research in which those wellsprings are aged men in rural regions. To ignore them as sources of history, however, does disservice to the past. Meticulously detailed descriptions of the "spells" once used by secret witchcraft guilds, for instance, could only have been learned from the practitioners. Not to cite these men dishonors their contribution and disappoints their descendants. Saying nothing of the circumstances wherein they learned and practiced what they now retell leaves the descriptions historically incomplete. Accordingly, in addition to providing conventional citations, I also cite the men (and women) that I interviewed for this book. Along with their names, I have indicated a "MOS" (Meru oral source) number, which corresponds to a listing in the Bibliography that describes each informant. There I note relevant facts about them, including full name, approximate age, precolonial status, and so forth.

DO AFRICANS DISTORT DATA?

Informants may also distort information. In Meru they often desire to upgrade their historical roles. In Tigania, for instance, few elders described their warrior years without claiming they were once commanders, even when their relative youth (or sheer lack of size) cast doubt on the claim. In Imenti some elders glorified their lineages by claiming descent from "exotic" peoples (e.g., Egyptians) or by extending their family genealogies, recalling individual ancestors older than the tribe itself. Conversely, some informants, raised to power under colonialism, sharply magnified their roles in spreading English ways, as was the case with one former Mwimbi chief who claimed to have "stopped all tribal customs" in his area.

Informants may have also reshaped their recollections out of tribal, traditional, or religious patriotism. In narratives recounting a decade of "civil war" (actually, reciprocal cattle raiding) between Imenti and Tigania in the 1890s, for example, all the informants claimed victory in every battle, a problem for any investigator. Informants may have also minimized (or omitted) those portions of their past of which they thought non-Africans might disapprove. In Mwimbi, for instance, descriptions of contact with ancestral spirits (Nkoma) may have been altered because prior experience with whites taught informants to be wary of their Christian bias. Conversely, Christian informants may have magnified those aspects of their histories that dealt with the early missions, speaking ecstatically about the spread of the faith but omitting all mention of the social disruption it may have caused.

Finally, the narratives may have been affected by the informant's age. The spokesmen-of-spokesmen are Meru's oldest men. The very fact of their advancing years qualifies them to speak of the past. All, however, were ill, infirm, and subject to memory lapses. When asked to identify a term connected with his warriorhood, for instance, one Mwimbi elder threw back his head and laughed in sheer joy at the pleasure the memories gave him. He settled down to describe them, opened his mouth, closed it, and then declared that he had forgotten what he knew. Nor did he ever remember.

ORAL HISTORY IS SWIFTLY DYING

Possible distortions, however, do not diminish the fact that each narration is a window, however fragile, through which we can glimpse aspects of the Meru past. In Imenti, for example, no fewer than twenty aged and respected elders recited the story of an "alien" (non-Meru African) said to have accompanied the tribe on its migration to Mount Kenya in the mid-1700s. Upon arrival, tradition states that he was executed ("lest he betray the tribal location to his own people") and buried with all his tribal ornaments at a specific spot. The twenty elders all agreed upon that spot. Their agreement, however, guarantees neither that such a man existed nor that his burial in fact took place. It does, however, provide the investigator of such narrations a basis for deciding whether to buy a shovel!

This oral history, therefore, is not presented as a faithful record of the Meru past. Rather, it is a collection of verbal beacons suggesting its existence. Thus, if a search such as that urged by the twenty elders were successful, it would still be incomplete. One would need to identify any artifacts found and link them to other cultures, to learn which ones had been in contact with the Meru at that time. Nevertheless, without consideration of the existing oral record, no search would be conducted and we would have nothing to identify.

Thus in Meru, as in other societies across Africa, all verbal communication contains potential clues. A child's riddle, a grandmother's cookfire tale, the quavering chant of a curse detector, or a circumcision song may all allude to some fragment of data, which once recognized and related to other fragments may lead to reconstruction of the African past. The continued presence of these fragile verbal clues motivated this investigation. But the inquiry is near its end, for in the words of one informant, "we Murungi are like sparks within the cookfires. One by one we are going out." His statement is both correct and prophetic, for the oral history of Meru is swiftly dying.

The demands of tradition were unrelenting and clear: the young were required to solicit knowledge from the old. The acquisition of the elders' wisdom was prerequisite to their own entry into elderhood. Only by visiting the eldest men in Meru, to "buy their wisdom" through presenting the traditional gifts, could they learn enough about the Meru past to guide the future.

Today, however, the oldest men in Meru wait out their years alone, but still hoping that younger men will once more come to seek them out. I once sat for seven hours listening to a spokesman-of-spokesmen tell the story of every battle in the history of his region. The narration began in the mid-1800s and dealt with a seemingly endless sequence of raids and counterraids between Maasai and Meru, Imenti and Tigania, British and African. His words spilled out across an afternoon and stretched back a century. They flowed past sundown and well into the night. As the moon rose, four pots of glowing coals were placed silently around the squatting elder to keep him warm and thus prevent an interruption of the chronicle. He continued until the moon was high. Finally, the flow of words came to an end and the spokesman-of-spokesmen sat crumpled in near exhaustion. Awed, I softly asked how often he had recounted the entire chronicle. "Twice," he answered bitterly, "and the other one who asked was white like you. Our young men have forgotten that elders have wisdom. They have been taught it lies in books and root in them like bush pigs."

But books do not contain the elders' wisdom. Few studies of the Meru have ever been published, and almost none deal with the precolonial past from their own uniquely African perspective. After conquest by Britain, much of Meru culture was dismantled. Christianity absorbed the Meru spirit world. The revered elders' councils were either anglicized or driven underground. Warrior bands were replaced by battalions of youths who sought adventure on colonial tea plantations and fought for shillings instead of military glory. The core of Meru childhood shifted from the hearth and family flocks to the blackboard of a Christian mission school.

In short, much of what was uniquely Meru has been obliterated. It now exists only within the memories of those few aged men and women who still recall the tribal past. This book is intended, therefore, not as the "definitive" history of Meru but as its oral history, the past as perceived by those who lived it. This book is their collective voice.

CHAPTER I

Traditions of Origin: Mysterious Mbwaa

"We began on Mbwaa, a small island surrounded by water. No one remembers where it was, but it lay on the edge of a sea, at a place where the waters would go to eat grass."[1]

Gaichungi Baibuatho M'mbarui
Kilamunya age-set
Age: Mid-nineties

The earliest Meru tradition discusses the origin of the tribe. Everyone in Meru retells portions of it. Detailed descriptions, however, can be recounted only be the region's most aged men, the last survivors of the Kiramana (in Tigania and Igembe, Kilamunya) and Murungi age-sets, the oldest in Meru. In 1969–1970, when these narrations were last recounted, all of these men were either in or near their nineties. Several remained mentally vigorous, retelling the tradition as they had learned it from their own grandfathers. Notwithstanding, of the thousands of men who had once made up their age-sets, fewer than a dozen remained.

MBWAA: THE MERU BEGINNINGS

"We began on Mbwaa," the chronicles declare, then go on to describe an orderly, prosperous island community, set on the edge of a large body of water, the name of which is no longer recalled. "It was the time when the men of Ntangi [age-set] were warriors [ca. 1700]; a time when we lived near the mouth of a large river that ran red into a great sea. It was a time when we lived on an island we recall as Mbwaa."[2]

Traditions describe the island as having been encircled by bitter (salt) water that no one could drink. It lay sufficiently near a "mainland," however, for both people and animals to have been visible from a northwestern shore. The island was irregularly shaped ("like a crooked gourd"), set in a circular coral reef, and small enough to cross on foot within a single day. The earth consisted of coral and sand, although freshwater springs near its center allowed small-scale herding and agriculture.

The islanders' economy, however, was based largely on fish. Men carved small wooden hooks to catch tiny fish along the reefs. Larger fish would either crush or break the hooks, thereby sharply limiting what could be taken. Men of Mbwaa also kept goats, sheep, and short-horned cattle. Through trade they acquired donkeys from a people re-called as Cucu (Somali). The donkeys drew water from shallow wells dug near the island's center. The wells also supported crops of millet and yams, supplemented by sugar cane, bananas, and sap from a palm that was brewed into beer.

The only "wild" animal on Mbwaa was a long-haired goat. Its skin was sought, periodically, to make simple bellows for forging iron. The chronicles declare that iron was found "everywhere" on Mbwaa. In consequence each clan contained ironsmiths who gathered the ore to forge into spear points and knives.

The island's most unusual feature was the behavior of its tides. In-formants from every Meru community described these with the phrase "ruuji rugwita kuria nyaki" (the water has gone to eat grass). The ref-erence is to times, once in daylight and once at night, when the tide would flow swiftly toward the mainland ("to eat grass"), leaving an area recalled as "dry," but which in fact was actually mud, sprinkled with tidal pools.

This dry period was very important to the economy. Women used it to gather cowry shells, which were worn on strings around their waists for use in trade. Little boys gathered larger shells for the community elders, who used them as containers for everything from snuff to magic herbs.

The tides served the islanders in other ways. After a certain time "it would return from eating grass" (from the mainland) with great force, flowing back into its channel with such speed that people caught out in the tide pools had to race for shore. Traditions dwell upon the water's swiftness ("watchmen would shout"), as well as the fear that women, in particular, felt at being caught in its flow. This return tide would even sometimes catch and drown wild animals, most often elephants, which moved between Mbwaa and the mainland. The islanders seized such occasions with great joy, stripping each corpse of ivory and meat, then saving the tusks for subsequent trade with the mainlanders.

The economic portrait that emerges from these narrations is surprisingly consistent. Mbwaa is remembered as sheltering a relatively well-ordered community, which worked steadily to survive but never knew hunger. The availability of iron for tools permitted construction of a diverse economic base, in which fishing, shellfish gathering, herding, and grain production all had roles. Beyond that the island's location, evidently adjacent to other communities on the mainland clearly provided both the desire and opportunity for trade. The occasional acquisition of ivory must have provided further stimulus for trade, although in subsequent traditions it appears to have contributed directly to the community's eventual demise.

WHERE WAS MBWAA?

No living elder recalled the location of Mbwaa. Nor, informants declare, did their grandfathers remember it. Nothing in the entire body of tradition speaks directly of the island's location. Yet the narratives are rich in clues. Much of the existing oral evidence suggests that the Meru ancestral homeland lay off the northern Kenya coast, on the northwestern edge of the contemporary island of Manda.

Linguistic evidence supports this contention. H. E. Lambert, a notable linguist and former commissioner of Meru district (in 1933–1935 and 1940–1941), suggests, for example, that the Meru word *Mbwaa* (or *Mbwa*) is derived from the Swahili term *pwani* (beach, shore). Linguistically, the only difference is that the Swahili word "has [added] the locative ending (-ni) while . . . discarding the nasalization ("b") in favor of aspiration ("p"), whereas the Meru word . . . having retained the "m" has kept the "b"; "n" becomes "m" before a labial.[3] Lambert also believed that the fundamental meaning of the Swahili stem *pwa* denoted not only "shore" but also "place where the tide ebbs." As an example he gives the term *pwayi*, which in the dialect of neighboring Pate Island suggests a creek that dries up at low tide.

Lambert, writing in the 1940s, was unable to locate Mbwaa. Yet his linguistic suggestions are supported by examination of historical variants of the word. The most recent recordings of this specific tradition, those collected between 1930 and 1970, spell the island of origin as "Mbwa." The very earliest, however, collected between 1917 and 1925, use the longer variant "Mbwaa."[4] In many Bantu languages, including those of the contemporary Meru region, the ground, or *r* or *l* (the intervocalic *d), has tended over time to disappear when surrounded by vowels within a syllable; the three letters run together, gradually evolving into a single short vowel.[5]

Before this century, for example, the Tharaka, the tribe adjacent to contemporary Meru, were known as the *Thaaka*, both by neighboring African societies and the earlier European explorers. Logically, they should be known as the *Thaka* today, but the r was restored by conscientious twentieth-century British administrators who inquired into their past. Similarly, if *Mbwa* (1930s–1960s) was once *Mbwaa* (1920s), it may have been expressed still earlier as *Mbwara*, having gradually contracted in the same manner as *Tharaka*. The linkage is made stronger by the existence of a specific region—on the western side of Manda Island—known as Mbwara Matanga.

Similarity in names, of course, is inconclusive. Yet the word *matanga* is also worth examining. In the Manda dialect it means "sands" but refers to a type of sand containing iron ore. This type of sand has also been discovered on the adjacent island of Pate, particularly within an area similar to one on Manda. An iron-based technology could have developed with ease.[6] This seems to mesh quite clearly with the Mbwaa traditions, in which frequent references to ironworking (e.g., spear points, smelting, ironsmiths) suggest that easy access to the ore had made its use routine.

Geographic evidence also suggests Manda as the Meru point of origin. The most striking argument lies in the behavior of the island's tides. Two-thirds of Manda is surrounded by coral reefs, corresponding to the pattern described in the Mbwaa tradition. Northwest of Mbwara Matanga, however, lies a narrow channel known as the Mkanda. The term *Mkanda* does appear within the Mbwaa chronicles, to describe a people living separate from the ancestral Meru, on the mainland.

The modern Mkanda Channel, however, fills and empties twice daily from the action of a tidal bore. When empty, it leaves a landscape of steaming mud and tide pools, which hinders rapid movement. One investigator, surveying the phenomenon in 1913, remarked, "An enemy must come at high tide through this (Mkanda) channel . . . and in the event of defeat has no opportunity to retreat until next tide, lest he be caught in a sea of mud."[7] This surging tidal flow is central to the Mbwaa narrations and is constantly referred to. As examination of subsequent traditions reveals, knowledge of the ebb and flow of tides proved instrumental in allowing Meru supernatural specialists to rescue their entire community from what tradition records as enslavement.

Tidal patterns of this type are found elsewhere in Kenya, but nowhere are they so closely associated with a specific oral history.

Historical evidence also points to Manda, in this instance within the oral traditions of a neighboring people. The Pokomo-speaking peoples currently inhabit both banks of Kenya's Tana River, which reaches the Indian Ocean just south of the Lamu-Manda region. Meru traditions say nothing of contact with the Pokomo. They do, however, speak of the peoples of "Buu," "Nderi," and "Dzunda," who lived on an island near Mbwaa, remembered as "Bua."

Buu, Nderi, and Dzunda are names for contemporary sections of Pokomo. Oral traditions recorded among all three groups confirm that several of their clans did live on islands in the distant past. One group recalls that its home island was once called Bua; it is known today as Lamu Island and is located only a mile or so from Manda's western shore.[8]

No traditions predate existence on Mbwaa, and informants did not recognize place names or tribal names associated with the region or even the name itself. The pre-Meru home island lies within the Lamu Archipelago, however, less than one hundred miles south of Bur Kao.[9] It is thus theoretically possible that the pre-Meru peoples may have trekked southward prior to the 1700s, perhaps as part of an entirely different group of whom all oral record has been lost. Until proof of this appears, however, it seems wise to restrict the Meru point of origin to Manda Island.

ELDERS' KIAMAS: THE COUNCIL SYSTEM

Existing evidence suggests that the Mbwaa community was guided by three interrelated systems of thought. The first was a system of legal precedents, administered by elders' councils, which governed according to traditions passed down by tribal ancestors. The second was a system of beliefs involving the spirits of these ancestors, thought to remain in contact with the living to enforce obedience to the traditions. The final system was one of supernatural rituals, used by a class of specialists believed to be in contact with these spirits to regulate conflict within the tribe. In theory each system operated independently. In fact they combined as often as required to guide the society.

The island's limited economic base permitted little social specialization. The basic social unit was the clan, composed of families claiming descent from common ancestors. Within each clan, conflicts were

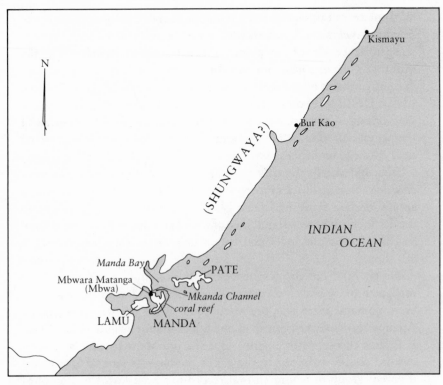

Map 2. Lamu archipelago

resolved by governing bodies known as councils (Biama; Kiama, the singular form, is used throughout for convenience). The council system ran parallel to that of the age-sets. At each stage of life males (and females) submitted to the authority of Kiamas composed of individuals their approximate age.[10] Thus, boys, youths, warriors, family heads, and ruling elders each formed councils of their own, intended to regulate whatever conflicts might emerge among themselves.[11]

Foremost among these was the council of ruling elders, composed of men whose sons had reached warrior age. In theory fathers and sons formed a partnership in which the ruling group could call upon its warrior sons to enforce communal decisions. In addition ruling elders could turn to survivors of their grandfathers' age-set, two above their own, for guidance in affairs that concerned the community as a whole. Ideally, the ties of blood bound those holding formal power into a coherent whole in which males of a single family line provided consultation, administration, and military enforcement.

The three age-sets—grandfathers, fathers, and warrior sons—thus formally shared power during the time required for a new generation of males to be born and reach puberty in numbers sufficient to fill the ranks of the war bands. Eventually, their numbers grew until they claimed a monopoly of military power, seizing it from the age group just above them by physically ejecting them from the military barracks. Those expelled in this fashion moved "up" into the next ranking, sought mates, and settled down to become both apprentice elders and the heads of families.

This action would then set every older age-set into social motion. The former family head/apprentice elders, having raised sons to warriorhood, ascended in turn into the role of ruling elders. In that capacity they then joined forces with their sons in governing the tribe. The age-set they displaced assumed administration of the people as a whole. The former ruling elders assumed the status of retired elders. Released from the responsibilities of government, they became free to turn their energies toward education of the newborn generation—their grandchildren—children of their sons, now family heads.

The oldest men in Meru—should any survive—rose to the ultimate status of ritual elders. As the age-set nearest death, they were also closest to the ancestors. Logic required, therefore, that they maintain the ancient rituals to ensure contact with the spirit world and thus advise the ruling elders and warriors—respectively, their sons and grandsons—as to the dictates of ancestral will.

Formal authority, therefore, alternated between one-half of male society and the other, passing back and forth every twelve to fifteen years. At any given moment three age-sets—grandfathers, fathers, and sons— were responsible for the spiritual, administrative, and military guardianship of society. The other three age-sets, also grandfathers, fathers, and (growing) sons would be released from such responsibilities in order to create and nurture families.

This division of the entire society into "ins" and "outs" was formalized, and had been since the beginning of Meru history, by assigning a "praise name" to each group. At any point in time members of the three related age-sets were known as "Ntiba." The other three, whether in or out of power, were called "Kiruka." The two names stayed with the members of each group throughout their lives, creating a political pattern in which it could be said that "first Kiruka and then Ntiba is in power."

Every elder joined his clan Kiama soon after leaving warriorhood. There were no exceptions. Membership was the mark of adulthood, to be sought soon after the acquisition of a wife. Applicants signified their desire for entry by donating livestock to the Kiama elders as they gathered, supplying the basis for a feast. By consuming the applicants' meat, members signified their willingness to include them in their ranks. On entry each man submitted to a ritualized beating, symbolizing his acceptance of the council's authority.

Once accepted, candidates entered into a period of instruction and apprenticeship. Instruction dealt primarily with the norms of behavior ("secrets of Kiama") to which new members were expected to conform. Beyond that, apprentice elders were expected to spend well over a decade silently listening to the manner in which their seniors settled conflicts within the community; they were expected to absorb and eventually master the vast body of ancestral traditions on which all facets of communal life were based.

Apprenticeship was followed by authority, which gradually increased within each council as an individual aged. Over time more charismatic individuals within each group of council members would begin to emerge as spokesmen for their fellows in specific areas of mutual concern. This "spokesman system" formed the core of decision making. There were no formal qualifications. Rather, selection resulted from general agreement among those concerned. Qualities that could lead to one's selection might include pleasing appearance, retentive memory, oratorical skill, or the ability to resolve conflicts among the young. Special expertise could also become a factor. For example, an elder may have acquired firsthand knowledge of specific regions, peoples, or situations unknown to the council as a whole. In such cases knowledgeable elders would become spokesmen on those topics for as long and often as their expertise was needed.

Conflicts between two or more clans were resolved by spokesmen drawn from each of the contenders. In questions involving the entire tribe, spokesmen could come from every clan to form a council-of-councils, empowered to resolve issues of significance to them all. The Kiama, however, was geared to intermittent functions. In times of crisis, whether among individuals or clans, a council of sufficient size and scope was formed to resolve it. Thereafter, however, the group would dissolve, and whatever knowledge had been gained would be dispersed.

While in operation, the system seems to have operated according to six universally accepted principles of thought. The first equated age with wisdom. Informants expressed this relation in terms of human blood. Youth was described as "hot blooded," and therefore emotional, violent, and selfish. It created conflict within the community, which only the aged could resolve. Aging, in contrast, cooled the blood, thus permitting elders to acquire wisdom. The elders' role, therefore, was to cool (resolve) the conflicts raised by youth and thus restore the harmony required for communal survival.

A second principle equated wisdom with consensus. All decisions were collective. No single elder could expect to gain such wisdom as to resolve completely the conflicts raised by younger members of society. Solutions could emerge only among elders gathering in council, as the result of measured deliberation based on an eventual consent of all concerned.

Wisdom was also equated with timelessness. Resolving conflict was perceived as the most important work of every elder, a function that was expected to occupy them for a lifetime. Because conflict among men was believed to be continual, the resolution of conflicts was also an unending task. Speed in reaching a decision was unimportant. True significance came from the formation of a Kiama to discuss the problem, since the very act of mutual deliberation created a common sense of purpose among those gathered, thus laying a basis for the harmony they intended to create.

Another Kiama principle was based upon the dual role of domestic livestock in reaching communal decisions. At one level specified types of livestock served as symbolic catalysts, their sacrifice having been required at each stage of the deliberations to permit them to continue. A conflict between younger clan members, for example, required the antagonists to sacrifice a specified number of goats for a Kiama feast. The goats symbolized the emerging conflict. By consuming them, council elders signified their willingness to resolve ("swallow") it.

On a second level livestock also served as a living currency of reconciliation. An individual judged by his Kiama to have wronged another, for example, would be compelled to make restitution to him in units of livestock, usually sheep, which symbolized harmony. This restitution, combined with the sacrifice of other livestock to the communal ancestors, symbolized the offender's desire to reinstate himself within society.[12]

Other punishments were also intended to reintegrate the offender. Guilt was considered collective, its stigma spreading from a single man to his entire clan. A beating, therefore, if ordered by a Kiama, was administered by the offender's closest relations. A livestock fine was intended as an exercise in collective expiation, because the animals were collected equally from the herds of every family in the clan. In contributing, kinspeople symbolically acknowledged both the offender's guilt and the need for reconciliation.

The system's final principle was based on oral precedent. In theory the Kiama's decisions were consensual. The consensus that emerged, however, was grounded not on personal emotion but on historic precedent. A vast body of traditions inherited from the tribe's founding members regulated every aspect of society's behavior. These founders had passed this collective wisdom on to their heirs, who in turn had transmitted it to future generations.

The original traditions were supposedly unambiguous. In fact they had been subject to interpretation by every generation of Kiama elders. In addition each generation wished to pass on the wisdom of its own interpretations. Over time, therefore, a body of oral case law grew up around the founders' teachings, to which new generations both turned for guidance and added interpretations of their own. This "wisdom," existing solely in people's memories, formed the core of the Kiama system.

ANCESTRAL SPIRITS: THE RELIGIOUS SYSTEM

No elders' council worked in isolation. As with other Bantu peoples, each Meru generation was closely linked to the ancestral dead, not only by bonds of kinship but also constant rituals intended to keep the relationship alive. To its members a clan consisted of the living and their ancestors. It "lived," therefore, within not just the temporal world but an interrelated spiritual sphere as well.[13] Reflecting this duality, the councils also existed within both secular and supernatural contexts. On earth they served as centers for conciliation, adjusting conflicts of human interest as they arose. Because all decisions were ultimately based on ancestral precedent, however, their ultimate task was to determine whether human quarrels had caused disharmony among their ancestors as well. If so, these also had to be resolved.

By implication, therefore, human conflict had both secular and supernatural significance. Because all violations of person or property were defined automatically as departures from ancestral tradition, they became the concern not merely of the instigators but also their families, clans, and ultimately the ancestors from whom everyone had descended.

This dual concept of justice reflected a philosophy in which the entire universe was believed to consist of earthly and supernatural spheres, each closely interwoven with its counterpart. Within these spheres elements were ranked in an organized hierarchy, according to the amount of life force they possessed. On earth humans were ranked higher than animals and plants. Among people, ranking was by age, with individuals possessing the power to command respect and obedience from those chronologically beneath them.

The supernatural, although only partially comprehensible to the living, contained identifiable elements that could be ranked in a similar manner. Highest among these was the concept of God. He was referred to only in the singular and envisioned as a distinct but remote entity. In contrast with Christian conceptions of an all-seeing god of love, the Meru god was essentially indifferent to mankind. If angered, He could withhold blessings. If placated by ritual, He could be beneficial. His relationship, however, was not with individuals but the tribe as a whole. He was thus considered beyond the reach of prayer by individuals or clans. His task had been to create and uphold the earthly framework within which people might live. Beyond this, no one could say.[14]

Below God in the supernatural hierarchy were the spirits. These existed in various forms, representing the life force believed to be incarnate in all physical objects. This life force could inhabit pools, rocks, trees, and living creatures. It was considered undying; among humans it remained intact after the moment of death, leaving the body but re-taining full awareness of its own identity and surroundings.

Collectively, these ancestral spirits were believed to resemble the liv-ing in several ways. They were said to look like normal humans, with each spirit retaining the age and physical characteristics of his or her body at the moment of death. They resided near the living, where they could pass continually and invisibly among their descendants and ob-serve their development and growth.

Ancestral spirits differed from other elements of the supernatural in the frequency of their contacts with the living. These could take several forms, all concerned with the ancestor's desire to prevent human devi-ation from traditional ways. Contact might seem accidental, occurring while the living gathered food or firewood. Its purpose, however, was to cause intense anxiety to the person concerned, as the mere fact of a spir-itual appearance was believed to signal human misbehavior.

Contact might also be made through the family flocks and herds. The cow, in particular, was believed to be a vehicle through which a spirit might make contact with the living world. Usually, this took the form of deviant behavior, if the animal went mad, for example. In such instances it was assumed that ancestral spirits were once more warning someone in the clan against a possible transgression.

Spirits might also appear to their descendants through dreams, usu-ally taking the dream form of a deceased grandparent. Invariably, the dream visitor delivered verbal warnings, intended either for the dreamer himself or for transmission to a kinsperson who was departing from tradition. Ultimately, the transgressor would have to either heed ancestral warnings or suffer the inevitable punishment.

MUGIRO: THE CURSE

The spirits' most frequent form of contact with the living was through placement of a "Mugiro," or curse. A curse, within Meru tradition, is defined as a verbal wish to cause harm. It was delivered in the form of a singsong chant, usually at the top of the lungs. The words themselves were believed to be "alive," in that they possessed an inherent life force of their own, able to inflict harm on the living. They could be uttered, however, only under one set of circumstances: when living persons vi-olated some aspect of ancestral tradition causing communal conflict.

Intent was irrelevant. Acts of seduction, rape, murder, or property damage obviously engendered conflict. But (men) accidentally catching sight of women bathing, of scavenging hyenas, or of human corpses had the same effect. The first set of actions meant conflict with the living; the second set, with the ancestral spirits.

All human conflicts were believed to create similar disharmony among the spirits, who always hovered invisibly at the edge of their descendant's lives. On one hand spirits might grow angry at their own descendants, should they depart from custom. On the other they might take sides in human quarrels, raging at those among the living who had harmed their kin.

Spirits were believed to respond to human conflict by cursing those who had angered them. The life force inherent within these words of the curse in turn placed their intended victim in a condition of "Mugiro," or ritually created impurity. If not rapidly corrected, the condition itself, in its turn, automatically and inevitably brought personal calamity upon the individual involved. This could take any form: physical illness, sudden accident, economic disaster, or even instant death. It could strike not only the violator but also anyone connected with him or her, whether guilty or even aware of the original offense. Thus the condition carried danger not only to the original offender but also to his or her family, crops, herds, clan, and ultimately the entire community.

Understandably, therefore, the curse, with its assurance of both impurity and calamity, was universally feared, particularly true because the community's concept of calamity assumed that the origin of any misfortune lay in someone's curse. The placing of a Mugiro on any person, therefore, caused an instant and universal reaction within that person's clan. The condition rendered victims impure to other members of society. They therefore shunned them, barring the victims from participation in communal activities, specifically those related to feasting, communal drinking, singing, and sex.

The society's response to each ritually created state of impurity, therefore, was an equally ritualized ostracism. It could be terminated only by further ritual, initiated by the victims to remove the curse. This in turn required that they discover and resolve whatever conflicts had sprung from their departures from tradition, by reconciling with those directly concerned.

CURSING RITUALS: THE "WITCHCRAFT" SYSTEM

The third system that regulated Meru thought was composed of supernatural rituals. They were practiced by a fluctuating number of specialists, who dealt with varying aspects of the spirit world. Ideally, they were men of great age, grandfathers of the ruling elders, and thus well suited to advise their grandchildren in their tasks. Formally, they served as spokesmen for the oldest living age-set, men who had completed their period of "ruling" eldership and reached the stage (ritual elder) when they could turn their thoughts toward contact with the ancestors.

In theory each spirit specialist worked alone, living within a zone of social isolation created by the mysterious nature of his work. In fact the rituals they dealt with formed an integrated system of which even the practitioners were wholly unaware, whose cooperation with both spirits and Kiamas maintained the community at large.

The system functioned through fear. To avoid or minimize the possibility of conflict with either living persons or ancestral spirits, an individual might seek the services of an appropriate specialist. Some of these were notable in every clan, men who were consistently able to perform whatever rituals were needed to invoke ancestral response.

UGWE, URORIA: PROPHECY

Foremost among the Meru supernatural rituals were those of prophecy, practiced by individuals whose contact with the supernatural enabled them to glimpse the future. In Meru tradition the term *prophet* had two meanings. One followed the biblical conception of a single man selected by God to transmit His word to an entire people. This task was filled by one individual during every generation who assumed the title of "Mugwe" (transmitter of blessings). His role was to serve as intermediary for his people, invoking God's blessing for each significant communal action and interpreting His wishes for the people as a whole.[15]

The term *prophet* could also refer to one who had the skill of foretelling, an examination of the future to avoid calamity. Most clans had several foretellers (Aroria; sing.: Muroria) who could be consulted by persons concerned with evading calamity in impending marriage, warfare, harvest, or trade.

Foretelling typically took two forms, examining goats and interpreting dreams. An individual anxious about some aspect of the future approached a Muroria with the traditional fee, usually livestock. "Foretellers of goats" then slaughtered the animal, examining its internal organs for signs of ancestral displeasure. "Foretellers of dreams" interpreted them and explained to the dreamer how to avoid impending harm. In both cases spirits directly ancestral to the prophet concerned were believed responsible for the answer. If misfortune was seen as inevitable, both types of seer could provide rituals appropriate to forestall it.

UROGI: CURSING

Of course, calamity could strike despite ritual precautions. Alternatively, one member of the community might harm another despite all prognostications. In such instances the injured party, angered by either real or imagined violations, could place a Mugiro (curse) directly on his or her enemy. In imitation of the ancestors this was done verbally. The curse could take two forms. It could be a plea to one's own ancestors: "Spirit of my grandfather, let he who has harmed me sicken." Or it could be hurled directly against the enemy, relying on the life force inherent in the words: "He who has wronged me, let him sicken." In either case the victims of such a formal curse would find themselves in a condition of impurity and be forced to choose between acts of expiation or social ostracism and impending calamity.

Anyone could place a curse. Children could do so only against others in their age groups, women only against their own sex. Men, however, could curse anyone, and as they aged (thus growing closer to the ancestors) the power of their curses intensified. That power could be further increased by collective action. Thus in serious conflicts an entire elders' council might assemble to chant somber maledictions against a single individual, whose transgression against some aspect of tradition threatened them all.

If the conflict between two people intensified, however, they might seek aid from a second type of ritualist, one who specialized in placing curses for others. In Ki-Meru (Meru language) these were called Arogi (cursers, sorcerers, ritual poisoners; sing.: Murogi). Officially, they had no place within society, for no one would admit knowledge of their work. In fact everyone knew of the curser's services and sought them as often as required.

The rituals of cursing were passed from father to son. Traditionally, practitioners concealed their skills from the community by posing as a different type of specialist. At night, however, they stole away from inhabited areas to gather plants, minerals, and animal organs known to be toxic. They then ground these to powder or burnt them to ash, then placed the residue in a series of tiny containers, usually made from shells, gourds, bamboo, or animal horn. The collection was placed in goatskin carrying cases, then stored for future use.

The curser worked only on request. A party to some conflict would approach his hut at night, requesting vengeance and bearing the gifts required in such instances by custom. In response the specialist would mix his powdered substances with goat blood, symbolic of conflict, then place them in a ritually broken gourd. Typically, he then buried the gourd near the homestead of the intended victim, with one edge exposed to ensure its discovery. The curser then marched, alone or accompanied by others, a specified number of times around the victim's homestead, chanting a single meaningless sound intended to gain the attention of every listener in range (e.g., "tui-i-i, tui-i-i, tui-i-i").

The curse followed the chant. It was phrased in general terms ("Let he who has harmed us . . ."), naming neither specific individuals nor particular transgressions. The intention, obviously, was to strike fear in everyone within the homestead, because anyone might inadvertently have transgressed tradition.

At first glance the curser seems pointlessly malevolent, a figure most akin to the diabolical witch or warlock of European tradition. On one hand his rituals were specifically meant to induce fear of impending calamity. On the other they were clearly for hire, extending the specialized placement of curses into every corner of society. Through the presence of a Murogi any man could be a "witchman," placing maledictions on the enemy of his choice.

It seems inadequate, however, to dismiss the curser as nothing more than the Meru parallel to a modern hired gun. In fact cursers were of far more value to Meru society than as simple channels for personal vengeance. Nor were they in any way malevolent. Rather they served as social catalysts, using verbal ritual to create the need for counterrituals, to undo what had been done. These, in turn, provided the basis for still other rituals, creating a ripple effect throughout society, until the conflict that had appeared among its members had been wholly reconciled.

UGA: CURSE REMOVAL

Clearly, the very existence of ritualized cursing required the development of equally potent rituals to counteract its effects. An individual might first become aware of a curse by actually hearing it chanted or by finding a gourd filled with "magic" powders at the rear of a hut. More frequently, one would recognize the Mugiro through the onset of physical symptoms known to the entire community as evidence of either human or ancestral malevolence. The most common of these was internal pain, its location in the body indicating the type of transgression that had occurred. Chest pains, for example, suggested adultery; pain in the fingers indicated theft.

General physical symptoms that lacked obvious explanation (e.g., fever or nausea) might also be attributed to someone's curse, as would the absence of other symptoms, for example a woman's consistent failure to conceive a child. By extension the same reason might be accepted for other personal misfortunes, including crop failure, livestock loss, or attack by predators. The onset of any ill fortune could mean that the victim had been cursed.

The first reaction of an afflicted individual was to remove the curse before the threatened calamity could possibly occur. The initial step in that process was to approach a member of the class of supernaturalists skilled in the rituals of "Uga" (curse removal, ritualized healing). This third group of specialists were known as "Aga" (curse removers, ritual healers; sing.: Muga).

The first stages of Uga rituals were similar to those of cursing, in that the practitioners searched remote forest regions for the mineral, plant, and animal matter that formed the core of their rites. The curse removers also reduced their acquisitions to ash or powder, storing them in tiny tubes of bamboo, gourd, or antelope horn and carried them about in special goatskin bags that were used for no other purpose.

The curse remover also resembled the curser in that he too worked only on request. Typically, the afflicted individual approached his hut with gifts of livestock. The ritualist responded by blending several of his magic powders into an unbroken gourd, meant deliberately to contrast with the broken vessel of the curser and thus signify his more benign intention.

The remover might also demonstrate his intended benevolence by publicly tasting his own medicines, licking the powders from his fingers in the presence of onlookers. Here, too, the purpose was to prove that his own preparations contained nothing harmful to the living and were intended only to remove impurity and to heal. These demonstrations were intended to combat widespread suspicions that many curse removers were cursers as well.

With his credentials established, the curse remover could begin the rituals of Uga. One of the oldest began with the slaughter of goats received in payment from the victim. The Muga would then unravel the intestines, inspecting them for signs indicating ancestral disapproval. If none were found, he wound the organs deliberately around the victim's body, binding arms, wrists, and knees. Next he cut the entrails from the body and buried them while chanting rituals of removal: "Let the curse be cut as I cut these strings [intestines]. Let the impurity be buried as I bury these remains." The healer's purpose, of course, was symbolically to remove the feeling of impurity from the victim's mind, thus dissipating whatever psychological anxieties it had produced. The resulting physical symptoms inevitably disappeared as well.

URINGIA: CURSE DETECTION

Rites of removal could not in themselves eliminate the anxieties of the individual concerned. No victim of a verbal curse could feel fully secure until certain who had caused it, whether human or spirit. Failure to seek out the ultimate cause of that agent's anger would simply lead to reimposition of the curse, thus reinforcing rather than resolving the conflict between them.

A victim's next step, therefore, was to approach still another type of specialist, this one skilled in the rituals of ("Uringia," or curse detection or divination). Curse detectors (Aringia; sing.: Muringia) differed in their methods of detection and even in the problems they resolved. One might specialize in detecting livestock losses, a second in locating thieves, a third in learning who had committed adultery. The purpose of these practitioners was to identify the originators, living or ancestral, of each human calamity, thereby allowing the victim to undertake whatever further rituals might be required to appease them.

The detection process had two stages. The first involved a public interrogation. A male victim, for example, having presented a noted curse detector with sufficient numbers of livestock, was asked to describe the misfortune that had befallen him, as well as his own suspicions as to its origin. The specialist then publicly inquired into the victim's past activities, focusing on behavior that had been most likely to provoke conflict with others in the community: "Have you spoken to any elder in such a manner as to anger him? Have you spoken to any woman in such a manner as to anger men within her family?"

Since the interrogation was public, both victim and diviner were inevitably surrounded by a crowd of interested and highly vocal spectators. These performed an essential part in the process, qualifying the victim's own convictions as to his previous behavior with a continuous

flow of often derogatory comments. For example, an adulterous male
would be prone to deny all interest in the woman concerned. In such
instances the watchers served as a necessary corrective, laughingly calling out incident after incident in which the two alleged lovers had gone
off alone.

The interrogation could continue for hours or even days. Its purpose
was gradually to expose each instance of the victim's social behavior,
and thereby, identify each ancestral or living individual he might have
antagonized. It was considered complete when the number of potential suspects, whether ancestral or human, had been reduced to two
or three.

At this point the actual divination began. The Muringia, or diviner,
had several methods. One involved filling a single gourd with several
powders, which the Muringia mixed together with appropriate chants.
The diviner then selected a number of objects (e.g., sticks, beads, peb-
bles), each of which symbolized a possible suspect. If the living were
suspected, he gave each object the name of a living person; if spirits, the
identity of a known ancestor.

The Muringia next dropped the objects into the gourd, where he
covered them with the powders, the contact serving to intensify their
power. The diviner shook the gourd and asked it: "Was it he who . . . ?"
He then cast the objects in the gourd onto the ground and determined
the answer from the pattern in which they fell.

Victims were free to vary the process in an effort to test a diviner's
skill. They could rotate the names assigned to specific objects, request
that new ones be chosen, insert the names of additional suspects, or try
to divert the line of questioning. Similarly, the diviner was free to vary
the process in whatever manner he felt was required to demonstrate his
supernatural capacities. Once he reached a conclusion using one set of
objects, he collected a second group and repeated the process. The rep-
etitions continued until diviner, victim, and onlookers had agreed on
two points. One was the ultimate source of the curse, whether spirit or
man. The second was the ultimate reason for the curser's anger.

RETURNING TO KIAMA:
THE RITUALS OF RECONCILIATION

Only after acquiring knowledge of the source of and reason for a curse
could victims pass through the final steps of this process, those of judgment, redress, and reconciliation. If a curse had been imposed through

ancestral anger, the diviner himself could arrange appropriate rituals of redress, typically the sacrifice of more livestock. If the agent was human, the victims had two further choices. One was to seek supernatural redress, usually by placing a curse in turn on whomever the diviner had named. This, however, would also intensify conflict within the community and thus cause universal social condemnation.

Alternatively, victims could seek earthly redress for their sufferings through appeal to an appropriate Kiama. Any male adult could call a meeting of his council. If one man accused a second of having cursed him, citing the diviner's work as proof, the incident might be swiftly settled by the accused admitting his guilt and placating the victim by payment of livestock. In such cases the elders decided the size and frequency of payment and saw that it was made. More frequently, the accused denied his guilt. Or he might admit it but justify his act by citing prior harm inflicted by the victim. In such instances the elders' council passed judgment. If they failed to reach a verdict, the ancestors themselves were consulted for a final decision, the secular and supernatural combining in search of truth.

A Kiama had three tools at its disposal that permitted contact with the spirits in questions of justice. The first was the ancestral oath. Meru tradition defined the oath as a public declaration, in which individuals staked every facet of their existence on the truth of the words they uttered. One's oath was directed both to members of one's own community and to the always listening ancestors. As always, the words, once spoken, acquired a life force of their own. If they were false, they angered both the living and the dead, creating the preconditions for calamity.

The Kiama's second tool was livestock sacrifice. Goats, sheep, and cattle were considered points of contact between the spirits and humankind, living channels through which both sides expressed their wishes. Ancestors showed displeasure by driving animals mad or into unnatural acts of behavior. The living, in turn, could contact the ancestral realm by sacrificing animals, thereby propelling them into the spirit world as message bearers.

The message carried in such cases was a public oath. It was usually linked to a specific pattern of renunciation—often sexual—until its terms had been fulfilled: "If I lie, may this oath kill me. If I touch a woman before one [cycle of the] moon, may this oath kill me." Livestock sacrifice and personal renunciation were both deemed necessary to attract the spirits' attention. Those concerned were believed to join in a council of their own in which they passed judgment on the words of their descendant, sending or withholding calamity according to the interpretation of the victim's vow.

The Kiama's third tool was trial by ordeal. If unable to reach a collective decision, the elders could appeal for ancestral intervention, a higher judgment on the conflict. The ordeal, in fact, was little more than a variation of the public oath, but physical pain rather than renunciation drew ancestral attention to a public vow. It was a final resort, used only when the eldest of the elders found themselves unable to reach consensus on matters crucial to communal harmony.

There were several ordeals, each intended to symbolize whatever violation had been committed. In one of the oldest, for example, individuals accused of murder were asked to drink water from the victim's skull, then proclaim their innocence regarding the victim's death. If they were guilty, the water itself was believed to join forces with the words of their oaths to kill them in turn.

The most common, however, was the ordeal of iron. It was initiated by the oldest member of an elders' council, whose nearness to death (and thus to the spirit world) was believed able to induce the ancestors to intervene. Acting in both secular and supernatural capacities, this elder first heated a bar of iron (often a sword) in a huge fire. Seizing it, he raised the iron skyward, gesturing symbolically toward the hovering spirits and calling in his capacity as council elder for their judgment on the case in question. Having allegedly gained their attention, he slowly licked the iron across its entire length and chanted the appropriate oath: "If I am guilty in the matter, let this iron burn me." He then displayed an unburned tongue to the watching elders, thereby symbolically establishing both the effectiveness of his appeal to the spirits and his own noninvolvement or impartiality in the case.

Victims and suspects each followed suit, symbolically laying their families, herds, crops, and indeed every facet of their lives at the disposal of the ancestors by inviting their vengeance as punishment for untruths. Each oath taker was then inspected for burns. If one suffered more than the others, it was taken as ancestral indication of that person's guilt. If all seemed to have suffered equally, victims and suspects alike were proclaimed ritually impure. Thereafter, they were excluded from communal and sexual activities until the inevitable onset of calamity defined the guilt.

Once a decision was reached, whether by elders' debate or ancestral acts of vengeance, individuals judged guilty were required to make adequate restitution for the harm they had caused, thus restoring the harmony between themselves and their antagonists. The first step was payment of some portion of one's property to the aggrieved party, invariably in livestock, with the numbers rising in proportion to the seriousness of the offense.

The second step involved another livestock payment, this time to the elders' council that had sat in judgment. The animals delivered included sheep, symbolic of the guilty individual's desire for reconciliation. The meat was eaten not only by council elders but also by parties to the conflict, the act of shared feasting serving to symbolize the desire of those present to restore the harmony that had previously existed among them. Ancestral concurrence with the council's judgment was assured by a symbolic "third payment." Here, small portions of the meat were set aside on wooden skewers at appropriate moments throughout the feasting for the spirits to savor at their leisure, thereby transmitting their acceptance of the quarrel's end.

THREE SYSTEMS: MERU SOCIAL CONTROLS

There are certain similarities between the three systems of thought that guided the Meru and those operating among other Bantu-speaking peoples. All have been based on the premise that ancestral spirits exist, keep in contact with the living, and respond to human situations. Many believed, as in Meru, that every social deviation brought on their anger. Those societies therefore responded to these beliefs by developing secular, spiritual, and ritual systems designed to regulate conflict.

The role of the elders' council in these systems has received adequate investigation, and several studies have been made of the East African spirit world. Less has been written, however, about the cursing rituals and those who practice them. Throughout the colonial era, African specialists in every aspect of the supernatural were lumped together as witch doctors and dismissed as practitioners of witchcraft. That day has passed, but even modern African nations have not progressed beyond belated legal recognition of curse removers—now dubbed "herbalists" and valued not for their rituals but for the medicinal value of their wares. All other specialists remain in limbo, condemned for generalized malevolence and thus confined to books about the past.

It may be time, therefore, to reexamine the redeeming social value of the curse itself, as well as the degree to which *all* of its practitioners were integrated into both the spiritual and secular sides of communal life, solely to uphold the social order. Certainly, it may be time to evaluate this possibility within a single tribe, on the assumption that trends occurring in one society may also appear in others.

In Meru, for example, supernatural practitioners certainly did *not* work in isolation from one another, whatever tradition may suggest. On the contrary they not only cooperated but also covertly practiced one another's specialties, assuming whatever role their work required. Nor, despite the testimony of tradition, were they either isolated from or in opposition to the community at large. Even those agents that tradition claimed as entirely malevolent (the cursers) had roles identical to those of their allegedly benevolent counterparts, so that both functioned to make the larger system work.

At an individual level each specialist, regardless of his malevolence, gave other people feelings of security, by permitting them to believe at least temporarily that they could manipulate the supernatural forces on which they so depended to explain calamity within their lives. At the communal level ritualists interacted with both Kiama elders and ancestral spirits to make up a single, three-stranded system blending secular and spiritual justice in ways at least roughly comparable to our own.

Within the framework of this larger system, concepts such as prophecy, cursing, curse removal, and divination meshed with those of public interrogation, livestock sacrifice, trial by ordeal, and communal decisions. Their purpose, simply stated, was to manage social conflict: to channel, publicize, redress, and finally reconcile each case of individual contention as it appeared, by redirecting it into the hands of specialized practitioners at the moment it became violent and thus visible to society as a whole.

A cuckolded husband, for example, might wish to kill a suspected lover. Alternatively, he could seek the ritual services of a specialist. By accepting this responsibility, the curser, curse remover, and all the others of their class functioned solely to maintain communal stability and continuous survival, making what the British would later label "witchcraft" the servant of society.

Society's second servant was the curse. Meru tradition maintains that its only purpose was to express hostility, in the form of a wish to cause physical harm. It seems evident, however, that resolution, not revenge, was intended. Someone angry enough to curse another—whether personally or through a specialist—was, in fact, publicizing a state of conflict between himself (or herself) and a specific enemy. This exposure, furthermore, was meant to force that enemy to take actions which would reveal that conflict to the community in a manner that could ensure its eventual resolution.

A cuckolded husband, for example, unable either to stop the suspected infidelities of his wife or discern the identity of her lover, might seek the services of a cursing specialist to cast a generalized curse. Superficially, the verbal intent would be purely malevolent: "He who has harmed me, let his chest burst from pains. . . ." The underlying intent, however, would be not physically to destroy the lover but force him to reveal his activities. This revelation would be ritualized so as to not only stifle the actual transgression by publicizing it but also gain the husband material redress (livestock) for the harm that had been done. In short, the formal curse was intended neither to harm nor destroy. Its purpose was to serve justice.

Three underlying principles within the cursing system support this contention. One is that every curse, regardless of its origin, could swiftly be removed by a visit to the appropriate supernatural specialist. Several of these existed within every clan. Obviously, with supernatural assistance instantly available, no one was expected to sicken and die.

A second principle can be found in the practice of giving such aid only in exchange for specified fees. Each stage in the entire process required the sacrifice of considerable numbers of livestock, whether to the various specialists or to the elders involved in final judgments and reconciliation. Clearly, every Meru must have realized that violation of social norms would lead eventually to heavy economic loss.

The third principle lies in the series of social, sexual, and spiritual sanctions that acted to ensure universal participation in the system. The ritualized isolation must have been particularly painful to a communally oriented people like the Meru, and the loneliness of separation, as well as sexual pressures, would in themselves have acted to spur victims into swift and decisive action. To have refused or evaded full participation at any stage would have exposed the entire community to the same psychological stresses as the victims, lest they too be implicated in the inevitable disaster. To relieve their own anxieties, they would have forced recalcitrants into action. Under such circumstances refusal to participate in the required rituals would have been psychologically impossible.

The formal curse, then, and by implication the entire system of supernatural specialization, was something far different from what colonial observers understood as undirected malevolence "witchcraft."

Rather, the system was a ritualized means of generating economic penalties for the violation of communal norms. It combined the threat of supernatural retribution with the certainty of economic loss—a system of religion, secular law, and social order that seems not so different from that which Europe's missionaries and administrators imposed in its place.

CHAPTER II

Enslavement Traditions: Persecution and Flight

"They [Nguo Ntuni] came wearing red cloth and curved
swords, and there was no end to how cruel they could
be. . . . The final task they set . . . was to make a spear so
long its point would touch the sky."[1]

M'Ikieni M'Itimbere
Murungi age-set
Age: Early eighties

The most beloved and widely known among Meru oral traditions are
those concerned with a people known only as the Nguo Ntuni (red
clothes). They are recalled as the most powerful of those tribes neighboring Mbwaa and the only group without a single identifiable location. Rather, they lived within small log stockades ("walled villages")
that were scattered at various points on the mainland and used as trading centers. The Nguo Ntuni also sailed, and islanders could see their
ships pass ("like clouds") across their eastern horizon, disappearing in
the direction of the rising sun.

Around 1700 ("when the men of Ntangi were warriors"), a group of
Nguo Ntuni attacked Mbwaa. They appeared in a large sailing vessel
that landed on the mainland, opposite the island's western shore. The
ship's crew then crossed the intervening waters on crude wooden rafts.

NGUO NTUNI: THE INVADERS

The invaders are remembered as taller and lighter skinned than the islanders. They wore a single red cloth tied around their waists and at
one shoulder, and bound another around their heads. Each carried a
short sword of the scimitar type, of which the blade curved backward
and only the outer edge was honed. They also carried several guns.

Informants differ on the nature of the conquest. Some state that there
was a single battle in which the use of the guns proved decisive. Others
believe that the islanders did not resist. All agree, however, that the

Nguo Ntuni victory was complete and that the pre-Meru entered a period of enslavement.

The Nguo Ntuni proved harsh and efficient masters. They seized existing food and livestock, and then set the islanders to work producing more. To prevent their escape, recalcitrant workers were pierced behind an ankle. A rope was passed through the opening and secured to a post in the ground. Males were also forced to "gather" ivory—whether from their existing stocks or by hunting is unclear—and carry it across the channel to a separate group of Nguo Ntuni on the mainland.

The invaders also brought certain innovations that were considered blessings. One was a type of plow that replaced the islanders' simple digging stick. More significant, the newcomers introduced an iron fish trap, one large enough to entrap the fish that had previously broken their wooden hooks. Finally, a new kind of cow ("like a buffalo, without a hump") was brought onto the island, and the defeated were set to tending what were now their masters' herds.

Contemporary informants refer unanimously to this period in their history as one of outright slavery. More likely, it consisted of an initial theft of whatever wealth was available, followed by the development of some form of tribute relationship. This hypothesis would seem to be substantiated by Nguo Ntuni behavior after the conquest. Evidently, some or all of them returned to the mainland, reappearing only at certain seasons ("they had their times"). They normally lived on the mainland behind a log stockade. They had other slaves whom they used to cultivate their mainland gardens but spoke to them in a language that no islander could understand.

WHO WERE THE NGUO NTUNI?

The Nguo Ntuni were most likely East African coastal Arabs, descendants of one of the earlier Middle Eastern migrant groups that had formed numerous commercial communities along the Kenya-Somalia coast. Descriptions of their appearance, clothes, and weapons tend to confirm this identification, as do the informants themselves.

A variant of the Nguo Ntuni tradition suggests non-African invaders. In some versions the conquerors are recalled as "Nguruntune," a pejorative with the implication of "red legs."[2] In the past, light-skinned non-Africans such as Europeans, Persians, and Arabs were commonly perceived as red by Bantu-speaking peoples. Thus, if the tradition refers to the invaders' skin color rather than their clothes, they may well have been non-African.

Linguistic data also provide clues to the invaders' origin. Informants state that the Nguo Ntuni did not speak Swahili yet could be quickly understood. In fact subsequent traditions recount considerable and often heated dialogue between victors and vanquished. This would seem to eliminate the possibility of an invading group that had sailed from distant regions in favor of one of the more local Arab communities that had settled adjoining island or mainland areas.

Nor would such a community have spoken Swahili. That language, since its inception, has always been a lingua franca, rather than a mother tongue, for many coastal peoples, including those of the Lamu Archipelago of which Manda Island (Mbwaa) is a part. It seems probable, therefore, that the invaders spoke a seventeenth-century variant of the dialect (Ki-Amu) then current in the archipelago, which islanders could understand.

Further support for this contention can be drawn from examination of a related Meru tradition that deals with the Mbwaa period ("when the men of Ntangi . . ."), the story of Mukuna Ruku. This tradition appears within the oral histories of the Gikuyu, Embu, and Meru peoples of Mount Kenya, as well as the adjacent Tharaka, Kamba, and Mbeere. The Meru version, however, appears at two widely separated points of tribal history. During the first (Ntangi age-set, ca. 1700), Mukuna Ruku is described as having lived behind a log stockade that the Nguo Ntuni had constructed on the mainland. He had red skin, which he kept covered at all times with cloth, a fact the islanders found odd.

Mukuna Ruku was also unique in that he never appeared or spoke to the islanders. Instead, men of Mbwaa who appeared at the barricade with heavy loads of ivory were instructed to drop them at the narrow gate. Then they beat upon a piece of wood that hung nearby (*gakuna ruku:* to beat a piece of wood). Having drawn attention, they withdrew from view.

The gate then opened, and Mukuna Ruku took the tusks, leaving prescribed amounts of beads in exchange ("placing *tucu, marutia,* and *ngambi* [beads] into the horn"). He beat the wood once more to attract the islanders' attention, then left. No word was spoken on either side, and the islanders, never able to learn the identity of the figure within the stockade, may gradually have raised it first to literary and then mythological stature.[3]

The figure of Mukuna Ruku disappears, however, from the traditions of subsequent age-sets. The story recurs only in narrations that deal with the mid-nineteenth century, when interest in ivory was reawakened by the initial appearance of Kamba traders in the Meru region. Men of that era (Kubai age-set) inquired as to where the tusks would be taken. The Kamba replied with a story similar to that which the Meru themselves had brought from Mbwaa. In this version the tusks were taken, by middlemen recalled as the Baruku, once again to Mukuna (or Mukuno) Ruku, this time explicitly identified as an Arab trader who had come from the direction of the sunrise and who required the "silent" trading system to do business.

It seems probable that the Meru, recalling their own experiences with "silent" traders, simply incorporated the Kamba tradition into their own body of folklore, where it has overlaid and perhaps distorted the earlier Mbwaa version. Nonetheless, the fact that the nineteenth-century accounts explicitly identify the figure of this silent trader with the Arabs makes it possible to identify the earlier pre-Meru trading figure with them as well.

The ultimate check on the validity of Meru tradition, of course, is the degree to which it corresponds with other historical data for the area. For instance, informants are unable to identify significant Arab towns, either on the mainland or adjacent islands. At first glance this inability seems hard to understand, in view of the proximity of Lamu, Pate, and other Arabized trading centers, each of which should greatly have influenced their immediate African neighbors. However, the period immediately prior to that in which Meru history begins (1770) was marked by continual conflict between the Arabized populations of all archipelago principalities and the Portuguese, struggles in which the latter were usually successful.

The rulers of Pate, to select only one example, revolted unsuccessfully against Portuguese domination in 1637, 1660, 1678–1679, and 1686–1688. The conflict of 1678–1679 cost the rulers of Pate and Lamu their heads. The battles of 1686–1688 took the life of Pate's next king and twelve of his counselors. Two years later Lamu was ravaged, with the Portuguese taking huge numbers of prisoners.[4] In short, the era was marked by rebellion on one side and repression on the other, a situation that ended only when the Portuguese were defeated at Mombasa in 1698, thus allowing the archipelago communities to regain their strength.

It seems possible, therefore, to accept the Meru assumption that the Nguo Ntuni of this era lived in scattered and heavily fortified stockades rather than in a few large towns that might well have been sacked, evacuated, or destroyed. If we further assume the attack on Mbwaa to have taken place around 1700, as tradition suggests, it would fit in with that period in which Arabized trading centers throughout the archipelago were merely beginning to reorganize their resources and expand.

It also seems possible to assume that the first need of a resurgent commercial community would be the acquisition of sufficient farmland to feed its rising population as well as whatever labor might be needed to till it. These needs would logically be sought on the community's own or adjacent islands, because their population could be more easily controlled than mainland societies with the chance to flee.

This type of speculation fits rather easily into the Meru tradition of their conquest. The Nguo Ntuni may originally have come merely to plunder, perhaps attracted by the occasional tusks the islanders brought to trade. They remained, however, to force their victims to herd, fish, and cultivate. The ultimate goal was production of food.

PERSECUTION AND FLIGHT

Further insight into the Arabic nature of the Nguo Ntuni can be found in examination of the Meru tradition describing the invaders' persecution of their people and their own subsequent flight from the island. The earliest version of this tradition was recorded in 1910.[5] Longer versions were gathered by early district commissioners in 1913, 1918, and 1925, as well as by a missionary in 1934.[6] The story has changed surprisingly little throughout the years, with earlier versions corresponding closely to those I recorded in 1969.

After a period of submission to their conquerors the pre-Meru grew increasingly hostile, refusing to herd the flocks and till the fields as commanded. Angered, the Nguo Ntuni summoned the elders' Kiama before them for judgment. Mocking their alleged collective wisdom, the invaders set them a series of increasingly unreasonable tasks. The first called for the elders to drop a small round fruit into a deep hole, then recover it without using either hands or sticks. Baffled, they turned to the community's ritual specialists, as was traditional in times of crisis. In this instance a Muga (curse remover), recalled by the Meru as Koome Njoe, suggested they fill the hole with water, then float the fruit to the top. The 1913 version reads: "The Kiama held a shauri [meeting] and decided . . . to fill the hole with water until it overflowed and the fruit floated out with the water. This they did, and the Nguntuni [sic] said yes you have performed the task but now we want you to do something else."[7]

The second task was to provide the Nguo Ntuni with an "eight-sided cloth," a problem that again baffled the Kiama. Koome Njoe responded, however, by providing the council with a cob of maize. The husk, when peeled, had eight sides. A third task called for the provision of a calf that would produce white dung. Koome Njoe reacted by starving the calf for a week, then feeding it milk and lime for four days more. Thereafter, its droppings were white. The Nguo Ntuni then demanded a sandal with hair on both sides. This was accomplished by using the dewlap of an ox, which was cut from the still-living animal and stitched into the desired shape while still sufficiently fresh enough to be flexible.

There were several other tasks, each more difficult than the last as the conquerors grew increasingly angry. One demand was for a "dog with horns," a problem that momentarily baffled even Koome Njoe. In the earliest versions, however, he advised the Kiama as follows: "They [the elders] caught a dik-dik [a tiny antelope], took its horns, then put them into the head of a dog, carefully sewing up the cuts [they had made] in the skin."[8] The elders completed the operation by smearing gum around the base of each horn, placing the animal's hair in the gum to conceal it, then immobilizing the animal until the entire incision had healed.

At this point, according to several versions of the tale, the Nguo Ntuni grew angry, demanding the death of several Kiama elders. The old men responded by withdrawing from the invaders' camp to hold a final feast, at which every family was to present a goat. When the time came, blood from the slaughtered animals was allowed to run into the waters that flowed from the point the elders had chosen for their feasting into the Nguo Ntuni camp. Spokesmen for the islanders' warriors then appeared with the blood of the slain animals still on their spears to report to the Nguo Ntuni that the executions had been carried out.

The Nguo Ntuni then gathered the remaining elders together and assigned what was to prove their final task—the forging of a single spear so long that it would reach the clouds. This time neither the Kiama nor Koome Njoe could offer a solution. In desperation they turned to another ritual specialist, a prophet who claimed in time of crisis to speak for the entire tribe.

The prophet, variously described as a Mururia (foreteller) or Mugwe (transmitter of ancestral blessings), could offer no direct solution to the problem of the spear. He declared, however, that he had been having "dreams of suffering," in which he saw the entire people fleeing their burning homes. Fearful now of the consequences should they fail in this final task, he proposed that the islanders flee.

As a first step the prophet suggested an elaborate scheme to deceive the Nguo Ntuni until preparations for the flight could be made. Initially, elders from the oldest age-set were sent daily to the conquerors, bearing ever longer pieces of rope, which they reported as reflecting the slowly lengthening spear.

In due time these elders informed their masters that the smiths had completed construction of a gigantic forge, which would send a great glow into the sky that same evening. The Nguo Ntuni were warned to keep away from the forge, lest they be burned by the supernatural power of its flame.

At the same time, elaborate plans were made for the flight. Specific clans were designated to carry and protect certain objects while on the march. The yam, for example, was carried by the clan now known as Abwekana (*gikana:* yam stem). The goat (*mburi*) was carried by the clan of Kiniamburi, and so forth. The objects held sacred to the community were carried by the Omo, the clan believed closest to the ancestral spirits and from which the men of Mbwaa drew their Mugwe, the prophet who transmitted all ancestral blessings.

The tribe then divided into three marching bands, with individual clans represented in each "so that if one [band] was lost, all clans would survive." The first unit was composed wholly of warriors and was to act as an advance guard. The second was made up of apprentice elders, men of middle age, but who could fight if needed. The final group consisted solely of the women, aged, and children. It was led by the prophet himself, because only the power of magic and the blessings of ancestors could provide such a group with protection. When night fell, every dwelling in the village was set afire, thereby providing the great glow in the sky that the elders had promised their persecutors. The warrior band set out immediately afterward, leaving by the light of the moon. Thereafter, the descendants of this group would be known by the name Nyaga (moon) or Njiru (darkness, black). The second group set out at dawn, subsequently receiving the name Ntuni (red). The final group left in full daylight and was thereafter called Njeru (white).

The first stage of the flight stopped almost before it began. Whether by miscalculation or chance, the channel between Mbwaa and the mainland was under water and no one dared to cross. The prophet responded by requesting three men willing to sacrifice themselves for the people. The first of these, Muthetu, was to be a human altar upon which the sacrifice could be performed. The second, Gaita (or Aita), permitted his stomach to be opened by the prophet's knife, so that the latter could read omens from his intestines—the crisis having become too severe for the traditional opening of a goat to have sufficed. The third, Kiuna, stood by in reserve in case Gaita's courage failed. With the sacrifice complete, the prophet placed magic powder on the tail of an animal that he held in his hand, then scattered it onto the waters that barred their way. These moved obligingly to one side—whether by tidal action or the prophet's magic—and the entire community crossed to safety.

WHY DID THEY FLEE?

Obviously, an oral tradition concerned with persecution, fulfillment of impossible tasks, and evasion by flight across a conveniently retreating body of water is too similar to biblical themes to be accepted literally. These themes are frequently repeated within both Arabic and Hebrew literature, from which they passed not only to the Western world but to those African peoples with whom the Arabs made contact. Traditions of the Bajun, for instance, a people immediately north of the Lamu-Manda area, describe their own alleged migration from southern Arabia to the Somali coast in a similar manner. Passage across the intervening waters, in this case too, was achieved only after a leading ritual specialist (here, a sheikh) forced the waters to move aside.[9]

It seems possible to assume, therefore, that the ancestral Meru also acquired the basic elements of this tradition through contact with an Arabized people, at a time when their own conquest and enslavement permitted equation of the ancient Hebrew theme of persecution (e.g., "bricks from straw") with their own. Tradition implies that their prophets seized upon the second theme—escape across the receding waters—as a solution to their plight, then led their people into exile. It seems more likely, however, that the pre-Meru initially learned an earlier, more Islamized version of the story from their conquerors, transposing it subsequently into their own cultural context only after completing the escape.

This still leaves the question of why they fled at all. Traditions from other northeastern Bantu tribes, particularly those who are said to have migrated from the Somali coastal regions of Shungwaya, cite pressure from the southward-moving Galla or the desiccation of farmlands as the cause of their flight. Neither of these possibilities appears in any form within Meru tradition, and it seems we need look no further than the rise of one of the archipelago principalities (most likely Pate) to a position of power over adjacent African peoples. The traumatic shock of conquest and enslavement together with the introduction of an ideology glorifying persecution, prophecy, and flight seem to have been the catalysts that set these people on their way.

THE MIGRATION

The similarity to biblical themes continues in the earliest of the migration traditions then fades as the migrants moved inland. As they reached the mainland, informants state that the group was forced to "climb a mountain" and then file across a narrow "gate" to avoid leaving tracks for their pursuers. On descending, they reached the banks of what is remembered as the "red sea" (*irea itune*). Informants are unanimous in their descriptions: its waters were red, fresh ("we could drink it"), slow flowing, shallow, and evidently very wide, since the migrants took an unusually long time ("many days") to cross. Tradition records that they thereafter followed the "left" (south) bank of the river, moving steadily "westward."

It seems probable that this second water crossing was made near the mouth of the Tana River. At present the river bank would permit westward migration only between the contemporary communities of Anasa and Kau. At certain seasons the waters in this area become reddish and extend miles beyond the normal river channels, through at a shallow depth.

However, the Tana River mouth has shifted at least once within the last century and its position during the early 1700s may have been different from any we now know. Moreover, detailed maps of the Tana show a series of cliffs or escarpments along the southern portion of the present river mouth and the entire length of the former one. A single "mountain," Milima Kitanga (174 feet), also forms part of the escarpment near the former river mouth. Any of these could conceivably be the height referred to by tradition, since their stony crests would indeed conceal the tracks of refugees. Finally, only a crossing of the Tana during its period of shallow flooding, whether at its current outlet or some former variation, would have permitted the refugees to continue westward while remaining on its left, or southern, bank.

The term *westward,* however, can be deceiving. Among contemporary Meru informants it carries connotations of both "inland" and "uphill," the consequence of life spent on a steep mountain slope, where all three terms are synonymous. Laughton notes that the Ki-Meru (Meru language) words for "right hand" (*urio*), "left hand" (*umotho*), and "high" (*ruguru*), also mean "north," "south," and "west," respectively.[10] From this he concludes that the Meru language developed at a time when the westerly direction was uphill.

In fact the best translation of the term *westward* is probably "inland," for tradition records that the migrants spent the next four seasons moving along the Tana River's southern bank. During this period, recalled as one of fear and hardship, they lived primarily from the few goats and sheep they had managed to bring with them, as well as whatever crops they could manage to raise. They also supplemented their diet by fishing, reverting to the traditional wooden hooks they had used prior to their period of conquest. Oddly, no attempt was made to duplicate the Nguo Ntuni's iron-cage method of fish trapping, perhaps because of the lack of iron-bearing sands in the lower Tana region.[11] The migrants developed a new trapping technique, however, using a simple lasso made of tightly woven goat's hair; this could be dropped around a fish in such a way as to snag it by the gills, at least long enough for the fishermen to complete the job.

After four seasons the migrants left the river entirely, turning "westward" into what tradition explicitly calls a "desert." They named this area Ngaaruni (arid place), or Maliankanga (holes of the guinea fowl), which also carries a linguistic implication of aridity. At this point the migrants began to call themselves Ngaa, a word possibly derived from the thorns (*migaa*) they used to protect themselves at night, but which may also have referred to the "disappearance" (drying up) of the river they had left behind.[12] In either case the migrants henceforth referred to themselves as the Ngaa until their eventual fragmentation near Mount Kenya.

WHY INTO THE DESERT?

The decision of a coastal, water-oriented group of migrants to leave the security of their only known source of water and march into what they perceived as desert is so striking as to require further examination. The existing oral evidence suggests two possible reasons.

Tradition declares the decision was based on their fear of recapture, either by the Nguo Ntuni or by other peoples they might meet along the river route. At the beginning of their flight the migrants were fully conscious of their own military weakness. They had few warriors, and these were armed only with small bows, wood-tipped arrows, and iron knives. They were further burdened by the need to defend their livestock and eventually their growing crops.

The result was a series of half-formed settlements along the river bank. Huts were established, crops sown, and food gathered from the surrounding lands and river. Nevertheless, their fears eventually caught up with them, as their very immobility led them to expect the Nguo Ntuni to reappear. Predictably, one or another of their ritual specialists prophesied their foe's appearance, and the entire group seized their goods and fled, leaving half-ripened crops behind.

A related reason may have come from their reliance on prophecy. Since the first moments of flight every stage of the Ngaa migration had been guided by their prophets, in contact with communal ancestors through the medium of dreams. During the final period of their march along the river, prophetic dreams had shown their former captors searching along its opposite (northern) bank for a crossing that would permit their recapture. Fear of this in turn engendered further prophecies in which the hardships of travel in a "desert" would be followed by entry into a more promising land, where they could live in peace and economic plenty. One of these, recalled only among the elders of Igembe region, is as follows:

> Tutigatura rwanda rururu kenya na kenya indi tukauma guntu guku na tukinye nthugure iingi injega nkukuki.
>
> (We shall not be in this desert forever, but shall leave this place and get to better land.)
>
> Gikiri giakwa kia mithega gigantongeria guntu kuu kweru. Tugiita tukauma naja tukamba nthiguru ngeni na antu banao tukabona ndweene iinyingi na tubenge baumeku na n'gombe cia tugataa.
>
> (My magic gourd will direct me to the new place. As we leave, we will settle in a foreign land, whose people we will defeat in battles and whose cattle we will seize.)[13]

Of course, more than fear and prophecy might be required to force a riverine people into a true desert. In fact, no such desert existed. Had the Ngaa moved either north or west from any point on the lowest reaches of the Tana, they would not have encountered desert in the sense of an ecological wasteland but an area of light bush and scattered trees, broken by several seasonal river systems and a large number of permanent papyrus swamps.

The traditions, when examined closely, suggest precisely this type of terrain, declaring that the first area crossed after leaving the river was open, stony, and nearly treeless but with sufficient foliage ("white" grasses) for livestock to graze. Thus, though the migrants may have been catalyzed by the power of prophecy as tradition suggests, they may equally have decided to follow an existing seasonal waterway. The seasonal river Laga Buna, which drains into the lower Tana at Kibusa, provides one such possible route, and there are several others.

THE FRINGE COMMUNITIES

The chronicles state that the migrants fled the island in three distinct bands. Each was named for the time of its departure. Thus, the black, white, and red clans left at night, dawn, and sunset, respectively. The three colors providing one of the tribe's earliest social divisions; these identities are retained today.

A second type of fission, this one economic, began soon after the migration began. Once the Ngaa were well launched on their journey up the Tana River, three increasingly distinct groups emerged. The main body of migrants remained close to the river, using its waters to reestablish their traditional herding, agricultural, and fishing economy. Their political and judicial institutions also stayed unchanged. The system of Kiamas continued to function, resolving conflicts within each age-set precisely as before. The ritual specialists continued to prophecy, curse, divine, and heal, maintaining contact with ancestors through the medium of dreams and providing direction to the flight.

The authority of those institutions, however, did not apply equally to all members of the society. Over time the change in economic conditions forced at least two sections of the community into positions of increasing estrangement. They did not split off from the main body but developed increasingly distinct identities of their own, which forced them gradually onto the community's fringe.

ATURI: THE IRONSMITHS

This process can be envisioned most clearly by examining the economic evolution of the Aturi, or ironsmiths. While on Mbwaa, traditions suggest, their craft was considered neither mysterious nor exotic. The iron they used was derived from iron sand, a magnite with a black metallic luster. It was easily visible, thus simple to collect; during heavy rains noticeable quantities were washed out of streambeds, gullies, or even pathways and could be quickly gathered. It also occurred in permanent watercourses, where it could be gathered in sufficient quantities for smelting.[14] Iron ore was thus both abundant and accessible. It was smelted through the use of a triangular goatskin bag, which when filled and compressed formed an adequate bellows.

Like other coastal Bantu, the smiths of Mbwaa did not form a single clan. Rather, each clan had its own ironworkers, often from one family, who drew apprentices from among its own or others' sons. Relations between the smiths and other islanders were evidently cordial, because traditions state they participated in feasts and were allowed to marry whom they pleased. Within an economy of abundance their craft lacked mystery. Land was limited, but every family had its source of iron sand. More important, there was enough for all.

Every one of these conditions changed with the commencement of the migration. Since land was now limitless, boundaries were now unknown. The traditions that had established them, thereby protecting sources of supply, had disappeared. More important, the lower regions of the Tana River area through which the migrants passed revealed no iron sand at all, precisely when the psychological need for iron-tipped weapons must have been strongest.[15] This need was not only military but supernatural. Iron was believed to have a life force of its own, an intrinsic power to either harm or protect men. Without it neither hunters nor warriors could face the wilderness with confidence.

The ironsmiths thus extended their search. Banding together for the first time in tribal history, they moved away from the security of the river and began to search inland. Over time, small, scattered supplies of ore were discovered, but these failed to provide the smiths with their former sense of security. To protect what little had been found, the smiths jointly sought that security within the supernatural, developing rituals and practices that had no precedent in island tradition. In consequence, these rites progressively estranged them from the cultivator/herders that made up the mainstream of the migrants.

A-ATHI: THE HUNTERS

The same type of transformation occurred among those families who from the beginning of their migration had chosen to hunt wild game or gather honey, rather than fish, herd, or farm. Tradition records nothing of either meat or honey hunting in Mbwaa, suggesting it did not occur. Once on migration, however, the lack of grain or livestock must have led men from the poorest clans to seek new sources of food.

Banding together in the same manner as the ironsmiths, they formed themselves into hunting bands (A-Athi; sing: Mwathi or Mu-Athi) sharing whatever was scavenged or speared. As the regions nearest the river were exhausted, they penetrated deeper and deeper inland. As their proficiency grew, they spent more and more time apart from the main community, developing customs, rituals, and even vocabularies known only to themselves.

As their estrangement from the river migrants intensified, the hunters found themselves in the same position as the ironsmiths. Their very successes raised the problem of preserving sources of supply. A-Athi clan traditions speak, even today, of the joy with which the first hives were discovered ("in tree caves"), as well as of the feasts that took place once substantial wild game had been found. Their inevitable second thought, however, was to protect what was found. A beehive could be stripped by any passerby; "mainstream" herders or cultivators could swiftly disperse concentrations of game.

Consequently, both ironsmiths and hunters gradually drifted away from the migrants' communal tradition. For herders and cultivators, people of the migrant mainstream, the patterns of social control could continue unchanged, for the simple reason that land for both farming and grazing was unlimited, thus needed no protection. The same was not true for either hunters or smiths. The commodities they sought, and perceived as prerequisite to their own survival, were undependable, limited, and could be rapidly depleted once found.

Both groups thus reacted by expanding the traditional curse, extending and reshaping it to fit their economic needs. On Mbwaa, cursing was a private affair, used to ritualize and thereby resolve conflicts between individuals. Only the council of ruling elders, acting in concert against a recalcitrant individual, was permitted to intensify the impact of a curse by reciting it collectively.

Now, both smiths and hunters adapted the tradition to their needs. The smiths, drawing on their beliefs in the intrinsic power of iron, adapted a communal form of cursing to its creation. Gathering their entire band around a single blazing fire, they began a chant in time to the systematic pound of their hammers against a single giant forge: "Let he who touches iron be as dry [hot] as this piece that I strike. Let he who touches iron be as dry [hot] as my hammer itself. No more trouble. No more trouble."

The curse was intended, of course, to be heard by the entire community. It would then strike at anyone who felt guilty. Having "troubled" any member of the smiths in some fashion, individuals would develop appropriate physical and mental symptoms. The community would react by isolating the victims, and the entire process of ritualized reconciliation would begin.

The hunters followed a similar pattern. Successful kills or the discovery of hives would be followed by nighttime feasts of meat or honey. These would ostensibly be set "in the bush." In fact they were always within earshot of the settled community. A curse was chanted by the entire company, followed by a single meaningless sound intended to carry through the night air to every migrant hut.

The words of the hunters' curse followed mainstream tradition. No specific names were mentioned. The proposed punishments were both socially appropriate and physically visible ("he who touches [this hive] . . . let his arm shrivel"). Only the crime had changed, and with it the intent of the curse itself. Formerly an instrument of personal vengeance, it was transformed into one of economic protection, levied by increasingly deviant minorities against the mainstream community itself.

The duplication of other mainstream social institutions occurred in turn, as both hunters and ironsmiths followed the logic of what each had begun. The casting of curses to protect a single group required the emergence of specialists unique to that group to deal with the consequences as well as Kiamas (councils of elders) subsequently to reconcile the persons most concerned.

In consequence hunters and smiths developed a "duplicate" series of councils (Kiama Kia A-Athi: council of hunters; Kiama Kia Aturi: council of ironsmiths) for each of its age-sets, patterned precisely like those of the mainstream but outside of its control. Similarly, each group created its own class of ritualists who prophesied, cursed, divined, and healed only among members of their own subcommunity.

Thus a curse, with its attendant condition of impurity, could be imposed by members of the "mainstream" cultivator-herders, the hunters, or the smiths. Victims had to appeal to specialists from the appropriate group for physical and mental relief and thereafter to that group's ruling council for judgment, restitution, and eventual reconciliation. A honey thief, for example, had to deal with the ritualists and ruling elders of the A-Athi hunters; a livestock thief, with those of the mainstream.

Over time the progressive estrangement among these groups was formalized by the creation of taboos, forbidding members of one occupation to share food and drink with those of the other two, thereby eliminating what is perhaps the single most important act of Bantu hospitality. Men who ate wild game, for example, were forbidden to touch cow's milk or millet, even in the form of beer. Those who did not were forbidden to consume the meat of wild animals. The smiths followed similar patterns. In consequence both groups found themselves ritually barred from the meat feasts and beer drinking that were the core of social interaction within the mainstream community. Although still part of society, they were restricted to its fringes, a development that would significantly affect the evolution of Meru history.

NGAARUNI: INTO THE DESERT

Tradition records that after having left the safety of their river for the uncertainty of what they perceived as desert, the migrants first drew water from the "elephant's footsteps." This phrase, in fact, is an ancient Meru euphemism for areas of shallow papyrus swamp so large they took several days to walk around. These swamps were also seasonal, drying up wholly or partially at the end of each rainy season and thus forcing the migrants to periodically move on.

At the first of these swamps, recalled as Kirorero (dreaming to a purpose; prophecy), the group swore an oath to stand and destroy the Nguo Ntuni, should the latter still pursue them. No enemy appeared, so the migrants dwelt peacefully for several seasons, long enough to initiate a new age-set (Nkuthuku), perhaps in the 1720s. Thereafter, the migrants moved on, always heading either north or west. Several more seasons of wandering elapsed before a second area of swampland large enough to sustain the group was discovered. This was named Thingithu, and it supported them for three seasons. They then moved to a third area (Rurii), a fourth (Tubaranya), and a fifth (Irikinu). Thereafter, still moving either north or west, they passed on to other sites, whose names have since been lost.

At some time in this period of the march, however, the Ngaa passed an area remembered as Kiiru (raised place), where "four white peaks" could be seen. These may possibly refer to the mountains of Kathiliwa, Mutito, Makongo, and Endau, among the highest points in this area, whose peaks are covered with white mist at certain times of the day.[16] An actual crossing of this area is doubtful, because it would probably have led to encounters with the Kamba groups, which informants deny occurred. Because the "four peaks" can be observed from any point in the lowlands between seasonal swamps formed by the Thua and Hiraman rivers, however, it seems possible to assume that the migrants passed that way.

After leaving the Hiraman River, however, a northwesterly march would have brought the migrants into increasingly arid regions, devoid of swamps, where dry-season water could be found only by digging. Traditions recall such periods, stating that the Ngaa survived later stages of their journey only by digging holes ("to the height of two men") in seasonal riverbeds. In addition only narrations of this "arid" period mention the hunting of Grevey's zebra and the reticulated giraffe, species found only in Kenya's dry northern regions.

Similarly, a continued northwesterly movement from the Hiraman River would have caused the migrants to cross an area where Kamba oral history recalls an old caravan route, which once ran in a rough line between present-day Garissa and Nguni.[17] Meru traditions offer no direct information on the existence of such a route but do mention wild donkeys in the "arid" areas, which were caught by Ngaa scouts. Because donkeys are not indigenous to this region, it seems possible to assume they had been introduced by trading caravans from the north and that the migrants did indeed pass near the place where such caravans once ran.

North of the "caravan route" the terrain changes rapidly to dense bush, a circumstance that may have forced the migrants to turn more sharply west. At this point the name Thingithu (given, according to tradition, to one of the seasonal swamps) is worth recalling. Thingithu is the current name of a river in central Meru. A similar term, however, "Thunguthu," describes a large seasonal river system that flows eastward from the Kamba highlands becoming the Nthunguthu, the Tula, and the Lower Tula before draining into the Tana River. It is the area north of the Lower Tula River that changes swiftly into bush, making a trek northwest along that river an attractive alternative to migrants approaching from the south.

A migrant community that chose to follow the Lower Tula–Tula-Nthunguthu-Thunguthu river system, moreover, would "emerge" from it just southeast of Mount Kenya, near the area of present-day Mbeere. This is precisely what Meru traditions record; clan elders from every section have declared that their ancestors "passed through" Mbeere and approached Mount Kenya from the south.

Several of the landmarks passed during this stage have also been recalled. One of these, Machanca (come to a point; sharp peak), appears to refer to the single peak of Kiambere Hill, for it is always mentioned in connection with a second, Mbacacca (many peaks), which informants recall as a range of hills along the right bank of the Tana River. This may refer to the Mumoni Hills, because these (along with the Kiambere) would be the first "peaks" that a migrant group would pass after leaving the Nthunguthu waterway. A final landmark, Orimba (papyrus), appears in old European maps in this area as a hill, now known as Kiburu, just north of Mbeere.

This stage in the migration can be said to have ended with a final crossing of another "great river." Traditions refer to this as the Kiluluma, Kinunuma, Kilunkuma, or similar variants—all words used by various central highland peoples to denote the Tana River. On first reaching the river, the Ngaa found themselves unable to cross without losing their livestock. They therefore moved north along the right bank to a point (or several points) where other rivers flowed into the Tana (the Mutonga and Ena rivers have been frequently mentioned), making the waters relatively shallow. Here they remained long enough to unite a new age-set (Mukuruma), perhaps in the 1730s, then crossed the river and moved north beyond its bank toward Mount Kenya, the ice-capped peak of which could be seen clearly in the distance.

KAGAIRO: THE SECOND FRAGMENTATION

During the 1730s the Ngaa traveled north and west through today's Mbeere region, moving along a line of forested hills that run from the modern Mount Kiburu (then, Orimba Hill), to Mount Kiaga. In so doing, they impinged upon a territory then inhabited by two other peoples, subsequently to be known as the Cuka (or Chuka) and Tharaka.

At that time both those societies were divided into two smaller sections. The early Cuka were then known as Chabugi and Irari; the Tharaka as Mbugi (or Diacho) and Chagala (or Murutu). The sharing of one name between the two societies suggests a long association between them, including frequent intermarriage. This in turn would appear to reflect the growth of economic interdependence between peoples who lived in a mountain forest and those who herded livestock on an arid plain.

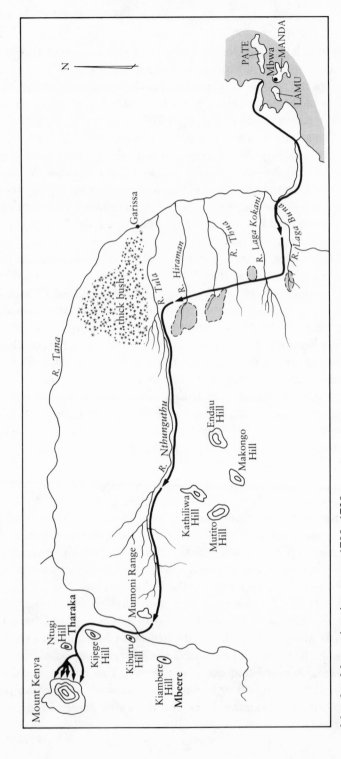

Map 3. Meru migration route: 1700–1730

Initially, the Ngaa appear to have been drawn toward the shelter of Mount Kenya's forest. Tradition states that they first settled at a point along the lower forest fringes, where they encountered the already resident Cuka. After a severe clash, the Cuka drove the migrants off; the Ngaa fled downhill into the plain, then north into the area now known as Tharaka.

Perhaps to their own amazement, they were received there in peace and dwelt for a considerable length of time in that section of the plain which then belonged to the Mbugi/Diacho clans. Traditions from both societies confirm they lived in harmony and that considerable intermarriage occurred. Perhaps for this reason the earlier unity of the Ngaa gradually dissolved, and they entered an era recalled in both Meru and Tharaka tradition as "the time of dividing" (Meru: *kagairo;* Tharaka; *igaironi*).

During this period, perhaps in the late 1730s, the original Ngaa nucleus separated into two segments, each of which took on an identity of its own. One was known as Mukunga (or Muku Ngaa: people of Ngaa). The other became Murutu, a name that may have been taken because of intermarriage with the Chagala/Murutu section of pre-Tharaka.

Initially, these two sections maintained their traditional (northwestern) direction of march. At a point that tradition places near today's Ntugi Hill, however, they fragmented once more. The Murutu appear to have divided into three smaller sections. One, retaining the name, remained on the plain to become part of the contemporary Tharaka. A second group moved westward toward Mount Kenya, eventually reaching the mountain base at the modern region of Mwimbi. The third segment pressed north into a then heavily wooded plain, known today as Tigania. In the years to come all three groups would remember their period of common identity ("Mwimbi, Tigania, and Murutu were once one") by creating rituals of pretended kinship that would eventually form the basis of military alliances between all three.

The second major segment of the original Ngaa fragmented in similar fashion, dividing into four and possibly five smaller sections. One moved northward toward the heavily forested mountains of the Nyambeni range, which stretches northeast from the base of Mount Kenya. Three others moved west, into the foothills that make up the lowest portions of modern Igoji, Abogeta (South Imenti), and Abothoguchi (North Imenti). The final group drifted south, eventually entering that part of the Mwimbi region that lies adjacent to modern Muthambi—an area they eventually seized from the Cuka in the 1880s. These groups too would commemorate their period of common identity ("Igoji, Igembe, Imenti, and Muthambi had one father") by establishing rituals of kinship that would evolve into military alliances, bonds that would set them against the clans of Mwimbi and Tigania and form the basis for future internecine war.

Tradition suggests that each migrant group may have adopted the Tharaka name for the mountain regions into which they climbed, a suggestion also advocated by H. E. Lambert. Lambert, using linguistic data, believes the migrants needed only to apply the prefix *amu-* (people of) or *iga-* (place of) to the Tharaka root word for each region. Thereafter, the original Ngaa prefix may have been incorporated into the compound word, eventually losing its separate meaning.[18]

Traditions from at least two regions support this theory to the south, the earlier "Amu-imbi," a name still recalled by informants, became "Mwimbi" (or Muimbi) rather than "Aimbi." If one applies the principle elsewhere, "Amu-thambi" becomes "Muthambi," and "Amu-iru" ("black" clans—those who fled Mbwaa at night) becomes "Mwiru," a form by which sections of contemporary Meru were known during the 1890s and which they still use to refer to themselves.

Similarly, tradition declares that the prefix *iga-* clearly applied to Igembe, whose people were known simply as the Mbe until 1900. When applied elsewhere, the concept suggests that those migrant groups entering Igoji (*iga-oji*), Imenti (*iga-mente*), and Tigania (*iga-nia*) may have followed similar patterns, each adopting the previous Tharaka name as their own. Certainly, tradition emerging from this point in time (1740s) up to the twentieth century says nothing more of the Ngaa; the name disappears entirely from the flow of oral history, which is recounted only from the perspective of these smaller social units (i.e., the Igoji, Imenti, and so forth), until the European conquest.

A question still remains, however, as to the reason for this fragmentation. Why would a band of migrants, sharing language, culture, and a common past trek thirty years through what must have seemed an arid wilderness only to break apart upon reaching more promising land? Neither the Meru nor Tharaka chronicles provide reasons for such fragmentation, other than to confirm it was not caused by war.

The answer, therefore, may be simply that various components of the original migrant group were faced with the lure of a wholly new type of topography. At that time the rugged lower slope of northeastern Mount Kenya and the neighboring Nyambeni Mountains were thickly forested. To the migrants they must have promised cool grazing, virgin cropland, inexhaustible water, and refuge against enemy attack. The choice was whether to seek the more favorable altitude or remain on the Tharaka Plain.

The slopes of this section of Mount Kenya, however, are also divided into steep, precipitous ridges, separated by swift rivers that are frequently in flood. Meru clan traditions invariably declare that their ancestors settled their respective sections by moving up along these rivers.[19] This seems consistent with their behavior throughout the migration and helps to answer the larger question of how a coastal island community settled finally on a forested mountainside. Because every portion of their earlier journey seems to have followed some form of swamp or river system, it is not difficult to imagine fragmentation occurring when they were faced with many smaller water systems emerging from a single mountain.

In their efforts to exploit this new environment, therefore, numbers of the migrants may simply have drifted out of contact with one another, becoming separated by the forest and the rugged ridges that they climbed, until gradually their common identity and even their common name had disappeared. Politically fragmented and demographically few, each band began to climb Kirima Kia Maara (now Kirimaara), the shining mountain, today's Mount Kenya.[20]

CHAPTER III

Mount Kenya Traditions: Fragmentation and War

"We [Meru] approached the Kirimaara [Mount Kenya] like a line of spears, with each [clan] marching upward toward the forest. For Mukuruma and Michubu [age-sets] it was a time of ax and firestick and fear."[1]

Hezikiah M'Mukiri
Murungi age-set
Age: Eighties

The chronicles suggest that every segment of the now fragmented Ngaa (pre-Meru) migrants reached the base of Mount Kenya, the Nyambeni Mountains, and the Tigania Plain during the late 1730s–1740s (Mukuruma age-set). What they saw must have awed and frightened them, for the landscape was completely outside their collective experience. Then as now, Mount Kenya rears up out of the flat surrounding plain like a lion crouching silently in dust. Its ice-capped peaks stand more than 17,000 feet high, providing a shining crown that the approaching migrants may have seen from almost sixty miles away.

Below them the mountain slope consisted of several zones, each with a distinct ecology that posed new problems to the approaching clans. The peaks themselves were ringed between 11,000 and 12,000 feet by a single belt of open moor. Tufts of grass and flowers bloomed in the shallow bogs, but chilling mists and icy winds made it impossible to remain for any length of time.

Between 9,000 and 11,000 feet the moor gave way to a zone of bamboo. Although interspersed with trees, it provided a nearly impenetrable barrier to man. In some areas bamboo groves grew 24 feet high. In others older plants had fallen to form tangled barriers, through which younger shoots struggled to grow. Except for paths forced open by rhino, buffalo, or elephant, this zone was also barred to man.

At 9,000 feet, however, the bamboo gave way to a zone of montaine rain forest, known subsequently among the Meru as the "black" forest. Currently, the black forest zone extends downslope to 7,000 feet, although originally it may have dipped nearly to the mountain's base. The trees were large, often 6 feet in diameter and 150 feet high. A thick canopy of branches shut out the sky, inhibiting undergrowth so that wild game slipped easily between the tree trunks.

To the Ngaa, however, the black forest contributed psychologically to the estrangement that had appeared between the core and fringe elements of the pre-Meru community. On one hand the forest offered A-Athi hunters hope of both honey and meat. On the other an annual rainfall of more than sixty inches, combined with months of chilling cold, made permanent habitation too difficult for mainstream cultivators and herders.

Below 7,000 feet, however, the black forest gave way to a narrow zone of bracken, a fern of no use to the migrants. Interspersed in this zone, however, occurring most often at 5,500 feet was a type of "sweet grass" that proved beneficial to cattle. Soil within this zone was unsuitable for cultivation, and the heavy rains and low temperatures deterred permanent residence. Nonetheless, this "bracken zone" was profitably used for dry-season grazing by people willing to live at a lower level.

Below 5,000 feet the bracken was replaced by a transitional forest of mixed deciduous and evergreen trees. Within this zone trees were smaller, ranging from 30 to 90 feet high. A thinner, more intermittent tree canopy permitted dense undergrowth, and the combination of adequate cover, moderate temperatures, and substantial rainfall attracted vast quantities of wildlife. These in turn drew hunters, and occasional glades of open grassland proved attractive both to herders and cultivators seeking grazing or agricultural sites.

Traditions suggest that earlier agriculturalists had cleared certain areas of this transitional forest prior to the migrants' arrival. At this elevation removal of the tree cover permitted the appearance of a second grass species, (star grass), indicative of highly fertile soil. This star-grass zone was narrow, occurring only between 4,000 and 5,000 feet. It combined adequate rainfall, fertile soil, and moderate temperatures with trees small enough to clear quickly away, however, thus permitting cultivation of an entire range of subsistence-level crops.

The star-grass zone was also characterized, however, by giant gorges, formed by the rivers that fanned radially out from Mount Kenya's peaks. Although the slope itself was gentle at this altitude, water runoffs from higher elevations had cut deep clefts through the bedrock. On reaching the star grass, many of these were 100 feet deep, with slopes too steep to climb. Even the smaller gorges ran 30 feet down and became impassable in rain.

Occupants of the star-grass zone were influenced in several ways by the gorges' depth and impassability. Ecologically, their steep sides made irrigation impossible, forcing potential cultivators to rely wholly on rain. Socially, their presence also isolated settlers from one another, restricting both casual communication and feelings of shared destiny.

Thus the gorges became political as well as geographic boundaries. Migrants entering the star-grass area from lower altitudes inevitably ascended along the ridgetops, following (and clearing) those areas where the vegetation was least dense. In settling along the narrow spines between the gorges, they invariably established them as the outer limits of their land claims, preferring to advance upward (rather than outward) each time new areas were cleared. In the process each migrant band—usually several clans—became a social unit unto itself, steadily decreasing its contact with more distant segments of the other Meru-speaking peoples, causing their sense of shared identity to virtually disappear. No longer, at this point in time, do the chronicles speak of "the migrants" or "the Ngaa" or even subtribes such as the Imenti. Rather, the only names recalled are those of individual ridgetop communities—Mwiriga ya Kigene, Mwiriga ya Ngomante, and so forth—as these emerged to form the boundaries of the migrants' mental world.

Few settlers established homesteads below 4,000 feet. Below that altitude the star grass vanished, and the land could grow only limited crops of millet and beans. Where not cleared, the vegetation consisted of "woodlands," a zone of underbrush ("bush") and thorntrees dotting an open plain. Lack of rain meant little agriculture. Livestock could graze the grasslands, but below 2,000 feet they and those herding them were subject to attack by tsetse flies and mosquitoes, both of which carried diseases potentially fatal to humans and animals. In consequence the zone was mostly used by transients: honey hunters, passing herders, or women en route to scattered gardens.

From the perspective of approaching migrants the region below 2,000 feet was virtual wasteland. One exception was the Tigania Plain, which lay above a tongue of mountain lava and which was able to hold rainwater and thus allow the growth of head-high grass. Beyond that, however, the plains around Mount Kenya's base combined high temperatures, infrequent rain, and leached-out, fragile soils that permitted no more than bare subsistence. The peoples of Tharaka survived by

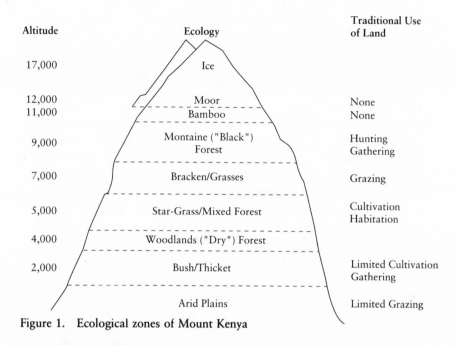

Figure 1.   Ecological zones of Mount Kenya

keeping small herds of livestock and growing millet in a few more favored spots. Most of this area, however, was uninhabited.

AX, RED CLAY, AND FIRESTICK: FORMING "RIDGETOP" COMMUNITIES

Meru traditions recall the era of the migrants' entry onto Mount Kenya as the time of ax and firestick. As each group of clans separated from the original migrant nucleus, it followed one of Mount Kenya's many riverlines up toward the lowest fringe of the mountain forest. The first to enter the forested zone were the hunters, armed only with small bows, axes, and iron knives. Traditions declare that no forest hunter of this era used either shield or spear. Instead they relied on magic to protect them, chanting protective curses to ward off harm.

On entering one section of the forest, each Mwathi (or Mu-Athi, "man of Athi," i.e., a hunter; pl.: A-Athi) marked off a specific hunting region, often adjacent to that of hunter neighbors from other clans. Using "ax, red clay, and firestick" to stake his claim, he and his companions then moved "west" (uphill) into the forest, seeking both meat and honey, but remaining always within their self-selected boundaries. If their quest produced a surplus, one or more of them returned to the forest's lower edge to barter it with those cultivator-herders with whom they were kin.

At the same time, the cultivator-herders were staking their own claims along the forest's lower edge by clearing off whatever vegetation barred their way. Thereafter, exploitation of each zone followed a standard pattern. Small bands of kin-related hunters pushed steadily uphill along specific ridgelines, marking them with ax and firestick as they progressed. Behind them cultivators and herders exploited the forest in their turn, dividing the land among existing clans whose members also moved uphill as they exhausted grass and soil.

In theory the migration could have been reversed, because any clan member could have returned to land used by his ancestors. In practice the migrants continued "west," as they had done since leaving Mbwaa, for each uphill transition brought them into a cooler climate, virgin grazing, and untouched soil.

Informants compare this migration pattern to a line of spears moving in roughly parallel formation up the mountain's face. Its consequence was that each group of clans found itself master of one or more steeply sloping ridges, broad at the mountain's base then sharply narrowing as they rose upward. Boundaries between these units were imposed by the giant gorges and racing rivers that divided the fertile areas. The result was the creation of a series of long, narrow "ridgetop" communities (Miiriga; sing.: Mwiriga), each containing both hunters and cultivators who gradually extended the land under their control.

Each ridgetop community was ruled by a Kiama of its own elders that might embrace one large or several smaller clans. Each was defended by the elders' warrior sons, who were banded together in whatever numbers were necessary to provide security. When necessary, members of any two or more of these communities could combine into larger social units. These were usually military alliances, for which elders gathered from various ridgetops to adjudicate conflicts.

In theory several of the ridgetops could combine to form a region, such as the lower Mwimbi. In turn, two or more regions could unite to form a subtribe; for example, the clans of upper and lower Mwimbi might join together against a common foe. Such larger combinations rarely occurred, however, and they never endured. Traditions mention almost no instances in which entire regions joined together and none in which they remained allied. Rather, between the time these groups reached Mount Kenya (1730s–1740s) and the British conquest of 1907,

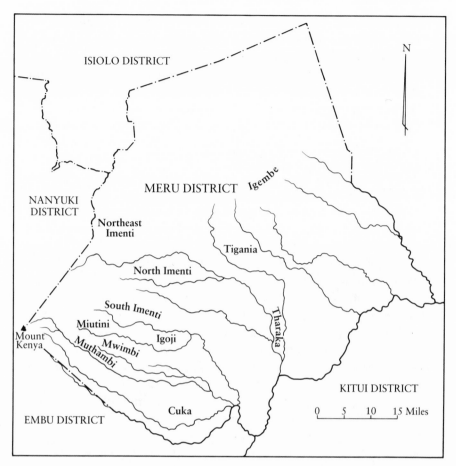

Map 4.   Meru: major subgroups

communal interaction occurred solely at the ridgetop level. No war was ever waged, for instance, between the theoretical regions of Mwimbi and Imenti. Rather, hostilities would erupt between two ridgetops, each from different regions, and continue until resolved by elders from both sides. In war and peace the primary social unit was not the region but the ridgetop.

MEN OF THE MAINSTREAM:
CONTINUED FRAGMENTATION

The physical fragmentation imposed upon the migrants through the circumstance of Mount Kenya's geography was reflected by a corresponding social fragmentation, which occurred in at least three of the traditional institutions. Faced with the division of the Ngaa into progressively smaller units, the system of supernatural institutions seems to have fragmented as well.

This trend is most clearly illustrated by Rev. B. Bernardi's research into the institution of "Ugwe," through which the blessings of God and the ancestors were transmitted to the living.[2] Any Meru could hope for contact with the ancestors. Contact with God, however, was reserved to a single individual within each age-set, the Mugwe, or "transmitter of blessings."

The Mugwe was the most revered figure in Meru tradition, the man who stood closest to God. He appears as the central figure in the narrations of every age-set, always as the person to whom all others appeal in times of change or crisis. At such times his blessing was virtually required for the society to function, as tangible proof that both God and the ancestors approved of whatever changes had been made. Thus, no rising generation of warriors could seize power from their predecessors without approval from the Mugwe. No wars could be fought, no conflict settled, without his ritual blessing of all concerned.

Bernardi did his research on this institution in the 1950s. In Imenti and Igembe he found this function carried out, as expected, by a Mugwe. In Tigania, however, the traditional rituals had been divided between two figures, a "Mugwe" and a "Mukamia," each of whom served one-half of the Tiganian people. In Mwimbi, Muthambi, and Igoji, no Mugwe could be found. Instead, the same functions were performed by foretellers (Aroria; sing.: Muroria), although traditions in each region suggested that they had "known Mugwe" in the past. The pattern implies a prior period of fragmentation. Because it may have proved impossible for every migrant band to include each type of ritualist, the required powers were probably transferred instead, passing from an originator to whatever type of ritualist proved most appropriate as the need arose.

The physical fragmentation of the Ngaa was also reflected in the system of Kiamas. As the segments split off from what had been the Ngaa core, they retained concepts of the council system, duplicating it once established in their new environments. In consequence Kiamas emerged everywhere along the mountain base, extending upward as the migrants climbed.

Soon, however, the need arose to form contacts between the elders' councils. While on the march, interclan and individual conflicts had been settled simply by calling spokesmen from each faction into council on a temporary basis. Now, as topography scattered the clans, the spokesmen-of-spokesmen concept took more permanent form. Beginning in Tigania after the 1740s (Michubu age-set), then spreading north to Igembe and more slowly thereafter into the southern regions, leading members of every elders' council withdrew from the gatherings of fellow elders to form more exclusive associations of their own.

In Tigania, and later in adjoining regions, these more exclusive units were called Njuri (secludedness, or the "councils of few"). Their initial purpose was to act as living repositories for the "secrets" now required for their communities to survive. Dissemination of such knowledge—always protected by oath—meant death.

Entry into an Njuri was restricted to elders already accepted as spokesmen for some larger group. Every lineage was represented, and a balance was maintained between both halves of the tribe (Kiruka and Ntiba) as well as between representatives of the black, red, and white clans. Large numbers of livestock were required to join, provided as "gifts" to form the basis of each candidate's initiation feast. Entry was thereby restricted to the wealthy. In Meru terms this meant that prestigious elders needed equally successful warrior sons, capable raiders who could supply their fathers with the livestock required for Njuri fees. Once achieved, however, membership was for life. A special walking stick served to identify its owner as a "man of Njuri" and thus one worthy of respect.

Inevitably, the concept of elitist councils was duplicated within younger age-sets of each community. Warriors, adolescents, and women are all known to have created corresponding councils, each with its inner circle of spokesmen or spokeswomen charged with protecting

TABLE 4   NAMES OF COUNCILS
(ca. 1740s)

Type of Council	Tigania-Igembe	Imenti-Igoji	Mwimbi-Muthambi
Warriors' council	Kiama Kia Lamale	Kiama Kia Ramare	Kiama Kia Lamale
Elders' council	Kiama Kia Otha	Kiama Kia Nkomango	Kiama Kia Kibogo or Kiama Kia Njuguma
Elders' elite council	Njuri Nceke	Kiama Kia Njuri	Njuri Nkome or Nkoma

"secret knowledge" from all members of the opposite sex and those of their own sex younger than themselves. Even the smallest children imitated their elders, with members of their own "elite" meeting within the "secludedness" of grain storage bins to pass on whatever "secret knowledge" they had learned.

In consequence a Meru living through this period could expect to pass from Kiama to Kiama as he aged. At each level, if he proved distinguished, he might gain entry into the ranks of that council's Njuri. The names of the various elitist councils varied among the major Meru regions. Over time, however, it appears that three major subsystems emerged, initially in Tigania-Igembe, then spreading gradually south (table 4).

In theory, conflicts between ridgetop communities from different regions were settled by joining two or more Njuris into a committee of them all, a process that could ascend indefinitely until entire regions could convene through choosing spokesmen. In crisis, tradition states that Mwimbi and Muthambi joined as one and that the Njuri of Tigania resolved conflicts that extended into adjacent regions of Igembe. Nonetheless, like the Kiama system from which it sprang, Njuris functioned mainly in response to crisis, disbanding once each issue was resolved.

"FRINGEMEN": THE EVOLUTION OF A-ATHI

One of the major fringe communities was also affected by the migrants' ecological transition. The pre-Meru entry into Mount Kenya's forests left the cursing patterns used by ironsmiths essentially unchanged. Over time clans on each ridgetop located adequate supplies, both to perpetuate their craft and to retain their former supernatural methods of protecting them.

The magic available to meat and honey hunters, however, continued slowly to evolve. To a hunter the "black" forest belt initially meant fear, primarily of large animals such as buffalo, which could lie unmoving within a shadow until a Mwathi (single hunter) moved too near. Tradition declares that all hunting groups responded to the problem by adopting a number of defensive rituals, intended to create a zone of safety around them as they moved within the forest. One of these, perhaps the earliest, was known either as "blow" (*ua*) or "bite" (*uma*).

It could be prepared only by curse removers (Aga) who were also A-Athi (hunters). Initially, the curse remover gathered various combinations of herbs, roots, and the sap of a tree (*Cacothanthera fresiorum*) known to be poisonous.[3] The materials were mixed with water, placed in a tightly sealed clay pot, and boiled for several days. Gradually, all the liquid evaporated, leaving a hard, black, waxy residue. This was either kept intact ("bite") or ground into fine powder ("blow"), then stored in tiny bamboo tubes, gourds, or animal horn. The contents were placed in a squared-off bag of antelope hide that A-Athi and all other Meru curse removers carried on one shoulder at all times.[4]

The magic substance within the containers was intended as a "gift" to other hunters. Tradition required, however, that it be "given" on request and that receivers reciprocate with specified amounts of honey, skins, horns (for use as containers), or meat. In this way both hunters and ritualist healers assured their economic survival.

Both bite and blow were transferred to recipients with precise instructions on their use. Blow, for example, was used at the beginning of each trek into the forest. On reaching an unknown or potentially dangerous area—such as a heavily tangled bamboo-edged glade that might conceal buffalo—the hunter would pause, uncap the powder, and blow it in all four directions. He would then chant: "Njira mno muthwa aki. Tukana gintu giku." (Only ants on the paths. We shall see no bad things.)[5] This ritual had the psychological effect of creating a moving zone of safety within which the hunter could carry on his work, protected from "seeing bad things," whether animal or human, that might harm him.

A-Athi traditions suggest that this concept was subsequently adopted for the creation of stationary zones of safety around the more permanent hunting encampments. These became increasingly isolated as individual hunters ventured higher and farther "westward" into the forests. The magic used to guard these camps was known as "Nkima," a word that carries linguistic connotations of "stiffness," but which A-Athi translate as "skull."

In some regions Nkima was simply an antelope horn, filled with the black, waxy mixture previously described. In others, strips of buffalo, bushbuck, and antelope hide were coated with the substance and then interwoven into a rounded mass the size of a human skull. Whatever its shape, an Nkima hung prominently in the center of each hunting camp, psychologically creating a second zone of safety for those sleeping therein.

A-Athi traditions suggest that the concepts of "bite," "blow," and "skull" were adopted ("bought") from earlier hunting peoples whom the Meru encountered as they entered the forest. These were most likely Ogiek, who lived in scattered bands across the mountain and who had adapted totally to a hunting- and honey-based ecology.[6] The A-Athi, however, as forerunners of much larger groups of cultivator-herders, faced different problems. During the prior decades of migration, both meat and honey hunters had begun to reserve specific areas for exclusive use. They had responded to mainstream incursions by developing the traditional curse into an instrument of group protection.

Once on the mountain, however, the pressures were intensified. Within a given ridgetop *all* the areas initially used for hunting and gathering were eventually coveted and claimed by herders and cultivators, themselves forced uphill by the continued exhaustion of both grass and soil. Inevitably, their very presence dispersed the game. Thereafter, as the forest was cleared to provide cropland, the habitat needed for honey disappeared as well. In consequence both hunting and honey A-Athi from every region of the mountain found themselves forced steadily uphill in turn, into regions that grew progressively colder, steeper, and less favorable to both beehives and game.

Initially, A-Athi councils of elders reacted to agricultural encroachments with the traditional patterns of communally chanted curses that had served them throughout the migration. Within the forest, however, these were frequently robbed of their effectiveness by the hunters' inability to learn whether men of the mainstream had penetrated their regions and where. Dispersed wildlife and empty beehives told no tales.

Nor were the Meru cultivator-herders always aware of their transgressions. They saw the forests as vast, unknown, "black," and endless. They could therefore pass through A-Athi hunting zones, or even cultivate them, without experiencing the anxiety and guilt required for the traditional cursing system to work.

The earlier system of chanted curses, therefore, was supplemented at some point in the 1700s by a second concept, probably springing from the traditional "ax, red earth, and firestick" used by Meru everywhere to mark their land. The firestick was also used in slightly different fashion by the Ogiek hunting peoples with whom the A-Athi may have been in contact. Hunters from this culture traditionally notched their firesticks in highly personal fashion and set them at intervals along traditional hunting trails in such a manner as to advertise the identity of each hunter.[7]

Tradition suggests that the A-Athi adopted both concepts, reshaping their use of the traditional firesticks (Ndindi; sing.: Rurindi) to meet economic needs by intensifying the ritual associated with their use. Initially, A-Athi ritualists from several ridgetops gathered in a solemn Kiama. With great ceremony they selected several long sticks from the *mwinkithia*, a tree held sacred to the group. Unlike the traditional firesticks these were gradually hollowed out at one end, then sharpened at the other. The hollowed space was filled with black powder ("blow") or a grey ash created by burning a number of poisonous roots.

The opening was capped with feathers from the marabou stork, one of the largest and most aggressive of East Africa's carrion eaters. The meat-eating bird was intended to symbolize that the stick would "devour" those who angered it. Each stick was then carved with the markings of its Kiama, smeared with bright red ocher (clay) to enhance visibility, and communally cursed.[8]

The curse was delivered in traditional fashion. Members of the council, having prepared the firesticks, moved several times around them, jointly chanting the words required to give them power. Thus empowered, the "Ndindi" were no longer simple firesticks. To the A-Athi they became "bones," empowered automatically to impose the hunters' curse on every person who passed by. Anyone catching sight of Ndindi, by definition, had penetrated an A-Athi hunting or honey zone, and their simple realization of this allowed the cursing sequence to begin.

This supplementary cursing system had several advantages over its predecessor, each of which served to alleviate the hunters' problems over the use of land. One was its service as a warning system, since even the thought of bypassing Ndindi kept cultivators and herders away. A second lay in the element of doubt engendered by the cursing process. The forests were vast, but neither herders nor cultivators could penetrate them at *any* point without fear of supernatural retribution. Consequently, contact between the two communities diminished steadily, an isolation wholly welcomed by the hunters.

The system's third advantage was its automatic nature. Since imposition of a curse was automatic, hunters had no further need to guard their zones, nor did they have to tour herding and farming communities proclaiming general curses on those who might have caused them harm. Instead, under the Ndindi system victims worked the curse upon themselves, their anxiety and guilt at seeing the sticks proving sufficient to induce whatever physical, mental, or social calamities they believed must follow. The onset of these, in turn, left victims with no choice but to voluntarily disclose their transgressions to the A-Athi themselves, because only their ritualists could remove a hunter's curse.

People of the mainstream, however, faced economic pressures of their own. Livestock could destroy a grassy glade, exhausting it for future use. Once cleared, the mountain soil was porous and could be leached by heavy rains. Too often it also wore out, leaving the users no choice but to seek new lands uphill. Inevitably, the core communities moved upward, nibbling constantly at the lower fringe of every A-Athi zone. Women sought firewood. Boys sought grass for their goats. Warriors took shelter from potential enemies. Ritualists searched for the plants and parts of animals that were required to activate their magic. Every incursion, no matter how unwitting or innocent, worked to disperse the wild game.

Wherever possible the hunters struck back, developing new applications of the cursing system to halt the upward flow. Where Ndindi sticks were ineffective, A-Athi communities intensified the concept, resorting to the creation of a stick they called "Nguchua" (claw).[9]

The sticks of Nguchua were cut from the same sacred tree as the Ndindi. They were said to be eighteen inches long, one inch in diameter, and smeared with red ocher. Following much of the Ndindi ritual, the sticks were hollowed at one end, split at the other, then slowly heated on one side to make them curve into the shape of claws. They were then filled with the same types of powder or ash used in making Ndindi. The hole was blocked with the tail of a mongoose, then tied with cords made from a creeping tree vine.

The completed "claw" was activated in the same manner as Ndindi, with appropriate verbal incantations to empower it to curse. The Nguchua, however, were placed in the ground, claws up, before the huts of those known to have offended the A-Athi. Members of the hunting Kiama then circled the offender's homestead, chanting, for example: "Those who eat [the food of] A-Athi, let them now die." Thus warned, the intended victims discovered the "claw" and reacted appropriately, developing physical symptoms that led to isolation by their own community and the need to seek out the A-Athi for reconciliation.

In more serious instances, however, entire agricultural and herding communities were propelled by their own needs into outright defiance of an A-Athi ban. Ridgetop traditions record dozens of instances in which whole clans fled upward into the forest, seeking shelter from locusts, drought, raiders, or exhausted soil. Communities placed in these circumstances usually tried to buy the goodwill of local hunting bands by giving gifts. If angered, however, A-Athi frequently responded with their most potent malediction, the ritual of *kallai* (gazelle).

"Gazelle" appears to have been an intensification of the practice of "claw." Instead of placing a stick before the homesteads of offenders, however, the entire A-Athi hunting band circled an offending cluster of homesteads, its leading members carrying the corpse of a freshly killed gazelle. The animal had been disemboweled, then hollowed out in the same fashion as the Ndindi and Nguchua to become a "stick" of flesh. The hollow was filled with the traditional magic powders, composed in this instance of ash from a newly cremated hyena cub, colobus monkey, and *keiea,* a parasitical vine that grew upon the hunters' sacred tree.[10]

While circling, the entire group chanted the curse in unison, thereby ritually intensifying its power. In theory the entire mainstream village then either sickened or reconciled with the hunters by giving gifts until the A-Athi ritualists decided to remove the curse.

At some point, however, the A-Athi added a new element to the rituals of curse removal. Unlike the rites used by curse removers of the Meru mainstream, A-Athi rituals of removal began not only to "lift" a communal curse but also to create additional conditions intended to prevent recurrence of the violation that induced it. This was achieved by imposing a "kinship clause" upon the transgressor. In Meru terms this meant that to complete the rituals of removal an A-Athi curse remover created a wholly artificial condition of kinship between the victim and every member of the hunters' Kiama concerned. In essence, an individual man of the mainstream, whether cultivator or herder, was forced to become the "brother" of every hunter in the region, as they all became "brothers" to him.

In theory the creation of such a relationship provided the basis for future harmony between cursers and victim, thereby neutralizing whatever hostility had been aroused by the initial conflict. In practice the oath of kinship bound each victim to the hunters' Kiama so that future submission to its authority was ensured.

Although permitted to remain a cultivator or herdsman, the victim of a hunter's curse was required to submit all future conflicts to the elders of an A-Athi Kiama (to the Kiama of his "kin") for resolution, rather than the council of elders that governed his ridgetop. At a more practical level, this also meant the contribution of livestock to the hunting Kiama's feasts. Because A-Athi taboos forbade consumption of either milk or meat from domestic livestock, the animals thus delivered were approximately renamed, the bulls becoming *magara* (an old word for buffalo) and goats, *nkurungu*, or bushbuck. Evasion of these obligations, or additional transgressions against A-Athi interests, led automatically to reimposition of the original curse, thereby reimposing the choice of further livestock levies as alternatives to calamity and threatened death.

However, the A-Athi system of supernatural manipulation continued to evolve along solely defensive lines. On one hand, each stage in its development, as with the system of the ironsmiths, reflected the efforts of a numerically insignificant ecological minority to protect their livelihoods from encroachers who sought however unintentionally to destroy it. On the other, the encroachers were kin, Meru who had entered a separate and often hostile ecological niche but with whom the hunters still shared common cultures, dialects, and ancestry. It does not seem surprising, therefore, that the smallest of the Meru fringe communities should have embraced the supernatural for protection against kin. Nor is it odd that the system that developed was designed first to neutralize and then incorporate transgressors rather than harm or kill them, despite the ferocity of the chanted curses themselves. By forcing cultivators to be kin, the curses made them subject to the A-Athi elders, thereby placing any violator in a position where no further transgressions could occur. At this stage in Meru history, therefore, the ultimate purpose of the dreaded "hunters' curse" was simply to impose a state of harmony upon those within the hunters' world.

MOUNT KENYA: EXPULSION OF EARLIER OCCUPANTS

The rate and direction of migration inevitably brought each of the major Meru subtribes into contact and conflict with earlier occupants of the Mount Kenya region.[11] The traditions emerging from this period are told almost wholly from the perspective of single clans, as they advanced upward into the forests or across the Tigania Plain. In every instance representatives of the Mukuruma, Michubu, and subsequent age-sets (1730s–1860s) seem to have met with an initially bewildering variety of enemies, with whom they fought and over whom they won.

Existing evidence suggests, however, that most of these migrating communities encountered representatives of three non-Bantu cultures, scattered in small numbers along the mountain's lower slope and northeast into the adjacent Tigania Plain. Analysis of Meru traditions that spring from this area suggests the following patterns of occupation: (a) small groups of Eastern Cushitic–speaking (Galla) peoples within the woodland zone, along the mountain's arid base and into the Tigania Plain; (b) small groups of Kalenjin-speaking (Ogiek) peoples, inhabiting the higher star-grass zone and lower fringes of the montaine ("black") forest; (c) somewhat larger communities of Maa-speaking (Maasai, Ogiek) peoples within the Tigania Plain and adjacent grasslands, north of the mountain itself.[12]

CUSHITIC SPEAKERS: MUKUGURU, UKARA, MUOKO

Contact with Cushitic-speaking peoples occurred before the pre-Meru migrants had even reached the mountain. Informants recall these early occupants by names that vary among the major subtribes (table 5). Traditions from several regions and other evidence suggest that these groups belonged to one or more sections of the Oromo-speaking peoples (Galla-Boran, Oromo, etc.). Their language forms part of the Eastern Cushitic language cluster, which extends across the Horn of Africa into the Middle East.[13] Thus, Muthambi informants often pronounce "Ukara" as "Ugalla," blending the letters r and l into the intervocalic $*d$ and g and k into a single sound. Mwimbi elders describe Ukara cattle, seized in warfare by their ancestors, as identical to those now herded by the Galla and Boran. Imenti traditions state that Ikara (or Agira) of that area were also known as Muoko (or mwoko).

Additional oral evidence is provided by descriptions of their burial customs. Traditions in each region describe Ukara, Agira, and Muoko (in various spellings) alike as having "buried their dead in a sitting position, covering each grave with stones." Pre-Meru found the custom both fascinating and repulsive, because their own tradition required that the dead be left for hyenas. The alien burial details became part of their fireside chronicles, thereby passing into oral history. After the British conquest an early colonial administrator confirmed the tradition by uncovering several alleged Muoko graves, pointed out to him by Meru elders, which substantiated the practice of burial in a sitting position.[14]

TABLE 5 NAMES GIVEN CUSHITIC SPEAKERS (PRECONTACT)

| Zone | | Meru Subtribe | | | |
	Muthambi	Mwimbi	Igoji-Imenti	Tigania	Igembe
Lower forest	—	Mukoko or Mukuru (hunters)	Mukuguru or Mu-Uthiu (hunters)	Mukuguru or Aruguru	—
Plains	Ukara (herders)	Ukara (herders) and Mu-Oko	Ikara or Agira and Mwoko	Muoko or Ma-Uoko	Ukara or Agira and Muoko

In the 1920s a Methodist missionary noted the similarity between the Muoko burials and those still practiced by the Tana River Galla.[15]

Physical descriptions also support this possibility. Informants describe each of the cattle-keeping peoples as "taller and more slender" than themselves. Their shields were small and narrow; their spears, short and tipped with the leaf-shaped blade once used by the Galla-Boran. More conclusive, perhaps, is that no fewer than three of these groups are described as linked to groups of forest hunters, in the same manner as the early Tharaka and Cuka. In Mwimbi, for example, the forest hunters were called Mukoko or Mukuru and were joined with livestock-owning Ukara. In Imenti, they are recalled as Mukuguru or Mu-Uthiu and linked with cattle-keeping Ikara or Agira. Tiganians describe Mukuguru (or Aruguru) as allied to the Muoko herders of their region.

Existing evidence thus suggests that the names of every group within the forest zone are variants of the Mokogodo, a contemporary Ogiek people, whose original language was part of the Cushitic cluster. Because the plains-dwelling Oromo, Galla, and Boran also speak Cushitic dialects, both forest and plains dwellers may have been able to communicate. This overlap, in turn, may have led to the creation of an intermittent hunter-herder symbiosis, based on trade and intermarriage, that benefited both sides.

Early Galla history also supports the possibility of hunter-herder symbiosis. After 1500, Oromo-speaking peoples (Galla, Boran, Oromo, etc.) began to migrate south from the Ethiopian highlands. Following their herds, they had reached deep into Kenya by the 1700s. The Boran, in particular, had moved into grasslands on both sides of the Tana River, while other Cushitic-speaking herders may have even penetrated Tanganyika. Bands of these herders were therefore probably attracted first by sight of the mountain, then the grazing opportunities at its forest base. Thereafter, they may have wandered in small groups along the lowest forest fringes, in contact with the Mokogodo, until the pre-Meru appeared.

Tradition states that both Ukara and Mokogodo fled the slopes of Mount Kenya soon after the migrants arrived. Unable to defend themselves, they are said to have "turned into birds and flown away." On the Tigania Plain, however, the more numerous Muoko chose to fight. Tiganian narrations from this era describe how men of the Mukuruma age-set (mid-1730s), sent ahead of the migrants to examine the plain, returned to describe an entire "sea of grass filled with few people and many cows."[16]

To fulfill the prophecy that had sent them westward since the migration's beginning, their prophets ordered them to seize the herds. As the narration is retold today, Tiganian warriors took the Muoko by surprise, seizing "four great herds" in an initial skirmish, then moved livestock, women, children, and the aged into a single, defensible camp. The Muoko, perhaps initially outnumbered, reacted by barring the intruders from both water and salt, systematically burying salt licks and springs to prevent their discovery and use. The Muoko also had stabbing spears, a weapon Tiganians could not forge. They responded with bow and arrow, ambushing Muoko herders in the long grass ("they crept like rats" sang the Muoko of their foes) and stampeding their herds.

Tradition speaks of "decades" of war. More likely, there was a time of dry-season raiding on both sides. At some point the Tiganians mastered the art of forging spears. Thereafter, the Muoko found themselves forced steadily into the arid northeast away from the fertile grassland region. In so doing, they evidently moved within the raiding range of the Il Tikirri (recalled in Tigania as Ngiithi) and Mumunyot (recalled as Rimunyo), two Maa-speaking (Maasai-speaking) Ogiek peoples who also herded—and coveted—cattle.

Both groups began to raid the Muoko from the north at the same time that Tiganian pressure intensified in the south. Consequently, Muoko communities gradually disintegrated as their herds were seized and absorbed by former foes. Early traditions record skirmishes between Muoko and Tiganian, Igembe, or even North Imenti warriors for many years. The later narrations, however, deal primarily with the seizure of Muoko children for Meru homesteads or the adoption of captive Muoko warriors into Tiganian clans.

The extent of such incorporation can never be known, because Meru elders swore oaths never to reveal that it occurred. Nonetheless, Mahner's (1970) research in Tigania suggests that the Muoko were incorporated into that region's "black" clans, the Il Tikirri into the "red," and the original Meru (who trace their roots to Mbwaa) still predominated among the "white."[17] The absorption of former foes may have therefore significantly modified Tigania institutions and, indirectly, those of adjacent Meru regions as well.

KALENJIN SPEAKERS: UMPUA, AGUMBA

The expulsion of peoples from the regions near Mount Kenya's base was repeated higher up the slopes. The victims, who lived either in the

TABLE 6   NAMES GIVEN KALENJIN SPEAKERS
BY MERU SUBGROUPS

Muthambi	Igoji	South Imenti	North Imenti
Agumba (hunters)	—	—	—
Umpua (herders)	Umpua (herders)	Umbua, Mbumbua	Umbua, Lumbua

Mwimbi	Northeast Imenti	Tigania	Igembe
Agumba (hunters)	—	—	—
Umpua (herders)	Lumbua	—	—

star-grass zone or lower forest ranges, are remembered in traditions either as Agumba or Umpua. The Agumba form a segment of the folklore told by every tribe on Mount Kenya. They appear in tales of the Gikuyu, Embu, and Cuka peoples, as well as the chronicles of Meru. Among other tribes Agumba are described as "little people" (*tuuji tukuru:* old children) or shy, hairy dwarfs, who lived in the forests above the Bantu (Gikuyu, Embu, Cuka, etc.) settlements. Routledge, Kenyatta, Leakey, Lambert, Orde-Browne and, more recently, Mwaniki and Muriuki, have all collected "Gumba" (i.e., Agumba) oral traditions that describe them as Pygmy hunter-gatherers, who lived in "caves" into which they fled at the approach of Bantu migrant bands.[18]

The Meru also share traditions with the Cuka, Embu, and sections of Gikuyu that describe the "Agumba pits," large or squarish depressions, within which the Agumba (or Gumba) once lived. Within Meru the pits are located along a line that runs roughly along the zone at 7,000–7,500 feet which delineates the lowest edge of the forest from the highest point in the star-grass (populated) zone. Today they form an irregular line that can be followed from ridge to ridge, along a region that is largely farmland, but which two hundred years ago must have been thickly forested. The largest pits average 16 to 24 feet across.[19] Traditions from every area describe the pits as having "holes" into which the "little Gumba" would flee. The Agumba traditions, however, are shared by primarily two of the Meru subtribes, those closest to the Cuku-Embu-Gikuyu region, and who reside on Mount Kenya itself. Elders of Muthambi and Mwimbi recall peoples living in the forest as their respective ancestors arrived (table 6).

Igoji and Imenti informants, however, provide accounts of these groups that differ sharply from the traditions of their two southern neighbors. The majority of their narrations speak neither of dwarfs nor Agumba. Rather, they describe a tall, slender, cattle-keeping people recalled (with variations) as Umpua. The Umpua wore shoulder-length hair, plaited into braids. In contrast with Agumba traditions, they are not recalled as hairy or as having any of the physical traits attributed to either Pygmoid or Khoisan (Bushmen) cultures. Rather, they are said to have looked like the Meru themselves.

The Umpua are also remembered in tradition as herders, not hunters, guarding small numbers of cattle and goats and living solely from the milk and meat of their herds. At night, livestock were kept in pits, dug by the herders themselves, which were gradually deepened as mud was removed after the rains. The earth and dung were heaped next to the pit to form a mound, within which the Umpua are recalled as having placed their dead.

Only the Muthambi and Mwimbi differentiate between Umpua and Agumba. Their descriptions of the Umpua correspond with those of other Meru subtribes. Narrations of the Agumba, however, describe hunters. Beyond that, the physical descriptions of both groups are identical, as are descriptions of their weapons (triangular iron spears, arrowheads with barbs on both sides), their dwelling places ("pits," "holes," "caves"), and their flight at each Mwimbi or Muthambi approach. The puzzle may be resolved, however, by suggesting the prior occupation of both Mwimbi and Muthambi by two separate sections of one tribe, sharing portions of an iron-age material culture but diverging in their economic base in much the fashion suggested for the forest Mokogodo- and plains Oromo-speaking peoples. The barbed weapons, for example, are similar (identical?) to spear- and arrowheads used by related groups of forest hunters *and* grassland cattle herders among the Kalenjin-speaking Ogiek who now live west of Mount Kenya.[20]

Both of the names recalled by tradition also suggest Ogiek origins. Certainly, "Agumba," "Umpua," "Umbua," "Mbumbua," and "Lumbua" all sound like reasonable variations of the Maasai "Il Lumbua." The term, which means simply "cultivator" in the Maasai language, was once used by pastoral Maasai to denote those Maa-speaking peoples who had adopted agriculture.

Certain of these cultivators, however, were once Kalenjin-speaking Ogiek. In the course of their own history they had come so deeply under Maasai influence that they accepted the language and traditions of that people as their own. One relevant example of this cultural transition can be found in the contemporary Il Mosiro, originally a Kalenjin-speaking Ogiek community, which has adopted both the language and material culture of Tanzania's pastoral Maasai. "Il Mosiro" is their name for themselves. Among their Maasai and Bantu neighbors, however, they are known as the Il Lumbua (in Maasai dialects) and Wahumbua (in Bantu dialects).[21] The similarity to Meru oral variants (i.e., Lumbua, Umbua, Umpua, Agumba), although not conclusive, certainly illustrates how Kalenjin-speaking peoples could once have been known as the Umpua or Agumba, the designation stemming from an era when at least one section cultivated and was in contact with Maasai.

Descriptions of the Umpua and Agumba "dwellings" (i.e., pits, caves) also suggest Ogiek origins, as well as the presence of two coexisting groups. Like the Gikuyu Gumba, both Umpua and Agumba are alleged to have lived in either pits, holes, or caves. More detailed investigations, however, have elicited two sharply different descriptions of the dwellings in which each people lived. One group is said to have lived in caves scooped from under the roots of trees. The second inhabited circular pits over which cow skins were laid to make roofs. Both patterns recur throughout Mwimbi-Muthambi. The association of cow hides in the second description suggests one possible function for each of the two types of Gumba pit. The large, square depressions may have been used to contain Umpua-Agumba herds, the smaller round ones to shelter herders.

Both dwelling patterns have, in fact, been found among Kalenjin speakers. Among the previously mentioned Il Mosiro (the Il Lumbua or Wahumbua of Tanzania), research completed in the 1940s described them as divided into two sections, each with its own ecology. One group lived within shallow depressions covered "by a rude shelter of skins," and the other section of the same community lived in "dugouts . . . scooped out beneath the roots of a suitable tree."[22] If this pattern of dual habitation was once typical for other Kalenjin-speaking Ogiek, it would seem possible to place Mount Kenya's Umpua and Agumba among their ancestors.

The most interesting evidence, however, comes through examination of what may be the last recorded fragment of the Umpua-Agumba language. No oral narrative in all Meru speaks of the Agumba dialect in any form. In Mwimbi, however, a single aged informant claimed to remember four "Umpua words" (for *one* and *two,* and two separate

TABLE 7   COMPARISON OF UMPUA
AND OGIEK WORDS

English	Umpua (Mwimbi Oral Tradition, 1969)	Il Mosiro (Maguire, Tanzania, 1948)	Kiriita (Lambert, Mount Kenya, 1939)
one	agenge	akeenge	agengi
two	uii	aen	oii
male (first variant)	chito	chiich	chiito
male (second variant)	ngeta		ng'etat

words for *man*), which had been sung in songs about (the Umpua) when he was a child. These can be compared with independently collected word lists for two widely separated groups of Kalenjin-speaking Ogiek (table 7).[23]

The existing evidence suggests, therefore, that the Umpua (and Agumba?) of the mid-1700s may well have been ancestral to the Kalenjin-speaking Ogiek of today. At some time in their past, groups of them may have adopted the title of Il Lumbua (in Meru: Umbua) from pastoral Maasai. They may also have adopted Maasai military methods, to the extent required to seize the herds of cattle they are said to have possessed. In consequence they may have decided to abandon agriculture, moving instead to an economy based both on herding and a partial symbiosis with related groups of hunter-gatherers within Mount Kenya's forests.

Meru traditions barely suggest the existence of hunter-herder symbiosis between the two communities, merely noting that they "waged no war and . . . gave honey for milk." If true, the trading pattern is supported by Blackburn's investigation into the Ogiek honey culture.[24] Among Mau Ogiek, for example, he reported that the average hunter could collect two hundred pounds of surplus honey per year, above the two pounds per day gathered for personal consumption.

Traditionally, that surplus was exchanged with cattle peoples at the (Mau) forest's lower fringe. They would ferment it (as do the Ogiek) to create an intoxicating honey wine as well as a honeyed water that forms the essential ingredient of every ritual requiring contact with ancestral spirits. Without honey, no rituals could be performed. Without ritual, no ancestral contact could be made. Without ancestral blessing, no actions could be taken, and human society would cease to function.

In consequence Ogiek hunters and those herders in Blackburn's research zone formed an interdependent relationship, based both on exchanging produce and intermarrying, in much the same manner suggested by Meru tradition for the Umpua and Agumba in the 1700s. Aside from economic benefit, both groups may have become psychologically dependent, seeking each other out to ritually, and therefore spiritually, survive.

If so, that pattern was shattered after the 1730s by the appearance of pre-Meru raiders on every section of the mountain. In Mwimbi, where traditions are representative of the whole, forest hunters from the ascending clans are said to have met peacefully with the Agumba, from whom they claim to have learned the use of magic. The Umpua, however, found their herds the targets of constant raids, as Mwimbi men of the mainstream sought both glory and cows.

A pattern of mutual warfare developed that lasted well over a decade, since warriors from at least two age-sets are recalled as having taken part. During that time, Umpua in every region were gradually forced up the mountain. Initially they attempted to shelter their herds in pits dug deep in the forests. When this no longer proved possible, they fled ("around the mountain, like birds") and disappeared.

The dates and directions of expulsion vary slightly among Meru regions. The Umbua of Imenti, for instance, are said to have been pushed northeast, onto Mount Kenya's northern plains, where they held out until scattered years later by raiding Maasai. The Umbua of Mwimbi are said to have fled south. Nonetheless, the pattern of conflict described in every region is identical: the Umpua fighting to preserve their herds, the migrants battling to seize them. In every case victory came through Meru numerical superiority, and by the end of the 1700s—except for children and captives adopted into Meru clans—the Agumba and Umpua were gone.

MAA SPEAKERS: IL TIKIRRI, IL MAASAI

Contact with the third non-Bantu language group, the Maa-speaking peoples, occurred during the warrior years of Githarie, Michubu, and Ratanya age-sets (1750s–1780s), after the pre-Meru clans had seized control of both Mount Kenya's lower forests and Tigania Plain. Contemporary Meru refer both to the Maa language and those who speak it as Uru, a term including the pastoral Maasai proper, those among them who have adopted agriculture, and specific Ogiek groups that have adopted their linguistic, cattle-keeping, and military orientation. The Maasai themselves refer to those who share their language—currently six tribes—as Ol Maa (the Maa speakers). Within that community they classify all members as either pastoral (Il Maasai) or agricultural (Il Oikop).[25]

Detailed examination of Meru relations with both pastoral and agricultural Maasai communities is beyond this chapter's scope. Suffice to say that every Meru region came under intermittent attack from both types, as well as their Ogiek imitators, from the time the Ngaa reached Mount Kenya until the era of colonial control. Warriors of every age-set fought often with "fierce Uru," and descriptions of these battles make up the bulk of every oral history in the Meru region.

Notwithstanding, more detailed analysis suggests that these Uru raiders were not always Maasai proper, but Maa-speaking Ogiek. Traditions from Tigania, for instance, report first contacts with Maa-speaking raiders as early as the 1730s, when the men of the Mukuruma age-set fought the Muoko to possess the plain. In this instance their foes were the Il Tikirri and Mumunyot, who raided Muoko from the north at the same time Tiganians pressed them from the south.

The subsequent dissolution of the Muoko placed the three remaining peoples into contact, at a time when the Tiganians had absorbed the greater portion of the former Muoko herds. Because both sides valued cattle, conflict soon began. The first attacks by both Maa raiders were successful, causing great loss in the Tiganian herds. The Mumunyot, however, were unable to hold their ground, as a series of fierce Tigania raids drove them from the plain.

The Il Tikirri reacted differently, forming an alliance with several Tigania clans that prohibited mutual raiding. This brought a time of peace, broken by Tiganian warriors of the following age-set, who sought their own glory at the expense of Il Tikirri herds. This pattern of alliance and attack may have recurred, for the Il Tikirri also found themselves forced northward off the plain, and they retreated finally beyond the Oasu-Nyiro River to Tigania's north. Here they remained, however, a seasonal threat to Tiganian herds, thereby setting the pattern for Meru-Maa relations for decades to come.

Contact with the Maasai proper occurred some time in the mid-1700s, when "Ratanya and Githangaria [in Imenti] were warriors," (1760s–1780s?), when Meru moving uphill into the Katheri region of contemporary North Imenti became aware of Uru on the other side of the forest that lay to their west. The evidence suggests that Maa-speaking groups of cultivators (Il Oikop) had occupied the grasslands of Northeast Imenti and were moving around a forest barrier that separated them from the advancing Meru.

The two sides fought with results comparable to those in Tigania. A period of raiding began, in which each side strove to seize the other's flocks and herds. Outnumbered, the Maasai were pushed off the grass-lands and moved northeast onto the arid plain. There, however, they re-mained, regarding the Imenti as seasonal prey, in the same way the Il Tikirri had viewed the Tigania. Each dry season they would appear to harry the herds, and every age-set fought them in its turn.

The Maasai, however, also came in times of peace, often sending women to exchange milk for sugarcane or millet. This led in turn to the exchange of brides and the emergence of kinship between certain Maa-sai and Meru clans. The Meru refer to this condition as *gichiaro,* or "birth," implying the birth of a relationship between two sides. The Maasai call it *a seriani* (peace), a condition that can occur only with groups with whom they have exchanged livestock and wives.[26] The ex-change creates a condition of kinship that serves to prohibit further at-tacks, lest the blood of "brothers" be shed.

This kinship could also be created through adopting Maasai as "sons." Within Northeast Imenti, Igembe, and Tigania this occurred through capture. Warriors taken in battle were held until ransomed by kin. If no ransom was paid, they could be speared or adopted into their captor's clan. Adoption took place during every age-set, with significant numbers of Maasai joining clans in Tigania. Adoption was by oath, in which the captive became "son" to the warrior who captured him. Having become ritually absorbed into his "father's" age-set, he was free to raid any group with whom he had no ties, whether by blood or cre-ated by ritual.

In consequence many Maasai settled easily among the northern Meru subtribes. Their impact was particularly strong among the Tiga-nia. Living on a lava grassland that offered no shelter from attack, Tiganians had no choice but to develop a system of continual prepared-ness if they were to survive. The Maasai model, based on circumcision, age-sets, a standing force of warriors, and ten years' duty in a war hut, fully met their needs.[27]

Warriors in every Meru region, however, adopted aspects of Maasai warfare: styles of dress, decoration, and weaponry, including long spearheads, wooden clubs, and buffalo-skin shields. A more striking aspect of this adaptation, however, was how certain segments of the Meru began to see themselves. The change was sharpest in Tigania, particularly among clans settling in the regions of Kianjahi and perhaps Muthara. Over time warriors from these regions began to perceive themselves as Uru, and referred to the forest peoples of Igembe, Imenti, and all other regions to their south as *kangiri* (little diggers), a pejorative word for cultivator. In short, earlier feelings of common ancestry were steadily eroded, replaced by purely Maasai conceptions linking contempt for agriculture, pursuit of cattle, proof of manhood and personal honor to the waging of a seasonal, highly stylized method of war.

This same transformation took place, to a lesser degree, in every other Meru region that absorbed Maasai. In consequence, during the last half of the 1700s, a new dimension of war emerged in which the Meru did battle not only with raiders from outside their region but also with one another as well, seeking their neighbors' herds with the same courage and enthusiasm they had formerly reserved for foes. Gradually the entire region engaged in internecine warfare, governed by convention and limited in intensity, but so deeply rooted in the Meru way of life that it endured until the advent of colonialism.

It can be argued, on the basis of existing oral evidence, that contact with Maa-speaking peoples has proven one of the dominant events in Meru history, and one which requires additional investigation. The Maasai, for example, may have given the Meru-speaking peoples their contemporary name.[28] Imenti traditions suggest that the forests of their region were called Miru (or Meiru) by Maa-speaking peoples of the plains, a term that was also given to those who lived within them.

In the major Maasai dialects the word carries a double connotation: a place where people do not hear (speak) the Maasai language (and who are therefore deaf and dumb); and a cold place that is silent (dead) and still (i.e., a forest, which Maasai find repellent). When the earliest migrants entered the "silent and still" forests of Mount Kenya, they may simply have adopted the name given to the region by adjacent occupants of the plains. To the surrounding pastoral communities the Meiru would have become a forest people, "silent and still," in that they spoke no language heard upon the plains. This would certainly correspond to the pattern in which groups entering the three southern regions (*-imbe, -ambe, -oji*) as well as Igembe (*-mbe*) may each have adopted previously existing Tharaka designations for the areas they chose. It may also shed light on the origins of the Meru people of Tanzania, also a Bantu-speaking people living in a mountain forest, who may have accepted the term given to their region by the Maa-speaking Maasai and Arusha who lived at the mountain's base. In all events, only after years of contact with the Maasai raiders did the former migrants of Ngaa perceive themselves as Meru.

CHAPTER IV

Traditions of Deviance: Evolution on the Fringes

"People will come with clothes [tied at the waist] like but-
terflies [to whom] we must give cattle, goats, and even our
daughters, so that we may survive."[1]

Kiariga the Prophet
North Imenti, 1860s–1870s (?)

NTHAKA: THE WARRIORS

During the late 1700s and most of the 1800s, the Meru-speaking peoples endured an era of internecine war.[2] Twice yearly, at the beginning
of each dry season, warrior bands set off from every ridgetop to raid the
livestock of adjacent areas. Raiding was universal, continuing until onset of the rains. The prize was livestock, particularly cattle, as well as
the chance for every warrior to earn not only glory but also wives. As
a result every Meru male spent his entire youth in preparation for the
warrior years, and every Meru community lived in constant expectation of attack.

Yet, although totally militarized, the Meru waged sharply limited
forms of war. Every conceivable type of military action was regulated
by a rigid but universally accepted series of military conventions ("ancestral traditions"), intended both to provoke the violence necessary for
successful livestock rustling and limit it at levels tolerable to the society
as a whole.

The most notable of these conventions was a quasi-military system
of ritualized alliances, based both on military strategies and kinship
ties, that regulated which ridgetop communities were potential opponents. Mount Kenya's relative isolation had left the Meru with few
neighbors and thus little choice of targets. The Gikuyu and Embu peoples inhabited the mountain's southern and western slopes but could be
reached only after arduous marches across the mountain gorges. The

Maasai, Galla, Ogiek, Mbeere, and Kamba were either too distant or too mobile, as were peoples of the northern plains. The Tharaka and Cuka, although near at hand, were livestock poor.

A preferred alternative was to wage war among themselves, essentially by dividing into "opponents" and "allies." The system that regulated this division was called *gichiaro* (in Mwimbi-Muthambi: *kijiaro*), which means "birth." The underlying implication is one of military alliance based on kinship or, in Meru terms, of war brothers related by common blood. Thus, if two ridgetops were allied through *gichiaro,* they believed themselves to be descended from common ancestors. As kin they were forbidden to do battle, lest "common blood" be shed.

Gichiaro could be natural, for example, if the men of two adjacent ridgetops had sprung from a single known ancestor. Alternatively, it could be artificially "born" through a ritual of mutual adoption, in which two groups mingled the blood of the respective elders and warriors to make it one.

In theory any single ridgetop could have acquired total protection by systematically forging this type of alliance with every Meru on the mountain. This would have left it with no one against whom to wage war, and thus no honorable way to acquire cattle. In addition, the alliance imposed a second obligation on those it bound. If ritually created "brothers" could not spill common blood, neither could they seek wives (or sex) among *gichiaro*-related women, since these too would be perceived as kin ("sisters"). The system thus required that certain ridgetops remain unrelated (potentially hostile), thereby providing the sources for both livestock in war and wives in time of peace.

In essence, three chains of alliance emerged among the Meru, each reflecting not only military but also ancestral ties remembered from the Meru past.[3] From a military perspective most of Tigania was joined with most of Mwimbi, reflecting the earlier period when both groups had formed the unit recalled as Murutu ("Tigania, Mwimbi, and Murutu were once one"), during the period of *Kagairo,* the time of the second fragmentation. Similarly, most ridgetops in Igembe, Imenti, Igoji, and Muthambi formed a second alliance, reflecting their common descent from Mukunga ("Igoji, Igembe, Imenti, and Muthambi had one father"), during the same era. A third chain consisted of the region's earlier occupiers, Tharaka, Cuka, and a tiny former Cuka region known as Miutini.[4]

In reality this division is too simple. During this entire period, *gichiaro* operated at the single ridgetop level rather than on a regional basis. In consequence alliances could be formed at every level of the Meru social system. "Most" clans within Tigania, for example, were hostile to "most" in Imenti. One, however, (Igoki, North Imenti), had made *gichiaro* with one area of Tigania (Athuana). Within Igoki one clan was hostile to Athuana, having allied itself to an adjacent Tigania group before migrating to Igoki. Within that clan a single family could have forged still other ties, for historical or military reasons of its own.

The result, on first examination, was a decentralized and apparently disorderly form of war, in which no one could be certain who was kin and thus taboo. The participants, however, found it clear, highly structured, and profoundly reassuring. By casting military alliances into a kinship context, the system protected every Meru warrior from both fratricide and incest. By limiting the number of potential raiders, it provided participants with a degree of security. Yet by defining others as potential targets, the system, inevitably, drove its members into battle. The result was a system intended to both limit and encourage a uniquely Meru form of war.

A second set of conventions also governed the intensity with which war could be waged, which functioned to protect property. War was fought to acquire livestock. Cattle, goats, and sheep were considered legitimate plunder and could be seized at will. All other types of property, however, were sacrosanct; no damage to them was allowed. Ripening crops, for instance, could not be pillaged. Raiders passing through a foe's banana groves were permitted to snatch what they required to still hunger but were forbidden to cut trees. The same principle applied to fields of millet, yams, and arrowroot. Raiders driving stolen cattle through such fields could afterward be "sued for damage to crops, with the amount (repaid in livestock) to be decided by elders of both sides, meeting in a special Kiama for the purpose.

Nor could raiders plunder homesteads. They might move swiftly through a group of huts, peering into each and seizing what could be swiftly carried. However, the structures could not be cut down or burned merely to make enemies suffer. Convention also regulated precisely what could be seized. Spears, swords, and similar weapons were considered trophies of war; agricultural, herding, and household implements were not, nor were beads, cloth, salt, or similar trade items. War was not waged for material enrichment but for livestock and glory.

Warriors were also forbidden to interfere with existing trade routes, whether local or linked with non-Meru societies. In many cases, for example, a river or large stream formed a recognized border between two potentially hostile communities. In such instances several crossing places (usually three) were set aside at the upper, middle, and lower sections of the populated (star-grass) zone.

During periods of peace these crossings were sanctified as trade routes, through livestock sacrifices and formal proclamations by the leading spokesmen of both sides. In war they remained open to any member of either group except warriors dressed for battle. Interarea barter could thus continue without restriction, even during periods of extreme hostility. In sum the Meru seem to have intended that the spheres of agricultural and commercial productivity—the domains of women—remain as distant as possible from the sphere of war.

Still other military conventions operated solely to preserve human life. The aged and very young were usually spared the problems of warfare altogether, because much of the action took place far from their homesteads. Women were protected for the same reason, as well as by traditions "dishonoring" any warrior who harmed them. Women were sought as war booty and could be captured, yet if cooperative they were neither harmed nor sexually abused. Neither unmarried women nor brides who had not yet conceived could be claimed by their captors, either as wives or as concubines. Instead, tradition required that they be regarded as their captors' daughters. After a reasonable interval each woman would usually be returned to the men of her own clan in exchange for a ransom of cattle. If no ransom was forthcoming, the captive would be married to another man of her captor's clan, with the warrior and his father acting jointly during the negotiations. The captor was thus rewarded in any case with livestock, in this instance as a part of the required bride-wealth, and the woman acquired a secure position within society.

Male captives were equally well treated. Surrender, although not encouraged, was considered honorable, the procedure having become standardized. If two warriors fought, the weaker could save his life by shouting "Take cattle!" (*ngua ng'ombe*), which was accepted as a declaration of surrender. Alternatively, he could place all his weapons in both hands, points upward, then push them toward his opponent. The victor would seize them, tear off his own skin cloak, and place it over his captive's shoulders, thus symbolically eliminating him from the fight. As with women, however, the cooperative prisoner was rarely harmed. The purpose of capture was simply to exchange him for as much livestock as his freedom would buy. After each battle elders from the hostile communities met to negotiate livestock claims. Usually, after suitable bargaining, a number of livestock were exchanged, both for captives and in compensation for damage. Thereafter, hostilities were considered at an end.

Other conventions, however, acted to inhibit warriors from taking lives once battle had begun. Although sparing opponents by capturing them was eventually rewarded in cattle, deciding to kill, even in combat, actually "cost" the killer livestock from his family herds. Each killing placed the warrior automatically in the condition of impurity (Mugiro) that shut him off from his community and required the sacrifice of livestock to remove. To kill, in short, meant to be cursed, a condition that could be removed only through giving up one's cattle.

Certain conventions operated to make raiding virtually inevitable. No herds, for instance, were ever well concealed within thick forest, placed behind log barricades, or hidden within pits.[5] Rather, each night the herds were driven to an open glade within the forest and guarded only by the least experienced members of a warrior band. All others slept within a single war hut at the clearing's edge, near enough to take up weapons if attacked but far enough to let the herds present a tempting target. To defend more effectively would dishonor the defenders, for only conflict could bring either side the chance of honor.

Warfare was essentially the same when waged outside Meru. Raiding strategies, whether directed against neighboring mountain communities or pastoralist tribes in the plains, stressed speed, stealth, silence, cunning, and successful evasion, rather than bloodshed, rapine, and destruction, to achieve "victory." Victory was most clearly achieved through the silent, bloodless, and undiscovered rustling of an opponent's herds, returning home with the animals while leaving the defeated community intact. Indeed, tradition required several of the captured livestock to be released in such cases, to provide the nucleus of future herds, "so that the next generation might raid them . . . and earn praise names in turn."

After a raid each warrior received his portion of the captured livestock then drove the animals to his father's home. Having transferred them into his father's herds, he returned to his age-set's communal war hut as poor as he had begun, richer only by a father's blessing and a promise to one day use the animals to find his son a bride.

A warrior's own reward, however, was the acquisition of a praise name. His father first bestowed it on him in gratitude for the livestock entering his herds. It was then publicly proclaimed that night during a "dance of praising," at which numbers of the captured livestock were slaughtered for a feast. Thereafter, warriors whose animals had been selected presented the hides to the young unmarried women they favored. As the feasting ended, the dancing began, and each warrior who had taken trophies, captured livestock, or done well in single combat danced one by one into the center of the field, singing out of his actions during that day's raid. The mother of each man then stepped forward to strip off his skin cloak, and he stood armed and naked while the women of his ridgetop chanted the praise name by which he would thereafter be known.

Names were chosen to reflect behavior during battle, and not all were flattering. A warrior returning with an enemy's sword might be called "sword harvester." Another man might be named for speaking loudly at a moment that required quiet ("silence breaker"), a third for momentarily opposing the leader of his unit ("stubbornness"), a fourth for cutting down an unusually tall opponent ("tree harvester"). Others, particularly new warriors on their first raid, might earn no praise name at all. The system's value lay, therefore, in its impermanence. Unwanted names could be wiped out by displays of courage on subsequent raids, and those who lacked reputations were spurred on to acquire them. The result was a system that rewarded both individual aggressiveness and obedience to authority, the very qualities required to both provoke and limit war.

ARORIA: THE PROPHETS

At every stage in their history the Meru have relied on prophets with sufficient vision to advise them during crises. Their traditions of origin, for example, recall that the prophet Mpaatha led his people during their original exodus from Mbwaa (Manda Island). His descendant, the prophet Kironge, is said to have guided the migrants along the Tana River, and Kironge's son, in turn, urged them to cross the river and enter what they believed to be a desert.[6]

The prophet (Muroria; pl.: Aroria) therefore held an honored place among the Meru. His principal task, after consulting ancestral spirits, was to predict impending calamity, thereby permitting those concerned to avoid it ritually. In times of crisis a notable Muroria could assume leadership of the entire people, striving to avert disaster with advice, ritual, ancestral assistance, and an eventual blessing.

The art of foretelling was usually hereditary. It passed from fathers to unusually gifted sons, through training and signs from the ancestors themselves. A young man could be taught to foresee impending crisis by examining the entrails of a goat. Sometimes, though, the spirits themselves appeared to the youth they had chosen, to reveal the approaching calamity in his dreams.

In war, warrior leaders from every band turned to the prophets for ancestral blessings, practical guidance, and approval of their plans. Men of Imenti sought out the Mugwe (transmitter of blessings) to provide this approval. Those of Mwimbi, Muthambi, and Igoji came to the Aroria, the prophets who foretold the future through dreams. Warriors of other regions sought specialists with other names. The procedures, however, were always the same.

War leaders appeared before the prophet as a single group, each in his capacity as warrior-spokesman for his band. One, speaking for them all, laid down detailed plans for an impending raid. The prophet listened in total silence, as did a slowly growing circle of elders, men of his own age-set, who appeared to lend the weight of their authority to his decision. The assembled warriors presented the ritualist with a goat, symbolic of the impending conflict. It was strangled, opened, and its entrails examined to ascertain the future of the proposed battle plan. If the forecast showed failure, the prophet concluded that some action of one (or all) of the warriors present had violated ancestral tradition, causing the ancestors to withhold their traditional blessings until the transgressors acted to reconcile.

Goat after goat might be provided to the ritualist by each warrior in turn, all to be slaughtered and the entrails used to ritually cleanse their owners of transgressions. Thereafter, still another goat was killed and the forecast repeated until the warriors either abandoned the project or obtained a favorable prediction. Only then could the assembled warriors anticipate the traditional blessing, given with a mouthful of watered honey or millet beer spit by the prophet on the forehead of each warrior-spokesman and followed by the traditional incantations that assured the raid's success.

The blessing was accompanied, however, by the protective magic substances used in war. The concept, which existed previously only among the Meru forest hunters, had retained its earlier names of "bite" and "blow," but at some point in the 1800s it had been extended to men of the core communities for use in war. Imenti tradition, for example, records that certain war leaders from their most powerful clans approached forest hunters with whom they were kin to buy the magic with gifts of goats, which they called bushbuck. They were followed by ritualists from all of the mainstream clans, who came to learn to prepare what their warriors now required.

By the mid-1800s, war magic was made in much the same way as its hunter derivative, from substances gathered in the forest and boiled in clay pots to form black paste. In war, however, "bite" was wrapped in green leaves then personally placed by the prophet on the point of each warrior's spear. "Blow," once ground to powder, was poured into tiny bamboo tubes, to be hung around the necks of leading warriors. Bite's function remained unchanged. War bands led by those possessing it would "see no bad things"—either human or animal—en route to an objective. Blow, however, was to be used only at the moment of attack. If blown toward the war hut of an opposing band, it symbolically obscured their vision until the raiders had seized their herds.

No raids were ever waged without the use of appropriate magic. Nor was it obtainable except as part of the prophet's blessing. This, in turn, could be acquired only by gaining the approval not only of the specific ritualist but also of all the elders who assembled to support him. In practice this group included men of the prophet's own age-set (ritual elders) and their sons (ruling elders). The warriors who wished to launch the raid, of course, were the sons and grandsons of the two older age-sets who came to hear them.

In theory (and according to tradition) the warriors' appeal was decided solely by the prophet's examination of the entrails of a sacrificial goat. In fact, because all decisions were collective, the ruling and ritual elders would withdraw into Kiama, pool their wisdom, and pass judgment on the proposed plan. The foreteller would then return to the waiting war leaders and prophesy accordingly, lending ancestral authority to the communal decision. Without this collective approval, however, no warrior dared wage war! To launch even the smallest raid without the elders' collective blessing was to raise spears against the ancestors themselves, an action so horrifying as to be psychologically impossible.

In retrospect, then, one can appreciate the feelings of warriors throughout Meru when spiritualists in every region began to prophesy the coming of an entirely new type of warrior, against whom no resistance would be permitted. In North Imenti the first mention of these people came from the prophet Kiariga, descended from the prophetic family of Kironge and Mpaatha, which extended back to Mbwaa.

During the 1860s, Kiariga prophesied a new form of calamity among the Meru. This was to be brought by men with "red" (white) skins and "women's clothing," a reference to female garments binding tightly at the waist.[7] Within a decade similar prophecies were heard throughout every region in Meru. With allowance for variations in wording, the basic elements of each prophecy were identical. Even foretellers preached the coming of "red" men. In some versions they wore "fur" on their faces and blew smoke from their mouths. In others they rode huge "dogs" (horses?). Every version foretold that their arrival meant conquest and the end of war. The prophets symbolized this for their listeners by predicting huge gatherings of warriors from every region at a single place, something that would have been impossible under existing military conditions. This would be followed by a period of total peace, during which warriors would walk the length of Meru without displaying the special "staff of Kiama" that guaranteed their safety. Nor would such peace staffs be needed to enter the country of their enemies, for these too would walk safely, even when near the warriors of Meru.

Later (in the 1880s–1890s) the prophets spoke of a single "great snake" (railway) that would extend from the east, moving closer to Meru with every westward coil. They spoke of warriors digging dirt with their hands, laboring for this snake as though they were women. Most bewildering and infuriating to the listening warriors, the prophets agreed unanimously on the hopelessness of armed resistance. In a prophecy totally without ancestral precedent they decreed that no Meru warrior was to so much as raise a spear against the red men. On the contrary everything conceivable should be done to placate them, by offering up livestock, goods, and even women. The alternative was nothing less than the destruction of the entire tribe.[8]

Such prophecies may have been based on something other than contact with ancestors. In several instances traditions mention noted prophets who spent their warrior years traveling far beyond the Meru boundaries, following a custom that allowed them to visit clans in neighboring or even distant tribes with whom they had some form of kinship. M'Agocorua, for instance, a noted Mwimbi prophet of the 1870s–1880s, traveled several times as a young warrior into the Kamba territories. There he had ample opportunity to learn of trading caravans passing inland from the coast, each protected by its quota of guns. Only in his later years, however, having perhaps digested the implications of what he had experienced, did he begin to prophesy the defeat of his people.[9]

The impact of such prophecies upon the warriors, however, was devastating, ultimately straining bonds between the age-sets. The prophecies were angrily disputed throughout Meru by enraged contingents of warriors interested in neither abject surrender nor an end to war. This type of conflict had no precedent. Often prophets refused to approve raids that warriors felt were well planned. Enraged, the warriors would verbally attack the decision, "shouting aloud for the right to wage war" and even threatening the ritualist with their weapons.

This response, in turn, would bring both groups of elders together in heated support of their age-mate. Equally angry, they would meet in their Kiama to denounce the hot blood of their warrior sons as reflecting contempt for the men of their age-sets. Chastened and faced with the threat of the elders' communal curse, the warriors would grudgingly abandon their initial plan, placing alternative after alternative before the elders, secure in the certainty that one would be approved.

The prophecies, however, were without precedent for either side. For the warriors to have followed the prophetic injunctions, despite their support by the ruling elders, would have meant violating all their military training and abandoning warriorhood itself. Accordingly, at some point between the 1860s and 1880s war bands throughout Meru rose up against the collective wisdom of their elders, denouncing the prophecies, deriding the prophets themselves, and refusing to retreat before the anger of the aged.

In Mwimbi the prophets themselves are said to have been roughly handled and physically driven ("with the butts of spears") from their places of prophecy, despite efforts by a Kiama of angered elders to intervene. In other areas, notably Igoji and Imenti, the prophecies were universally rejected, as warriors throughout both regions took formal battle oaths to kill such red men as should appear.

THE "DEVIANTS"

By the 1870s–1880s, however, there were other precedents for conflict between the ruling elders and their warrior sons. These had emerged because of the behavior of deviant elements among the Aruau, men who had become family heads/apprentice elders. According to tradition the decade after release from warriorhood was a time of relative ease. The former warrior was expected to court and acquire a wife, establish a homestead, and produce and raise children. Only after his children grew to warrior- and womanhood would the family head become a senior or (ruling) elder and assume—with all his age-mates—responsibility for governing the tribe.

Most family heads followed tradition. Those who lived closest to the forest, however, found themselves increasingly influenced by practices of the fringe communities, notably the magic of A-Athi hunters. As a result the various cursing practices that had developed within the hunting communities spread "downhill" to men of the mainstream, where they continued to evolve.

The supernatural cursing systems developed initially by both the ironsmith and A-Athi hunting groups were invariably defensive, the chanted response of an outnumbered group to threats against their territory and supplies. The refinements adopted by both meat and honey A-Athi within Mount Kenya's forests simply intensified this defensive trend. The communal curse, whether publicly proclaimed or inherent in a wooden boundary marker, was directed only against those who first encroached upon the interests of the fringe community.

THE UPLANDERS: KIAMAS OF CROP PROTECTION

Inevitably, A-Athi magic proved attractive to other minorities, specifically the pioneer wave of cultivators whose croplands pressed most closely on the lower edges of the forest. At some point in the mid-1800s a third form of supernatural protection appeared as those groups in closest contact with the forest adapted A-Athi concepts.

The initial change was reflected in the emergence of several new supernatural councils (Kiama Kia Mithega: council of magic), within every Meru region adjoining the montaine forest.[10] The earliest of these new agrarian groups hewed closely to the A-Athi model, adapting both verbal and symbolic rituals to their own economic needs. Like the A-Athi the existence of these groups was public knowledge, their members perceiving the adoption of the hunters' cursing rituals as no more than logical solutions to their own economic situation.

The most detailed traditions of this type of Kiama are recalled by the elders of Wathua, a supernatural council once known in every Meru region but Tigania. The Wathua was clearly derived from contacts with the A-Athi. The very name of the organization suggests "derivative." Its members were alternately known as *aathigani,* or "scouts," a name traditionally used by the A-Athi themselves when acting as scouts for their cultivator kin in war.

The men of Wathua, however, were not scouts in the military sense. Rather, they were pioneers, the first wave of the rising flood of cultivators who would someday clear the forests. As pioneers they had problems not always shared by those on lower slopes. Their tiny farms were always hacked from lower forest edges. In consequence the fledgling seeds were always placed on rich and fertile earth, but the richness of the rising crops made them targets for both forest animals and hungry men. Too often, therefore, owners of rich lands would find their harvests plundered. In normal years some depredation could be borne. But famine lower down the slopes might bring hungry clansmen like locust swarms into their unprotected fields. It does not seem surprising, therefore, that these pioneering clans adopted whatever protective devices were available.

Wathua traditions from Muthambi, for example, record that group's emergence as a supernatural association during the Kubai age-set (1870s). It began, according to tradition, when a forest hunter approached a Muthambi elder remembered as M'Kaumbatu, one of the pioneer cultivators of that era. The Mwathi (man of A-Athi) is said to have offered M'Kaumbatu "a new Kiama" in honor of a distant common ancestor.

The phrase, in this instance, meant a new kind of formal curse. It was contained, figuratively, in a sacred bundle of seven carved Ndindi sticks, cut from the A-Athi's sacred *mwinkithia* tree. The sticks were notched in forest-hunter fashion, daubed with red ocher and white chalk, then lashed together with a gazelle-skin sandal.

The bundle was exchanged for a goat. With it, the hunter passed on certain sacred oaths, techniques of sacrifice, and other rituals needed to make the power inherent in the sticks "leap into life" against the user's enemies. He also taught the rites required to lift whatever calamities should be imposed.

M'Kaumbatu reacted in traditional Meru fashion. He sought out fellow elders one by one, "selling" his knowledge to those willing to enter into his "Kiama." Fees took the form of goats, honey, and seven gourds of millet beer. With equal predictability the new Kiama based its existence on exclusiveness, restricting membership to propertied family heads. Women, warriors, and the landless were excluded.

The Wathua was typical of several supernaturally oriented agrarian groups emerging throughout Meru at this time. All of them followed practices derived from those of the A-Athi, transforming them to the degree required to meet their local needs. Each of these groups assumed the form of an elders' Kiama. Each Kiama produced its own curse removers, elders charged with collecting the ingredients required to either activate or cure its particular form of ritually created impurity.

The magic itself was drawn directly from the earlier practices of the hunting Kiamas. In Muthambi, for example, Wathua sliced Ndindi wands from the same *mwinkithia* trees as the A-Athi, notching, dying, and binding them in the same manner as the hunters. The completed bundle, however, was lashed to a goatskin sandal, symbolically imitating the A-Athi use of gazelle. When used, each stick in the bundle was cut away, then cursed by its owner. Thereafter, the sticks were placed separately around the edges of a cultivated plot of land, to protect it against intrusion, exactly as A-Athi hunting Kiamas of an earlier generation had protected their forest hunting grounds.

The A-Athi concept of "Nkima" (skull) was also adapted to agricultural use. Among forest hunters, the skull-like Nkima ball of beeswax and gazelle skin served symbolically to protect their camps. Among pioneer cultivators this protective function was transferred to a specific vine, the *miogo jwa Nkima* (vine of Nkima, i.e., skull vine). Even here the hunting traditions were followed, for the vine selected was the *keiea*, the long, wire-thin, mistletoe look-alike that hung from the *mwinkithia* tree, used by hunters to create their most potent curse, that of *kallai* (gazelle).

The cultivators, however, adapted the *keiea* vine to their own needs. Many vines were tied together, then looped entirely around whatever cropland was to be protected, except for a single gate ("gate of Nkima") known only to the field's owner. The circle was never closed lest the cultivator himself be barred from his crop.

The vines were always highly visible. Some supernatural Kiamas looped them from low tree branches. Others ran them ostentatiously along the ground. In Muthambi, Wathua members carefully strung them three feet above the ground. Every group made certain that their vines touched each of the ritually prepared sticks ("the Nkima touched all Ndindi"), thereby linking and reinforcing their initial power.

Violators passing into the protected zone incurred an automatic curse, again in the manner of A-Athi. Physical symptoms varied among localities but were always visible ones (e.g., boils at the joints or blood in the urine), invariably painful and frightening. As with the A-Athi recognition of the condition effectively isolated the offender from the mainstream of his society. Again, as with the hunters, the condition could be removed only by a ritualist (Muga Jwa Wathua, Wathua curse remover) from the cultivator's society itself.

The cleansing substances (Mithega: "magics," literally, medicines) were also derived in part from A-Athi practices. In Muthambi, for example, the *keiea* vine was used once more. For this use it was shredded, then placed in the traditional sealed clay pot. The pot was heated in a raging fire until its bottom cracked, with the ritualist urging the process on by chanting: "Tubu . . . tubu . . . tubu . . . turika!" ("Burst . . . burst.")

The substance within the broken pot was mixed with honey, dust collected from papyrus groves, and the blood of a newly killed goat. The mixture was heated over an open fire until fully charred, then ground to powder. The completed product was placed in a tiny gourd, bamboo tube, or antelope horn to be stored in the healer's goatskin medicine bag until needed.

Actual removal of the curse was almost wholly symbolic. An afflicted man, for example, usually knew whom he had offended, particularly because specific symptoms were always associated with equally specific groups within his region. If uncertain, he could seek the services of a diviner, who would identify the curse's origin.

Among Wathua, removal of the symptoms took two stages. Initially, the victim was asked to lick a mixture of the *keiea* preparation and the blood of a newly slaughtered goat. The purpose was to induce an attack of vomiting in which the healer would symbolically urge the victim to "vomit out what he had eaten," (i.e., the curse): "Taika, taika, warire mpingo ya Wathua" (Vomit, vomit, if you ate what was prohibited by Wathua). If the victim was physically unable to comply, he simply spit drops of saliva as a symbolic affirmation of his compliance with the cure.

The healer then produced a length of cord, made from the bark of a tree (*mugijo*) respected for its usefulness to humans. He looped this between two sticks driven into the ground, thereby symbolically recreating the pattern of Ndindi-Nkima used by Wathua to protect their farms.

The victim was asked to cross once again over the vine of protection, then back over it once more, thereby symbolically undoing his earlier transgression: "Ka ngukinya muugu ya Wathua? Tagaruka! Utichokere baria waukira!" (Are you crossing the vine of Wathua? Go back! Return through the same spot!")

The victim was then considered cured. As with the A-Athi this cure also required entry into a condition of kinship with the Wathua and thus into their Kiama. During the precolonial period, however, incorporation into this type of society really meant the required contribution to and participation in a series of communal feasts.

These feasts were usually given after the harvest, "when the goats were at their fattest and there was sufficient millet to make endless gourds" (of beer). At that time individuals who had been cured by Wathua were commanded to join the festivities, providing "the seven quantities of food" (goats, millet, beans, honey, and so forth) that were due to the council as fees. Those who evaded the obligation might fall once again under the Wathua curse. In good harvest years, however, few if any did. In consequence membership in these crop-protection councils slowly increased until the late 1890s.

THE LOWLANDERS: KIAMAS OF THE STOMACH

Initially, membership in these new agrarian councils was restricted to the wealthy: in Meru terms those having sufficiently large and productive holdings to require crop protection. During the late 1880s, however, an unprecedented series of natural disasters struck the Meru-speaking regions, producing for the first time in their history classes of "haves" and "have-nots."

In 1887–1888, the Meru cattle herds were decimated by rinderpest, part of a larger epidemic that swept through African cattle communities from Sudan to South Africa. In 1891 the region was afflicted by drought, while certain areas were struck once more by overwhelming swarms of locusts. In 1892 the already weakened Meru communities were decimated by smallpox. It struck some areas with sufficient ferocity to disperse entire clans, either through death or mass flight from an afflicted area. The social consequence, inevitably, was the emergence of a rural proletariat, temporarily landless, bereft of livestock, and perhaps even without kin. Seeking security, many such victims turned to tradition, presenting themselves (and their women) for ritual adoption to clans in which they had distant or even fictionalized blood ties. Others, however, found themselves turned from every sanctuary—perhaps by fear of the disease—and began to group together to survive.

These food-acquiring groups were detested by the more prosperous Meru agrarians. Informants from the fertile regions near the forest denounced them without exception as "Kiamas of the stomach, with no function other than to consume the property [goats] of men who in every way remained their betters." The force of these denunciations, still violent after decades, suggest the food-acquiring societies were once indeed something to be feared.

They were certainly numerous. Oral evidence suggests that "stomach Kiamas" such as Wathi, Gatanga, Muundu, Kagita, Mwaa, and several others, appeared within this period among the land-poor inhabiting the lower, drier regions across the mountain. In every instance they were composed of the family heads/apprentice elders, men in their late twenties and thirties, whose plans to found homesteads and families after leaving warriorhood had been based on possession of large numbers of livestock. Where the herds had been dispersed or decimated, whether by raiders or natural calamity, all hope of wives and wealth was gone. Under such circumstances the landless and livestock-poor had little choice but to seek sustenance by banding together and gain security by turning toward the supernatural.

It is hardly surprising, therefore, that this third wave of supernatural councils drew from both the hunters and crop protectors in creating their own types of ritual. Former members of the Kiama Kia Wathi, for example, one of the stomach Kiamas that appeared in Igembe, declared that the founders of their council "bought Kiama" (i.e., the rituals) from A-Athi hunters.

As dry zone cultivator-herders, however, they adapted those rituals to their own needs. To establish the now traditional zone of safety, for example, this group planted one branch (Ndindi) from a sacred tree (again, the *mwinkithia*) in the clearing that was to become their gathering ground. That zone was then encircled by the entire group, chanting and sprinkling the liquid dung of a goat to keep out intruders, just as the crop-protecting Wathua had used the pattern of sticks and vines. With the zone secure a large circular hut, sufficient to hold thirty-five to forty men, was constructed of banana leaves. At its peak the Wathi hung a "magic gourd," in imitation of the A-Athi Nkima but containing seven short Ndindi sticks. Ndindi were also used to light the fire that signaled the start of each feast. As it blazed, messengers would run swiftly through the surrounding homesteads, a wooden cowbell hanging from each hip. Its beat alerted every member to appear—and eat.

The acquisition of food supplies varied sharply among the various stomach societies, possibly reflecting the relative degree of economic disruption suffered in Meru's different regions. Groups higher up the mountain, for example, had once held croplands of their own, perhaps even using the stick and vine concept to protect them. When subsequently struck by catastrophe, some began to ensure a supply of victims by placing stakes and vines along the public paths. Others began to enclose the croplands of wealthier landowners, leaving themselves inside. To remove them, each owner was forced to "invite them to feast," thereby paying the customary fees (in grain, beer, and goats) for removal of their curse.

Other stomach societies were more direct. The Wathi of Igembe, for example, selected a wealthy victim, then descended directly on his homestead, chanting a communal curse. Circling his hut, they ritually isolated the homeowner within his dwelling, again by sprinkling liquid goat dung in the same manner used to protect their meeting place. Thereafter, they gathered before the victim, requested the feast, then removed the spell, by chanting an oath:

> Tubu, turika! Tubu, turika!
> Uma mugiro wa gukiranga Wathi
> Urogi bwa Wathi Butithuraa muringwa nibu
> Ukorokiranga inya na Wathi kairi wija gukua
> Keere nja yaku nayo itikeji gutukiranga
> Inya yaku nituure na twakuringiria
> Ugie na into bibingi ng'ombe na irio.

> (Clay pot, burst! Clay pot, burst! [Curse, disappear!]
> Get out [disappear], curse of the A-Athi;
> Never again trespass against the A-Athi, lest you die.
> Warn your family never to trespass against us.
> [Now] grow strong. We predict [that you will have]
> Many cows and much [millet] porridge
> [To consume, now that our curse has been lifted].)

THE FLATLANDERS: KIAMAS OF KIDNAPPERS

Other groups adopted still more violent tactics, reflecting their rising desperation as normal means of economic security were swept away. Perhaps the most striking were those of the Kiama of Kirimu, which emerged among Tharaka clans that lived along the Sagana (Tana) River but also drew from those Mwimbi, Igoji, and South Imenti peoples that lived nearest to the Tharaka Plain.

Kirimu was originally a figure in Tharakan mythology. Oral tradition refers to him as a huge animal, most frequently a snake, that lived in the depths of the Sagana River, emerging only to swallow young men and older boys. Before 1900, Kirimu was also a recognized Tharakan Kiama, whose members sprung from a ritually protected riverbank stronghold to catch and "swallow" young males of great promise. In this instance seizure was an honor. The man concerned became a member of the group, gaining thereby the honorific of *nkara* (elder), which suggested he could no longer be treated as a child.

By 1900, however, the catastrophes of the preceding years had caused at least one section of Kirimu (and probably others) to evolve into a stomach Kiama. Its base was now an island in the Sagana River, the largest in Tharaka's otherwise almost arid plain. Its emergence now took the form of a procession of Kirimu elders, protected by a "swaying forest of Ndindi," in fact, a waving sea of the wooden sticks held up in members' hands, and by the "crying of Kirimu"—the rhythmic noise of drums and horns and whistles.

The band would leave the riverbank at dusk, then march inland toward someone's preselected homestead. Once in darkness the members fell silent, moving stealthily onward until their goal was reached. Still silent, the band raced from hut to hut seeking to seize young boys with nets of sewn goatskin. The victims, always predetermined, were taken only from the wealthy families. Having seized its prey, the band withdrew into the bush that ringed each homestead. There they began "Kirimu's cry," and surrounded by the safety of their music, marched triumphantly away.

Informants declare unanimously that Kirimu's magic was too powerful to resist. It seems more likely, however, that parents accepted the seizure of their sons only because they were aware that the children would return. Without exception, kidnapped boys were taken to the Kirimu island stronghold, a tradition known by every parent. After three days the "stricken" elders appeared along the river to invite Kirimu to a feast. Once fed, tradition stated that the real Kirimu would "spit out" the males he had swallowed. The Kiama that bore his name could do no less.

The victims, however, were released only after they had been smeared from head to foot with castor oil. Their hair was also "strangely" shaved, to serve as a symbolic reminder of the monster's teeth that had grazed them while being swallowed and spit back. Thus returned, they served for months as living advertisements of the kidnappers' power, as well as proof that any further boys seized in this manner would promptly be returned.

Both the relative gentleness with which victims were treated and the limited nature of their kidnappers' demands suggest that the various stomach societies may not have been so widely detested as current informants suggest. Certainly, still-living members of these societies describe them in a more positive light. On one level these groups were perceived by their own members as a ritualized means of food sharing, in which food-poor communities could commit limited aggression against their wealthier neighbors in exchange for limited amounts of food.

FROM NKOMA TO MWAA: AN EVOLVING KIAMA

The pattern of limited aggression–limited reward is illustrated even more clearly in the next generation of Kiamas. Traditions record that at least two of the food-gathering (stomach) councils evolved from Kiamas of crop protection into what might best be described as Kiamas of clowns. At least one of these, the Kiama Kia Nkoma (council of the spirits) was composed of males wishing to act out the role of females in some fashion that would win social approval.

Originally, Kiama Kia Nkoma appeared during either the Kubai or Kaburia age-set (1850s–1870s) as one among several other crop-protecting groups. Nkoma's sacred tree was the *mwinu*, the leaves of which have a repugnant smell. A ritualist wishing to start a new section of this Kiama gathered its leaves and branches with appropriate incantations. Thereafter, seven of the *mwinu* sticks were lashed together with a vine, then placed in the healer's medicine bag to form the basis of both his ritual and power. Leaves of *mwinu* were also used to construct the hut in which members would meet for feasting. The protective Nkima was supplied by mixing millet paste with water and honey, then molding it to form a skull-like ball, which hung at the hut's peak.

The Nkoma's pattern of crop protection differed little from that of the other agrarian groups of this period. Vines were gathered, bound together, then roughly looped along the branches of whatever vegetation surrounded the cropland. Leafy tips of the *mwinu* branches were then laid across the vine at its most visible points, thereby identifying it instantly as a "vine of Nkoma."

The protection must have been potent, for the Nkoma alone among the crop-protecting Kiamas seems to have spawned imitators. Informants in at least two regions speak with disgust of cultivators who though not part of the society had "dared" to cut large branches off the *mwinu* tree, then plant them upright around their fields as if they too were under the group's supernatural protection.

Violation of the Nkoma barrier also followed standard Meru patterns. Violators suffered either visible illness or physical calamity. Their subsequent visits to a local diviner would indicate that the condition had been caused by Nkoma. A further visit to the curse remover of that Kiama lifted the curse, alleviated the illness, and led to the victims' incorporation into the Nkoma itself.

The rituals of removal, in this instance recalled by informants in great detail, reflected each major step in this council's evolution. Each victim was led into the hut of Nkoma by two members of the band. The curse remover produced a sacred object, most often a cow horn wrapped in small iron chains. This was ceremoniously placed in a shallow pit at the hut's center and covered with the skin of an unblemished white goat. The actual curse removal took the form of a series of sworn oaths, each intended to create bonds of kinship between victim and his new "brothers" in Nkoma. In fact, each oath laid a specific obligation on new members.

There were many oaths, some obviously dating back to the group's beginnings. Interestingly, all of the earlier ones deal with crop protection: "If my [Kiama] brother comes to me for seed, let this oath kill me if I fail to share. . . . If I see goats in my [Kiama] brother's garden, let this oath kill me if I fail to chase." Later oaths deal largely with the sharing of food: "If my [Kiama] brother sees me with millet beer, let this oath kill me if I fail to share." The final oaths, however, are not only exclusively sexual but also antisocial as well: "If I find my [Kiama] brother with another man's wife, let this oath kill me if I tell her husband. If I find my [Kiama] brother with another man's wife, let this oath kill me if I tell anyone else at all." The explanation for this shift of emphasis lies in the evolution of the society itself. Over time the original council of crop protection evolved into what could best be described as a Kiama of food-seeking clowns.

MWAA: A KIAMA OF CLOWNS

During the 1890s a series of agricultural calamities seem to have jolted the members of Kiama Kia Nkoma away from cultivation and crop protection. Like other famine-stricken peoples, they became food gatherers, forming stomach Kiamas and using magic to seek whatever food could still be found. Unlike other groups, however, the Nkoma reemerged as several smaller bands of clowns, blending the powers of both magic and music to provide members with sustenance and security.

It was at this time that the Kiama Kia Nkoma also became known as the Mwaa. In Ki-Meru, *waa* means both "foolish" and "stupid." A "man of Waa" (Mu-Waa or Mwaa) is defined as one who has embraced foolishness or folly.[11] Nevertheless, the term carries overtones of joyous clownishness rather than of ignorance or imbecility.

Traditions suggest that the transition from landed cultivators to dancing clowns occurred gradually. At first during periods of famine, but eventually at the onset of each dry season, groups of Nkoma would band together as "fools" or clowns, often only in groups of two or three. Thereafter, they would tour surrounding homesteads singing for their sustenance in the manner of English minstrels.

During this early period their reward was never more than a handful of castor seeds, flung into their goatskin sacks in exchange for each burst of song. When sufficient quantities had been collected, the singers could trade them at local markets, thereby sustaining themselves, however meagerly, throughout a famine.

By the early 1900s, however, Kiama Kia Mwaa had evolved into groups of polished entertainers, with branches on virtually every Meru ridgetop. They had also become increasingly deviant and predatory. Their dancing costume was blatantly feminine, consisting of numerous strings of *minyugu* (beads), worn around the neck and waist in women's fashion, and a skirt made either from shredded strings of goatskin or palm leaves.

Each member also wore the wide shoulder blade of a cow, tied with vine around his neck so that it dangled across his chest. A wooden cowbell, similarly bound with vine around his throat, lay against the cow bone. When dancing, the bone and wooden bell and clapper provided the basic rhythm. It was supplemented by the whistling of a *karambeta*, half-flute, half-horn, made from a hollowed stick to which a small round gourd had been attached, its base punched out to amplify the sound.

Members also dressed to remind others of their power. Often they danced with tiny bows and arrows, symbolic of the weapons carried by apprentice elders in time of war, when tradition forbade them a warrior's spear. Their real power, however, lay in the magic substances carried in goatskin sacks. Slung across the shoulders of each man, they continuously rattled as he danced. The constant noise was intended to remind all listeners of the magic contained within each bag, "lest anyone forget to fear."

As an obviously deviant minority, the Mwaa were highly sensitive to verbal insult, whether directed at single members or their Kiama as a whole. Their choice of homesteads at which to dance was often dictated by reports of who among the rich and powerful had spoken ill of them. To ensure sufficient victims, they often formed processions, dancing down the public paths while considering the comments and even the expressions of those they passed for evidence of disrespect.

Performances took place at dusk, when people were returning from their fields and could take time for leisure. By prearrangement a Mwaa troop would dance their way into a wealthy homestead, singing and cavorting in exchange for a reward. Over time the earlier handfuls of castor seeds expanded into full-scale feasts. During the early 1900s, cultivators forced to host Mwaa dancers were required to donate enough millet beer, vegetables, and later, goats to feed the entire company. In theory these donations were freely exchanged in return for the entertainment. In fact failure to provide what was expected led to the usual curse being placed on the entire homestead.

Mwaa councils followed cursing practices all their own, however. Surrounding the hut of a recalcitrant cultivator, a troop would dance noisily around it, chanting verbal maledictions in traditional Meru fashion. They also purposely defecated, ringing the property with human feces that had been liquified by a substance the group had previously consumed. Borrowing, perhaps, from the earlier practice of Wathua (who used goat dung as protective magic), the Mwaa provided a more powerful substitute for the earlier cursing pattern of visible sticks and vines. Human feces, of course, could be smelled as well as seen, and were used to isolate a "violator" within his home, in such a manner as to express the troupe's extreme contempt. To remove the condition, the cultivator had only to pay over the required foods, in the form of invitations to a feast.

Few homestead heads dared resist this type of threat. A host's most frequent reaction was to accept the appearance of a Mwaa Kiama with whatever courtesy he could muster. Spectators shared no such inhibitions, and the chaos of a band of wildly dancing Mwaa could bring them running from every direction to enjoy the show.

The songs themselves were rough and aggressively sexual. Both words and rhythms were extemporaneous and explicitly intended to both mock and shame either the host or any spectator that caught a singer's eye. In practice both songs and dances could combine bursts of extemporaneous eloquence with the crudest displays of juvenile toilet humor, always to the rising laughter of the crowd. One of these, for example, described a series of increasingly hilarious misfortunes befalling a man of Meru (the host) who went into the forest to hunt buffalo. The "gunshots" with which each stanza invariably ended were provided by the entire Mwaa chorus and consisted of the air expelled in unison from their assembled anuses.

The dancing was also spectacularly female. The humor came from the dancers' imitation of female body movements, especially urination, defecation, and sexual intercourse. These, when combined with song and story, were intended to provoke lust and laughter. ("Mwaa dances were so funny and insolent that it was too great a burden not to laugh.")

Sometimes during a performance, onlookers might be so moved that they joined in, unconsciously swaying to the dancers' rhythm and laughing deeply at the songs. In such instances the attraction might operate on either of two levels. One was clearly sexual: the chance to join others who wore women's clothes and thereby imitate female roles in a way that brought at least limited social approval. On another level, the Mwaa might also attract men who simply took pleasure in singing and dancing.

When a man responded, however, whether moved by sexual or musical motives, the performers redoubled their efforts, trying to lure him out of the audience to join them in the dancing ring. Succeeding, they would embrace him, ritually welcoming him into their group. Failing, they would suddenly turn on him, with the entire troupe seizing small rocks from their shoulder bags to stone him.

Faced with such a barrage, the man usually turned and ran, often still laughing at his memories of the spectacle without realizing he was now part of it. The entire troupe of dancers gave chase, finally seizing him in a mixture of laughter, good fellowship, and physical force. The captive was borne away to be "taught Mwaa," whereby he swore both the agrarian and sexual oaths that now bound him to the dancers' Kiama.

It must be noted, however, that contemporary informants who were once members of Mwaa declare that the element of compulsion was more ritualized than real. Many family heads, dangling in the double noose of unhappy marriage and inadequate land, saw the Mwaa as the gate to their freedom. The capture was generally used as a method to allow those who wished to join to do so without loss of face. In particular, men uncertain of their sexual identities were shielded from social disapproval by the element of compulsion. The method was also valid, however, for men who simply wearied of their drought- and insect-ridden land and for whom the joys of song and dance offered more than years of pointless toil.

Despite their antisocial aspects, therefore, the supernatural dancing societies such as that of the Mwaa seemingly provided several positive functions within Meru society. At the most obvious level they offered increasingly polished entertainment to a people always burdened with toil, as well as the beginnings of an entertainer class within a still relatively undifferentiated and classless society. In times of hunger they offered famine relief, providing a socially acceptable option whereby those most fearfully stricken could band together and sing to ensure their survival.

Finally, the Mwaa offered a socially acceptable alternative to sexual deviants. Sexual deviation was not condoned in Meru, but now family heads who proved unwilling or unable to restrict themselves to male roles could act out feminine behavior in a way that brought at least minimal social approval. Alternatively, if that approval was withheld, Mwaa could strike back at those denying it, combining sexual and supernatural actions that ensured that even deviance commanded respect.[12]

PROPHETS, WARRIORS, DEVIANTS: CONTINUED FRAGMENTATION

By the final decades of the 1800s, two further splits had occurred within the Meru core. First, members of the warrior age-set began to challenge the authority of both the ruling and ritual elders to define with whom they might wage war, a situation unprecedented in tribal history. On another level, deviant and increasingly antisocial members of the age-set out of power (the family heads) essentially defied the collective authority of elders and warriors alike by forming duplicate administrative systems of their own, once more a situation without precedent within the tribe.

Of the two the split created by the deviant family heads was initially more threatening to Meru society. The fringe Kiamas not only openly defied mainstream authority but also actively recruited mainstream members, thereby steadily increasing their own ranks. Nor could the threat provided by these fringe groups be considered a passing one. The very intangibility of the cursing system would periodically suggest new variants to its practitioners. Thus over time the initially beneficial concept of a chanted curse, originally meant to maintain communal harmony, evolved into an ongoing series of derivative practices that grew steadily more threatening to society.

Why then did mainstream Kiamas fail to meet the threat, eliminate deviant practitioners, and restore the status quo? If, for example, the elders of a specific ridgetop disapproved of deviant groupings on their fringe, why did they not gather in Kiama, then order their warrior sons out to destroy them?

One reason may be that the deviant groups were small. Informants describe them as "few" and "scattered." Other evidence supports this fact, suggesting that both the original fringe communities (hunters, ironsmiths) and their later derivatives (crop protectors, food seekers, child extortionists, clown dancers) were, in fact, too few in number to endanger the Meru core. Nor did Mount Kenya's topography allow them to merge. Several deviant groups had branches in every major Meru region but were subject to the same geographic restrictions as men of the mainstream. Thus, they could function only at the ridgetop level throughout their history.

A second reason was that deviant groups were kin, however distant. Warriors sent out to crush them would have been attacking members of their own community, nonwarriors, and males older than themselves. None of these were "permitted" opponents. To attack any of them would have violated both ancestral teachings and the most basic concepts of warrior honor.

A third reason was that deviant groups were feared. Warriors fought according to universally accepted military conventions. They were not prepared to move against a force that fought only with chanted curses, capable of causing subsequent calamity among their livestock, families, or entire clans.

The most important reason, however, was that mainstream Kiamas throughout Meru were apparently immobilized by their own traditions. Several of these had developed during prior generations, to cope with the evolution of the two older fringe communities into duplicate administrative entities. This development had created a sense of ambivalence among mainstream elders. On one hand the duplication of their institutions diminished their authority and power. On the other both hunters and ironsmiths rendered valuable services to the community. In consequence mainstream attitudes toward both groups wavered between fear and respect. Mainstream Meru reacted by developing customs intended to isolate men of the fringe, yet never harm them. Dietary taboos, for example, prevented hunters and cultivators from eating together or sharing food, thereby inhibiting social intercourse and prohibiting marriage. Similar isolating rituals surrounded the ironsmiths. The same principle applied to the work of Kiamas. Mainstream elders resolved conflicts solely among their own members, the cultivator-herder clans along their ridgetop. No hunter or ironsmith could approach them seeking redress. The concerns of fringemen were isolated from mainstream justice.

This isolation was subsequently applied to each of the derivative fringe communities as they appeared. The crop-protection Kiamas were received with ambivalence; their use of land was respected, but their use of magic was despised. Mainstream Meru detested the food-seeking groups, yet feared their power. In consequence they officially ignored them, shutting off their participation in communal life. Nor rituals were shared. None of their women was ever courted. No deviant could join a mainstream council or seek its judgment. All the honors of elderhood were denied. Notwithstanding, this policy had its price. By adhering to tradition, the elders abandoned thoughts of action. By ignoring the people, they ignored the problem as well.

WARRIORS VERSUS ELDERS; WARRIORS VERSUS DEVIANTS

The mainstream elders' ambivalence was not reflected in their warrior sons. Sharing their fathers dislike of the fringe groups, war bands often tried to move against the "dancing jackals" that despoiled their family crops and herds. War leaders across Meru repeatedly petitioned their respective elders to let them wage war on the deviants. Every petition was denied.

At some point in this period, however, warriors began to rebel against the elders' authority. Striking at night, in itself a violation of Meru military tradition, they attacked groups of deviants at their feasts, beating and scattering them with their spear shafts, then burning both their huts and sacred symbols. Furious and fearful, the elders' Kiama most directly concerned would call their sons collectively to task, punishing the entire band with fines of livestock. Since the animals, in fact, were drawn from their own herds (tradition required that warriors give all captured livestock to their fathers), the punishment was pointless. So were the raids. After each incident, since no lives had been taken, the deviants would reassemble.

In fact, the warriors rage may have been more ritualized than real, since their limited actions were never intended to resolve the problem but were merely to keep it in bounds. Like the earlier concept of cursing, the later types of deviance survived because they served society. Indeed, Meru psychology may have required their survival as permitted options for those unable to perform traditional masculine roles. In Meru such options took supernatural forms. In the early teens, for instance, boys inclined toward homosexuality, and thus unwilling to become warriors, retreated into witchcraft. This meant establishing supernatural Kiamas of their own, to protect themselves, by use of the collectively chanted curse, against beatings and taunts from the militarized majority. As young adults, men could opt out of warriorhood by apprenticing themselves to practicing ritualists. As middle-aged family heads, men failing to meet traditional masculine expectations could choose the limited female role-playing offered by some of the fringe Kiamas. Other deviant groups presented similar options, each attractive to small minorities as alternatives to their traditional roles.

The deviants may also have benefited the very warriors that tormented them. By the final decades of the 1800s, increasing numbers of fringe Kiamas had provided warriors in every region with the precedent of disobedience to the elders. By unspoken agreement, warriors across Meru struck out at those groups that angered them, yet never so effectively as to prevent their reappearance. Their elders raged against such disobedience, yet took no steps to prevent its recurrence. Thus by tacit compromise, the social contract that bound both groups remained intact. However, ruling elders in every Meru region found their authority challenged both by warriors and the middle-aged, and Meru society once again began to break apart. For the moment the social fabric was patched by tacit compromise. In years to come, however, men beyond the Meru regions would provide all groups with sterner tests.

CHAPTER V

Capitulation Traditions:
The Coming of England

"If you stand behind a tree, you are killed.
If you stand behind a shield, you are killed.
If you stand behind a hill, you are killed."[1]
As told to (Mrs.) Mwamucheke wa Gakuru
(Muthambi, 1906) by a kinswoman
fleeing the conquest of Embu

ACHUNKU: RED STRANGERS

The first appearance of Achunku ("red" men, i.e., Europeans; sing.:
Muchunku) in the Meru regions caused the smoldering conflict between
elders and warriors to burst into full flame.[2] The whites first came as
guests and later leaders of the Kamba, Swahili, Somali, or Zanzibari-
Arab caravans that habitually journeyed to Mount Kenya every dry season, exchanging cloth, trinkets, and coastal beads for tusks, honey, and
sufficient goats and grain to feed their porters. Collectively, the Meru
labeled all of these peoples as Acomba (or Achomba), men of the coast.

The Europeans initially saw themselves as part of this commercial
pattern and wished only to maintain it, hunting and trading for tusks,
meat, and millet, before traveling north or west of the mountain. Unfortunately, British and German conceptions of trading demanded that
transactions take place instantly, whether the indigenous peoples were
willing or not. Whereas a party of Swahili, Somali, or Arabs might be
prepared to sit and haggle for days over the price of each item, Europeans expected instant service for fair value. Having once offered what
they considered adequate goods for grain and livestock, they expected
the offer to be taken and the requested commodities to appear. Any delay in negotiations or, worse, any refusal to trade, was taken as an act
of hostility akin to declaring war. With the survival of their expeditions
dependent on continued resupply, most Europeans felt no qualms in
seizing what they required. Accordingly, they plundered cattle, sheep,

121

goats, donkeys, and occasionally women, leaving a trail of burned-out villages to mark their passing.

Meru warriors, in their turn, had no difficulty in fitting both the aliens and their activities into their own traditional framework, reacting to the expeditions as they would any other cattle raiders and attacking them in defense of their livestock. In these instances, however, their traditional and expected aggressiveness brought them into repeated conflict with the prophets, whose fears were echoed by the ruling elders. Thus, in every Meru region an ominous split emerged between warriors and elders, with the former still seeking glory in traditional fashion and the latter forbidding them to do so. The result was a period of wavering and indecision in which the entire Meru social system began to fray.

Meru ambivalence toward the Europeans was perhaps most clearly demonstrated with the arrival of William Astor Chanler, an American, in 1892.[3] His caravan was composed of two Europeans, four Somali guardsmen armed with rifles, and about sixty Swahili porters.

Chanler was not the first white to reach Meru. He had been preceded by two Germans, Karl Peters and Herman Tiedemann, who passed briefly through the Tharaka region in the autumn of 1889. Peters, later to become known both for exploration and for his mistreatment of Africans, reacted to the Tharaka in his customary manner. Brushing aside initial attempts at trade, he plundered six hundred head of cattle, successfully repulsing Tharaka attempts to retrieve them as he fought his way out of the district.[4] The peoples of adjoining Tigania had better fortune, attacking and overwhelming a Swahili-led caravan that entered their district the following year.

Chanler's caravan then appeared to the north of these regions, penetrating the foothills of Embe, today's Igembe. In view of the region's obvious fertility, the whites decided to ensure the success of their trading venture by seizing two "old men" as hostages. In so doing, they violated Meru military conventions, which restricted hostilities to men of warrior age and imprisonment to women. When a unit of fifty outraged warriors appeared, Chanler instantly seized four of them, scattering the rest with gunfire. He then demanded trade.

The Igembe contingent reacted predictably by calling in reinforcements from the adjoining communities. By the next morning Chanler found his group ringed by more than four hundred spearmen, all sounding a war cry and spoiling to fight. In this moment of crisis they were overruled by the elders, who to Chanler's amazement permitted the caravan to leave in peace, merely redirecting it to an adjacent community in Tigania with which the Igembe were continually at war.

The pattern repeated itself, however, in Tigania. Chanler's initial demands for instant trade were met by the appearance of "hundreds" of Tiganian warriors, in this instance reinforced by family head/apprentice elders carrying bows and poison-tipped arrows. Evidently, the caravan's reputation had preceded it, with sufficient force to cause full-scale mobilization.

The whites requested millet and livestock to feed their porters, offering what they felt to be adequate trade goods in exchange. The Tiganians refused, boasting of their previous massacre of the Swahili caravan and threatening the intruders with extermination. Once again, as tension rose between both sides, the ruling elders intervened, effectively neutralizing their own warriors by offering the rituals of common blood and military alliance (*gichiaro*) to the entire caravan.

Chanler, however, decided to fight. After taking still another ruling elder (to Chanler, "a chief") as hostage, he sent foraging parties into every nearby village, seizing goats, cattle, and sheep. Two hundred warriors blocked their return, enveloping them in the traditional manner while still burdened with their plunder.[5] Rifle fire broke the blockade, scattering the defenders with more than thirty casualties. Thereafter, having collected sufficient booty, the caravan marched back to Igembe, surrounded by a moving screen of enraged pursuers, who rained poisoned arrows from the thickets and set water ambushes at every stream. One final time the elders intervened. Once again they restrained their warriors, this time long enough to complete the previously proposed ritual alliance. As "brothers" the Europeans were no longer subject to attack, and they thereupon left the area without further incident.

This pattern of plunder, counterattack, rifle fire, and subsequent alliance was repeated for the next decade by every European to enter Meru. In each case the decision for peace on the intruder's terms was made by Meru elders over the violent objections of leading warriors. In some instances European demands were so objectionable that the elders themselves "rose to their feet and danced in fury."[6] Yet, in the end, they always submitted.

There were several reasons for this acquiescence. One was an increasing inclination among Meru elders everywhere to heed the prophecies, which had already proven accurate in several ways and still threatened resisters with death. The second was an increasing appreciation of the intruders' military effectiveness, as the Meru gained a clearer understanding of the relationship between the casualties and the European weapons. Warriors, still frozen within their traditional concepts, tended to dismiss gunfire as something ("the popping of beans") that could be overcome by still greater displays of personal courage. Elders, both more experienced and reflective, became less certain, increasingly choosing to temporize in the interests of survival.

Strife between warriors and elders also intensified in communities where whites were able to establish stable trading relationships without the need of guns. This tended to occur when European-led caravans entered weakly defended regions, whose herds were perpetually plundered by more powerful neighbors. Chanler's wanderings, for example, brought him to the territory of Daicho (today's Thaicho), a small community between Tigania, Imenti, and Tharaka, whose warriors had been unable to protect its herds from its neighbors, including the Tiganians against whom Chanler had fought. At that time Daicho's warriors were led by M'Minuki (to Chanler, Dominuki), a canny, thoughtful man seeking constantly for military advantage. The relative weakness of his own community made him welcome anyone hostile to his foes, and he offered Chanler grain and goats in exchange for his protection.

The next logical step, from a Meru perspective, was to ensure the permanence of this protection by offering *gichiaro* and thereby creating a condition of kinship between the leaders of both sides. This in turn made it logical—again, to Meru thinking—to suggest that these ritually created "kin" join them in a punitive raid against their former common enemies. Invariably, such joint ventures proved successful because of European firepower, and the victors gained large numbers of livestock.

At some point, however, the European sponsors would depart, usually storing surplus tusks, trade goods, and livestock with their newfound ally. That departure, unfortunately, left the client community once more open to its neighbors' raids, which frequently resulted in the loss of both cattle and goods. When this occurred, subsequent punitive expeditions by the returning Europeans radically shifted the balance of local wealth and power toward the client community. This in turn set off a small-scale arms race, as neighboring groups vied to acquire European sponsors of their own, able to protect with one hand and bestow trade goods with the other.

The material rewards, however, were restricted to the ruling elders. Their warrior sons, it will be recalled, were forbidden by tradition to acquire wealth except through raiding. To "seize" trade goods was dishonorable, and even livestock presented by the whites had to be transferred to their fathers' herds. Moreover, the sheer volume of potential wealth that could be acquired from every passing caravan staggered the imaginations of both age-sets. In consequence, discord between the two groups reached unprecedented heights as caravans penetrated every Meru region throughout the 1890s. Many of these were led by Europeans, and each came with its quantity of goods, guns, and arrogance. Warriors viewed each intrusion as a chance to gain goods, livestock, and glory by traditional attacks. Their elders, in contrast, saw each caravan's appearance as the means to acquire the same things by inhibiting the warriors' work.

Many thoughtful elders also opposed attacks upon the caravans because of their straightforward fear of military defeat. Already shaken by the prophecies, this faction became even more fearful in the 1890s as tales began to come in from various Gikuyu communities to the south and east of Meru. Many of these were told by Meru warriors themselves, men of unquestioned courage and integrity, who had wandered abroad to visit distant kin. They returned to their homesteads with startling tales of Gikuyu surrender, of sticks that threw fire at a distance, of the killing of children, of the destruction of homes, banana groves, and millet fields—acts so far removed from Meru military tradition they were difficult to accept and believe.

Wilder stories followed. Gikuyu and even Maasai warriors were said to have laid aside their spears in favor of the woman's digging stick and now to be making paths that extended like snakes across their ridges and north toward Meru. Each tale occasioned furious discussion within the elders' councils and warrior barracks, as both age-sets grew more uncertain of what to do.

THE BATTLE OF EMBU

Meru's fears grew even greater after 1906, as they learned of the conquest of neighboring Embu.[7] The Embu-speaking peoples inhabited that section of Mount Kenya just south of the regions of the Meru and the Cuka. Fierce and defiant in the shelter of their mountain forests, they had long refused to deal with Europeans, attacking their caravans and denying them foodstuffs with an arrogance that verged on contempt.

Nor did the subjugation of their neighbors, whether in Gikuyu or the adjoining flatlands of Mbeere, change their position. Several early military successes against both European and Swahili-led caravans had given them a number of workable guns. Although these were fired primarily for their noise, rather than for their destructiveness, their possession gave the Embu a self-confidence that far surpassed their military capacities.

By 1904, British military power, supported by levies of Maasai spearmen, had conquered the Iriani Gikuyu region immediately to the south of Embu. The British had also extended military protection to Mbeere, the arid, thinly populated, thornbush flatlands that bordered Embu on the east. Thereafter, demands went up from three separate quarters for the subjugation of Embu itself.

The conquest was proposed for several reasons. British colonial officials objected in principle to the existence of a hostile force adjacent to their own and desired to humble the Embu for nothing more than their perceived truculence toward whites. Nonofficials, whether settlers or concession seekers, coveted the fertile Embu lands and forest produce.

However, the demand for conquest was shared equally by Britain's African allies. The Gikuyu, having themselves fallen to British power, now envied the Embu, both for their freedom and their vast cattle herds that could be used to replenish their own. The Mbeere also thirsted for conquest. Having suffered through generations of successful Embu raiding, they now anticipated the chance for both looting and revenge.

The first step in the invasion took place at the instigation of Gutu, an Mbeere war leader who had chosen cooperation with the British. Through his influence one of the most respected Embu commanders was invited into the conquered area in June 1906 to witness British firepower and discuss surrender terms. The Embu leader, Mugane of the highland Ngandori region, was severely shaken by what he saw and returned to his people bearing a letter demanding one thousand cattle, to be paid as a fine and collective apology for past transgressions.

The Ngandori warriors massively rejected the demands and reviled their spokesman for cowardice, finally driving him bodily from the council. Their reply to the surrender terms was symbolic rather than formal. They returned the paper with a basket of millet, asking the whites to count each grain if they wished to learn how many warriors awaited their invasion. Other Embu areas, notably the lowland communities near the Mbeere border, reacted similarly, returning British surrender ultimatums with pieces of leopard skin or war clubs to indicate the fierceness of their warriors.

The Embu contempt for European power was most clearly displayed in the decision of several of the highland communities to launch a massive raid on Cuka, their northern neighbor, in the dry season of 1906. In July an unusually large number of warriors assembled from both lowland and upper forest communities. Numbering several hundred and encouraged by the possession of a dozen operable guns, they set off for Cuka and a traditional war.[8]

In this instance the Cuka were prepared. As the second smallest and the militarily weakest society on Mount Kenya, they had long since acted to ensure their survival by constructing immense barriers along their region's outer boundaries. These barriers were based initially on the thick forest cover that grew along the banks of the two rivers marking Cuka's northern and southern borders. The Cuka had improved on nature, however, by felling scores of trees along each riverbank, then weaving elaborate barriers of vine and thornbush into the gaps.

Over generations these barriers had grown together to form two irregular but effectively "living" walls that ran from plains to forest, screening the entire population. In some places the barriers were more than twenty feet high and nine feet thick. In others the Cuka had cut narrow, twisting paths, designed to permit intruders only in single file. One by one potential invaders emerged into cleared areas in which defenders had open fields of arrow fire from every side.

Habitually, Embu raiding expeditions took advantage of spies within the Cuka areas to learn of weak points in their defense. Given time and the advantage of surprise, they could cut their way through a thin or rotting portion of the barrier, emerge in force, and raid at will. This time, however, the raiders cut their gap only to be met by an equally large and steadily increasing legion of defenders. Although fighting steadily, the Embu found themselves gradually forced back through the opening they had made, having failed to seize a single animal.

Weary, angry, and discouraged by their failure, the retreating warriors were met outside the barrier by runners from their home areas. Hysterical and exhausted, these gasped out the news that Embu itself had been attacked from the west and south and that their women and herds were being driven off in all directions. Overwhelmed by the news, the entire body of warriors shook off their fatigue and set off at a dead run.

They arrived to find all of Embu thrown into chaos. Invaders had struck at five points along the Gikuyu-Embu border in early July, crossing the river that separated their regions and penetrating far inland. Embu elders remember this as a Gikuyu rather than British invasion, as Gikuyu commanders served as guides for the whites, and their spearmen made up most of the intruders' rank and file.

The heart of the invaders, however, was the Third Battalion, King's African Rifles (KAR), which had been formed only ten years before. The attacking contingent consisted of two KAR companies of one hundred men each, as well as one column of African *askari* (guards, police). All were armed with Martin-Enfield .303 rifles, a breech-loading weapon known for its high rate of fire. Although led by three British officers, the KAR ranks consisted solely of "alien" Africans, mercenaries drawn from places as diverse and distant as Sudan, Abyssinia (now Ethiopia), and Nyasaland (now Malawi).[9] Cut off from Mount Kenya's peoples by differences in language, geography, traditions, and training, they proved able and obedient soldiers who inspired fear in those who fought them. Even so, they made up only a small percentage of the invasion forces, and with so few aliens and Europeans in the battles it can be understood why the Embu perceived their invaders as none other than their traditional Gikuyu enemies.

A second major thrust came from the Embu-Mbeere border. Here the Mbeere had gathered themselves under three of their most noted war leaders to launch a concerted attack on their Embu neighbor. Like the Gikuyu, Mbeere forces had been stiffened by the acquisition of several guns. Crossing the Embu boundary, they initially met only scattered opposition, as most of the lowland warriors were still off on the Cuka raid. Accordingly, they began to scour the border districts for captives, goats, and cattle.

Deprived of the major portion of their fighting strength, most Embu communities could do nothing but flee before the invasion. Elders, women, children, and the few remaining warriors drove their herds desperately northward up the mountain slope, racing deep into the forests as the only possible avenue of escape.

Nor could the return of the Cuka invasion force transform the situation. The Embu warriors arrived, exhausted from both the prior battle and the speed of their return, to find their enemies ranging at will throughout the region. In consequence war leaders found it impossible to keep the returning warriors together. As cries of "Mbu-u-u!" (danger!) rose from every side, each military contingent split off from the main body and raced to protect its own homesteads—lowlanders to throw back the Mbeere, highland peoples to battle the Gikuyu and whites.

The upper regions were quickly overwhelmed, as each attempt to concentrate defending Embu forces was broken by the crack of rifles. The Embu fought with notable courage, ambushing the enemy from trees and often charging directly into KAR bayonets. At first they also plunged directly at the riflemen, shouting that the guns could only fire water. Their resistance swiftly crumbled, however, and the invaders spread unchecked among the Embu herds.

In the lowlands, resistance was more successful, perhaps because both sides attempted to fight according to traditional rules. In several instances Embu war leaders greeted Mbeere forces with personal challenges, demanding that the issues be settled by personal combat between commanders. The lowlanders also proved unable to concentrate their forces against rifle fire, however, and resistance swiftly ebbed away.

For nine days the Embu survived their invaders by hiding and starving in forest retreats or large caves along the river fringes. During this time, enemy columns scoured the region at will, driving off more than ten thousand head of cattle, sheep, and goats. Nearly all of the conventions of war were violated, not only by the whites and their alien allies but by the Gikuyu as well. Hundreds of livestock were uselessly slaughtered and piled in the ashes of burned-out homesteads. Banana groves and millet fields were razed. Warriors who attempted surrender were often shot or speared. Elders, women, and even children—traditionally exempt from combat—were beaten, abused, and sometimes killed. Only after this nine-day period were the whites able to control their allies and reestablish order. Nevertheless, the shock of conquest had been one that no Embu would forget. Nor would their Meru-speaking neighbors to the north.

THE COMING OF ENGLAND

The shock of conquest was no less great among the peoples of Cuka, Muthambi, and Mwimbi, who stood next in line of conquest. From the invasion's inception all three groups had been deluged with requests from frantic Embu kinspeople to shelter livestock that had been driven swiftly along the forest's lower fringe to safety. The herds had been followed by bands of terrified elders, women, and children, fleeing the approach of the invaders. Rumors of the violence reached new heights as frightened noncombatants passed on reports of the white man's bullets: "If you stand behind a tree, you are killed. If you stand behind a shield, you are killed. If you stand behind a hill, you are killed."[10]

The Muthambi and Mwimbi decided, in late July 1906 to call a joint meeting of their Nkomes, the highest elders' councils. Traditionally, the two councils had met only as adversaries, to reconcile conflicts that had appeared between them. In this instance, however, events in Embu were considered sufficiently serious to bring not only both groups of Nkome elders but also their respective warrior contingents together in a single field. As the older men deliberated, their warrior sons danced alongside them, displaying their weapons and shouting out vows.

The elders argued for several days over what should be done. Traditional defensive tactics, such as cutting the log bridges across the river separating them from Cuka or digging ambush pits along the river paths, were rejected as inadequate. Nor was it felt that the two peoples had sufficient military strength to hold off attackers even if reinforcements were sent them by traditional allies.

The meeting broke up in indecision, as both elders and warriors wavered between the desire for courage and a fear of its consequences. A second meeting lasted several days but produced the same result. A week went by, as elders everywhere gathered in their homesteads to reflect and talk. Finally, a third council reached a decision. Spies were to be sent to Embu to act as "eyes" for the elders, to aid them in further decisions. The peoples of upper Mwimbi had created *gichiaro* alliances with several Embu communities, including Ngandori, home of war-leader Mugane, where the fighting was reported heaviest. Accordingly, two of their number were selected to visit his area.

The spies returned within forty-eight hours to report that the worst of the rumors were true. They declared that the entire population of upper Embu seemed to have abandoned all resistance and were now scattered and starving in their northern forests. Their great herds were now in the hands of the invaders, some of whom had guns that fired far more rapidly than those previously experienced. Many warriors were aware of the firing rate of muzzle-loading rifles. These new stories, however, so disheartened them that they were almost unwilling to fight. The psychological weight of the prophecies, combined with the defeat of two much larger and more powerful neighbors, finally penetrated their collective thinking. As a result, the Mwimbi elders made a separate decision, to sue for peace.

The implementation was swift. Two spokesmen, one for each ruling age-set, were selected to enter the battle zone. The ruling elders chose M'Rigi Cania, a man respected for his caution. The warriors selected Mbogore M'Mwendo, foremost commander of the upper Mwimbe region and widely acclaimed for his physical courage. Accompanied by an honor guard of twenty other warriors, the two set off for Embu, each bearing the wooden staff of Kiama, the traditional sign of peace.

Skirting the Cuka regions, the party arrived during the last of the "nine days" unrestricted plunder. The Embu they met filled their imaginations with often exaggerated reports of atrocities. However, one individual, Ciriani wa Karwa, had just been appointed "chief" (Munene: the big [fat] one; pl.: Anene) over his region by one of the Europeans.

Ciriani, also of warrior age, advised Mbogore both on the futility of armed resistance and the procedures for making peace. Because the leading white man was also of warrior age, it was decided best for Mbogore to approach alone. He was to present the European with the gifts traditional in such circumstances, a ram (the symbol of peace) and a cask of honey.

Mbogore followed Ciriani's advice. On presenting the gifts he was ushered into the presence of Edward Butler Horne, then twenty-six years old.[11] Horne had participated fully in the Embu campaign and had been selected by colonial authority to extend British influence northward around the slopes of Mount Kenya. He had been born in 1881, the youngest of eight brothers, and came from a family distinguished for service to the empire. After receiving a conventional British education he had yielded to a sense of adventure. He spent several years in Canada and Wyoming, working as both a lumberjack and ranch hand. In Wyoming he acquired the name "Shorthorn," a reflection of his lack of height in contrast to a taller brother, nicknamed "Longhorn."

Horne was a fanatical hunter, and it was big game that had lured him to Africa. Having entered the colonial service, he discovered in himself an unsuspected capacity for languages. In the course of his career he at least partially mastered Swahili, Gikuyu, Meru, Embu, Maasai, and Nandi.

In Embu, Horne was known among Africans as "Bwana Mdogo" (Mr. Small), again because of his height. His meeting with Mbogore took place in July 1906. Mbogore began the conversation by stating that he had come from a region "far to the north" of Embu, where the warriors were extremely fierce but nonetheless prepared for peace. Horne replied by praising Mbogore's size and imposing physical appearance, then appointed him "Munene [chief] of Mwimbi."

The post was formalized by Horne's presentation of a symbol of the office, a *kanga,* or black cotton blanket. As a "blanket chief" (Munene ya Kanga), Mbogore was to return to his people and prepare them for Horne's arrival. In addition, on his return he was to seek out other "chiefs" among neighboring peoples and send them to the

European's Embu headquarters. Each one who came would be given the black blanket of chieftainship, thereby preserving his people from military destruction.

Mbogore and indeed the entire Mwimbi contingent were more than a little confused about the term "chief." To Europeans it meant the single leader of a people, but the Meru had no such concept. Their leadership was collective, with no individual able to serve as more than temporary spokesman for the rest. Thus Mbogore's announcement, upon his return to Mwimbi, that he had been given the European title of "chief" was greeted by both elders and warriors with joy and relief. In actuality, the term was translated into Mwimbi dialect to suggest "spokesman" (Mugambe; pl.: Agambe) and was restricted to those matters concerning whites. Mbogore, therefore, already a Mugambe for his warriors' council, was thereafter to be spokesman for the elders' Kiama as well—although only in matters concerned with white men, for which he would serve in the capacity of "spokesman for the whites."

To formalize this status, as well as to ensure their own continued control, members of the elders' council initiated Mbogore into their ranks, an act not unprecedented, but unusual for so young a man. By so doing, they sought not only to honor his achievement but also to assure that the new "spokesman" stayed under their authority.

MBOGORE: BLANKET CHIEFTAIN

With hindsight one may wonder why a highly trained war leader, proud of his skills and at the peak of his military existence, would so quickly accept the subordination of his people in exchange for a title and blanket. Obviously fear, both of the prophecy and of military defeat, must have played a dominant part. However, there were also other reasons. Mbogore, like many other Meru war leaders, was a man of unusual intellectual curiosity. Like his comrades he had followed the tradition that permitted him to spend his earlier warrior years wandering to distant regions. Always accompanied by a single companion, he had traveled through the Gikuyu, Kamba, and Maasai areas, once going nearly to the boundaries of present-day Tanzania.

During his travels, he had had ample opportunity to compare the customs of other people with his own. Mbogore's fascination with problems of warfare went far beyond military strategies and tactics. He became concerned, for example, about the relatively small population of Mwimbi as compared with the far larger numbers of their traditional enemies. On reflection, he decided the cause of this lay in the inability of Mwimbi women to bear many children. This in turn, he decided, was the result of their circumcision at puberty.

Female circumcision was practiced by every tribe in central Kenya. Usually, it consisted of removing a woman's clitoris at puberty. In Mwimbi, however, portions of the major and minor labia were removed as well, causing scarring that could seriously hinder childbirth.[12] Mbogore was shocked to learn of the differences between his own and other peoples' practices on this issue. On his return he defied tradition and launched what appears to have been a one-warrior crusade to modify the custom, in the interest of increasing Mwimbi numbers and thereby military strength.

His efforts were unsuccessful, as were similar attempts to eradicate other practices that ran counter to military efficiency. The traditions surrounding his early years, however, suggest a man far less bound than his contemporaries to ancestral custom and far more ready to accept whatever innovations might increase his sense of security and power.

On his travels Mbogore undoubtedly had had frequent opportunity to hear tales of Europeans and their distant-killing guns. Although he had never handled firearms, he had viewed muzzle-loading rifles at a distance and was generally acquainted with their principles and effects. While in Embu, however, he was shocked by tales of the high firing rate of the Martin-Enfield rifle, tales that had grown with the telling until they nearly surpassed belief. Disheartened, Mbogore seems to have acted with his usual mental flexibility, abandoning his prior drive for Mwimbi military power in favor of incorporating that of the whites.

On assuming his chiefship, Mbogore also carried out Horne's second injunction. After fulfilling the rites for his entry into the Kiama of elders, he journeyed to neighboring Muthambi to seek out "other chiefs" to send to Embu. Because Muthambi also lacked a single leader, Mbogore sought out his war-leader counterpart, Njage wa Kathiore. Like Mbogore, Njage was in his late twenties and had achieved the distinction of "commander" within upper Muthambi. After hearing Mbogore's description of his journey to Embu, the Muthambi elders' council hastened to obtain what seemed to be the same advantages. Meeting hurriedly, they authorized Njage to lead a delegation to the white's headquarters at Embu, to obtain the black blanket and with it the promised peace. He did so, following much the same procedures as Mbogore, then returned to spread the word still further north, to Igosi (today's Igoji), Miutini, Imenti, and beyond.

In every region reactions to his message were the same. Warriors, half fearful but ready to wage war, were thwarted by the refusal of their respective ritualists and elders' councils to sanction an attack. Withholding their blessing implied ancestral disapproval of the warriors' intent. But the invaders of Embu were not men of the Meru fringe, to be attacked and scattered by the whacks of a dozen spears with no loss of life to either side. Neither tradition nor prior acts of disobedience offered adequate solutions. Without them the warrior contingents remained immobile, armed but unwilling to cast a single spear.

Their elders proved more decisive. In every region, from Igoji to Imenti, the ruling Kiamas sued for peace along the lines already taken by their two small southern neighbors. Communities from Igoji, Miutini, Abogeta (South Imenti), and Miiriga Mieru (North Imenti) all sent delegations, headed by their most noted war leaders.

Many of these spokesmen had traveled as widely as Mbogore. At least one, M'Mwitaria wa Karandu of North Imenti, had already received a black blanket as the result of an expedition to Nyeri, a Gikuyu area on the western side of Mount Kenya. While there, Gikuyu kinsmen had directed him to a European, who had received M'Mwitaria's declaration of peaceful welcome in good spirits and had rewarded it with a blanket. Throughout the remainder of 1906 the Meru delegations appeared in Embu, to make their submission and receive their blankets. As newly styled chiefs they returned to their respective regions with the news that a "red (white) warrior" would soon arrive.

E. B. HORNE ("KANGANGI"): THE MOMENT OF CONQUEST

British power expanded northward in July 1907 with the arrival of E. B. Horne, accompanied by one company of the King's African Rifles and supported by levies of Maasai spearmen. Gikuyu and Embu warriors also accompanied him as porters, their reduced status a silent but eloquent message of things to come.

Horne had been instructed to proceed north through Cuka, Muthambi, Mwimbi, and Igoji, establishing the colonial presence in each area. Preferably, this was to be done without war, because their submission had already been declared. Passing through Cuka without incident, Horne and his entourage appeared at the Nithi River, which separated the Cuka people from Muthambi. Anticipating his arrival, Njage had isolated his warriors from the main community. Through ritual many of them had begun to work up courage for an attack on the invaders, and there was considerable feeling both against the ruling elders and Njage himself.

To maximize his initial impact, Horne chose to ride a white horse, the first seen on Mount Kenya. He moved surrounded by a guard of picked Maasai spearmen, chosen for their height and fierceness. On arrival, he was guided to Mkui, meeting place for the Muthambi elders' council and Njage's home. On greeting Njage, Horne first asked about the whereabouts of the conspicuously absent warriors. Njage answered that he had hidden them in the bush lest their ferocity harm the white man who was now his guest.

Horne responded that he had come not to visit but to rule. He then demanded that the warriors appear before him immediately. When they came, beating spears against shields and hurling battle cries at the intruders, Horne treated them immediately to a demonstration of his gun.

Initially, he selected a black bull that stood some one hundred yards away from the assembled warriors. Dropping it with a single shot, he then contemptuously presented it to them "for meat." Thereafter, he seized a Muthambi shield, asking if its owner could penetrate it with a spear. On hearing the reply that this was impossible, he asked several other warriors to stack their shields in a row, then riddled them with a display of rapid firing. The demonstration was convincing, and the shouting warriors subsided into silence.

Horne then spoke to them all. He began by asking how they ruled themselves. The reply was, "through the Kiama of our elders." He then asked how they dealt with their neighbors. The response, proudly given, was, "by waging war." Horne then informed them that he had been sent by his king to bring peace to their peoples. Thereafter, all raiding for livestock was to stop. No further seizure of women would be permitted, and all quarrels between men were to be submitted to himself rather than settled with war clubs and spears.

At this the warriors sent up a concerted howl of rage, asking in one hundred voices how they would acquire the livestock needed for brides. "Through trade and other peaceful means," came the reply, punctuated with a single gunshot as the warriors howled out their anger and despair.

Horne then informed them that they would not be idle. He declared that a gigantic road was being built across the land that would one day stretch clear around their mountain. To see this, however, each community would have to do its part. The Cuka had already begun their section, and the Mwimbi were to join in. This raised another shout of anger from the warriors, who informed the white man that digging the earth was work for women. "Now it is work for men," came the reply. "Begin it!"

Horne then turned to Njage, asking him to name the leading "chiefs" of the other regions of Muthambi. Taken by surprise, Njage named prominent commanders of his own age-set, who led warrior contingents in three other Muthambi areas. He was then somewhat stunned to see them named as blanket chiefs alongside himself.

Each new appointee was then asked to provide a specified number of warriors to accompany Horne to the neighboring Meru regions. Most of these were designated as porters. A few, the tallest and strongest, were incorporated into the corps of guards and also given blankets as symbols of their responsibilities. Horne referred to them by the traditional Swahili term *askari* (police), but among Meru they subsequently became known either as Askari ya Kanga (blanket police) or, more satirically, Kanga ya Muchunku (blankets of the "red," i.e., white man).

The pattern was repeated in each of the other Meru-speaking regions. With Njage as guide, Horne's entourage moved north into upper Mwimbi. There they were greeted by the blanket-clad Mbogore as well as his assembled warrior contingents, dancing and chanting to honor the white man's arrival. Having established his authority, Horne then passed onward to Igoji. Subsequently, after a return to Embu and several months' administrative delay, he resumed his travels, moving north in January 1908 into Imenti, Tigania, Igembe, and beyond.

At most stages in his two journeys Horne was met by spokesmen who had already visited Embu or other conquered regions and received black blankets. In each community warrior hostility was met with firepower demonstrations that grew more elaborate as Horne worked out what could be done with his weapons. The speech, however, never varied: he had come to end war in the name of his sovereign, and conflicts should henceforth be brought to him instead. After appointing chiefs and selecting police and porters, he would then journey on. In later years the Meru would recall his constant movement and rename him Kangangi, the "little wanderer." It is the only name by which he is recalled today.

Not every Meru warrior accepted the surrender of his people with equal grace. Although the elders effectively neutralized mass actions, there were several instances of individual resistance. In one such incident, an Imenti warrior is said to have stood before Horne fully armed and bellowing out a challenge to single combat. He was shot and wounded. Another, also from Imenti, is recalled as having suddenly wheeled and slapped Horne's face. His father's property was confiscated and burned. Two Igoji warriors, the youngest of their age-set, are said to have hit him from ambush with rocks. They were publicly whipped, and only the elders' interventions saved thirty of their warrior age-mates from suffering similar fates.

In another instance Horne seems to have collided with the Meru custom that permitted small bands of Nkuru ("old" ones), former warriors recently expelled by members of the age-set just below their own, to roam the countryside for a period, seeking "aliens" (any male non-Meru) on whom to blood their spears. The act of spearing an alien— even without killing the victim—by any member ritually cleansed the whole age-set of the stain incurred by its members' expulsion, and by symbolically drawing off their anger allowed the warriors to enter elderhood. A skirmish with one of the Nkuru bands within Imenti resulted in several warrior casualties and a decision by Horne to break up similar groups throughout the entire region.[13]

The most dramatic form of resistance, however, and by far the most painful to all Meru, came from a single man in Miutini. Miutini, the smallest Meru region, was located high in the forest between Imenti and Igoji. Although originally populated by Cuka, it had been overrun in recent times by pioneers and refugees from several other regions. Nevertheless, by the late 1900s it had developed fierce military traditions that had enabled it to survive despite its lack of size. Moreover, the region's relative isolation from traditional caravan routes had shielded its warriors from direct experience with gunfire.

By the time Horne first entered this area, he had already imposed his authority as far north as Tigania, but then decided to establish a headquarters in Imenti. On reaching Miutini's southern boundary, he rode through the ridgetop community of Kathigu, a cluster of homesteads at that time defended by a war band of forty men. Without warning, one of these warriors bellowed ("like a bull"), then struck Horne heavily with a long yam stem, almost knocking him from his horse.

Because the man's act seemed to be backed by his entire band, Horne gave no immediate response. Instead he returned to his Imenti headquarters and gathered warriors from at least four of its largest communities. These were ordered to attack Kathigu and whomever came to its aid. Every hut was to be burned and all livestock taken to Kangangi's (Horne's) camp.

The Imenti fell on the village. The Kathigu warriors, outnumbered, sent to every ridgetop in Miutini for assistance, as Meru military tradition required. These responded instantly, perceiving the invaders in traditional terms, as Imenti cattle raiders. As a result Miutini reinforcements began to appear within minutes of the intrusion, prepared to support their compatriots and fight.

At this point Horne himself intervened with a fusillade of gunfire. Four Miutini warriors were killed. The others encouraged one another to stand fast, calling out that the gunfire would do them no harm. As other shots rang out, however, they finally broke and ran.

Horne's Imenti allies then began a cattle sweep that threatened to extend far beyond the "guilty" ridgetop and include all Miutini. At this point the highest elders' councils from both Imenti and Igoji intervened. Tradition states that their spokesmen scolded Kangangi, accusing him of willfully violating the very peace he sought to impose. They admitted the guilt of the Miutini community. They also approved the use of Imenti warriors, since Kathigu had also violated their own injunction of nonresistance. Nevertheless, they declared that making peace was the traditional prerogative of elders, and as a man of warrior age Kangangi should stand back and allow them to proceed. Horne saw the wisdom of accepting their invitation, and peace was restored by the Meru themselves.

CREATING COLONIALISM:
THE BLANKET CHIEFDOMS

By May 1908, Horne's entourage was firmly encamped at Mwitari's (homestead), a site about nine miles from the present area of Meru Town.[14] The Miutini incident had made him aware of his military limitations, however, and he decided to construct a more defensible permanent camp.

Spokesmen from several of the local Kiamas recommended a ridge of partially uncultivated land near the Kazita River, just below the forest fringe. From Horne's perspective it had several advantages. The ridge was high, sharply defined, and thus easily defended. It lay near a permanent water source and was also open to cooling winds. Known earlier as Kaithe, it was then called Mutindwa's (place), after its war leader, and today forms the core of the modern Meru township.

The Meru elders, however, saw other advantages in the proposed site. It was exposed, thus potentially open to attack from lowland raiders, such as the plains Maasai. More important, it was partially covered by a sacred forest grove, "sacred" in that it was reserved for habitation by spirits of the Meru dead. These groves, it will be recalled, were found throughout Meru. For generations no living person had entered them, lest their presence incur supernatural wrath. Now, it seemed only fitting to direct an unwanted alien conqueror into an area where he could be dealt with, either by ancestral spirits or warlike Maasai.

Horne shrugged off the warnings of his interpreters and began work, forcing Imenti warriors to clear the forested and cultivated sections with equal thoroughness and a fine disregard for either ancestral anger or previous property rights. The next step was to erect two Canadian-style log cabins, built in the manner he had learned as a lumberjack.[15] These became his house and office. Thereafter, a line of grass and thatch huts was constructed, set in a permanent square in traditional British military style. Local warriors were then set to digging a six-foot trench, again in a square, around the complete encampment. Finally, water from the neighboring river was diverted into the square by means of trenches, and the headquarters was complete.

Throughout the building period Imenti elders had waited eagerly for the first signs of ancestral retribution to strike the intruders, in the form of catastrophic illness. They were initially quite encouraged when Horne consistently refused his interpreters' pleas to placate the supernatural by sacrificing goats. However, calamity failed to strike in any form, a failure that deeply shook the elders' faith in their traditions and cast many into apathetic despair.

Meanwhile, with their base complete, the invaders turned their attention to the construction of roads. That action brought them directly into conflict with the traditions of warriorhood. Horne's desire to create communication and supply routes back to his own administrative center can be understood, especially in view of his exposed military position. In full agreement the colonial administration had called for the simultaneous construction of a roadbed ten feet wide, to run from Embu through each of the Meru regions, pass through Horne's encampment, and extend thirty miles beyond into Tigania. Eventually, it would extend northward to include the Nyambeni Mountains (Igembe) and east around Mount Kenya into Gikuyu. The "simultaneous" element was to occur through the coercion of every African community along the route to undertake its construction.

In some regions the work was little more than the clearing of paths through the bush. In others, and particularly those of Meru, the road was required to traverse the same steep gorges and swift-flowing rivers that had so influenced traditional military development for generations. Nor were there European tools available to facilitate the job. Axes, shovels, and iron-tipped hoes were still in the future. Trees and thorn-bush could only be cleared with bush knives made of local iron, and rocks dislodged with wooden digging sticks.

Nor were the Meru eager for the task. The warriors were outraged at the orders to "dig," traditionally a woman's task. Their spokesmen appealed to Horne, explaining this facet of their customs and offering their services in clearing bush but leaving the actual road construction to women.

Tradition states that Kangangi was absolute in his refusal. Locked firmly into his European perspective, he came from a world in which men dug, women languished, and idleness was sin. Accordingly, he objected initially that Meru women lacked the strength for the work at hand. Thereafter, he pointed out the young men's current idleness and their need for "useful" labor. Once again, when customs clashed it was African warriorhood that suffered.

In fact, men and women participated equally in the road building. Newly appointed chiefs were made responsible for recruiting labor from each area. Their orders were enforced by other appointees, usually war leaders of secondary status. These acted as overseers and enforcers, thereby escaping the need to dig themselves. Every young adult had to be present. Absenteeism was eliminated by requiring workers to sleep at their work site. Each evening rough shelters were put up beside the half-formed roadbed, where men and women alike stayed in place until dawn.

At sunrise the work itself was in fact divided by sex, but according to British conceptions. Men dug, heaving at the packed earth and buried rock. Women carried dirt to the roadsides, using their hands to fill traditional woven baskets. The work was particularly exhausting when the roadbed had to be forced up (or down) the precipitous Meru gorges, through streams still raging from the recent rains, or over giant boulders that needed heating until they split and could be cleared away. Slackness or resistance was punished with the whip, with warriors being whipped before their women in flagrant disregard of military custom.

In consequence it was Meru warriorhood that began to die as the road emerged within the forests. The transformation of war leaders into chiefs and enforcers and of their rank and file into manual laborers did far more to kill the military ethic than mere surrender without battle. For the first time in their history warriors of an entire generation were forced to take a role reserved for women, working as equals beside them and sharing identical punishment. For the first time men could no longer take pride in their warrior role. Instead, as redefined by conquest, it had become a source of shame. Nor did war leaders escape the transformation. By serving the conqueror to the point of enforcing his conquest on their comrades, they escaped the humiliation of "women's" labor. But in so doing, they too lost all pride in their warrior identity. In the words of a former comrade: "they were no longer our [Meru] Agambe [spokesmen] but his. They were no longer men of Meru but simply Kamuchunku . . . little whites."[16]

Having established both a defensible headquarters and adequate lines of communication, Horne turned to the creation of a "native" administration. His task was considerably lightened by a British decision to divide the Meru-speaking regions into two administrative districts. Between 1908 and 1933 the peoples of Mwimbi, Muthambi, Cuka, and Tharaka were ruled from Embu, with direct control stemming from a subheadquarters in Cuka.[17] The northern regions, including Igoji, Miutini, Imenti, Tigania, and Igembe were labeled "Meru District" and placed directly under Horne. With two other Europeans to assist him, Horne turned to the task of forming an administration.

His initial assumption of authority had been backed only by the single company of the King's African Rifles and such non-Meru as had accompanied him on his march. Horne's first step, therefore, had been to supplement his force of aliens with warriors drawn from among the conquered groups themselves. This was done initially by requiring each blanket chief to select two warriors to serve as "blanket askari" (police) on his initial march.[18]

Those chosen were selected personally by Horne from the potential candidates sent forward by the chiefs. Occasionally, those selected were reluctant to go. More often, they sought out the position, seeing it as a means to adventure, military action, and future praise. Kangangi always looked for men of outstanding size and physical vigor. As these criteria became widely known, warriors began to present themselves at his camp for selection. At least once, as Horne told the story, a huge war leader, well over six feet, was so anxious to be taken that he appeared before Horne with a "prisoner" under one arm and a sheep under the other.[19]

The blanket askari were permitted to retain their traditional shields and spears, thereby subordinating them to the "gun askari" who provided the core of Horne's force. Nonetheless, they proved of enormous value to him, forming his first breach in the wall of Meru resistance. Their initial task was to construct a traditional military war hut adjacent to Horne's headquarters. There, guaranteed an unceasing supply of meat from their white "commander," they lived more or less according to warrior tradition, feasting, singing, and honing their fighting skills while waiting for his call to war.

After 1908, Horne's few initial appointees were supplemented by the systematic selection of two chiefs for each area. Essentially, the war hut was selected as the basic unit of administration. Before the British conquest each mountain ridge was guarded by its band of warriors, who lived together in a single *gaaru*, a huge hut that served as a military barracks. Each barracks was governed by a selected council of senior warriors who in turn were subject to the authority of the elders' council that contained men of their fathers' generation. Horne, upon learning something of this system, reacted initially by trying to restructure it in British terms, appointing a single "chief" for each age-set and labeling them "chief elder" and "chief warrior," respectively.

The system proved unwieldy and unworkable. The chief warrior, for instance, soon discovered he had no duties other than to assemble his entire warrior contingent for labor at the white man's command. In consequence the post became unpopular and then impossible to fill.

The position of chief elder also created problems, both for the Meru and their solitary conqueror. From Horne's perspective the sheer number of appointees required must have been staggering. Early sources suggest the creation of at least ninety-one "chiefdoms" of two chiefs apiece. Of these, thirty retained their initial status, but the other sixty-one were gradually reduced to being led by "headmen."[20] Nonetheless, the complexity of the problem remained.

In theory Horne made every effort to select leaders he felt would fit perfectly into the existing Meru administrative system. In fact, his selection was conducted strictly along European lines, thereby confusing and subsequently dividing Meru society. Like other Europeans of that era, Horne chose native leaders for what he termed "administrative vigor" and commanding physical presence. These requirements excluded men of small stature, great age, or physical infirmity, regardless of their experience, wisdom, or status within the Meru community.

In consequence Horne's criteria led to the exclusive selection of senior warriors, men in their late twenties, and an occasional family head of middle age. The concept initially horrified those chosen, since subordination to the authority of elders had formed the core of Meru communal thought. Horne, however, was apparently unable to comprehend the concepts of leadership implied in the Meru term "Ugambe" ("spokesmanship"), for these would have suggested the need to choose leaders of great age, known for their wisdom. What he needed, moreover, were not interpreters of tradition, but enforcers of his commands. Once more an African concept of social order was forced to give way as "kids began to lead the goats" (the young began to lead the old), a reversal that not only cost the elders their authority but also the respect in which they formerly were held.

THE DEATH OF WARRIORHOOD

Horne's major effort, of course, was directed against the Meru way of war, and his success in establishing a native administration enabled him to finish dismantling its immobilized remains. The first step lay in completing his network of both formal and informal appointees, who could be relied on to tell him whenever raids occurred.

The formal system was composed of the chiefs and headmen. Under threat of fine and imprisonment, they were required by colonial law to report the appearance of "alien" cattle in their locations. These were to be impounded by the chief himself, then turned over to Horne, together with the names of every warrior suspected of having seized them. Those concerned were then interrogated. If believed to be guilty, they were subject to the whip, imprisonment, and compulsory shaving of their warrior hairstyle. All three penalties, inconceivable to the Meru before their conquest, were regarded as deep humiliations for those concerned and proved effective deterrents to other warrior observers.

This formal system was supplemented by the activities of "informers." Many proved glad to volunteer whatever information was required in return for a reward of livestock, even if warriors of their own community were involved. Their efforts were complemented by complaints from the "losers" in each raid, as elders from a defeated community learned that an approach to the whites might lead to the return of all lost cattle, as well as whippings for those who seized them.

After 1908 these initial efforts were supplemented by increasingly effective restrictions on movement. In essence this meant that as the boundaries of each location were mapped it was designated as a small-scale native reserve. Thereafter, a form of "pass system" was introduced, similar to that formerly used in South Africa. Natives were forbidden to leave their own locations for any reason, except with the permission of their chiefs. If they traveled outside their designated areas, they were required to hand carry a *chiti* (chit, pass), proving their right to do so. No one was permitted to travel uphill into the forested areas, which were reserved for the crown, and travel in groups of any size was totally forbidden.

Because large bodies of armed men could thus be reported by any chief through whose area they traveled, raids became difficult and then impossible to stage. The change came gradually, extending slowly outward from the center of authority at Meru Town.[21] Warriors in more remote regions tended to react at first by slashing the scale of their activities and sneaking out in bands of two to five for night attacks. Nonetheless, the white man's system closed steadily around them. Homesteads found outside the designated native locations were forced to move within them. Seasonal movement of cattle to the star-grass areas was prohibited. Successful raids by single warriors were exposed and met by collective fines and mass whippings of entire warrior age-sets. Worse, more and more men of warrior age found themselves spending every day of the dry (raiding) season in endless labor for the white man. Faced with these conditions, the Meru way of warfare died away.

The second custom to expire was the warrior "battle vow" and the magnificent feasts, songs, and dancing that accompanied it. Before the conquest the public battle vow had been the culmination of an entire series of rites intended to bring warriors to the physical and psychological peak required to risk their lives in war. Before each raid all warriors within a war band went into formal isolation. Free from the "softening" influence of women and male elders, they would devour the meat from bull after bull—supplied in silence by their fathers—to build strength for the impending ordeal. As they ate, they sang "cry songs" (the songs of crying), to prepare them for the pain they knew must come.

Finally, with their sense of unity and courage at a peak, they would burst free of isolation, racing fully armed and as a single body from their bush camp to the dancing ground. There they would "hold Authi," a bounding stiff-legged dance, in which each warrior in turn would cast aside the skins that cloaked his body. Armed and naked, he would dance before the women and the elders of his community, shouting out the formal battle vows by which he would live from that day on: "If I return without spoils [war trophies], May this oath kill me. If I return without blood [having drawn blood], May this oath kill me. If I return without cows, May this oath kill me."[22]

The isolation, the bull feasts, the cry songs, the nakedness of Authi, and the final proclamation of a public battle vow were all techniques to prepare warriors to actually wage war. Now, with war itself forbidden, all military vows but one grew meaningless. The exception was the vow to ignore Kangangi and his prohibition and continue to raid. In barracks after barracks, individuals of singular courage and dedication swore publicly to evade the Europeans and seek cattle in traditional ways.

The whites responded at first by permitting the feasts and dancing but forbidding those parts of the ritual that gave them meaning, that is, the vows themselves. In Mwimbi-Muthambi, for example, the local district officer permitted the Authi dancing to continue but required the warriors to blood their spears on goats rather than on "enemies" as custom mandated.[23] In Meru proper, Horne allowed continuation of both feasts and dancing but required oaths to be eliminated altogether. He also objected to the warriors' nakedness, demanding that they cover their loins with cloth while dancing. Thereafter, shorn of both sexual symbolism and military purpose, the bull feasts, cry songs, Authi dance, and battle vows all died away for lack of warriors willing to perform them.

The tradition of bearing weapons met the same fate. Despite the shock of conquest no warrior ever went without his spear and shield, symbolizing as they did his state of manhood. Yet the very presence of these weapons psychologically compelled their use, if not against enemies then among themselves. As a result, although war was forbidden, military training still continued as warrior battled warrior within the regiments in vain attempts to recapture military pride.

Inevitably, the previously unyielding self-discipline ebbed, as the warriors' feelings of rage and frustration overcame the traditional restraints and exploded against their own age-mates. What had originally been carefully structured combat training became pitched battles, or even large-scale brawls in which entire war bands would pit themselves against each other in a frenzy of violence that neither custom nor protesting elders could stop.

Eventually, Horne decided to ban arms altogether, with the exception of those bearing them in the service of his king. He began by calling in the warriors from several of the more truculent Imenti barracks, asking them to perform an Authi dance, for which he would provide the feasting bulls.

When all had assembled, Horne addressed them angrily, accusing them of violating their own military traditions by brawling and injuring one another. Several senior spokesmen among the listeners loudly agreed, intending thereby to imply they would welcome a return to the traditional restraints that governed single combat. Instead Horne called for them to lay shields and spears aside completely, stating that thereafter he alone would keep the peace. The warriors' united roar of rage was cut short by Horne's shouted command. Startled, they turned to find themselves surrounded and under the guns of the King's African Rifles.

All weapons were then collected, to be stored under Horne's personal control. The shields, however, were gathered and thrown into the Kazita, the small swift-flowing river that flowed near colonial headquarters. There they formed a small but temporarily effective dam that remains in the memory of today's living elders as symbolic of the death of their warrior status.

This single incident had its intended effect on the surrounding military contingents. Horne's subsequent commands to disarm were met by sullen yet uniform compliance. Some bands tried to evade the rules, for example, by giving up only their oldest weapons while concealing the new. Nevertheless, the disarming of Meru was virtually complete from the moment the first war band laid down its spears. No longer could weapons be carried openly and with pride. No longer, therefore, could they serve as a symbol of manhood. And without weapons new warriors could no longer be trained. The loss of weapons was the death knell.

The impact on warrior behavior was devastating. Deprived of their reasons for personal restraint, they began to question every facet of their previously inviolate codes of conduct. One of the first to crumble was the injunction against drinking. No warrior drank before the conquest. Drinking, whether of the traditional millet beer or the stronger honey wine, was a specific prerogative of elderhood. The aging could enjoy the luxury of drunkenness knowing that the young were sober, and thus strong and alert against surprise attack. Conversely, the young took equal pride in their decade-long period of abstinence, realizing that drunkenness by one member of the age-set might jeopardize the entire community.

An individual who violated the drinking code was brought before his own warrior Kiama and beaten with a particular whip known for the visible marks it would leave on his back. He was then marked for the community to notice as a man to watch, lest he endanger their safety. Repeated offenses were punished with beatings of such severity as to lead to his total incapacitation or with expulsion from the war barracks.

After 1907, however, the need for perpetual self-discipline disappeared. Cattle raiding, defensive ambush, and surprise attacks were the concern of Europeans. With no logical reason for temperance, the warriors began to drink. Remonstrations by their elders, and a series of threats and proclamations by Horne, had no effect. Worse, the pattern of drunkenness spread from warriors to the unmarried girls, an even greater violation of tradition.

Horne, deeply concerned at this new development, ordered at one point that any woman or warrior found drunk would be publicly whipped. A day or so later a girl and warrior were brought together into his headquarters, both obviously drunk. Horne was painfully embarrassed but refused to go back on his word, even when the warrior offered to take the girl's share of the beating as well as his own. Refusing, Horne ordered them both to lie on the ground, beat the warrior soundly, then gave the girl six timid strokes with his rhino-skin whip. "For a while, drunkenness among unmarried women stopped like magic,"[24] but the problem was too deep-rooted to be cured by a single beating. Swiftly, the pattern of drunkenness intensified among the warriors, as the enforced idleness of their new existence began to take hold.

The codes that governed sexual relations between warriors and unmarried women began to erode as well. Before the conquest, warriors were forbidden all forms of sexual contact, whether physical or verbal, until the final months before their entry into elder status. The purpose, as with the ban on drinking, was to maintain their strength and alertness at a peak. In practice this meant well over a decade of sexual abstinence, a burden welcomed by those in their warrior years as a sign of their courage and strength.

The first easing of these restrictions came with an increasingly widespread acceptance of the Gikuyu custom of Ngweko.[25] In its essence the term suggests "fondling." In practice Ngweko was similar to the custom of "bundling" practiced in certain American pioneer communities. In bundling, courting couples could lie alone together, fully clothed, and were permitted to caress one another. Disrobing and sexual intercourse were forbidden.

Among the Gikuyu, restraint was aided by a leather pubic apron that covered the woman's vagina and the end of her long leather skirt. This was drawn between her thighs and tucked in at the waist. Thus protected, she was permitted to lie with and fondle her partner, receiving his caresses in turn. The apron could never be raised, nor was any form of intercourse permitted. The young man who even attempted it risked public denunciation by the woman, ridicule from his age-mates, and the disapproval of communal ancestors. The Gikuyu considered Ngweko an acceptable means of teaching sexual discipline, one that permitted young men to relieve their physical needs without risking the impregnation of their partners.[26]

After conquest the custom spread north, through Embu, Cuka, Mwimbi-Muthambi, and finally into Meru itself, where it was known as Nguiko. In each area it was initiated by those Gikuyu who had accompanied Horne as porters or *askari* (police). From them the idea spread to Horne's Meru *askari*, and thereafter to the chiefs and retainers. These, relatively free of restraints of tradition, began to use their newly acquired power to command the unmarried women of their communities to participate. Parents who objected to the inclusion of their daughters were arbitrarily fined as many goats as were required to impose compliance. Complaints passed upward to Horne were rewarded by stern warnings. Even so, enforcement proved impossible, and most officials found the sexual temptation too powerful to resist.

Eventually, the custom spread into the ranks of the increasingly demoralized warriors. Numbers of them would often creep out of their sleeping places to the long, shallow trenches they had been forced to dig throughout the day. They lined these thickly with dry banana leaves, then sought out partners and indulged themselves throughout the night.

The breakdown of sexual discipline had tragic results for both men and women. Abandonment of their own traditions led to increasing conflict between men of the warrior age-sets and those immediately above and beneath their own. Older boys, now on the fringe of their own warrior years, showed their contempt for the existing military age-set in traditional fashion, taunting and mocking their neglect of tradition in chants, shouts, and extemporaneous song.

More disturbing, they also began to usurp existing military prerogatives. Many adopted the warrior hairstyle and dress, refusing to give way to members of the existing age-set on pathways and even offering to fight any veteran who objected. Both sides, of course, had been disarmed, but as each could call in age-mates, sudden strife between individuals could lead to conflicts involving dozens and then scores of men on each side.

The warriors had even sharper conflicts with the age-set just above their own. Incensed at their juniors' usurpation of those women reserved by tradition for themselves, the family heads/apprentice elders were loudest in their protests against the entire concept of Nguiko. When the administration proved unable to stop it, they took the cause into their own hands, attacking and beating any warrior whom they found in the company of girls. Those beaten responded in turn with ap-

peals to their age-mates, until once again a jealous spat between two individuals could involve entire age-sets in a nonstop conflict too embittered and widespread for even the ruling elders to reconcile. Thus at the
very time when men of every age-set should have joined to resist or at
least lighten the effects of conquest, they dissipated their strength in
endless status and sexual conflicts that killed all hope of future unity
against the conqueror.

The impact on young women was equally tragic. Shorn of the protection provided by tradition and equally disheartened by the demoraliza-
tion of their men, the women of every age-set proved unable to resist the
attractions of drink and Nguiko. All too often these led to full intercourse. The result, predictably, was a sharp increase in pregnancies,
attributable to fathers who were neither able nor prepared to marry.

The wave of pregnancies was matched by a parallel increase in the
number of abortions. Abortion has always been known in Meru. It was
performed by midwives using a combination of herbs and beatings until the fetus was expelled from the womb. Inevitably, the procedure had
also produced its percentage of fatalities, but never on such a scale as
now occurred.

Alarmed, both Horne and several of the more British-oriented chiefs
moved to stop the abortion trend. In upper Mwimbi, for example,
Mbogore M'Mwendo moved with predictable enthusiasm, jailing all of
the women who customarily served as midwives, as well as heavily fining the parents of those who sought their service. The result, most dramatically visible in those areas where the antiabortion campaign was
successful, was a dramatic rise in the birth of fatherless children.

This situation too was without precedent in Meru history. Penalties
for conceiving out of wedlock had always been severe. As a result
young people usually chose to avoid the consequences by agreeing to
marry before an actual birth. Marriage required bride-wealth, however,
which in turn meant possession of livestock. Many younger warriors,
had not yet collected sufficient numbers of animals through the traditional rites of raiding. Nor would they ever have the opportunity. They
therefore saw themselves as unable to marry in honor and thus provide
legitimacy to the children they fathered.

One consequence was an increasing number of abandoned children—once again, a condition previously unheard of in Meru—to be
gathered in as future Christians by newly appearing missionaries. The
second was the creation of a class of angry and embittered women,
scorned by their elders and viewed as "damaged" by potential mates.

Made outcasts by forces outside their control, members of this group turned to Christianity, concubinage, or prostitution.

In time the Meru-speaking peoples would follow patterns similar to those arising in the colonized societies of Kenya, across Africa, and throughout the world. In time white concern for the idleness of warriors would be replaced by the decision to let them labor. At first the young men would hear of new types of Europeans, who had come to settle on Mount Kenya's lower slopes in regions other than their own. Thereafter, they would meet the labor recruiters, for whom each of their chiefs would supply quotas. Finally, the warriors of Meru would be led off in batches—peacefully or bound by ropes—to work for pittances in regions far from home.

In time the missions would also take root. They would offer not only Jesus but also literacy, with its chance for work somewhere within the white man's world and the acquisition of some fraction of its wealth. In time the first few outcast converts would grow into a legion so large that the work of ritualists and even worship of the ancestors were pushed into the shadowed realm of history.

In time there would even be new wars, and the call would go out for warriors to fight them. Young men would still go off to battle, initially as unskilled porters for the British in Tanganyika, but subsequently as warriors in their own right in such places as "Jambo Hill" in Burma in 1942. But for the men of the Murungi age-set, the last generation of true cattle raiders, real warriorhood died with the coming of England.

CHAPTER VI

The Extortion Traditions:
Dancing Deviants

"I am [of the] Kagita
I am [a] Mosquito
Yes-s-s, I bite man at the heels."[1]

Oldest chant
of the Kagita Society

RESPONSES TO CONQUEST:
THE FAMILY HEADS (ARUAU)

The shock of conquest fell with equal force upon all age-sets and both sexes. For warriors it meant the collapse of both military and moral traditions. Most of the rank and file turned to alcohol and brawling. Many abandoned their vows of celibacy, initially adopting the limited sexual pleasure allowed by Nguiko, then gradually abandoning even the restriction of its leather apron in favor of outright intercourse. Former war leaders, appointed as colonial servants, turned to patterns of material and sexual extortion, in which the livestock, beer, wives, and daughters of the elders soon became fair game.

Middle-aged men followed the same paths. If the warrior youths of the Murungi (age-set) could no longer follow traditions related to war, those of the Kiramana (age-set) were equally barred from assuming the dual roles of family head and apprentice elder, known in Meru as the Aruau (sing.: Muruau).

Both roles were required by tradition. The years immediately after warriorhood were intended to be ones of peace. Every man entering family elderhood had devoted twelve to sixteen years to both celibacy and war. He was rewarded by the chance to court and marry a girl just reaching puberty, thus twelve to sixteen years his junior. During the following twelve to sixteen years, family heads/apprentice elders were to devote themselves to conceiving and raising the sons who would

151

someday serve as warriors in their turn. With their wives they were also expected to create family homesteads, based both on produce from the fields and livestock brought into the marriage by the bride.

Simultaneously, new elders were expected to redirect their thoughts beyond war and procreation to maintaining harmony within the community at large. Once established, they sought membership in their ridgetop Kiama, where they came in constant contact with the aged. Within the council they became "apprentices," subordinating themselves to the ruling elders (in 1907, the Kaburia age-set), whose guidance they sought on matters of tradition.

Overawed—at least in theory—by their entry into the presence of such wisdom, the family heads spent the subsequent thirteen years in silent apprenticeship. Their only function was to listen. Freed for the first time in their lives from ceaseless military training, they had only to sit silently, at the edges of the council's conversations. Over the coming years, until the sons they were producing grew to puberty, they could share freely in the millet beer and public drunkenness that formed the main prerogative of elderhood. Secure in the knowledge that new warriors would now defend their herds, they had only to absorb the verbal wisdom of those older than themselves against that time—years hence—when their sons would pass through circumcision, and their age-set would finally come to power.

Tradition taught that learning the "wisdom of Kiama" would take the balance of their lifetimes. It was believed that every imaginable aspect of human conflict would eventually emerge within an elders' council. Apprentice members had only to listen, therefore, to the ways in which each conflict was resolved and to the specific oral precedents ("ancestral traditions") upon which elders drew for their decisions. Over years those who listened would acquire a vast and constantly expanding knowledge of such precedents, which they would use to settle conflicts as they came to power in their turn.

The conquest slashed across every aspect of these expectations. Colonial levies on livestock drained the flocks and herds and, with them, all sense of security. Worse, the conquest depredations of colonial appointees, whether official or self-appointed, gnawed ("like angry rats") upon their stores of grain, beer, remaining livestock, and the peace of mind of those who tended them.

Nor could new family heads feel secure about either the sexual loyalty or labor of their wives. No longer protected by tradition, their wives—always thirteen years younger than themselves—were subject to seduction by former warriors and extortion by those who once had led them, demands that could include field labor in the daytime and sexual service at night.

Neither were the family heads secure in themselves. The mantle of "elderhood," instantly apparent to every Meru, could be ripped aside at will by any European in search of men for communal labor. Within the first years after the conquest white demands for Meru labor multiplied each year as planters, missionaries, hunters, and entrepreneurs settled the surrounding regions, all with requests for native laborers to initiate their work.

As a result long lines of former warriors were roped together at the command of whites, then sent off to work for other whites in fields that seemed more distant every year. Each chief and headman received a certain quota to fill. If too few warriors were available, no headman would hesitate to seize family heads to avoid colonial wrath. In such circumstances the long-anticipated cloak of elderhood meant nothing.

Nor could the new apprentice elders seek help from the respective ruling councils, either to protect their livestock or themselves. The ruling Kiamas, struggling to preserve their own authority against both colonialists and chiefs, were powerless to do more than utter protests against the seizure of their junior members. Attempts to explain the differences in status between warriors and apprentice elders were beyond Horne's willingness to grasp. Among Europeans the sole criterion for labor was whether men were strong enough to do the work. In consequence the fledgling elders' expectation of sitting quietly in council to absorb ancestral wisdom was rendered hollow. The traditional role, anticipated with such pleasure, had simply disappeared.

Deprived of both security and status, the entire Kiramana age-set slid into despair. Family heads now carried fighting sticks to replace the now forbidden spear. Public drunkenness, acceptable in moderation, now expanded beyond all known bounds. Worse, it led to almost nightly brawling, as family heads across Meru expressed their rage through confrontations with those warriors they felt showed undue interest in their wives.

ARUAU WIVES: THE KIAMAS OF WOMEN

The despair of the Kiramana age-set was shared fully by the women intended as their wives. The conquest weighed heavily upon potential brides as well as those women already married. At one level they keenly shared the anguish of the men at submitting to an alien rule. At another they shared a fear that the steady erosion of sexual restraints would lead to pregnancy, abortion, infanticide, and unrecognized children. Beyond these they feared the ancestors, whose teachings had required sexual monogamy and promised of frightening punishments for those who transgressed.

Meru tradition had always separated the sexes. In childhood boys played at being warriors. Girls "played" at being wives, by working ceaselessly at home. As they grew to the age of impending adulthood, both sexes still played apart. Girls were taught to look down and fall silent in the presence of males, or at best to call out to them when in groups, at a distance.

Like boys, girls formed themselves into "secret" councils, organized chronologically, from early puberty into old age. These were secret in that their activities were carefully concealed from boys and men. Nevertheless, the women's Kiamas essentially reflected both the structure and functions of their male counterparts, in that each was intended to ensure the correct behavior of its members by training them to meet communal expectations at every stage of their lives.

Women married soon after reaching puberty, in their early teens. The youngest set of women's councils, therefore, were formed as sufficient numbers of girls within each ridgetop reached their early teens. A second level was composed of women who had married and produced at least one child, the time before first birth being one in which a woman had no status whatsoever. Above this was the ruling council, composed of senior women whose children had reached adulthood.

Each women's age-set was initially regarded as an extension of the male age-set into which they were to marry. Thus in Imenti during the early 1900s, women reaching puberty (age twelve to fifteen) were forming into a set intended to provide brides for the family heads/apprentice elders of Kiramana (age twenty-seven to thirty) as they left warriorhood. Publicly, this set was also known as the Kiramana (implying women of the Kiramana men). Among themselves they took the name Ncurubi, whose symbolic meaning remained secret to all men. Similarly, those women married to the ruling elders of that period had formed into women's councils known secretly as Munyange.[2] Beyond this level, survivors of the older women's sets appeared at dances, where they could observe and guide the rising generation and take pleasure in their growth.

Members of this oldest group, in consultation with the council of senior women, would also assemble the rising generation of eligible girls into their first Kiama. It was they who directed the act of female circumcision, the excision of clitoris and inner labia that proclaimed each girl to be an adult. It was also they who passed on "secrets" of the female Kiama to the initiates, to prepare them to be wives.

As in the male Kiamas, many of the secrets concealed so carefully by the women's councils were, in fact, roles of behavior ("ancestral traditions") concerned with the sexual aspects of growing up. The women's Kiama of Chigiira (seashell), for example, which functioned in Igoji and Mwimbi prior to the British conquest, was typical of women's groups throughout Meru. One aspect of its "secret" teaching dealt with the precise behavior to be expected during the moment of circumcision when the outer genitals were cut away. A second set of "secrets" dealt with social expectations during courtship. A third concerned itself with appropriate behavior during the bridal night, a fourth with behavior toward female in-laws.[3] Each body of teachings was presented both as secret (from men) and as ancestral tradition, thereby both dignifying and magnifying it in the minds of those involved, since the spirits themselves could strike out at any infraction.

The women's councils emphasized strict sexual fidelity. When courting, women could indulge in limited sex play with a number of lovers but were required to stop short of full intercourse. Once betrothed, however, monogamy was obligatory for life. Within councils such as Chigiira, girls were taught that acts of sexual infidelity would be actively watched by those ancestral spirits from whom both lovers were descended. They would respond by imposing a curse on both partners, leading to physical (and thus visible) pain in the breasts (in males, the chest) or genitals. Removal of the symptoms, as with other curses, could occur only through recourse to the appropriate supernatural specialists, payment of livestock, public investigation, disclosure, and termination of the adultery.

Sexual fidelity was also reinforced by peer pressure. Like their male counterparts, certain individuals within each council gradually emerged as spokeswomen for their age-mates, concealing their preeminence from men ("lest no one dare marry them") but assuming positions of leadership over their peers.[4] Much of their energy was directed toward reinforcing what had been taught, often in ways that no one could forget.

All members of a newly formed girls' Kiama, for example, were taught that a pregnancy in any one of them meant shame to all. If a member became pregnant, spokeswomen would run from hut to hut, assembling the other members of the offender's age-set. All of them would then proceed to the offender's hut, drive out the victim, then surround, beat, and spit on her—always urged on by the group's spokeswomen to display even greater rage at the transgression. Thereafter she was compelled—solely by her peers—to walk to the hut of the man who had impregnated her and stand silently before it ("for days, if necessary"), thereby providing a mute but highly eloquent testimony as to what had occurred.

Only by presenting her Kiama age-mates with a sheep ("the sheep to close her up again") could the man induce his partner to leave. Even then, the animal was accepted only as the first installment of a negotiated bride-wealth that would lead eventually to the transgressors' marriage.

DANCING DEVIANTS:
THE ORAL HISTORY OF THE KAGITA

The true Kiamas of women were honored throughout Meru. The content of their moral teachings, their concealment from men, and the severity with which they were enforced made women's councils objects of awe and respect among Meru males. All men adhered carefully, therefore, to the rigid segregation of the sexes, avoided all women when gathered "in Kiama" and learning as little as they could of what went on.

Horne had become aware of this sexual separation through discussions with those warriors who made up his immediate entourage. These often boasted of their years of warrior celibacy, declaring that it formed the basis of their strength and thus their manhood. Within the first years of his administration, therefore, Horne was increasingly disturbed to hear reports, again delivered by his warrior informants, of "Kiamas of women" that had begun to practice "witchcraft" throughout Meru. When pressed to explain, Horne's informants declared that these groups were "eating people's property" while simultaneously terrifying them with fearsome curses.

The warriors' angry declarations were periodically supported by their elders. Several times during Horne's first few years of rule he was approached by somber delegations of ruling elders, requesting that he allow them to take action against "witchcraft Kiamas" that had appeared within their region. The most feared of these, according to the spokesmen, were the "Kiamas of women who drank and danced and cursed all who crossed their way."[5]

The image presented by these delegations was too similar to the witch's coven in European folklore not to capture Horne's early attention. Like many other first-generation administrators of that era, Horne had a lively interest in Africa's witchcraft. Denouncing it as quackery, he was amused as its continued existence, believing that the "witch doctor" would simply disappear when faced with Christianity. Nonetheless, as an administrator he was quite interested in learning "how things worked" among the people he had come to rule.[6]

On occasion he therefore closely questioned both women and elders on the functions of "witchcraft societies," male and female. Lacking both a common frame of reference and mastery of each other's language, neither group proved able to reply. Often the Meru fell back on clichés and stereotypes they believed he might understand, a pattern repeated with other British administrators during subsequent decades.

In turn both Horne and those who came after him equated the stereotypes with those they knew from Europe, where terms such as *sorcerer, witch, spell,* and *curse* carried satanic implications that had no parallel in African society. As a result Horne emerged from these discussions with misunderstandings regarding the precise nature of these women's "witchcraft" societies that would have significant impact on later Meru history. One of these came from Horne's misunderstanding of the term "women's Kiama," which he assumed referred to the traditional councils of women. In fact it was meant to refer to a new form of "dancing Kiama," involving both men and women, that had begun to assume unprecedented power.

Horne's initial confusion, compounded by subsequent British administrators, can easily be understood. Both types of council were secret, were dominated by women, and used supernatural curses to compel obedience. The traditional women's Kiamas, however, formed the bedrock of Meru society, teaching each generation the traditional moral codes. The dancing Kiamas, in contrast, were composed of deviants who joined to flout them.

Dancing Kiamas, of course, were not new in Meru. Nor were they composed solely of women. Earlier forms of deviant organizations, even the most predatory, had restricted their memberships to men. Even the dancing Kiama of Mwaa was composed wholly of men who had chosen to assume female roles. In the first years after British conquest, however, numbers of family heads, male and female, drifted even

)m tradition. Impoverished by colonial taxation, exploited by
.ket chiefs, deprived of status through their elderhood, and
ithout hope, they joined new types of Kiamas to survive.

made little pretense of having been formed for economic self-
protection, as had been the case with the A-Athi (hunting zones), ironsmiths (mineral sources), or crop protectors (cleared fields). Rather,
they were openly exploitive, turning to beer, feasting, all-night dancing,
and copulation as antidotes for living in a newly conquered world.
They were known in every Meru region. Collectively, they called themselves the Kiama of Kagita.

KAGITA ORIGINS: MBWAA

The British perceived the Kagita as merely one of several alleged
"witchcraft" societies that had emerged in Meru since their own arrival
and that survived by using deadly curses. Among Meru, however, the
name evoked memories of their most ancient tradition, extending back
to their island of origin.

The earliest Meru chronicle, as has been mentioned, describes the
flight from Mbwaa (Manda) Island in detail. One variant of the narration, most often heard in Tigania, relates the moment when the Meru
stopped their flight at the island's edge, blocked by the surging tides.
Most versions continue with the prophet striking the waters with his
stick, causing them to move aside. In Tigania, however, a variant occurs
in which the ritualist who led the flight

> called for three warriors to stand forth and be sacrificed, for their danger
> was too great to rely on the slaughter of an insignificant goat. The first to
> come forth was Gaita [the sacrifice]. He was followed by Muthetu [the soil],
> and Akiuna [the bellies]. Gaita was to be killed and his entrails examined to
> learn the future. Muthetu was to be the soil, forming the altar for his sac-
> rifice. Akiuna was to look on, his belly quaking in fear, and be sacrificed in
> turn, should the first set of entrails show nothing.[7]

Gaita's entrails must have shown the pre-Meru how to cross the intervening waters, for his name remained within their songs and dances
for the next two hundred years. In Igembe, "Gaita" became a woman's
dance of triumph, used to welcome warriors on their return from raids.
In Tigania and North Imenti it became a song sung by women at those
dances where men were allowed to appear.

As a song it continued to evolve. Even the name varied within the
major Meru-speaking regions, remaining "Gaita" only in Igembe. To

the south, however, it became "Kaiita" (Tigania), "Kagita" (Imenti, Igoji), and "Kagica" (Mwimbi, Muthambi). The verses also evolved. As each generation created new versions, they were woven into the existing songs and dances, while earlier verses were gradually lost. Thus, elders who had heard the songs of the Kagita in the early 1900s could remember only a single phrase that had come down to them from the earlier age-sets, and even the earlier meanings of this had been lost: "Ndi wa Kagita. Ndi rwagi. I-I-I-I, ndatha muntu itende." (I am [of the] Kagita. I am [a] mosquito. Yes-s-s, I bite man at the heels.)[8]

Former Kagita members declare that their group existed in Meru since the time of the Mukuruma age-set (1730), when the pre-Meru peoples first advanced uphill into the forest of Mount Kenya. Existing evidence, however, suggests that it probably emerged as one of the Kiamas of crop protection that appeared along the upper rim of the star-grass zone between the 1860s and 1880s to protect newly cleared fields against plunder. During that era small bands of Kagita (Kagica, Kaiita, Gaita, etc.) are recalled as having lived in every major region, often unknown to one another but sharing similar bodies of ritual as well as the ancient names.

During this period their magic was evidently derived from contact with both the forest hunters and other crop-protecting groups. Drawing from the A-Athi hunting rituals of "bite" and "blow," for example, they chose a sacred tree (the *mureema*), whose bark they ground to powder. This they mixed with beeswax, then "bit" or "blew" the compound to create zones of safety in the A-Athi fashion, within which they believed themselves free from attack. The Kagita also drew upon the A-Athi concepts of Ndindi and Nkima, cutting, hollowing, and daubing slender three-foot branches from their sacred tree as well as shaping a skull from beeswax, then using these to create the traditional safety zone around their huts.

The society departed from hunting rituals, however, by incorporating the crop-protecting concept of the guardian vine. The vine selected resembled telephone wire and was looped from Ndindi to Ndindi to form a circle. As with other crop-protecting rituals, a single gate was left open, known only to members. Once activated by appropriate verbal ritual, the sticks and vines were believed able to place the traditional automatic curse upon anyone trying to cross.

Verbal activation followed Meru tradition. The members of a specific Kagita branch would assemble, circle the sticks and vines seven times, then collectively chant an appropriate sequence of curses at the top of their lungs. Again following Meru tradition, the curses of Kagita explicitly asked for transgressors' death, a fact that would subsequently prey on the minds of colonial officials in decades to come: "Let he who crosses [this vine] die! If [the curse is] not lifted [let him] die!"[9]

The group's intent, as always among the Meru, was not to kill victims but to force them to seek alternatives, preferably by providing its members with gifts sufficient to induce removal of the curse. The society departed from Meru tradition, however, in having achieved a psychological monopoly over diseases of the legs. The "bite of the mosquito," symbolic of the society and central to their songs, was generally believed to be the cause of almost any type of foot or leg disease. The Kagita could be blamed for an outbreak of something as small as boils to elephantiasis, an enlarging of the feet to gigantic proportions. It was also held responsible for attacks of yaws, an affliction of ulcers to the feet, legs, and buttocks that was the most prevalent disease in Meru when the British appeared.

The Kagita eagerly concurred in these beliefs, claiming credit for causing every form of foot and leg affliction and thus generating considerable fear. Afflicted victims, having consulted ritualists within their own communities on the cause of their conditions, would be directed to the society. At a victim's appearance, all the Kagita members would assemble within the hut that formed their static zone of safety to deliberate.

The member who had set up ("owned") the vine a victim had crossed would formally agree to serve as the victim's patron ("father") during the rites of removal. In exchange, the Kagita member received the required fees ("gifts"), consisting in this early period of seven gourds of maize and beans, seven more of newly brewed millet beer, a single goatskin, and an iron knife. These things, in turn, would be offered to the entire gathering, to form the basis of a communal feast.

The rites of removal, in common with other crop-protecting Kiamas of the time, were entirely symbolic. The vine that served to surround and thus protect the greeting hut was solemnly removed from its original position, then wrapped around the victim's lower body. The Kagita's curse remover would thereafter smear the victim's legs, feet, and lower trunk with castor oil. In the process the vine that bound the victim was also smeared, thereby symbolically uniting the two. It was then cut away with the iron knife, slashed into pieces, and stomped into the ground, as the members chanted: "Let the curse be cut as we [the Kagita] cut this vine. Let the curse be crushed as we crush this vine. Depart, curse of Kagita."[10]

Interestingly, in certain areas the traditional rite of removal was intensified by use of a symbolic "brush." A leafy branch was cut from the group's sacred tree and used, with appropriate incantation, to "brush the curse" off the victim's body after the "vine of Kagita" had been cut away. The individual was brushed from head to toe, until the remnants of the affliction were symbolically scoured off onto the earth, where they could be crushed or burned. In theory the victim would be relieved of his anxiety. In practice the associated physical symptoms would disappear as well.

As with other Kiamas of this type, the Kagita's rites of curse removal were supplemented by what I have called a "kinship clause," whereby each victim was incorporated into the group. Symbolically, the man whose vine had been crossed, thus allowing him to assume the role of "father" to the victim during the removal rituals, remained in that capacity throughout his life—a position entitling him to frequent gifts. By association all other Kagita elders became kin in the more general sense, placing the victim in the role of "child" or "sibling" to them all.

The social, economic, and political consequences of this status were identical to those forced upon victims of other groups of this type. Socially, new members had to contribute gourds of maize, beans, and millet beer to each Kagita feast. Economically, they were allowed to "buy Kiama," in the sense of learning to use Kagita methods to protect their fields, often an attractive inducement as uncleared land at the higher rim of the star-grass zone grew increasingly scarce in the final decades of the 1800s. Politically, the Kagita forced new members to submit all future quarrels to the judgment of its elders alone, effectively withdrawing recruits from the administrative and judicial authority of their own Kiamas. Earlier fringe Kiamas, including A-Athi creators of the concept, had intended the kinship clause to eliminate future conflicts by making all contenders kin. Under the Kagita, the clause would lead to future conflict, both with men of the mainstream and the colonial British.

THE KAGITA AS STOMACH KIAMA

The oral histories of the Kagita change sharply as informants comment on the latter portion of the 1890s. The 1880s and early 1890s are remembered generally as years of good harvest, when members of the slowly growing Kagita councils appear to have worked lands of their own. The middle and latter 1890s, however, are recalled as times when almost every Meru region was devastated by a series of natural calamities.

In 1894, 1895, and 1896, certain localities were virtually stripped by clouds of locusts; even Europeans passing through the region commented on how little vegetation was to be found.[11] These infestations were followed by a prolonged drought, particularly severe at lower elevations throughout the region, that aborted both growing seasons during 1897 and continued well in 1898.

With the grain supplies devastated, Meru was then scourged by the infamous rinderpest epidemic of 1898, which killed large numbers of flocks and herds across Mount Kenya, wiping out livestock that had taken decades to acquire. The combined impact of these disasters allowed many weaker members of the population to fall prey to disease, at least partially because of the widespread starvation. British authorities operating within Gikuyu regions during this same period estimated a loss of more than half the population in the more devastated areas.[12]

This loss is exaggerated only in that it assumes the death of all concerned. Doubtless, many died. Far greater numbers, however, particularly on Mount Kenya's lower slopes, were simply driven from lands that could no longer support them. Meru tradition provided for such events, teaching each generation to respond to times of famine by mass flight into areas where food could still be found.

Trekking with entire families, with warriors holding tufts of grass as signs of peace, they would appear as supplicants among their distant kin. The aged, children, pregnant wives, and remnants of their livestock would be left with these relations until the famine had run its course. In exchange, those who offered shelter retained the calves and kids born during their owner's absence among the livestock left behind. Men would leave their wives behind only if desperate, fearing they would become pregnant by others. More often the family heads led their women homeward, seeking sustenance where they could while hoping to replant and rebuilt.

These men formed an expanding pool of possible recruits for the Kagita. The cattle plagues, locusts, and drought of the late 1890s all struck hardest at the youngest members of the Kaburia age-set, which in that era made up the Meru family heads/apprentice elders. Those who had married just prior to the catastrophes had had too few years to build up surplus herds or harvest. Nor had they had time to produce full-grown sons, who might have added to their livestock by success in war.

As a result the youngest family heads found themselves most frequently among the landless. With their livestock decimated and crops blighted or destroyed, they abandoned their original homesteads to seek sustenance where it could be found. Some turned to the Kagita. It was a time, informants say, when "the landless gathered in the landless and the poor sought out the poor to dig for food."[13] In consequence, by the end of the 1890s several bands of former crop protectors, among them the Kiama of Kagita, had evolved into "Kiamas of the stomach." To survive, they sang and danced in exchange for sustenance in much the same fashion previously described for Mwaa, the Kiama of clowns.

The evolution of the Kagita, however, took another direction. The Mwaa had departed from Meru tradition by depicting its males as women. The Kagita deviated by including women openly in its ranks. Both types of deviation must have seemed equally offensive to mainstream elders and warriors, because ancestral custom demanded that every Kiama be composed only of one sex. That tradition was as old as the Meru themselves. The earliest fringe groups of hunters and iron-smiths had adhered to it, as had the councils of crop protectors derived from them. The same principle held true for the various stomach-Kiamas previously described. Transvestite dancers such as the Mwaa shared a common purpose with the child snatching bands of the Kirimu: to practice limited forms of extortion in exchange for limited amounts of food. The drive behind their deviance was not sexual but economic. Their primary goal was simply to survive.

For the men of Kagita, however, women meant the difference between starvation and survival. Both sexes, of course, would have been driven from their newly founded homesteads by the unremitting sequence of calamities. Many family heads, however, refused to leave their teenage wives with distant kin, from fear that they might become pregnant or even decide to remain. As numbers of them were drawn into the Kagita, they found that the presence of women drew more spectators and larger portions of food or beer. Thereafter, the "Dancing" Kiamas of family heads/apprentice elders began to include both sexes in their work.

For this reason—and at this time—the various bands of the Kagita became known as "Kiamas of women," the phrase that subsequently proved confusing to colonial administrators. Among Meru, however, the term referred not only to women's participation in the Kagita dances but also to their unprecedented influence within the councils themselves.

This was an era, remember, when "women's things" were decided solely by women, meeting in whatever council proved appropriate to the issue involved. "Men's things" were similarly decided by councils of men, who communicated the relevant conclusions to women of their households. No issues whatsoever were decided jointly; the very concept lay outside the Meru frame of reference, and social intercourse between the sexes had always been structured by female subordination to the decisions of men.

Within the Kagita the traditions of segregation and subordination were gradually abandoned. Both women and men danced sexually and suggestively whenever the dancing groups appeared. In North Imenti women held subordinate positions of leadership within the councils. In South Imenti they led specified rituals during Kagita feasts, and women appear to have functioned as curse removers. In Igoji, Mwimbi, and Muthambi women also held positions of authority, as men joined their gatherings primarily to feast. Only in Tigania and Igembe, heavily influenced by the culture of the Maasai, did the Kagita remain wholly male, excluding women from its ranks as tradition commanded.

The Kagita also deviated from tradition in its relations with other males. Respect for the aged, a concept deeply ingrained within every Meru, kept them from directing their attention to the homesteads of ruling elders or the very old. Rather, they focused entirely on those members of their own age-set whose more favorable location—usually higher up the mountain—had allowed them to retain some portion of their harvests. As age-mates these more fortunate family heads were obligated to share their surplus to some degree, and the Kagita turned to them as suitable subjects for extortion.

Existing evidence does suggest a brief period when Kagita bands exchanged songs and dances for their suppers in much the same lighthearted fashion as the Mwaa Kiamas. After 1900, however, the techniques used to obtain daily food supplies acquired menacing overtones. Perhaps the simplest example can be found in the words of the group's traditional mosquito song. During the first years of this century only a few shifts in vocal emphasis were added, yet they proved sufficient to transform the ancient phrasing of "Yes-s-s, I bite man at the heels" into an implicit threat of supernatural extortion.

THE KAGITA BEFORE CONQUEST:
THE EVOLUTION OF EXTORTION

Meru tradition appears to have always sanctioned the appearance of limited forms of extortion in times of scarcity, which could be used against the richer members of society to procure limited amounts of food. The Kagita clearly followed this tradition from the crop-protecting into the food-seeking stage. Unlike many of its competitors, however, it continued to evolve, developing an increasingly effective sequence of techniques to acquire food. At first (in the late 1890s) these were used solely to ward off famine. Later as agricultural conditions improved (during 1900–1906), they provided the basis for continued feasts. Still later the impact of British administration (from 1970 onward) caused this evolution to continue, until the group became one of the most feared in Meru.

The earliest of these techniques, possibly dating back before the years of famine, might be labeled the task of "honest watchman." At some period, possibly during the 1880s or early 1890s, landholders from several ridgetop communities in Imenti and possibly Igoji seem to have "requested" Kagita groups within their region to collectively curse and thereby protect their ripening millet crops from night intruders. This single service did not require entry into the society itself. Rather, landowners simply "offered"—the degree of compulsion remains unclear—two feasts to members of the society, complete with the traditional seven gourds each of maize, beans, and beer.

The feast of planting took place at the time of year when both the crop and (the Kagita) curse could be set simultaneously in the ground, a ritual that involved surrounding the entire cultivated area with the Kagita variant of Ndindi sticks and vines. A harvesting feast was thus also required, so that Kiama members could collectively remove the protective cursing system, thereby allowing the owner to reap his crop.

The "honest watchman" period may have been brief, for traditions suggest it ended throughout Meru with the onset of the natural catastrophes of 1894–1899. Perhaps the very intangibility of Kagita ritual suggested more antisocial options to those proficient in its use. At any rate, in the years just prior to the British conquest, Kagita bands in several of the higher mountain regions had begun to place their sticks and vines across well-traveled public paths. Those who crossed them, however unintentionally, found themselves obligated to feed the entire group in the traditional manner or suffer the afflictions of its curse. During this same period, Kagita bands nearer the mountain's base began to place their sticks and vines around fields of standing millet and sugarcane, enclosing themselves within. Thereafter, they would devour portions of the harvest at their leisure, singing heartily to attract the attention of passersby and eventually the owner: "Ndiuria wimbi ikiuna, na ruuji ingikwira? Ndi kiria kiri miriini! Inyaina wone." (What is drying out my millet, despite my watering? Something [i.e., Kagita magic] in the roots! Dig out and see.)[14]

The landowner, of course, was expected to "dig Kagita out" of his fields, simply by offering to provide its members with the traditional feast. He was not required, in this instance, to join the group. Nevertheless, after completion of their feasting, the Kagita required the cultivator's children to give stalks of sugarcane (or measures of millet) from future harvests to its members on demand.

In other regions, notably North and Northeast Imenti, Kagita bands seem to have assumed a function that contemporary Westerners might label "ambulance chasing." The society had always claimed credit, as previously mentioned, for every type of illness that affected feet and legs. In prior years, however, they had patiently waited for the afflicted to seek them out and petition to be healed. After 1900, perhaps spurred on by their fear of famine, members of certain Kagita bands systematically sought out anyone, anywhere, who had been stricken in these areas. Claiming credit for the condition, the group would inform sufferers that they had offended the Kagita. Thereafter, simple logic impelled the victims to request removal of the symptoms in exchange for the customary feast.

At some point just prior to the conquest, however, these relatively limited forms of extortion were supplanted throughout Meru by the technique of placing collective curses directly on family head/apprentice elder compounds. In certain aspects Kagita methods were similar to those of the Mwaa. Meeting "in Kiama," elders of one branch of the society would select the homestead of a relatively prosperous family head as the source of their next bout of feasting. The man selected was usually a senior member of their age-set, often a dozen years older than themselves. In theory his early start and additional years had allowed him to acquire a food surplus sufficient to ensure his survival during famine.

Kagita elders, deciding that such an individual had "offended" one of their members, would send a message to his homestead, offering to sing and dance for him at sundown, three days hence. The invitation was courteously phrased, but tradition suggests that no one dared refuse. The three-day wait was mandatory, because that was the period required for brewing millet beer.

At dusk on the third day members would assemble to don dancing gear consisting of goatskins, wooden bells, and broken calabashes, set off with body paint of chalk and ocher (red clay). Unlike the men of

Mwaa, they made no attempt to blur their sexual identities. "Men dressed like men," informants declared, "and women like women." Instead, the group's ability to draw responsive audiences was based on the interaction of both sexes as they danced.

On arrival the dancers initially circled the selected homestead, chanting their traditional mosquito song. Simultaneously, they surrounded everyone within it—themselves included—by a network of their sticks, vines, and chanted curses. They then formed two lines, one for each sex, within the largest courtyard, habitually used as a gathering and dancing area. Thereafter, "they did things that people did not expect normal human beings to do, attracting people from everywhere to come and see."[15]

Kagita dancers were both acrobatic and sexually explicit. They made every effort to elicit ribald comment and bursts of laughter, both through the wit of their extemporaneously chanted verses and continuous reliance on sexual innuendo. The use of gestures and "body language" to simulate sexual relationships between the male and female dancers might seem tame by contemporary standards. It was, however, wholly in violation of ancestral custom and thus both shocking and offensive to the senior age-sets. This view was not completely shared, however, by members of the younger age-sets, particularly other family heads. Often, both male and female members of this group would gather just outside the Kagita's witchcraft barrier to watch and laugh, behavior sometimes noted by Kagita elders in their search for future sources of supply.

The evidence suggests that during the final years before colonialism Kagita activities fell well within the range of social deviation permitted within Meru. Its sexual displays were considered vulgar but posed no threat to established marriage patterns. Its economic demands were limited to maize, beans, and millet beer. The Kagita Kiama did not impound livestock, nor did it demand services beyond the occasional provision of additional quantities of food. In short, the society was perceived as little more than a Kiama of sexual exhibitionists, practicing limited forms of extortion and seeking equally limited rewards.

The response of elders' councils within every major Meru region was thus identical to that used with other deviant societies. Privately, members of the Kagita were discussed only in tones of loathing and contempt. Publicly, they were ostracized. No man of Kagita could meet in Kiama with other elders. Nor could he join in their solemn feasts or even the most casual beer-drinking sessions. In Meru terms this exclusion meant the individual "remained a boy," in that he was barred from every opportunity to acquire the wisdom of his elders. This penalty, it was believed, would weigh more heavily upon all deviants as they aged. Later in their lives they would want to abandon their deviation and return to their rightful positions as elders, men of the mainstream, and supporters of ancestral ways.

Interestingly, Kagita members appeared to have acquiesced in their own isolation, even from other deviant groups. As a tiny numerical minority they were probably aware that survival depended on drawing only minimal attention. Yet it seems odd that such fringe societies shunned any form of contact with each other, thereby making their isolation complete. Later, colonial administrators openly worried that the various witchcraft societies might eventually unite and then urge the entire Meru population to rise against them. In fact, the Kagita's "secret" teachings not only forbade such contacts but also prevented them through imposition of food taboos similar to those developed to separate earlier generations of mainstream Meru from the A-Athi hunting Kiamas.

Remember that those groups were kept apart from one another by injunctions that forbade hunters to drink milk, thus inhibiting their raising of domestic livestock. Conversely, Meru cultivator-herders were forbidden to eat wild game and thus discouraged from entering the forest. The effect intended by the originators of these traditions, of course, was to inhibit the social intercourse that arises from sharing food and drink, thereby ensuring the continued isolation of both sides. In the same vein Kagita dancers after 1900 sang: "I [Kagita] visited Mwathi [a Mu-Athi, a man of the forest]. He gave me only hooves [i.e., no meat, therefore no hospitality]. If he visits me, I will not give him beer" [i.e., no grain, therefore no hospitality].[16] The meaning of the verses, clear to every Meru of that era, was that every deviant segment within Meru wished to keep rigidly to itself, using its methods of supernatural cursing only to protect its members against intrusion while simultaneously assuring a reasonable supply of food and beer.

AFTER CONQUEST: THE KAGITA AS SAFETY ZONE

The Kagita's isolation was rarely shattered by the British conquest, in striking contrast to its impact on other members of their age-set. The status inherent in the Aruau role as family head/apprentice elder had disappeared. British concepts of taxation drained their wealth. Outside labor recruiters, more numerous each year, sent constant tremors through their ranks. But worse was still to come, for the colonial roles of "policeman," "district judge," "labor recruiter," and "tax man," initially held only by the English, were swiftly duplicated on a smaller scale by those Horne had chosen as chiefs.

There was no lack of appointees, all drawn by the hope of personal reward. At first this was perceived in terms of meat, to be acquired from the steady flow of livestock impounded by the government through levies, taxes, and fines. Later, as their horizons expanded, colonial appointees sought rewards of rupees (later, shillings), still more livestock, the power to make others labor, and illicit sex. In consequence the original British pattern of exploitation was duplicated on every ridgetop, as chiefs began to copy colonial methods on a smaller scale. Acting as local police, judges, labor recruiters, and tax men, they diverted steady streams of meat, beer, labor, and sexual service into their homesteads. In theory they were merely enforcing colonial law. In fact they fell easily into the Meru tradition of "limited extortion for limited reward," in ways not so different than those of the Kagita and other deviant societies.

None of the blanket chiefs' demands, however, fell on those deviants who lived through song and dance. Lacking warriors, the Kagita were not harmed by peace. Lacking herds, flocks, and harvests, they owned nothing for either whites or chiefs to tax. Best, the Meru fear of their defensive magic screened them from those who sought men for forced labor. Safe inside their zone of sticks and vines, the Kagita continued to feast in peace, perhaps the least disturbed of anyone in Meru by the onset of colonialism.

The society also benefited from a three- to four-year period of favorable weather (1908–1911?), which produced larger harvests and increased the availability of both grains and millet beer. As a result the Kagita's basic function evolved once more, from simple acquisition of its members' daily meals to large-scale, nightly beer drinking and feasting. More striking, the Kagita began to profit from the example set by local chiefs by extending its earlier practice of consuming food and beer to include all-night "hidden" dancing and random sexual intercourse.

Meru tradition had always made dancing a public occasion. Every dance was a communal event, held at a special dancing ground, lit by brightly blazing fires. Most dances were considered part of courtship, wherein younger people of both sexes could display their skills in such fashion as to attract mates. Dancing, therefore, was by age-set, with only members of a single sex on the field. Unmarried women danced to show their grace, agility, and beauty. Warriors displayed their strength and skill. Those men about to enter marriage scrutinized the girls, searching for potential mates. Elders of both sexes watched for budding romances, commenting on the suitability of a potential match. It was courtship in its most communal form, in which the interplay between potential lovers took place within a public forum where it could be observed and thus enjoyed by all.[17]

Premarital and extramarital intercourse, of course, were rigidly forbidden. Men were even forbidden to follow the women of their choice home from dances. Instead, custom allowed a man to pursue the courtship only by meeting with his intended as she walked in company with her mother—to and from their family fields. Subsequent visits were made to the girl's family compound but were conducted in a manner that inhibited physical intimacy at every stage, thereby assuring the girl's virginity at marriage.

Extramarital intercourse was equally taboo. When suspected, a husband had only to ask the appropriate ritualist (here, a Murogi, or curser) to place a curse on whoever had approached his wife. The adulterer, trapped by his own knowledge, developed physical symptoms sufficient to alert the whole community to what had occurred and perhaps with whom. The removal, of course, meant consultation with various specialists, payment of livestock, public disclosure, enforced restitution, and an end to the affair. Under the weight of such penalties extramarital conflicts were rare. In the first years of colonialism, however, the Kagita broke with these traditions. With grain, vegetables, and beer more plentiful, they were often provided with more than they could consume in a single session. Logically, Kagita bands began to gather up the surplus to carry with them into the night. Gradually their demands grew to include provision of a surplus, which also expanded over time. In turn, its continued availability led to a pattern of continuous feasting, now marked not only by consumption of surplus food and beer but also by nightly dancing, "hidden" in the pitch black and total secrecy of their communal huts, to the rumble of cowskin drums.

Clearly, the Kagita Kiamas continued to evolve, responding to external forces in ways allowing its members to survive. Originally crop protectors, they had been transformed by famine into dancing deviants. As harvests improved, they changed from Kiamas of food seekers to Kiamas of feasts. Certainly the purpose of their dancing changed, from a means to glean subsistence into a joyous nightly revel. The inclusion of heretofore forbidden sexual activities was also in response to external change, whether in imitation of chiefs or as one more reflection of the general collapse of morality that sprang from submitting to alien rule.

There is no question that these final changes deprived the Kagita of the social isolation it required to survive. On one hand its deviations had become so sharp as to draw the wrath of the ruling elders. On the other the prospect of nightly feasts, beer drinking, dancing, and sex proved more and more attractive to those family heads—and their women—whose status, security, and communal happiness had drained away. For some of these the Kagita offered a way to survive. For most it provided a safety zone for a pleasurably illicit alternative to life under British rule.

For these and perhaps other reasons family heads in every area began to join, appearing with their wives at the nightly revels, bearing gourds of food and beer. For women the decision must have been difficult. They were flouting the most explicit teachings of their own Kiamas, as well as their virtual certainties that the ancestors would be enraged. Set against this was the growing feeling that the world had changed, the ancestors had lost power, and that the old ways no longer brought them joy. If they could eat, drink, dance, or copulate, it might be possible to forget the life outside the sticks and vines.

KAGITA, KIAMA, AND KANGANGI

No evidence suggests, however, that many joined the deviant Kiamas. The Kagita was always a Kiama for the few. Most men, including family heads/apprentice elders, professed only loathing for its activities, even as they feared its curse. But at night, some joined in the festivities. In certain localities the simple beehive huts that housed the groups were rebuilt to larger scale, some approaching the size of a communal war hut, intended to hold scores of men. Within these huts, sheltered by darkness, the rumbling drums, and the sticks and vines, family heads throughout Meru found they could at least briefly defy both ancestral and British tradition, and carouse until dawn.

Before the conquest, reaction of the elders' councils to the Kagita's rising popularity within their areas might have remained indifferent. Even the night feasts might have been passed over, accepted as a type of safety valve for family heads unable to conform to the sexual restrictions of marriage. It must be remembered, however, that many other types of restraint had crumbled under the shock of military surrender and British rule. As a result, in several regions the dual lure of drums and darkness proved too strong, and traditions record the appearance of warriors at the feasts of Kagita, and even Mwaa.

At this point warrior contingents in each of these localities reacted as one. Enraged and shamed by the appearance of age-mates within the deviants' ranks, warrior bands in several areas defied their elders and launched sporadic attacks against the huts of known Kagita members. The raids were limited in scope, in keeping with traditions that forbade the slaughtering of kin. Raiders symbolized these restrictions by covering their spear heads with red ocher, which "was not to be removed by elders' [family heads'] blood." Should any warrior so forget his bearing as to stab an elder in the dark, the lack of ocher on his spear would both betray him and make him liable to his Kiama's justice.

In consequence each raid followed set patterns. Raiders who had scouted the area beforehand would stop well short of Kagita sticks and vines. From beyond that barrier, however, fire spears were launched against the hut, until the dry banana leaves of which it was composed began to burn. As the dancers scattered, the raiders beat them soundly with the shafts of spears, striking at men and women alike.

The dancers fled into the darkness, leaving their hut a smoking ruin. Whenever possible, the raiders destroyed their drums and tipped their beer gourds, pouring the beer onto the ground. Honor satisfied, they returned to their war hut. Simultaneously, the ruling elders of their ridge-top appeared and violently berated them for bringing shame upon their age-set by "beating on their mothers" (a phrase that implied that the Kagita was composed of women).

Before conquest the elders would have ended their harangue by fining the entire group a number of goats and cattle, to "cool their blood." Because the warriors would have none to give, the entire unit would be sent out raiding and permitted to return only when they had acquired livestock in sufficient numbers to "eat the shame" brought out by disobedience. Simultaneously, the deviants would assemble once more, rebuild their dancing huts, begin collection for their feasts, and initiate the cycle once again.

After 1908, however, both warriors and deviants were forced to contend with the increasing power of Kangangi. Horne's attention had initially been drawn to the Kagita by complaints against them from his warrior guards. He was pleased to receive delegations of ruling elders who echoed their complaints. He was considerably less pleased to learn that small groups of warriors had been raiding the societies, burning their huts, and beating the dancing members of what he perceived to be a "women's Kiama."

It was a time when Horne's first concern was to dismantle warriorhood. War, even in the guise of police work, had become a British monopoly. Only the crown's agents, as appointed by Horne, had the power to enforce law, even against alleged practitioners of witchcraft. Horne's first instinct, therefore, was to move against the dissident bands of warriors by arresting them all. Horrified, the elders explained that although the raiders had in fact transgressed against their own traditions they had been brought back under their Kiamas' control.

The first time, Horne simply accepted the elders' explanation and dropped the matter. As the raids sporadically recurred, his curiosity was sufficiently aroused by the accusations against the society to the point where he demanded to see them himself.

In keeping with what he believed to be Meru tradition, Horne slaughtered a bull, then sent out proclamations to the effect that all members of the Kagita should appear and share his feast. Although annoyed at the offer of meat, instead of maize and millet beer, Kagita groups within Imenti responded by choosing spokesmen. Following custom, only the eldest males were selected, both to present their cause and display their dancing.

Traditions record that the spokesmen addressed Horne by declaring that none of them feared him, since he in turn had nothing to fear from a "Kiama of poor people who must dance to find food." Thereafter, the spokesmen danced for Horne, minimizing the element of sexuality and emphasizing the dignity of the occasion.

Horne, always an admirer of traditional Meru dancing, was greatly impressed. Rejecting declarations by Kiamas of elders that the society was both deviant and antisocial, he permitted it to continue, firmly cautioning warriors that further raids against them would be swiftly punished.

Within a Meru context his remarks were catastrophic. Horne had probably intended to do little more than keep the peace, choosing to arrest neither the dancers nor the warriors who raided them. In no way did he encourage the Kagita to continue in anything other than dancing. Nonetheless, his implied approval of their continued existence caused the society's popularity to reach new heights. With nothing to fear from the white man, the Kagita saw no limits to what could be requisitioned to form the feast. As a result every band grew larger as more and more people dared to join.

For a time the Kiamas of elders persisted in their efforts to disburse the society, allowing small bands of warriors to "disobey" their orders and raid their huts whenever it seemed safe. Their spokesmen continued to deal with Horne as they had done before, expressing regret for the hot blood of their sons and promising to once more bring them under control. Subsequently, they found it more effective to emphasize the Kagita's "witchcraft," a term to which they found the British increasingly responsive as time went on.

Tradition suggests that Horne gave his permission for at least one punitive raid against the society in 1909 and perhaps a second during 1915. Others may have occurred in between; certainly, they continued for some years to come. None, however, would have a permanent effect. Kagita was the child of catastrophe, offering new ways of survival for impoverished and despairing men and women. As long as catastrophe continued within Meru, the society would continue to evolve.

CHAPTER VII

The Colonial Traditions: Dismantling Elderhood

"Short [E. B.] Horne had laid out a nice little golf course.
500 local girls were paid to cut the grass by plucking it out
with their fingers. Next to the golf course stood a large,
handsome log house, in which the door opened to reveal
mud floors on which a large hat-stand stood gaunt and
proud within a pool of water."[1]

Madeleine Laverne Platts
Wife of W. A. F. Platts,
First Assistant District Commissioner
Meru, 1912

KANGANGI AND KIRAUNE:
E. B. HORNE AND G. ST. J. ORDE-BROWNE

Horne's first five years in Meru were spent virtually alone; he was assisted only by the two British officers commanding his multitribal force
of the King's African Rifles (KAR), as well as a single Gikuyu translator. During this period he made great efforts to absorb Meru culture.
Informants gleefully declare, for example, that "Kangangi spent much
time courting Meru girls." In fact he often accepted gifts of food from
unmarried women he had hired to labor on his own expanding compound and joined on occasion in the dances of "his" (warrior) age-set.
From the Meru perspective accepting food from a woman's hands and
dancing among warriors were both acts intended to provide a symbolic
beginning to courtship. Evidently, those who saw "Kangangi" engage
in the initial stages assumed he would complete the rituals over time.

In 1912 Horne went briefly on leave. He was temporarily replaced by
W. A. F. Platts as acting district commissioner and no less than five as-
sistant district officers, none of whom had experience in the region.[2]
Three of these remained to assist Horne upon his return in mid-1913.
The difficulties encountered during his absence, however, convinced the
colonial administration in Nairobi that the Meru unit was simply too

large to administer effectively, even with the addition of three other men. This feeling was underscored by a series of "ridgetop risings" against British authority that occurred after 1912, each time among peoples in those regions—Mwimbi, Muthambi, and Cuka—geographically farthest from British military control.

The cause of the earliest uprisings was Horne's increasingly effective imposition of a hut tax. Between 1909 and 1911 he had decreed that each hut owner (in theory every male member of the tribe) was to pay stipulated amounts of tax, collectible either in currency (initially rupees, subsequently shillings), livestock, or labor for the whites. The decree was initially given force by Horne's selection of a large contingent of "hut counters," who were instructed to count and record every hut in Meru District. Because of close supervision by the King's African Rifles, the census was completed quickly. Thereafter, small units of "tribal police" (Horne's warrior bodyguards), backed by appropriate number of KAR, went from region to region to collect taxes.

Most Meru dealt with Horne's demands with either compliance or evasion. In Mwimbi, Muthambi, and Cuka, however, local groups of warriors greeted the appearance of the tax collectors—usually from Imenti—as they would any other band of fighting men that came to seize their cattle: they went to war. Generally each uprising followed a similar pattern. The original tax collectors would be driven off by a rain of spears, arrows, and rocks. They would return with members of the KAR, usually led by one of its British officers. The army unit would demand immediate surrender. The rebels, usually encouraged by a single senior warrior, would reply initially with spears. The KAR would open fire, killing one or more of the resisters. Often at this point the ridgetop elders would appear, handing the recalcitrant senior warrior over to the KAR, as well as the disputed livestock.[3]

Horne's taxation program also led to a second type of uprising, also by the warriors of Cuka, at that time Meru District's most southern region, against their traditional "northern" enemies in Imenti. The Imenti, as the people in most frequent contact with Horne, had been the first to feel the full weight of his taxation. In response bands of warriors began to gather and trek south, seeking work to pay the tax. In so doing, they passed through Mwimbi, Muthambi, and Cuka en route to the white farming areas near Nairobi.

Passage through Cuka would have been hazardous during the "best" of traditional times, because Imenti warriors had no *gichiaro* alliances with any Cuka clans. Their hostility was fully reciprocated, because the Cuka, only five years freed from the scourge of Imenti raiding, remained intensely fearful that it might begin again. The first Imenti labor seekers to enter Cuka after 1912, therefore, were met by local warriors, shaking whatever spears and shields remained to them and screaming threats of war. The Imenti retaliated in kind, although the ensuing skirmishes were initially smothered either by Cuka elders or the threats of a blanket chief to denounce the Imenti transients to the whites.

One of these Imenti bands, however, found itself unable to suppress its frustration and rage. Forced to back down from what they considered an honorable confrontation with Cuka counterparts, they wandered off the track that had been set aside for labor transients. By accident they met and traded angry words with a Cuka woman who was cultivating the southern bank of the river nearest today's Cuka Town. In total violation of military tradition, they speared her to death.

The offense was too great for the Cuka to bear. Warriors in every ridgetop cried out for war against the Imenti. In panic the blanket chief for upper Cuka, a former war leader named Kabandango, went at a run to Embu district headquarters to report the incident to that region's district commissioner, N. A. Kenyon-Slaney.

Kenyon-Slaney ordered the transients' arrest, sending out his own tribal police to make the capture. They were successful, but the Cuka warriors were unappeased. Initially, they objected that the white man had done nothing to assure that the parents of the murdered woman would be compensated in cattle by the clans of her killers. Nor did they see any reason why their land should be open to people (the Imenti) so demonstrably savage that they abandoned every warrior tradition and hunted down their wives and daughters. Nor did they understand, finally, why district commissioner barred them "as warriors and men, from taking justice onto the points of their own spears."

Unfortunately, as Kabandango was arguing these points with the Embu district commissioner, a second party of Imenti warriors appeared on the same track. This group knew nothing of the earlier killing. They were not, however, favorably disposed to the warriors of Cuka. Reverting to tradition, the Cuka war band with whom the slain girl was kin surrounded the Imenti. Waiting until they began to cross the Naka River, they attacked and killed the last six men.

The repercussions were felt from Meru Town to Embu. In the north, Imenti warriors began to rearm and sizably expand their labor-seeking expeditions southward, in joyous anticipation of taking justified revenge on killers of their tribesmen. In the south, Cuka messengers sped along the ridgetops shouting to prepare for the invasions yet to come.

British response to the increasing tension was a decision to quell it at the source. In early 1913 a separate administrative substation was designated for the Cuka region, to be placed near the site of today's Cuka Town. Initially, it was to be administered from Embu and to include not only Cuka but also Muthambi and Mwimbi, regions that would not be transferred back into the Meru administrative unit until 1933.

The first British administrator of this region was G. St. J. Orde-Browne.[4] Like Horne and many others among the first generation of colonial administrators, Orde-Browne was entranced by the culture of the tribes with whom he had to work. He admired Horne's linguistic achievements among the Meru but found himself unable to match them because of dialectical differences that caused their "tongue to spring up anew" at every ridgetop. Nonetheless, he threw himself enthusiastically into the task of learning all he could about the people he had come to rule.

Tradition records Orde-Browne's arrival as a major event. Blanket chiefs from Cuka, Mwimbi, and Muthambi had been asked to send delegations of warriors, partially to honor his arrival but also to labor on constructing his stockade. Following the tradition first set by Horne, Orde-Browne appeared on a horse. He arrived at the head of a column composed of three hundred Embu porters, a police detachment of Kamba, two British colonial officials, three Asians to supply the station, and the inevitable Gikuyu interpreter.[5]

Orde-Browne, later known to the peoples of his district as Kiraune, is remembered as a "senior warrior" (i.e., twenty-eight to thirty years old), stout and clean shaven. A serious man, he was extremely aware of the dignity inherent in his role as servant of the British king. Whereas Horne had come to power by his gun, however, Orde-Browne relied on a combination of a brass-bound medicine chest and his skill as a magician.

"In dealing with primitive people," he wrote later, "it was important to impress them with the knowledge and power of the white man." For Browne this meant that his first encampment became "a little like a circus, with various entertainments taking place, magic lanterns, fireworks, looking glasses, all served as great attractions. While the solid good work of the medicine chest could be backed up with . . . conjuring tricks."[6] Orde-Browne used his powers of conjuring as Horne had used his firepower, to overawe and thus compel obedience. On one occasion, for example, he proclaimed the appearance of a comet, having first carefully consulted an almanac for the expected date. Having foretold its arrival, Orde-Browne was pressed by his listeners to explain the meaning, comets usually having been considered by the peoples of Mount Kenya as harbingers of disaster. Shortly after, the death of King Edward was announced throughout Kenya. When Orde-Browne proclaimed it to the district, his reputation was assured.

Like Horne, Orde-Browne made use of his rising prestige to learn everything possible of the three southern cultures. In consequence both district officers gradually focused their attention on the regional systems of Kiamas that functioned within their respective areas, perceiving these as the key to building an administrative structure that would work for conquered and conqueror alike.

THE KIAMA OF THE FEW:
THE EVOLUTION OF THE NJURI

Horne and Orde-Browne had both become acquainted with the Kiama system during an earlier period of service in Embu. Both men perceived it as more useless than harmful, little more than the gathering of old men to settle arguments and drink beer. For that reason both administrators found themselves rather favorably inclined toward the Kiama systems they found functioning within their respective administrative jurisdictions, seeing them as a supplement to British law.

Horne was unaware, however, that the system in use among the northern Meru was undergoing extensive change. He was aware that his own appearance in Meru had ended an era of internecine warfare among the various subtribes. He knew nothing, however, of the intensity with which that warfare had been waged between the warriors of Tigania and those of North Imenti, a struggle that was smothered only through the imposition of his authority.

The northern wars had raged for almost three decades before the British conquest. Their origin lay in the continued incorporation of both pastoral and agricultural Maasai warriors (and women) into the clans inhabiting the Tigania Plain. In time both the pastoral and military orientation of Tiganians increased as a result. Using Maasai raiding strategies, they began to wage war against their neighbors, primarily in North Imenti. These groups, far more numerous, had responded with predictable enthusiasm, launching raids against Tiganian clans that have gone down in the oral histories of both peoples as major landmarks in their military pasts.

No conflict that rages over three decades can leave the social structures of the protagonists unchanged. One consequence of Tiganian military exertions, for example, had been the creation of *gichiaro* alliances with several regions in Igembe, breaking with prior tradition that had restricted such alliances to clans in Mwimbi and Tharaka. Their purpose was to free Tiganian warriors to focus on the more dangerous Imenti. These alliances, in turn, led to progressively more frequent contacts on both sides, as spokesmen from the allied Kiamas of each region met more and more often to coordinate military plans.

At some point in the late 1800s these meetings became formalized. The result was the gradual creation—initially solely on an ad hoc basis—of a new "Kiama of Kiamas." It was referred to as the Njuri Nceke, a term that carries connotations of "thinning out" (winnowing, selecting) both crops and men. The corresponding English might be "committee of the few." The second word refers to the Nceke Plain, which lies roughly equidistant between the Nyambeni forests of Igembe and those of North Imenti, thus near the more thickly settled sections of Tigania.[7] The field within that plain where the Njuri met was called Nciru. In subsequent decades all of these terms would acquire chilling meaning for colonial administrators.

The increasingly permanent nature of the Njuri Nceke was also facilitated by a steady expansion in the number of livestock available to Tiganian and (some) Igembe communities. Their growing military dominance over much of North Imenti, as well as successful forays farther south, led to a continuous expansion of their flocks and herds.

The warriors' success ushered in an era of plenty for their fathers. Family heads who had lived through their younger years in constant scarcity now found themselves the owners of livestock beyond their capacity to consume. In consequence the feasts required to dignify the Njuri convocations grew progressively more elaborate. This was particularly true for the bull feasts associated with initiation of new members into the Njuri Nceke itself. Between the 1870s and 1890s larger and larger numbers of livestock were required to buy one's way into the association. This was in striking contrast with the poverty of the corresponding two "Kiama of Kiamas" that appeared within subsequent years of Imenti-Igoji and Mwimbi-Muthambi, all of which remained relatively poor in livestock at least partially because of the Tiganian success in war.

In 1900, for example, a single goat bought entry into the highest elders' council of lower Muthambi, a region often stripped of its cattle by raiders. In South Imenti, candidates were asked to provide a bull. In Tigania several bulls were demanded over an indefinite period, as well as goats, a sheep, forty gourds of millet porridge, fifteen loads of firewood, several baskets of yams, and a quantity of *miraa* (*Cathus edulis*), a twig that served as a stimulant when chewed. In addition, applicants were required to provide sufficient beer to quench the thirst of the entire gathering, often a considerable task.[8]

This "fee," moreover, was far more than a simple ticket of entry. In Meru society it was impossible to find a gathering that did not value meat and beer as tools for building relationships among its members. Hence the "fees" were meant specifically to provide Njuri members with a feast—in Tigania a series of feasts—intended to forge close ties of fellowship between themselves and entering members. To feed so many, candidates had thus to prove themselves men of economic substance within their own localities. They could do so only through gathering sufficient livestock, acquired by successful warrior sons.

At some point during this same period, two new levels of administration appeared within the structure of the Njuri Nceke, each perceived as more selective and thus "higher" than the preceding one. Traditionally, failure to resolve a given issue by consensus had always led to the selection of a smaller body to reexamine it in isolation from the larger group. In Tigania, custom limited these smaller councils to eight, four representing each half (Kiruka or Ntiba) of the tribe. Where possible, each of the four also served as spokesmen for some smaller social unit, usually a cluster of clans within a given region.

The names given these smaller councils reflected their selective nature. One was known as Njuri Mpingiri, the second as Njuri Mpere (or Mbere). Both terms imply a further winnowing of growing things ("a winnowing of winnowings"), in reflection of the name bestowed upon their parent body.

Over time the Mpingiri and Mpere followed the development of the Njuri Nceke. Initially, both were temporary bodies, each assembling on an ad hoc basis to resolve two separate types of issue. Subsequently, they shed their temporary nature, assuming permanent form. Spurred on by the availability of millet and livestock, members of the Njuri Nceke gathered ever more frequently at the field of Nciru. The smaller Njuris of Mpingiri and Mpere would then break off from the larger gathering and seek "secret" places of their own.

These extensions of the Kiama system in Tigania were subsequently reflected in the south. Up to the mid-1800s the series of councils that governed the affairs of ridgetop communities in Igosi (later, Igoji), Abogeta (South Imenti), Abothoguchi (Northeast Imenti), and Miiriga Mieru (North Imenti) were collectively known as Nkomango, "councils of the throwing stones." The highest body within each region, the Kiama Kia Nkomango, met to resolve conflicts among smaller social units within its territory. On occasion spokesmen from all three regions would assemble as one unit to form a Kiama-Kia-Nkomango-of-them-all.

At some point in the final decades of the 1800s the members of this final council began to choose spokesmen to form a still more select body to resolve those issues on which they could not collectively agree. This smaller council, not surprisingly, became known as the Njuri ya Kiama (select council-of-councils), in reflection of the concept they had borrowed from the north. When deadlocked, this Njuri would choose a still smaller body to go into *nkireba* (secret sessions) to resolve the specific dispute. These daughter groups had several names. The one most frequently assembled, however, was the (Njuri) Kathaka Kai, "council of the small bush."[9] That name, like those of the daughter groups used by the Njuri of Tigania, was to give British officials deep cause for concern in the coming decades.

In the southern (Nithi) Meru region the Kiama system developed along similar lines. Generally, each ridgetop had its local council. These tended to cluster into "upper" (forest) and "lower" (woodland) regions, each of which developed identities of its own. Thus, people of upper Mwimbi, Muthambi, and Cuka saw their localities as distinct from those of the three lower sections of their respective subtribes. The Kiama systems that developed in each region followed these divisions, as six higher councils emerged to resolve disputes within their areas. Collectively, these were known as the Kiama Kya Kibogo (Cuka; meaning uncertain) and Kiama Kya Njuguma (Mwimbi, Muthambi: council of the throwing club). When required, the two highest councils of any one subtribe could unite to form a single body. Alternatively, two councils from any two subtribes could also join together. Thus, the highest elders' council from Igoji allied to both upper and lower Muthambi could meet with either to solve a conflict or plan a raid. Simultaneously, the two highest councils from both upper and lower Cuka could meet behind their forest barriers to organize a mutual defense.

No supracouncil held authority over all these regions. Instead, in a time of crisis, spokesmen were selected only by as many areas as felt involved. These would temporarily combine, to form what in Tigania or

Imenti would have been called an Njuri. In the south, however, that term was unknown. Rather, a gathering of this nature was known collectively as Nkome, a term probably borrowed from the name used for the highest elders' council (Ngome) from Igoji or the neighboring Embu. Usually, a crisis involved military conflict between two regions, most often upper Mwimbi and one area of either Igoji or Muthambi, neither of which were *gichiaro* (allied) to any Mwimbi clan. In such cases selected elders from one Nkome council would proclaim a gathering with the others. The proclamation went in total silence, with junior members of the group acting as silent messengers. The message was written on their bodies, in the form of a smear of red ocher on their brow, four streaks of chalk on one shoulder, and a carved wooden walking stick ("the staff of Kiama") in one hand. On seeing the message, selected ruling elders would don a heavily oiled goatskin shoulder-cloak, seize the staff that symbolized their own authority, and gather at the meeting point until the conflict was resolved.

Although the system functioned smoothly, these southern gatherings lacked permanence. When agreement failed, the joint Nkome might select a smaller group to meet in *kaundu* (darkness; i.e., in secret session) until agreement was reached. In Mwimbi one daughter group was thus called Kaundu (darkness). There were certainly others.

On reaching agreement, however, the entire council dissolved itself, with members of both "parent" and "daughter" Kiamas simply returning to their homes. Nor would the same individuals necessarily be selected to represent their ridgetops in subsequent disputes. The difficulty of traversing the region's mountain gorges (in contrast with the ease of crossing the Tigania Plain), as well as the comparative lack of livestock, inhibited opportunities of assembling primarily to feast. Thus, in contrast to its northern neighbors, the highest elders' council of the south remained impermanent. Both systems proved capable of growth, but only the Njuris of the north achieved stability.

HORNE: PENETRATING THE NJURIS

During the first months of his administration, Horne found himself increasingly fascinated by the little he could learn of the Njuri system. By the end of 1908 he decided to penetrate what he believed to be its "secrets" by attending its gatherings. On inquiry he focused his attention on Tigania's Njuri Nceke, which his informants had reported as the most powerful of these organizations, and which in fact had reached the point of representing not only its own region but many areas of Igembe as well.

Horne's intent was unquestionably honorable. As a conscientious administrator with a genuine interest in those he ruled, he wished nothing more than to discover whatever information might assist him in his work. The fact that elders might hold such things in secret merely intrigued him. To acquire the needed information, he was quite prepared to join the Njuri itself, learn what was needed, then keep its "secrets" while going on efficiently about his work.

His decision, however, placed Njuri elders in a quandary from which tradition promised no relief. The organization's soul lay in its use of secrecy. Ancestral traditions emphasized it as central to survival of the tribe. Each age-set, throughout Meru history, had contributed its wealth of stories in which only the use of secrecy (e.g., secret language, concealed weapons) had been able to preserve its warriors from defeat in war. The need for secrecy, as exemplified by the secrets kept by each sex from the other and within every age-set, permeated the society. Secrecy was a tool, used to sharpen the learners' minds and imbue the teachings with significance and dignity. This concept was perhaps most clearly reflected in the "secret oaths" that every elder swore when entering a Kiama. Through these oaths candidates bound themselves to die if they were ever to reveal what the society taught. What better way to emphasize the importance of collective knowledge than to promise individual death if it be misused?

In fact, as always in Meru, the "secrets" that elders swore so diligently to defend were nothing more startling than the rules of behavior for elderhood. As each man entered the council of elders that administered his own location, he was initiated into its "secrets" in the same manner than new warriors were introduced to the military secrets of their war band.

The elders also taught these secrets in ways similar to those used by warriors. To preserve the dignity of elderhood, they used no beatings to drive facts home. Rather, senior members gathered round the novices and imparted the lessons by means of repeated chants.

To intensify the lessons, each novice cut the throat of a goat that had been selected for the purpose from one of his own herds. He then inserted both the knife and a wooden splinter, charred at one end, into the opening. Holding both objects in that position he listened to and repeated a series of "secrets" in the form of oaths.

One by one, the precepts of elderhood were chanted by the group. "You are now elder. Elders do not lie. If you see younger men fighting, you must 'cool' [compose] them. If you see spouses fighting, you must 'cool' them. If you see animals in other's gardens, you must remove them. If you see women giving birth [without other women present], you must assist them. If you are chosen to judge others, you must 'cool' them. If you do not, let this oath kill you. If you reveal these things, let this oath kill you. If you reveal any secret of this Njuri, let this oath kill you."

The main thrust of Meru secrecy, of course, was directed against "strangers," including any nonmember of the tribe. In the past the very concept of a "stranger" settling permanently among them had been beyond the range of Meru thought. Non-Meru came to raid. Their women came to trade. Both behaved predictably, returning to their own regions when their work was done.

Occasionally, refugees from other tribes struck down by famine fled to Meru seeking food. Alternatively, warriors from distant regions whose own communities had been dispersed in war might ask a Meru clan to shelter them. Tradition covered all such cases. Refugees appeared unarmed, carrying tufts of grass in outstretched hands, to show they came in peace. Having symbolically cast themselves upon the elders' mercy, custom dictated that each man take on the role of a child, addressing the leading Meru elder as his father and asking for adoption as his son. This adoption was accomplished by slashing the wrists of both men, then mingling drops of their blood.

The result was to make the newcomer into "someone," a Meru person, by bringing him into a specific place within the kinship web. Through becoming the "son" of someone, he became "grandson," "nephew," "brother," and so on to others. His relationship to every other adult within the clan and, by extension, the entire tribe, was thereby defined. He thus symbolically abandoned his entire identity, assuming a Meru name, the obligations of kin, and eventually, the raising of descendants to carry on the Meru line into which he had come.

Such men were clearly eligible for entry into every level of the Kiama system. To assure their acceptance, even their non-Meru birth became one of its secrets, a fact protected by the oaths of every member, who swore never to reveal the former strangers' origins. In consequence men originally descended from the Galla, Ogiek, or Maa-speaking peoples that had once inhabited Meru were protected by a cloak of total secrecy. So, too, were those who had fled to Meru from adjoining regions such as Kamba or Mbeere during famines. From that moment they were and had always been Meru. As a result informants who speak of that era are correct when declaring: "All who enter Kiama are Meru. All who enter Njuri are Meru. We are a fist [i.e., united]! Others are fingers [i.e., separated]."

Tradition did not, however, provide methods of dealing with a "stranger" who had conquered the entire Meru tribe, then having completed his task, refused to leave. Nor did it provide for a stranger who refused adoption into the tribe and who was wholly unaware of the web of kinship into which he would enter and thus oblivious to its demands. Actually, Horne was sufficiently aware of the rites of adoption to offer to mingle his blood with men of the tribe. In so doing, however, he was actually offering to pass through the ritual in total unawareness of what he was to become on completing it and how his new status meant he should behave.

In early 1909, Horne received a delegation from the Tiganian Njuri Nceke. The elders explained at great length that those not of their blood were forbidden entry into their ranks. Horne responded agreeably, then demanded to attend their meetings as a guest. The question threw the elders back into a quandary, because he was not a guest among them but a conqueror, quite capable of seizing every cow they owned. Under such circumstances the elders reluctantly agreed, hoping he would take on the demeanor appropriate to his age-set and sit silently throughout the gathering.

Horne, however, proved anything but a silent observer. As his command of the language increased, he evolved swiftly from a seeker of knowledge to a decision maker. This was particularly true when Njuri decisions went against either British morality or colonial law. Thus, interridgetop conflicts involving acts of witchcraft, physical assault, cattle theft, wife beating, and adultery, among others, were invariably interpreted in different ways by the Njuri Nceke and its unexpected guest.

Soon, of course, Horne emerged as the Njuri's leading member, a status he then moved to formalize by requesting full membership within the group, pointing out that he was more than able to pay every one of the traditional fees required for entry. The Njuri elders were dumbfounded. For the first time in their collective experience tradition offered no precedent, and thus no guide. Refusal might end their collective existence but so might acceptance.

The council's first solution was to inform Horne of his acceptance. He was subsequently "initiated" through payment of the fees traditionally required of a senior warrior accepted into the elders' ranks. Horne was told, accurately, that such a selection was rare but not unprecedented and that several of the men selected as colonial officials (among them, Mbogore M'Mwendo of upper Mwimbi) had been inducted into their respective elders' councils at some time in the past. At the same time the accompanying verbal rituals, including the sacred oaths that would in fact have brought him into membership, were quietly ignored. Both sides were thus briefly content—Horne because he had entered the institution, the Njuri because he had not.

The elders had still to cope with the problem of Horne's attendance at meetings. Their second decision, reached only after long debate, was to conduct all relevant aspects of their work in proverbs, arguing every aspect of a given issue with oblique circumlocutions that took their meanings from extensive knowledge of the Meru past. The proverbs were understandable to everyone except Horne. When he inquired as to the meanings, they replied with still more proverbs, intent, as one informant put it, "to lose him in the forest of our tongues."

The concept worked until Horne began to learn the proverbs. As his linguistic skills improved, however, he began to ignore large portions of what must have seemed interminable discussion. To Horne what the elders said was less important than what they did, which was to dispense justice. As he saw more and more of how the elders' administered justice, Horne felt he had learned enough about the Njuri to begin reshaping it in the image of England.

HORNE: WESTERNIZING THE NJURI

Even with the best will in the world, Horne must have been deeply exasperated with the Njuri perception of time. To the colonial British of that era the purpose of any judicial gathering was to progress steadily toward a specific decision. To the Meru the purpose was to thoroughly examine an issue until no *indecision* remained, thereby creating communal harmony among the participants.

To facilitate consensus, it was imperative that everyone attend the meeting who had any involvement whatsoever in whichever conflict had emerged and that all be given the opportunity to express themselves. In a typical Njuri meeting the elders gathered in a circle. Spokesmen for each side of the conflict sat opposite one another. Once seated, one spokesman rose and began the debate, speaking directly to one of his opponents in the other half of the circle. Thus addressed, the opposing spokesman rose to present his side of the issue, speaking directly to someone else in turn. Thereafter, discussion shifted from one side of the circle to the other, until every elder had had his say. As each rose, he guaranteed himself an audience by directly addressing someone on the circle's opposite side.

If a consensus emerged, a decision could be swift. If not, discussion could become interminable, as then the oldest living men in Meru were called into the gathering, to search their memories for suitable precedents on which to resolve the issue. No other decision-making mechanism existed, other than the selection of a smaller council, representative of all factions within the larger one. This new body could then withdraw and reconsider the problem once again.[10]

The elders felt no need to hasten their decision. The very act of mutual deliberation produced the sense of harmony out of which they felt conflict could be resolved. Horne, dedicated to his Westernizing mission and locked psychologically into his European sense of time, might be forgiven if he looked upon these proceedings with rising impatience. Inevitably, he moved to replace them with as rigid a version of English law and parliamentary procedure as he could decently impose.

Horne's first attempt at intervention was a lamentable failure. In 1911 he ordered the two Njuris—and by extension the entire Kiama system beneath them—to cease consideration of "cases of debts, if all of the original parties [were] dead." Unfortunately, compliance with Horne's edict would have involved such massive changes in the Meru economic structure that it would have caused its total collapse. The proclamation was therefore courteously agreed to, then universally ignored. Horne was eventually forced to cancel it as unenforceable.[11]

Horne tried again in 1912, proclaiming the creation of one Kiama of Kiamas for all Meru to meet regularly at his administrative headquarters, ideally once per week. Always attempting to blend British institutions with Meru ways, his stated purpose was to "restore the previous condition of tribal unity which had been lost when different divisions lost touch with one another [just before the conquest] due to years of inter-tribal fighting."[12]

This idea, too, proved impossible to implement, since no Meru elder in the region wished to enter into a "previous" condition of unity, which all but Horne knew had never existed. Undaunted, Horne began once more in 1913. Still bound by the British concept of "regular" meeting times, he decided that the Njuris of both Imenti (Njuri ya Kiama) and Tigania-Igembe (Njuri Nceke) should meet precisely once a year. He had also learned, correctly, that decisions made by both bodies could be physically enforced by their respective warrior contingents.

Still determined to shape his reforms to fit local custom, he once more changed the place of meeting for both groups to his administrative center ("the Boma"), then appeared as the gathering began to lay down a precise itinerary of what he felt should be discussed. More significantly, he informed the elders that whatever decisions were reached would thereafter be enforced by warriors of the government. To ensure this, he had ordered his personal contingent of bodyguards to become the "warriors of Njuri." Now renamed the Askari ya Kanga (blanket police) and identifiable by their black blankets, they alone could carry out the elders' decisions among the people.

This innovation was successful, in part because neither body of elders could think of a way to rescind it. In subsequent years Horne carried out a virtual barrage of similar changes, each intended to gradually Westernize both elders' councils by slowly reshaping their outer structures to conform to the customs of England. Membership, for example, was sharply restricted to the number of elders Horne felt should be placed on an official membership list; this ruling eliminated the Meru concept of unlimited participation in the judicial process. Subsequently, Horne required written records of each conflict to be kept, thereby ensuring they assumed the format of a legal "case" as understood in English law. Since the use of written registers, instead of human memories, also eliminated the need to rely on oral precedent ("ancestral tradition") to guide decisions, there was no further need for consultation with the oldest members of the tribe. The very old were thus systematically eliminated from the councils, and with them the concept that judicial wisdom comes only through contact with the past.

Horne also sought to "bring order" into the payment of what he believed were "court fees"—meaning the gifts of livestock and millet beer presented by the parties to a conflict to members of the Njuri as they deliberated their case. Cattle, goats, and sheep, it will be recalled, were living catalysts, whose sacrifice at each stage of judicial deliberation was intended to gain attention (and thus approval) from the ancestors. Subsequent consumption of the meat and beer was intended to foster the spirit of fellowship and restore communal harmony. Horne saw the transfer of livestock as judicial bribery, consumption of beer as public drunkenness, and the continued feasting as evidence of the elders' unwillingness to work. In England judges worked, then feasted. Combining both, he felt, endangered justice.

Horne's reaction was to establish a fixed scale of court fees, to be paid in cash rather than cattle. The money thus collected was to be placed in an iron chest within Horne's office for safekeeping. Ultimately, he explained, the money thus collected would be used to finance the future laws that each Njuri would decide upon for all Meru. Once again, a principle of Meru justice gave way as the living link between the elders and ancestral spirits was forcibly dissolved.

Horne also tried, with less success, to regularize the local, regional, and interregional councils into a system of judicial appeals. Ideally, both civil and criminal actions would originate and be decided at local gatherings. Plaintiffs dissatisfied with the decisions could then appeal through each level of the system, with Horne himself serving as a court of last resort. For the system to meet European expectations, however, elders at every level were required to mete out "punishments" in European fashion. Usually this meant whipping, then incarceration in a "jail" constructed as an extension to Horne's log cabin.

In retrospect finding fault with Horne's intentions is hard. As part of a pioneer generation of administrators that respected African customs, he emerged as a gentle and gradual reformer. On one hand he wished to transform the Meru administrative and judicial structures into something resembling their counterparts in England. On the other he sought to move slowly, changing only as much as he believed the conquered would accept. His goal was to preserve the inner spirit of their institutions while gradually reshaping their outer forms. It seems relevant, therefore, to examine certain of Horne's reforms from the perspective of those who experienced them.

> At first, Kangangi [Horne] took interest in our Njuri [here, the Njuri ya Kiama of Imenti] and asked to attend our meetings. After he came, he let us do our work of settling quarrels but made changes so strange that no man could understand them.
>
> First, he forced Njuri to meet inside a building, as if guilty of some crime, rather than under our *mvuli* tree where all who knew [of] the quarrel could come and speak. Then he forced us to meet on every fourteenth day, rather than use our sensible system of meeting whenever a dispute arose that required elders to receive it. He then made lists of who was to attend and who might not, thereby excluding those who often had most interest in the case. Worse, each season it seemed he made these lists shorter, as this man and that man was proclaimed too old to decide such matters.
>
> Then he permitted "young men" to sit with us, not to sit quietly and "listen" to the wisdom of their elders but to write down whatever words their elders said . . . as if the words were important, rather than the spirit of what we were trying to settle. Then, finally, he and other white men informed us

that we had all grown too old and were no longer fit to judge our people. They told us that our places should be taken by younger men who had been trained in "the laws," by which he meant not ours but his. Thereafter, of course, it was not our Njuri, but his.[13]

Njuri elders met Horne's most gentle changes with a mixture of anxiety and bewilderment, feeling almost every principle of Meru justice was being violated. They were particularly confused, for example, by his insistence on basing each decision on "evidence." Often he would lecture them, to their amazement, that the "correct bench" to hear any case was one that knew nothing of the matter to be resolved beforehand and thus could pass judgment on the evidence alone. Elders who did know something of the case were to disqualify themselves voluntarily from hearing it, lest they enter the deliberations with preconceptions of what might have occurred.

The elders lectured in their turn, explaining that every member of an Njuri would of course know the facts of every conflict before it came to their court, the disagreement having grown sufficiently severe to disturb communal harmony. The issue to be settled was not "what happened" but which traditions could be interpreted in such a manner as to permit restoration of harmony among all contending parties and thereby of the community as a whole. Horne proved unable to understand.

The elders were also baffled by their conqueror's insistence upon prompt decisions, and indeed, upon any decisions at all. Justice had always been based on the concept of timelessness. The entire system of human relationships functioned through continual acts of reciprocity, the giving and receiving of livestock serving to symbolize the existence of ongoing relationships between those concerned.

To them, the relationships, not the decisions, were significant. If one man claimed another owed him five goats, for example, the second might deny the obligation. If the first then placed his claim before an Njuri and received their agreement as to its justice, a European would expect the goats to change hands immediately. If they did not, bribery and corruption were suspected or at the least deliberate evasion of the law.

In the eyes of the Meru, however, the conflict was resolved. The plaintiff, by appealing to the Njuri, sought only public agreement that the goats he claimed were indeed his. Verbal reaffirmation of that fact by an authority acceptable to both sides ended the conflict over who owned the goats. It also publicly reaffirmed the nature of the continuing relationship between them, a bond that defined each man's status in the eyes of peers and did so for as long as the relationship endured. Among the Meru it was enough to know who owed what. A decision on the physical possession of the goats was thus irrelevant to all concerned.[14]

The purpose of the judicial process itself provided a final area of misunderstanding. Horne and his successors were nurtured not only on British judicial traditions but the entire Judeo-Christian ethic, based on the principle of equitable retribution perhaps most eloquently expressed in the proverb "An eye for an eye and a tooth for a tooth."

The concept was perfectly familiar to the elders. However, it had nothing whatsoever to do with their system of justice. Born into a communal tradition, they felt that justice came not through punishment but reconciliation. To merely whip or jail the guilty failed to reimburse the victim. Both might then harbor resentments so intense that their conflict emerged once more.

The ultimate purpose of the Njuri, therefore, was not to decide guilt or innocence but to seek a third solution that would satisfy all sides, one that moved the parties to reconcile. "Guilt," where it could be determined, was perceived as collective. A livestock fine, therefore, was intended as an exercise in collective expiation, with the required animals being drawn equally from the herds of every homestead in the "guilty" person's clan. Moreover, because every conflict had two sides, the "victor" in a Njuri deliberation might also be instructed to draw livestock from among the herds of members of his own clan, with both sides thereby contributing to a final feast. In consuming the meat thus collected, elders, antagonists, and bystanders symbolically also swallowed the conflict that had led to its collection.

As Horne's reforms became more numerous, Njuri elders in both Tigania-Igembe and Imenti found themselves in an increasingly awkward position. On one hand both groups had to continue to meet the expectations of their conquerors. On the other they needed to continue serving their own people according to their own traditions. Both groups, abandoning their earlier hope that Horne would tire of attending their meetings, responded in three identifiable ways.

Their earliest tactic was simply to agree with whatever decisions Horne asked them to make, then continue to operate according to tradition. Informants discuss this period by citing the proverb: "Where elephants pass, grass must bend." ("What the white man asked, we bent to. When he had passed, we stood straight again and went on as before.")

This pattern of verbal evasion grew less effective as Horne perceived the elders' plan. Falling in with their intention, he countered by first seeking their collective approval of a specific measure. Having received it, he then commanded his force of tribal police to swiftly implement the decision in the Njuri's name.

The elders countered in their turn by turning from evasion to delay. Still acting and reacting within the framework of their own traditions, they began to take more and more time to decide each issue. Their unstated intention, of course, was to stave off enforcement of judgments contrary to their own traditions. Writing in 1915, for example, one of Horne's colonial officers dutifully logged that five hundred cases had been considered by the Njuri of Tigania and the highest elders' council of Igembe. In contrast, the Njuri of Imenti, more deeply Westernized due to contact with district headquarters, had begun passively to extend the entire process. As a clear forewarning of the trend to come, it had begun to let each case "drag out over months," simply by endless debate over each decision.[15]

By 1916, however, the highest elders' council in every region had reached the point of attempting administrative suicide. That year was particularly hard for Meru District, as the full impact of World War I began to be felt by everyone in the region. Hundreds upon hundreds of native men had been drafted into the Carrier Corps, to work as porters for the British Expeditionary Force in Tanzania. Their return triggered epidemics of dysentery, which when combined with the failure of seasonal rains threw the entire district into turmoil. As a result the highest elders' council within each of the four major regions—Igoji, Imenti, Tigania, and Igembe—reacted to the crisis by suspending further sittings: "The Kiama[s] this year have requested that sessions be adjourned owing to the danger of spreading dysentery."[16]

By 1917, the final year of Horne's administration, the higher elders' councils of Igoji and Imenti had stopped functioning entirely, and the number of cases heard by the Njuri Nceke had dropped from over one hundred (in 1916) to forty-one. By 1919 administrative reports referred to all of these bodies in the past tense. By 1920 the system was described as "having been allowed to fall into disuse." In 1921 the ranking district officer admitted he knew nothing of them, their "having been closed down" before his tenure.[17] By that time even the term *Njuri* had passed out of administrative use, and the dissolution of what had always been a horse-and-rider partnership was complete.

DUPLICATION OF NJURI: THE NATIVE TRIBUNAL

During his final five years of rule Horne worked assiduously to develop a purely colonial judicial system that would eventually expand first to duplicate and then ultimately absorb Njuri judicial functions. In 1912, official proclamation of the area surrounding the war hut of M'Mwitaria as a gazetted trading center permitted Horne to rename his headquarters Meru Town. It also allowed him to establish a European-style judicial court, to try cases wholly within the areas of British jurisdiction according to English law.

Horne's original intention was to create a handpicked tribunal of local natives, who would be initially empowered to settle conflicts among his non-Meru African retainers. By mid-1912, no fewer than 63 men were under his command, including Gikuyu, Embu, Maasai, Swahili, and Somali. By 1913 the number had risen to 130, including Africans from areas as distant as Uganda and Nyasaland (today's Malawi), as well as 37 Asians, 4 non-English-speaking Catholic priests from Italy, and 2 Methodist missionaries from England.[18]

As a result the Local Native Tribunal (LNT) was created in 1913. Its members quickly expanded. The original members were Horne himself (or a designated European assistant district commissioner), his Gikuyu interpreter, and a leading man from each of the other non-Meru communities. It soon became evident, however, that many conflicts occurred between the "alien" Africans and the Meru themselves. Horne responded by "nominating" his most trustworthy Meru as permanent members. Initially these were drawn from those previously selected as chiefs, or the most Westernized and receptive among the blanket police. Subsequently each of the newly established missions nominated representatives of their own, initially drawing upon Christianized Gikuyu who had accompanied them to Meru, then upon the first of their local converts.

The tribunal's powers expanded along with its membership. Often conflicts within the district were so serious that they required resolution under British law. For the crime of murder, for example, Horne would have been psychologically unwilling to accept an Njuri decision to punish the killer by transferring livestock to the victim's clan. Yet that is what Meru tradition would have required. As a result the LNT quickly assumed a judicial monopoly over a specified list of crimes, forbidding both local Kiamas or their selected Njuri to consider them further.

Horne's list was initially brief, claiming exclusive jurisdiction over murder, assault, cattle theft, and rape. During his leave of absence (June 1912–June 1913), however, Acting District Commissioner Platts, a firm believer in the civilizing power of British justice, swiftly expanded the court's jurisdiction into areas Horne would certainly have considered the prerogatives of the indigenous Kiamas. From its original jurisdiction over non-Meru Africans, the list expanded swiftly to include almost every category of criminal law, even when all parties were Meru. Beyond that Platts included certain moral and supernatural categories, such as "illicit fornication," "casting spells," "public cursing," and "practicing witchcraft," which may have had few precedents in British law.[19]

In theory the elders' councils remained free to decide cases of "civil law" involving only Meru, as well as disputes arriving from native custom. In practice Platts fully intended to expand the designated list of tribunal powers until it finally absorbed those of the Njuri.

In its first year, however, the Local Native Tribunal operated on much the same principles as a radio wave. LNT power was strongest within the Boma, Horne's administrative headquarters. Beyond it, its power weakened in direct proportion to the distance from the log stockade. Within the township and among non-Meru its word was law. Among those peoples of Imenti living nearest the township, its voice was clearly heard. In more distant areas, however, the LNT was virtually unknown, and the weight of British justice was felt in sharply different form.

NCAAMA ZHA ANENE: CHIEFS AND CHIEFS' MEN

In more distant regions colonialism was most frequently experienced at the hands of chiefs and chiefs' men. As previously mentioned, most chiefs were senior warriors, selected more for their size than for their community status. Unable to conceive of collective leadership in the Meru fashion, Horne had initially followed European practices by choosing one "chief" for each ridgetop he crossed. Unfortunately, he was burdened from the onset by the sheer number of ridgetops within Meru. Having begun by using the ridgetop community (Mwiriga) as his basic administrative unit, he felt trapped by a need for consistency. Consequently he felt obliged to name a chief for each ridge that came under his control, a system that initially led to the creation of ninety-one chiefdoms, with dozens of others demanding chiefs of their own.

Horne initially resolved the problem by redesignating many of his appointees "headmen," subordinate to his preferred selections, who remained "chiefs." On paper the system thus became a tidy pyramid, with authority running smoothly up from headmen to chiefs to Horne himself. Unfortunately, the Meru nominees universally refused to accept their rankings with regard to one another. Before colonialism the men of neighboring ridgetops might have been allies or enemies according to their place within the *gichiaro* alliance system. Now they were considered as either coconspirators or political rivals in the struggle to find favor with the whites.

In consequence no colonial appointee felt secure. During the first years of British administration, for example, Horne was baffled by the refusal of both chiefs and headmen to venture willingly into selected localities that lay formally under their administrative control while displaying perfect willingness to enter others. Efforts to make a chief enforce (or even transmit) orders to "his" headmen were met by evasion, delay, or alternatively an intrusion-in-force in which the chief would attempt to compel obedience from every warrior at his command.

White administrators, unaware of the complexities—or even existence—of the *gichiaro* system of military alliances found this behavior incomprehensible, usually dismissing it as symptomatic of the native mind. From a Meru perspective, however, the dilemma was nothing more than the inevitable consequence of serving two cultures simultaneously.

Most Meru, of course, including many of Horne's initial appointees, found it impossible to keep faith with both sides. The British were uncompromising in their view that chiefs were to be servants of the colonial government. They were to be chosen solely for their ability to implement its wishes. Their power, therefore, was derived wholly from the British king, owing nothing either to those they served or to their Kiamas.

Obviously, those blanket chiefs who saw themselves as spokesmen for these Kiamas soon found their positions untenable and swiftly resigned. Nor did men of equal caliber rush forth to fill their places. Gradually, as realization grew as to what becoming "chief" would really mean, the posts grew harder to fill. The administration therefore was forced to fill the places of the earliest appointees with whomever they could get.

Both the original and subsequent appointees, however, found themselves categorically unable to carry out the white man's work without a body of assistants. Throughout Meru the Kiamas initially responded by suggesting that spokesmen be appointed to assist both chiefs and headmen in their tasks. The elders saw the appointment of such representatives as softening influences, able to work with either chief or headman, implementing British orders on the basis of their common ideals. This proved universally impossible. Whereas assistants often did speak for their Kiamas, the chiefs found themselves either unable to evade colonial commands or even in agreement with them.

Horne's earlier pattern of administrative selection was therefore systematically duplicated at lower levels. As the district commissioner had ignored both tradition and communal status in selecting his assistants, so did the chiefs in selecting theirs. Potential supporters who perceived themselves as spokesmen for local Kiamas refused to perform the white man's work. This left both chiefs and headmen without means to enforce their orders. Logically, they chose men on whom they could rely, often of the same marginal status as themselves. The administration referred vaguely to these subordinate appointees as tribal retainers. As they were unpaid, they were forgotten.

The Meru, however, did not forget them. They became known as Ncaama Zha Anene, the "servants of chiefs" or "chiefs' men."[20] They were also known as a blight on the Meru communal soul. Following the pattern established by Horne and his original blanket police, each chief established a "boma" or administrative compound of his own. Adjoining it, his Ncaama (servants, men) would establish a war hut of their own. Within it they lived out a shallow parody of their former warriorhood, singing, training, and endlessly feasting on cattle impounded by their chief for violation of colonial law.

The Ncaama system extended itself in two directions. The original number of appointees tended to expand until the formally selected chief felt able to compel obedience by force of numbers. These in turn tended to select subordinates of their own, who became Ncaama of the original Ncaama. Over time a number of informal ranks emerged among them, corresponding vaguely to the levels of the Kiama. The "arms" of a chief, or head retainers, traveled with their leader to villages within his jurisdiction, lending the authority of their numbers to his commands. The "eyes," or subretainers, served as spies, in search of information that might enhance a chief's position. The "tongues" or "stomach" Ncaama held no permanent position but simply followed any higher-ranking man who promised meat.

The Ncaama rapidly became the most effective ruling power in the land, far more to be feared than was a distant British district officer. By 1917 leading Ncaama in every region had begun to speak of themselves as "spokesmen" (Agambe) for their respective chiefs, designating their pseudowarrior barracks as the "war hut of spokesmen."

From that point they required little imagination to retitle themselves the "Kiama of spokesmen" (Kiama Kia Agambe) or "Kiama of chiefs' men" (Kiama Kia Ncaama), and thereby duplicate the functions of both traditional elders' councils and colonial chiefs.

Ncaama, remember, received no pay, and thus no sustenance other than what was acquired by extortion. In consequence, throughout Meru the meeting places of Ncaama became the scenes of "public trials." Within their war huts the self-designated councils of chiefs' men held daily court, in what they believed was solemn imitation of colonial authority. There they passed collective judgment on what they decreed were violations of the white man's law, demanding fines of livestock for their feasts, in blatant imitation of their chiefs.

The impact of the Ncaama system is perhaps best illustrated by the emergence of the Kauganyama, a group composed of the subordinates selected by Mbogore M'Mwendo of upper Mwimbi.[21] Like other blanket chiefs, Mbogore found he needed aid in enforcing white authority on those within his jurisdiction. Like others he chose men personally loyal to himself, using them to locate and impound the often hidden flocks and herds of tax evaders.

This band, however, also reflected the vigor of their chief. Beginning with warriors drawn solely from Mbogore's own village, it soon expanded in all directions, attracting bored and embittered warriors from every war hut in the area. Encouraged by its rising membership, the band began to search out goats and bulls to fuel its nightly feasts. Initially it did this only on Mbogore's command. Later it began to supplement his wishes with actions of its own.

The Kauganyama was also notable, moreover, for its mounting contempt of Meru traditions, once again perhaps in pale reflection of the Western leaning of its chief. Within weeks of its formation, it was no longer content with livestock. Instead, it became customary for its members to enter vacant compounds illegally, and help themselves to milk, vegetables, and whatever else could be consumed.

Before the conquest genuine warrior bands were permitted by tradition to do this—within limits—while en route to a raid. They were required, however, to arrange the part-empty food containers in such a fashion as to convey their silent thanks for the homestead's hospitality. Mbogore's band, however, perhaps in deliberate contempt for their former traditions, broke the vessels they had drained, leaving them scattered in a manner that left no doubt as to who had done the stealing.

Later this contempt grew both more public and pronounced. Having impounded bulls or goats, the entire band would break into a chant of triumph: "Nitwi Kaburanyama. Nitwi Thirikari. Nitwi Achunku!" (We are meat searchers. We are government. We are white!)[22] Others in the district, either unable or unwilling to share in the plunder, labeled them the Kiama Kya Kauganyama, the "council of meat chewers."

Over time, again in imitation of their chiefs, the activities of the Ncaama councils gradually extended from feasting to sex. In upper Mwimbi, for example, Mbogore soon discovered that his position as chief permitted him to compel those under his authority to labor in his fields. Because agricultural work was done by women, the chief began to require that large numbers of them work from dawn to dusk within his compound and on his land. Gradually he also began forcing them to spend the night, in order to resume work on the following day. Thereafter, the combined lures or roasting meat, millet beer, and the dancing drums led them invariably into the compound of the Kauganyama and the sexual practice of Nguiko.

The rise of Kauganyama reflects a trend that emerged at this time throughout Meru. After an initial period of indecision, chiefs, headmen, and their ever growing army of retainers became enthusiastic participants in the colonial system, urging each other on to greater levels of extortion. Ruling elders who protested were threatened with "trial by Ncaama," or collective denunciation, before British officials and subsequent imprisonment. Those who appealed for the chiefs to return to traditional values were dismissed, arrested, or ignored. Indeed, newly scornful of tradition, many chiefs and headmen abandoned it completely, believing that their future lay in both implementing and imitating the tactics of their conquerors.

Similarly, most Ncaama felt their fortunes lay entirely with the chiefs and imitated their practices in turn. As a result colonial justice began to operate throughout the region at three simultaneous levels. At the core Horne's tribunal based its decisions on a law that no one in Meru could fully understand. At the fringes chiefs and headmen dispensed justice in what they felt was similar fashion, transferring the livestock of those they found guilty into their private herds. Beneath them Ncaama practiced the smaller-scale extortion required for their endless feasts, drawing beer, goats, and women into their compounds while the dance drums tapped into the nights. For some, conquest meant rule by white men. For most it meant rule by retainers and their ever more rapacious chiefs.

RESPONSES TO CONQUEST: KIAMAS VERSUS CHIEFS

The position of the Meru chiefs must be examined from a second perspective. Many were young, having barely emerged from their warriorhood. Nothing in Meru tradition had prepared them to carry out orders based on concepts fully alien to their own or to act against the wishes of their elders. To be caught between two such different sets of expectations must have been psychologically devastating to all of them.

Most of the colonial appointees reacted to the stresses inherent in their position with a mixture of evasion, extortion, and alcoholism. European reports of the first decades overflow with comment on headmen evading duties, extorting livestock, or sinking into drunken stupors, without once remarking on the probable causes of such behavior. Perhaps the most striking example can be gained from the brief comments made by district officers on the conduct of Chief M'Minuki, promoted from war leader of tiny Daicho, between Tigania, Tharaka, and Imenti, to chief of the major Tiganian district of Muthara. The earliest reports describe him as clever and enthusiastic, later ones as sullen and evasive, and the last as hopelessly alcoholic.[23] To the British, however, alcoholism among chiefs was viewed as a consequence of advancing age. Thus men too drunk to carry out their duties were simply sacked and replaced with younger substitutes.

A minority of the colonial appointees, impressed with the reality of Western military power, became Westernizers themselves, seeking to impose British concepts on their people with the fervor of the recently converted. The most striking of these converts was the previously mentioned Mbogore M'Mwendo, chief of upper Mwimbi. A man of unusual mental flexibility, he saw the British conquest as a tool to enhance the power of his region by allying it with that of the whites.

This initial positive impression was reinforced by the genuine friendship he was able to establish with Orde-Browne, during the latter's period as district officer. Out of Mbogore's hearing, the Englishman always referred to him as an "insufferable and arrogant rascal." Nonetheless, he respected the newly appointed chief for the "efficiency and ruthlessness with which he hastened to carry out one's [Orde-Browne's] orders."[24]

Mbogore, however, was not content merely to implement directives. His goal was to transmit Western ways to those placed under his jurisdiction, or at least those that he felt might increase Mwimbi power—and his own—relative to other newly conquered peoples.

His selection of Western concepts, however, was still influenced by military considerations. As a young warrior in the late 1890s, he had waged a one-man verbal war against circumcision, arguing that it hampered women in their production of future Mwimbi warriors. At that time his efforts had been universally ignored. Now as a newly appointed blanket chief he was delighted to find his British superiors in full agreement with his views.

Thoroughly encouraged, and armed with the approval of every European in the district, he launched a new campaign to eliminate the custom completely. As a warrior he had used powers of oratory and impassioned argument. As a blanket chief he used powers of arrest, levying livestock "fines" of unprecedented size upon both the fathers of children who were circumcised and the elders who actually performed the operations.

Again with British approval, Mbogore then expanded his drive to include abortion. Before conquest it had been virtually unknown, out-of-wedlock pregnancies having been settled by livestock fines to the dishonored and arranged marriages for those directly concerned. The disruption of traditional sexual relationships, primarily by the non-Meru Africans, had produced an unprecedented number of unwanted pregnancies. With no possibility of resolving the paternity in traditional fashion, many women turned to abortion. In consequence a "class" of abortionists emerged within each region, able to induce expulsion of the fetus through use of local herbs.

Mbogore's "war" against abortionists was marked by the same pattern of arrest and extortion that had marked his anticircumcision efforts. Consequently, a stream of livestock—and an occasional enraged group of "prisoners"—flowed into both his compound and Orde-Browne's district headquarters. As both the circumcisers and the abortionists were inevitably of advanced age, the Englishman could do little but scold them, reaffirm the fines, and send them on their way. Nonetheless, the rift between the former ruling elders and the blanket chief was soon too great to heal, a pattern occurring not only in Mwimbi but throughout the Meru-speaking regions.

In Mwimbi, however, Mbogore's third campaign struck directly at one of the major prerogatives of elderhood, the consumption of alcohol. The Meru, like most other African peoples, prided themselves on both the excellence of their alcohol and the rules regarding its consumption. Women in every region learned from childhood how to brew several varieties of millet beer as well as a potent honey wine. Actual consumption, however, was solely for male elders. Women were forbidden either brew, lest it lead them into immorality. Warriors abstained, lest even a moment of drunkenness dull their senses against enemy attack. Only elders, having passed beyond sexual temptation and securely defended by warrior sons, were permitted to indulge in the luxury of drunkenness as they believed—like many other peoples—in the power of drinking to "sharpen the edge of their words" in communal debates.

After the conquest, heavy drinking and public drunkenness spread swiftly among both warriors and women. Horne and Orde-Browne, understandably concerned, lectured all of their chiefs and headmen on the evils of alcohol. It is probable that both Europeans actually advocated a rather straightforward return to traditional custom, in which drunkenness would have remained a prerogative of age. It is certain, however, that Mbogore reacted to their teachings by declaring a total prohibition on both the making and consumption of alcohol in any form.

This was too much for the ruling elders. The ban symbolized the arrogance, ignorance, and high-handed disregard of tradition that they felt had characterized Mbogore from his first moment as a blanket chief. In early 1914 a large delegation of spokesmen for the Kiamas of Mwimbi appeared at Browne's headquarters to present their complaints. The presentation took hours and must have severely taxed the administrator's patience. It consisted of a highly detailed but frequently repetitive narration of Mbogore's every misdoing since the moment of his accession to power.

Unfortunately for their own cause, the elders' charges mixed violations against both British and Meru traditions, some of which must have been utterly incomprehensible to the district officer in charge. Thus a British administrator, listening carefully to the elders' recounting of incident after incident of livestock extortion, sexual oppression, or enforced labor, would suddenly find the narrative interrupted by complaints regarding the division of meat at feasts that had occurred more than ten years ago: ". . . and Mbogore took the hump of the cow for his own, which was not his way [prerogative] as a warrior but the way of an elder."[25]

Unsurprisingly, Orde-Browne found the elders unable to substantiate any of their charges, particularly when no other witnesses appeared to support their testimony against the colonial chief. The district commissioner felt it necessary, therefore, to "take a very severe attitude toward the elders," lecturing them publicly and at great length on the necessity of continuous and cheerful cooperation with their chief, and mentioning the possibility of imprisoning those who failed to do so.[26]

The pattern was the same in Horne's northern region. "Westernizing" chiefs had arisen in several sections of Imenti, extorting labor, sex, and livestock in the name of British law. Complaints by the exploited to their respective Kiamas proved ineffective. Council spokesmen took cases to the white man and found themselves unable to present them in terms the conquerors could comprehend. The accused chiefs, more familiar with British ways, spared no effort in denouncing their accusers, often bribing the interpreters to assist them in distorting what was said. Council elders soon learned, therefore, that complaints to Horne could lead to anything from scolding to imprisonment.

In desperation Kiama elders in at least two regions resorted to ancestral tradition. The most notable instance occurred in upper Mwimbi, where hostility to Mbogore reached unprecedented heights. In early 1914, shamed and embittered by Orde-Browne's public chastisement, the Kiama of upper Mwimbi resolved to subject Mbogore to its communal curse. At the same time, and perhaps in ignorance of the elders' intentions, Mbogore decided to extend his own power still further by creating a new village settlement, to be under his direct control.

Having carefully gained administration approval for the move, Mbogore commanded two hundred families to cluster together on the hillside, holding his own administrative compound. As the move was in process, the elders struck. That night, five of the oldest men in upper Mwimbi, acting as an Njuri for their whole Kiama, circled Mbogore's compound the prescribed seven times, chanting a curse against him. The entire Kiama then met as a whole to ritually curse every person willing to make the move or follow Mbogore in any way.

From a Meru perspective their intent was clear. By their curse they had hoped to ostracize him. To remove it, he had to come to them to reconcile. Having done so, he would rejoin them in good standing, having changed his deviant ways. In short, they wished him only well.

According to his sons Mbogore remained unmoved by the demonstration, trusting fully in the protective power of the whites.[27] His followers were less certain. Within days almost every one of the newly settled families had returned to their previous homesites, and Mbogore's authority lay in ruins.

Outraged and shamed in his turn, Mbogore brought charges against the entire Kiama and particularly the five Njuri elders who had initiated the proceedings. These five, despite their advanced age, were accordingly tried for the practice of witchcraft and sentenced from three months to one year in prison.[28]

As a sop to the community, Mbogore was formally reprimanded, and his wages were withheld for three months. But the damage had been done. Imprisonment, unknown in Meru prior to the British conquest, held special terrors for the aged. For members of a communal people to be deprived of the familiar patterns of home, herd, comrades, and kin was to suffer loneliness akin to death. For the very old, imprisonment was death. Unable to adjust, they simply ceased to function. In despair at the fate of their leaders and in fear for themselves, the Kiama of upper Mwimbi subsided into fatalistic acquiescence. So did the elders' councils in other parts of Meru. Both their ancestral traditions and warrior sons had failed them. For the time, the chiefs and chiefs' men reigned supreme.

CHAPTER VIII

Missionary Traditions:
Spreading God

"No tribe in Kenya is more deeply steeped in witchcraft
than the Ameru. Witchcraft is their religion and the Wizard,
their high priest."[1]

Early Christian missionary
Meru, 1913

SETTING OUT: THE ERA OF DISCOVERY

The first Christian missionary body to enter Meru was that of the British United Methodist Mission, later known as the United Methodist Church. The Methodists brought fifty years of East African experience to the venture, having initially entered the area in 1862. In that year Charles New established a mission on Kenya's Swahili coast. From there Methodists within Kenya focused their attention toward people of the Tana River, particularly the Pokomo. Their hope was to use the Tana as "Christ's Highroad to the Mighty Galla Peoples," whom they believed waited one million strong to receive the word of God.[2]

They had little success. A combination of extreme aridity, desolate landscape, unresponsive tribespeople, and virulent malaria reduced the mission by the early 1890s to little more than a token outpost. By 1898, however, completion of the Kenya railway survey confirmed earlier descriptions carried back to the coast by white leaders of trade caravans. These spoke of wealthy, war-like, and cattle-rich tribes, living in a fertile highland region that offered lush vegetation, flowing water, and a climate much like that of England.

The stories were also of interest to members of the Roman Catholic church. The first Catholic missionary body to take interest in these newly discovered highlands was the Consolata Mission Society of Turin, Italy. The order, at that time composed wholly of Italians, was founded on January 1, 1900, one of a number of similar religious orders created on that day expressively to carry both Christian teachings and Western technology into areas selected for conversion.[3]

Like the Methodists, members of this order had originally directed their attention toward penetration of the Galla regions, in this instance by proceeding south through Ethiopia. This project was blocked in late 1901, however, by the unexpected refusal of Ethiopia's emperor to allow new orders of Western missionaries into his kingdom. Instead the society turned its efforts toward the island of Zanzibar, responding to requests from the apostolic vicar of that island for Consolata to send him priests to support his work.[4]

The first four Consolata fathers reached Zanzibar in October 1902. They had expected to remain on the island. Instead they found themselves caught up in preparations for "the apostolic penetration of a wild, new country,"[5] the mountain region of what was then known to Europeans as Kikuyu (today's Gikuyu).[6] The idea appealed to the new arrivals, particularly Rev. Philipo Perlo, their senior member. At his insistence, the four priests entered the Gikuyu region in December 1903, having refused the military protection offered them by the colonial government, and established the first Consolata mission in January 1903.

The next few years were spent in learning how to evangelize. It proved simple to erect a mission station but far harder to convert a population wholly committed to its own traditions. The missionaries were also hampered by a then common European belief that Africans used "sounds" when speaking that could not be written out in European characters. Nonetheless, seven stations were constructed in the next six years. By 1909 the faith was sufficiently established for the region to be declared an apostolic vicarage, with Father Perlo as first vicar. In 1910 he received the rank of bishop and with it permission to seek out adjacent regions into which the order could expand.

Methodist leaders also avidly wished for expansion. One of the most outspoken was John B. Griffiths, a minister with many years' experience on the Kenya coast. A shy, intellectual Welshman, who had only learned English in his teens, Griffiths found himself inspired by the rapid conquest of Embu in 1906, followed by the bloodless surrender of Meru to E. B. Horne in 1907–1908.[7] On receiving the news, Griffiths first petitioned the colonial government to grant the entire Embu region to the Methodists as an exclusive religious sphere. The request was denied, initially because the government considered it unsafe. Griffiths then applied a second time, requesting that the comparatively "peaceful" Meru district be regarded as the exclusive sphere of the United Methodist church. In December 1909 the government agreed.[8]

SEEKING LAND: THE ERA OF EXPLORING

Griffiths lost no time in staking out his claim, receiving both funds and permission from the United Methodist Council of England. In 1909 he walked, with one European companion and twenty-four Gikuyu porters, around the entire eastern slope of Mount Kenya, traveling the 171 miles from Nairobi to Nyeri and on to Meru by footpaths that were often little more than traces in the bush.

Griffiths's party arrived at "Fort Meru" in October 1909, to be met by Horne. The district commissioner advised them against attempting to "penetrate deeper into the Meru country, which was still subject to the depredations and disturbances of young warrior bands," no doubt a reference to a band of former warriors with whom Horne had clashed as the year began. To ensure both social contact and military protection, Horne decided to allot the Methodists a plot of land less than two miles away from his administrative headquarters.

Griffiths's subsequent report of this expedition electrified Methodist leaders back in London. Describing Meru as a land of "hills, valleys, and innumerable streams," he found it "unlike any other area in Africa":

> Its hills are covered with ferns, hedges are thick with blackberry bushes, and in the streams watercress abounds . . . [and] mosquitoes are unknown. . . . We have been toiling for fifty years in the sweltering climate of the coast, contending with tremendous difficulties, bitter disappointments and deaths. We have been for years meditating upon seeking another and better country in which our men can live and labor and reap. SIR, HERE IT IS. THE FUTURE OF OUR EAST AFRICAN MISSION LIES HERE. I implore the committee to enter it.[9]

By 1910, London members of the United Methodist church had responded to Griffiths's glowing report with the decision to extend their mission into Meru. Efforts began immediately to recruit a missionary, carpenter, and doctor to launch the project. The carpenter's position ("industrial missionary") was granted, in 1911, to Rev. Frank Mimmack. In January 1912 he and Griffiths left England to occupy the allotted site and begin construction of the first buildings.

To search for a minister and doctor took longer, Griffiths having declined both positions in favor of returning to the Kenya coast. Eventually, the posts were combined and awarded to Rev. Reginald T. Worthington. Worthington had entered the Methodist ministry in 1910. After a period in the Home Service he began to look abroad and was overjoyed at the prospect of pioneering in a virgin field. As a minister, however, he lacked medical training; thus he delayed his departure several months to acquire a basic knowledge of medicine.

Worthington sailed for Kenya in December 1912, joining Griffiths at Mombasa. Thereafter the two traveled up-country, tracking around Mount Kenya's eastern flank, where they were joined by three Gikuyu youths, Maina, Kamau, and Wanjoe (to the missionaries, "George"), who offered to serve as translators among the Meru. The group then made the final trek across Mount Kenya's northern slope to North Imenti, where Mimmack eagerly awaited their arrival.[10]

Horne also greeted the new arrivals with pleasure. In anticipation of their coming he had supervised every detail of Griffiths's earlier negotiations for land. Arriving in March 1912, Griffiths had initially been dismayed to learn that government policy restricted him to a single five-acre plot. Horne, although bound to enforce the restriction, determined to place the Methodists on the most favorable site possible. Characteristically, he accompanied Griffiths to the area he had chosen, then proclaimed a *baraza* (public meeting) to discover who had the right to sell.

The land in question was owned collectively by elders of the Murathankari clan. Horne's demand placed them in a dilemma. On one hand they wished to see no further whites invade their homesteads. On the other they feared the consequences of a refusal. They resolved the problem by offering the single tract of land shunned by them all, the "spirit forest" (sacred grove) of Ka-Aga, today known as Kaaga.

Ka-Aga was indeed a spirit forest, known to the Meru as the "small place of curse removers [Aga]" and to Horne as the witch doctors' forest. Spirit forests existed everywhere in Meru, "sacred" in that they were reserved for the ancestors. Every clan had such a forest. Depending on the altitude, it consisted of a particularly dense tract of vegetation, woodland, or rainforest surrounding a gigantic wild fig tree. The tree was the most sacred point within the grove and home to the spirits that lived around it.

No living Meru dared enter a spirit forest. No one could hunt there, chase straying livestock, or even cut wood. To be caught and cursed by the spirits in such areas meant experiencing personal terror, subsequent physical illness, and communal ostracism, and requiring the services of a curse remover. In theory, therefore, the forests were never entered. In fact they were visited at night by Kiamas of the various Meru supernaturalists. Ka-Aga, for example, was used by the "Council of Aga," the curse removers, whom the British mislabeled as "witch doctors." Their songs, heard faintly through the darkness, were believed by the Meru to be sung by the spirits themselves.

This forest tract, always shunned by the men of Murathankari, was now offered to the Methodists in hope that the ancestral spirits would wreak traditional revenge. Horne, aware of the grove's reputation, initially objected. To his surprise, Griffiths accepted at once, declaring a forest of wizards and witches to be the most fitting spot possible to sow the seed of God.

The Roman Catholics had also grown interested in Meru. Bishop Perlo's imagination had also been kindled by the story of Horne's bloodless conquest. It seemed logical, as Horne's administration took root, to extend the influence of the Consolata into this untouched region, particularly because it was so near his own. Perlo's conviction was strengthened by the promise of future financial support. This appeared in the form of permission to engage in direct commercial activity to support the faith financially, actions previously forbidden by the Holy See.

Earlier funding for the mission's work in Kenya had come almost entirely from Canon Joseph Alamano, founder of the order. Now Perlo responded to his new commercial freedom by purchasing two sizable tracts of prime coffee land in the more distant regions of Gikuyu and arranging future purchase of a three-thousand-acre estate adjacent to the mission itself. Because Gikuyu labor was available in unlimited quantities and at minimal cost, the anticipated profits could be directed toward long-range financial support of apostolic expansion.

Thus in August 1910, Perlo sent Fathers J. Berlagnia and T. Gays to explore the Meru region. Like Griffiths one year earlier, they trekked across Mount Kenya's arid northern face, to enter what Gays later described as "a little earthly paradise . . . rich with forests and streams, . . . fertile with regular rains, . . . and holding about 40,000 primitive and courageous warriors."[11]

Like Griffiths the two priests proceeded initially to Fort Meru, intending to establish their station adjacent to Horne's administrative headquarters. On arrival they were crestfallen to learn of the earlier Methodist claim to the tract near Horne's log cabin. Colonial regulations, passed only months earlier, stipulated that each mission order be segregated from competitors, with Catholics and Protestants remaining at least ten miles apart and as far beyond that as geography would allow.[12]

If measured at its base, Imenti was ten miles wide. Thus Griffiths's earlier Methodist claim blocked off the entire region to the Consolata. Nor did Horne show sympathy for the Italians' plight. As an

Englishman and member of the Anglican church, he had little use for either Catholics or Italians, especially those unable to speak English. Speaking to the two priests through Gikuyu interpreters, he tried first to impress them with the "savage" nature of the district and its people in the hope they would simply leave. When that failed, he suggested they extend their search south of Meru proper into the adjacent Mwimbi region.

After returning briefly to the Consolata mission in Nyeri to consult with Bishop Perlo, Father Gays again set out for Meru in 1911, this time accompanied by Father Giovanni Toselli. Following Horne's advice, the pair passed through Imenti and Igoji to lower Mwimbi. Finding no site there that met their needs, they returned to Fort Meru. There they petitioned Horne to allow construction of a single mission station in the region of Kiija, a flat, marshy plain that bordered lower Imenti and Tharaka.

Kiija was precisely ten miles from district headquarters and thus just outside both Imenti and the Methodist religious zone. Privately Horne objected, preferring that his personal colony be restricted to the British. Officially, the priests had clearly complied with government policy. Horne therefore permitted them to occupy not only the requested site at Kiija but also a second, still undetermined plot of land to be located somewhat farther south.

Gays and Toselli then returned to Nyeri, where Toselli was immediately charged with organizing a third expedition. In December 1911 he led three other missionaries and a file of forty porters into Meru once again. He was accompanied by Fathers Luigi Olivero, Giovanni Balbo, and Giuseppi Aimo-Boot. The priests reached Horne's headquarters after a four-day trek. After resting, they decided to move south, searching out the second site that Horne had promised within the relatively unknown regions of Igoji or Mwimbi.

Initially, they selected a tract of land at Thigaa, today a part of lower Mwimbi, which they described in subsequent reports as "wild and very low from a morality point of view."[13] On further reflection they abandoned it completely, dividing into two parties to continue the search.

Aimo-Boot and Toselli traveled north and east (uphill) into Igoji, eventually settling on a site high on the mountain, on the banks of the Mutonga River and near today's Igoji Town. Thereafter they returned to ask Horne for permission to buy the tract from its original owner. Agreeing, Horne accompanied the two priests back to Igoji. On arrival he inquired of the person he had appointed blanket chief as to who owned the land. Four men stepped forward. The group spokesman, M'Riria, listened patiently while Horne explained the Consolata offer, then flatly refused it. The other three supported his decision.

M'Riria's curt refusal fell clearly within Meru tradition. Land transfers were not settled within moments but emerged through long-drawn and complex negotiations. Ideally, adequate compensation would have had to be offered, not only to the plot's actual owners but also to each of their tenants who had previously negotiated cultivation or grazing rights. Deciding who might be eligible would take time.

Every Meru present at the scene instantly understood M'Riria's position as a bargaining ploy, the prelude to a long and satisfying period of negotiation. Voices from both sides rose, as Horne's police began to argue with the Igoji clansmen over how many goats they would in fact accept from the new whites, who clearly could afford so many. Horne, however, had little patience with Meru commercial traditions and none at all with the time they consumed. Unexpectedly, he cut short the rising babble of voices by striking M'Riria to the ground. Stunned and thoroughly frightened, the four landholders agreed immediately to the sale on the priests' original terms.[14]

The other two members of the party were initially more fortunate. Fathers Balbo and Olivero had been selected to occupy the lowland site of Kiija. By prearrangement they were met at the location by R. A. B. Butler, Horne's newly assigned assistant district commissioner. Butler had no difficulty in convincing members of the Kiija Kiama to grant two pieces of land ("one for hut and one for garden") to the two priests in exchange for a specified number of goats. The real reason for their acceptance, however, lay in the elders' desire to acquire "white men of their own" to protect them from what they perceived as the rising power of Imenti clans higher up the mountain, increasingly arrogant because of their "possession" of Horne.

TAKING ROOT

With land secured, Catholics and Methodists alike faced the task of recruiting labor in numbers sufficient for construction of church buildings. The Methodists achieved this by compulsion. Horne, strongly supportive of their effort, made them a government grant of unlimited logs from the Imenti forest. He then distributed a number of half-rupee pieces, provided by Griffiths, to each of his personal police, charging them to round up the needed labor.

The bands of warriors who subsequently appeared were ambivalent but not wholly unwilling. By this time (1913) most had been made increasingly aware of the hut tax, to be paid either in money or the forced sale of livestock. Thus while openly angry at being forced to do what they considered as the work of women, many were privately pleased at the chance to earn rupees for taxes by doing what seemed like easy work.

The "easy work" began by cutting trees that often ran to four feet in diameter, then dragging them by hand to wherever the whites wished. Many of the new employees, however, had already worked for Europeans, some having traveled to the Gikuyu region of Nanyuki. These "Nanyuki Nthaka" (Nanyuki warriors), as they called themselves, had become sufficiently familiar with European construction methods to work efficiently. Under Mimmack's direction and advised by Horne, they constructed the region's second Canadian-style log cabin. Initially, it was to serve as home for both Mimmack and Worthington, after Griffiths's departure for the coast, and thereafter form the basis for a larger dwelling devoted entirely to God.

The Catholic priests at Kiija and Igoji had no expectations of assistance from Horne. The Igoji fathers, in particular, faced the problem of recruiting labor from among a population mistrustful of their presence. Both groups resolved the problem by simply appealing to local warriors to come and work for them "as warriors." By 1911–1912, of course, the warriors of Kiija and Igoji had been both demobilized and demoralized by the shock of conquest. Many looked with open envy on those "more fortunate" war bands of Imenti, who had found work and thus a new sense of purpose as bodyguards and blanket police for Horne. On reflection several in each region decided they could achieve similar status by seeking the same type of work with these whites who had settled near them.

Thus the first employees to appear at both missions, therefore, sought work only as guards and watchmen, returning to their warrior traditions by "protecting" the whites. At night they stood silent watch around each mission campsite. During the day they formed squads of armed guardsmen, following each priest wherever he went. Their request to serve as soldiers fitted easily into the fathers' tradition of militant Christianity. As warriors appeared in search of work, they were renamed the Nthaka ya Kristo, or "warriors (soldiers) of Christ."

The warriors refused, however, to construct lodgings, explaining to both sets of priests that such work was for women. Unlike the Methodists the fathers heeded them and set aside their European prejudices as to what constituted the appropriate sexual division of labor. As a result their initial request, which took the form of a "plea for trees," brought scores of singing women to their camps, each dragging three- to six-inch-thick tree trunks, which they then bound into the framework of as many traditional huts as the priests required. Each hut was then covered with banana leaves (Igoji) or papyrus (Kiija), woven in the latter case by groups of women into rainproof mats. Gradually these first church buildings took their somewhat untraditional form, and the first Holy Mass in Meru was celebrated on Christmas Eve in 1911.[15]

The choice of Kiija, however, soon proved a strategic disaster, because of its impact on the health of both priests. Set amidst a marshy plain at the mountain's base, the site was subject to several ecological extremes. Throughout the dry seasons it baked beneath a searing sun. During the rains it virtually dissolved into the rising waters of the marsh. Each evening brought mosquitoes in clouds too great to bear, and with them, of course, came malaria.

By early 1912 both Balbo and Olivero had become seriously concerned. Their rising fears were fully shared by Bishop Perlo, after an inspection of the Kiija setting in February of that year. The bishop's initial request for a new site, higher up the mountain, however, brought no response from Horne, other than a reminder that such a move would bring the priests too near to the emerging Methodist mission at Meru Town.

By October 1912, however, the appearance of heavy rains drove the two Kiija fathers to desperation. Their desire to move "uphill," away from the marshlands, was given further impetus, moreover, by Horne's decision, in October 1912, to begin construction of the regionwide roadbed (the Horne Road) that would eventually link Fort Meru with Fort Embu to its south.

The Methodists, unwittingly, had placed their mission along the very edge of the projected road. The Catholics felt that simple justice should allow them the same privilege. Thus, in November 1912, Father Balbo petitioned Horne once more, asking to move "directly uphill" from his present site, to the "edge of the road now in construction," thereby escaping the "perils of marsh malaria, heat, and flooding."[16] At the same time, Balbo argued that by placing themselves roughly equidistant between Forts Meru and Embu they could both remain under British Military protection and distant from the emerging Methodist church.

Once again Horne opposed the move but found himself overruled by colonial authorities in Nairobi. The new agreement thus allowed the Consolata to establish one new site "not more than one uphill walking hour" from the old one as far as possible from the Methodists in North Imenti. After a brisk uphill walk by Balbo the mission was resited on what only a few years earlier had been a warriors' dancing field, near the modern community of Gitie Mujua, in South Imenti. In keeping with the change, it was renamed Mujua (now Mujwa) Mission.

The actual transfer from Kiija to Mujua occurred in January 1913. During the same month, colonial authorities in Nairobi gave permission to extend Catholic religious activities into the regions farther north. To comply with the ten-mile rule of separation, the Consolata fathers were required to skip over Imenti and its Methodists but were allowed to establish stations in both Tigania and Igembe. The idea was deeply attractive, because it would provide a virtual religious monopoly over the Nyambeni Mountains.

Expansion was slower than expected. In 1913 two Catholic stations were established, one in Tigania (Athuana Mission) and a second in Igembe (Amun'Gente Mission). Each was manned by the now traditional pair of Consolata priests. Ten years passed, however, before additional stations were constructed in either northern region or before the Methodists sought to challenge the Consolata's monopoly by building a mission in Igembe. Meanwhile, local elders in both Tigania and Igembe proved eager to accept "new" whites, hoping to increase their power with respect to clans in Imenti. The same could not be said, however, for local willingness to accept the Christian message.

SOWING SEED

The search for converts began as soon as the first buildings were completed. Methodist and Catholic missionaries alike faced the problem of spreading God's word among peoples thoroughly content with their own religious system. For the Methodists the problem was intensified by their own preconceptions of African beliefs. For example, an early report back to England commented: "No tribe in Kenya is more deeply steeped in witchcraft than the Ameru. Witchcraft is their religion and the Wizard, their high priest."[17] The mission's directors in London, supported by the Kenya Mission Council in Nairobi, responded by asking Worthington to "engage in constant study of the evils particular to this [Meru] country, so as to devise ways to combat them."[18]

Considering both his lack of African experience and the religious bias characteristic of the era in which he worked, Worthington's study of the Meru religious system was relatively impartial. The Meru, he decided, did believe in a supreme being, whom they called either Murungu or Ngai. They perceived Him, however, as either indifferent or hostile to people's fate. It was Ngai, they told him, who sent famine by withholding rain. A run of good fortune, in contrast, simply meant He had turned His attention elsewhere.

For want of such attention, Worthington decided the Meru had turned to the worship of innumerable alleged spirits. Some were spirits of the bush, woodland, or forest that surrounded every hut. Others were the shades of ancestors, returning from the dead. Such spirits also alternated between hostility and indifference, never displaying love. Daily life, therefore, was lived in constant fear, briefly alleviated only by continued efforts to placate one or more of the spirits through the continual sacrifice of livestock.

Worthington's first act against these forces came unintentionally, through his party's need to cut daily loads of firewood for warmth and cooking. Without thinking, he ordered Wanjoe, the Gikuyu translator who also served as cook, to cut firewood from the forest groves that encircled his cabin. Having learned from neighboring Meru that the entire site was sacred to ancestral spirits, Wanjoe refused.

Worthington's response was to cut the wood himself, having decided that their belief in spirits was what cut the Meru off from God. The action stunned Imenti observers, as did Worthington's subsequent excellent health. Unable to explain why the spirits spared him, local elders decided they must have fled before his ax. That flight became part of Meru oral tradition. Those elders who once lived near Ka-Aga still claim they heard the spirits sing their final song: "Twathama, twathama. Tweta Rinyuri. Mugumo, mugumo. Jutigwe, ntiu." (We [the spirits] move, we move. We go to Rinyuri [a place]. The sacred fig tree, the sacred fig tree. It will be axed, when we are gone.)[19] Because the location of Rinyuri is unknown in Meru, the spirits were never seen again.

Having established the sanctity of his mission station, Worthington then attempted to venture out into the surrounding villages. Unable to speak Ki-Meru, he was accompanied by one of his Gikuyu interpreters, usually Maina. His method was simply to walk, greeting people as they passed in twos and threes by asking Maina to impart that "this day was God's day, and would they come to hear a message?"[20]

Without exception small crowds gathered at a designated point. Many came out of fascination with Worthington's "red" skin and the pleasure of hearing him talk using sounds they never had heard. Others enjoyed his attempts at song, participating cheerfully in simple chants, which they later learned were prayers. Only the elders interrupted his preaching, often to question one of his statements, but also occasionally to approve. Notwithstanding, Worthington himself grew swiftly disenchanted with what he saw as the "extensive method" of sowing God's seed. In establishing a new mission, he later wrote: "[a single, isolated missionary] must either sow widely, preaching to every village in reach, while trusting other hands to reap the harvest, or he must turn to the intensive method, gathering a chosen few around him, [then] surrounding them with a Christian atmosphere."[21]

Conditions within Meru, he decided, dictated the intensive approach. Too often the crowds he assembled failed to stay, drawn away by their work. In dry seasons the heat proved stupefying to both the missionary and his audience. In wet seasons the rains proved too heavy to permit extensive foot travel.

Over time, therefore, Worthington placed more and more emphasis on drawing people into his home. In theory men of his age-set (family heads/apprentice elders) and older would have responded with pleasure to such invitations, had he been willing to greet them, as tradition required, with servings of millet beer. Unfortunately, because Methodist tradition of that era abjured beer, Worthington refused to even bring it near his "house of God." He thereby placed himself outside the traditions of Meru hospitality. Affronted, few apprentice elders ever came.

The same, however, could not be said for children, particularly youths between eleven and fifteen. These were known as the Ndinguri, or "elder boys." Before the conquest, every moment of their time would have been spent in their Kiama Kia Ndinguri (council of eldest boyhood), training ceaselessly for their approaching time as warriors. By 1913, however, such training was pointless. Idled by forces they could not understand, many began to consider approaching the white strangers to seek either diversion or work.

Worthington responded swiftly. The first Ndinguri to approach his compound were rewarded with stories, salt, bits of sugar, and strips of cloth. Because at this age boys often went naked, the cloth was particularly prized as a symbol of their approaching adulthood. The salt and sugar also proved attractive, and many of the boys became regular visitors as they grew increasingly addicted to the "honey powder" with which the missionaries proved so generous. However, the stories often proved the strongest lure of all. As Worthington's mastery of the language improved, he became an artful storyteller, able to hold an entire circle of boys spellbound with his tales of the boyhood of Jesus.

In the long run, however, the greatest attraction—to boys of every age—was the pleasure of learning to read. Several of the Ndinguri who would subsequently form the first generation of Methodist converts were fascinated by the promise inherent in a printed page. The most notable among these was Filipo M'Inoti, later to become Meru's first author, Methodist minister, and regional chief.[22]

M'Inoti was the fifth of ten children. His father had died when he was five. His mother lived in relative poverty, near Ka-Aga. M'Inoti originally came to the mission seeking work. At age fifteen he was at the end of boyhood and deeply restless. His older brothers, all warriors, had refused to approach the white man, scorning the work he offered as women's labor. Worthington was struck immediately by M'Inoti's intelligence. When offered the chance to learn reading, M'Inoti in turn was initially stunned with the ease in which written words could be learned and understood. Thrilled by the chance to acquire a wholly new skill, he came daily and was soon far ahead of every other budding reader.

His example inspired several others of his age-set to join him. Together they resolved to follow both Meru and Methodist tradition, by forming a "Kiama of learners" (Kiama Kia Mabuku, or "council of 'bookers' "), which would live in a war hut, as warriors, next to the white man's church. There they would learn to be both men of war and men of books. Worthington, retranslating this concept into British form, was delighted to assist in the construction of what he perceived as a boy's dormitory, which in daytime could function as a school. By late 1913 the structure housed eleven youths who met as schoolboys during the day and as "almost warriors" at night. To Worthington it appeared that his intensive method of conversion had achieved considerable success.

In contrast the Consolata fathers in Igoji, South Imenti, and (later) Tigania and Igembe relied entirely on what Worthington would have called extensive methods, or "walking everywhere within the wilderness to spread the word of God."[23] Initially this "word" was spoken only in Gikuyu, the only local language the four pioneer fathers knew. For translators the priests initially drew upon the services of ten-year-old boys from the Gikuyu Catholic orphanage at Nyeri. These had all

learned some Italian and quickly proved able to bridge the gap between
their own and the Meru dialects. Inadvertently they also served as cultural interpreters, teaching the priests the courtesies associated with the
Meru language as they learned it.

The priests' first approach, therefore, was to visit the surrounding
homesteads and present gifts ("We began Christ's word by giving
greetings and tobacco").[24] The Kiija and Mujwa fathers offered native
snuff. The Igoji fathers gathered salt, then placed it in their saddle
bags and rode on horseback through the Meru homesteads dispensing
lumps as gifts.

These acts fell squarely, if inadvertently, within Meru traditions of
hospitality. Custom, within every Meru region, required that strangers
present gifts to the heads of each homestead they visited and accept
other gifts in return. The exchange was intended to generate feelings of
empathy that would transform host and visitor into friends.

The priests behaved precisely as tradition required, visiting favored
homesteads on a regular basis, each time with gifts of snuff or salt. In
response the elders asked their wives to brew huge gourds of beer on
days the strangers were expected. The priests shared the beer and then
asked their hosts to visit them in turn at their home on "God's day"
(Sunday). They hired the women who lived nearest to the mission to
brew fresh supplies of millet beer. Thus each Sunday found the mission
filled with visitors, all drinking happily from the Consolata's supply of
beer. The days were then spent in exchange of song and story, which
gave the priests unending opportunity to speak of God.

The visits were extended, zone by zone, into concentric circles
spreading outward from each mission. On occasion they took on somber tones, allowing priests to expand beyond their initial role as guests.
For example, the priests entered homes where occupants lay ill or dying. They responded according to their religious tradition, dispensing
such medicine as they carried while refusing to accept payment, even
when recovery was complete.

These refusals, however, clashed sharply with Meru tradition, trig-
gering suspicion among patients and relatives alike. In Meru those who
gave the gift of medicine without accepting gifts in return were believed
to be Arogi, or cursers. Father Balbo, in particular, was adamant in his
refusal to accept what he perceived as payment. Consequently several of
the elders he was treating denounced him as a curser and refused all
further medicine. To the consternation of the local community, they
soon died, but others who had accepted Balbo's treatments lived on and

grew well. His reputation restored, Balbo continued to practice, after modifying his approach once again to conform with Meru custom.

The Consolata fathers were sometimes faced with those their medicine could not save. Again following Western tradition, they administered both the rites of baptism and extreme unction. When questioned as to what they were doing, the priests replied they were cleaning the spirit, to prepare it for God. Their answer pleased the Meru. The rites of "cleansing" (i.e., curse removal) formed the very core of Meru religious belief and those of baptism and extreme unction allowed the Catholics to believe they were reclaiming souls. The first 155 of these "secret baptisms" were duly recorded in the early mission logbooks as evidence of the Meru's spiritual awakening, long before the first living candidates appeared.[25]

Many Meru displayed a lively interest in the new ideas, along with a total disinclination to accept them. Women proved too deeply wedded to their own traditions, with no room left for intellectual inquiry. The same could not be said for Meru men. The first to truly listen to the Consolata message were the ill and dying, "who would come every Sunday for [the fathers'] medicines and instruction, simply for the comfort that it gave them."[26] The next to reconsider were often half-castes: men of mixed tribal ancestry whose mothers had been seized in war. As boys they had noted that their mothers worshiped other spirits. As warriors many had visited their mothers' kin, learning of other ways. As elders, however, many were cattle poor, barred from social prominence by their heritage. These men were thus often least loyal to Meru traditions and most willing to examine the Catholic way.

The missions also proved attractive, on occasion, to "political" outcasts, cattle-rich elders who had incurred the greed or anger of Horne's blanket chiefs or more often their retainers. In such instances the elder might be seized and brought before the chief or the retainer's Kiama for a trial intended to drain off at least a portion of his flocks and herds. Having been judged guilty, he would be told to bring the animals in. Instead he sought refuge for them in the mission, where at the very least the priests would guarantee an accurate count.

The experience of Meru's third Catholic mission, founded at Athuana, Tigania, in August 1913, provides an interesting example of this trend. The mission, established by the now experienced Father Aimo-Boot, had been placed in the administrative chiefdom of Muthara, a district that had been given to the famous old warrior M'Minuki (Dominuki). M'Minuki, remember, had begun his career in the late

1880s as a war leader for the tiny border clan of Daicho. Caught between far larger forces in both Tigania and Imenti, he sought allies to survive, systematically befriending every Western caravan leader who crossed his land.

M'Minuki displayed an unusual ability to adapt to change. During the 1890s he passed from warriorhood and became a family head, intent solely on expanding his lands, flocks, and herds. He achieved this by becoming a "broker," selling ivory, which he had acquired from A-Athi and Ogiek hunters from Tigania to Mwimbi, to passing caravans. By the early 1900s he had become a ruling elder, cattle rich and the acknowledged spokesman for the Daicho clans. For him Horne's conquest meant an end to war and thus guaranteed safety for his growing herds.

On completing his subordination of the Tigania region, Horne acknowledged M'Minuki's position by appointing him blanket chief, not just of Daicho but of the entire Muthara District, a location that contained almost all of his traditional enemies. Trapped by circumstance, M'Minuki responded by seeking even greater numbers of livestock to bolster his own sense of security. He was thus deeply pleased, initially, to acquire a "missionary of his own," to counter both the resentment of his Tiganian enemies and the power of the Imenti at Fort Meru, who claimed to "own" both the Methodists and Horne. As a result he expansively invited Father Aimo-Boot, now joined by a second priest, Father A. Russo, to place their mission adjacent to his "chief's camp" in the heart of Muthara District.

Having done so, however, the priests refused emphatically to join in with M'Minuki's plan to drain the herds of his subjects by imposing constant livestock fines for alleged violations of colonial law. Worse, M'Minuki's most vocal opponents, elders fearful of losing their animals, began to look to the mission for refuge. Thus a predictable pattern of events emerged. A wealthy elder would speak out against the chief or his retainers. He would be seized, tried, and fined. Desperate, the victim would drive every animal to the mission, then refuse to return for fear of the chief's retribution. The priests, too often aware that the trials were unjust, felt bound in turn by their own traditions, which allowed the Catholic church to serve as sanctuary for the oppressed, to allow the outcasts to stay.

The missions also offered shelter to former warriors. The first warriors to work within the missions, of course, served as watchmen and guards. During this same period, however, all men of warrior age were conscripted to work on the roads. By 1913, military traditions had crumbled so much that the blanket chiefs began to practice conscription in their turn, seizing entire war bands to cultivate their private farms. The idea spread, in turn, into the ranks of each chief's troop of retainers, who began to imitate their supervisors, extorting labor on a smaller scale from men of an age-set now increasingly perceived as "idle" and "unemployed." Exceptions could be made, however, for warriors who worked for Europeans. Horne's private guards, for instance, were formally freed from conscription, and the Catholic mission warriors soon followed their example. As a result missions became increasingly attractive as possible havens for warriors particularly oppressed by demands for what amounted to indefinite involuntary servitude. On occasion those who angered either chiefs or chiefs' men sought security where they could and often found it in the church.

On occasion, a warrior might also join the mission because of his admiration for its details. Often these were not the central teachings of the faith; however, concepts peripheral to the Italians were often central to Meru thought. One early convert in Igoji, for example, explained his draw to the church thus:

> When I was a boy, a child died in my village. The body was eaten by hyenas. I swore an oath that hyenas would never eat me. Later a white man appeared, who said he carried word from God that no one should ever again be eaten by hyenas when they die. Instead they were to be placed safely in the ground. So I looked at what was happening in the world and decided to listen to what the white men would say.[27]

The Catholic missions' major successes, however, like those of the Methodists, were with children. This was especially true with youths falling within the eleven-to-fifteen-year-old age range (Ndinguri). Traditions governing this final stage of boyhood included learning wisdom from one's elders. This applied particularly to wisdom taught by strangers, because in former years they might have learned something of the regions where they might some day wage war. Thus as one source stated: "So it was the children who came. They approached out of curiosity, and took our medicine for the pleasure of spitting out the taste, and for the good it did them. They listened to our stories of Jesus as a boy like themselves, and generally took pleasure in our company."[28]

Inevitably, the focus of both the Methodist and Catholic missions shifted to the children. Having won their attention, both churches directed the second stage of their labors to providing schools. The

Catholics began constructing a considerable number of traditional beehive-shaped "school huts," initially within the villages they visited but subsequently also on the mission grounds. Like the Methodists, the priests lured the first generation of students into these huts with promises of sugar and cloth. The first schoolteachers, however, were often Gikuyu youths, still in their teens. Usually, each teacher lasted less than a month, remaining only until he had exhausted either the situation's novelty or his store of knowledge. Thereafter, to the pupils' intense amusement, their teacher would "escape to Kikuyuland."[29] The school would close, and the pupils returned to herding goats. In time, however, the priests provided new Gikuyu, and classes began again.

THE COSTS OF CONVERSION

In Meru both the Methodist and the Catholic forms of Christianity proved attractive only to a few. Despite persistent missionary efforts the number actually willing to accept the Christian faith proved astonishingly small. European estimates of the Meru population during the early colonial years ranged from 80,000 to 200,000. During their first seven years the four Catholic missions recorded only twenty-eight baptisms between them (twelve in Igoji, eight in Imenti, and eight more in the north).[30] Methodist efforts were no more effective, with six conversions in 1913 and only twenty-six by 1920.[31] These are small numbers for so many years of unremitting effort.

Neither faith, however, had underestimated the social, cultural, and psychological costs of conversion. "The supreme act of surrendering . . . to Jesus," a missionary wrote in 1919, "is an act of separation from the African's own people. He is called to give up so much which he has regarded as . . . African, . . . tribal dances, . . . customs, . . . traditions. The danger is that he must cease to be African . . . to become Christian."[32] These costs grew progressively greater as potential converts aged. The Catholic missions relied partially on the collection of abandoned infants to swell their ranks, reacting to Meru tradition that sanctioned the abandonment of certain types of newborn babies. Twins, the deformed, and those born feet first were believed cursed and were thus abandoned to the hyenas. The Catholics, aware of the tradition from their experience in "Kikuyuland," sought to collect and thereby save those babies. Thus over time a Catholic orphanage appeared at Mujwa Mission that provided a small but slowly increasing number of future converts.

Entry into the Christian faith was also easy during childhood. Children entering the mission, usually in search of schooling, found themselves subjected to the "European cleansing rites" of soap and water, as hair and bodies were scrubbed and goatskin clothes replaced by squares of cloth that could be kept clean by washing. Beyond the required rites of cleansing, however, little change was required. Like Meru children everywhere, they were required to do little more than sit, listen, and learn wisdom from their elders. Beyond that their decisions on whether to accept their "elders' wisdom" were essentially religious, touching few of the secular traditions that governed their childhood lives.

Upon entering the stage of elder boyhood, however, it became increasingly difficult to be both Christian and Meru. As each boy moved through adolescence, warriorhood, courtship, and marriage, he found himself gradually engulfed by a rising tide of religious prohibitions, intended to isolate him not only from his "pagan" age-mates but also from the life of the entire tribe. Boys choosing to join either religious faith during elder boyhood, for example, faced two immediate decisions, intended to separate them instantly from members of their age-set. The first was to shave off their warrior braid, the mark of an emerging warrior.

Younger boys wore their hair short. Only Ndinguri were allowed to let it grow into what would become a foot-long warrior braid. The braid could be further elongated by attaching it to a fifteen-inch-long wooden rod, after which the entire creation was decorated with strips of hide and wooden beads. The hair braid and rod were dyed bright red, using the ocher clay found in ponds along the mountain's base. The result was a unique, distinctive hairstyle for which all growing boys yearned, knowing it would distinguish them as warriors and men.

On entering the Catholic mission, men had their magnificent war braids shaved away. The red ocher used to enhance the beauty of women and warrior alike was scrubbed from hair and body. Beads, skins, and every form of ornament were cast aside. "We knew too much of symbols," a priest recalled. "We had to make them see that in accepting Christ they left all other things behind."[33]

The Methodists, in contrast, relied on peer pressure. Young men who joined the church soon realized that both the missionaries and the Gikuyu converts who became their teachers disapproved of warrior regalia, particularly the war braid. Thereafter, as their own perspectives changed, they followed "Christian fashion" by imitating Worthington's close-cropped hair. In so doing, however, they both distinguished and separated themselves from those of their age-mates who retained traditional ways, a separation that inevitably stimulated hostility.

This separation was further enhanced by Christian pressure on the elder boys to "close up their ears." Traditionally, entry into elder boyhood was marked by widening the earlobes. This was done by piercing them, inserting wooden plugs into the holes, then replacing each plug with wider versions until the earlobes reached a desired size. Both Catholics and Methodists abhorred the practice, declaring that any mutilation was against God's will. The priests required, therefore, that the earlobes be sewn up on entry into the church. The Methodists again relied on peer pressure, designating Paulo M'Ituke, an early convert trained in mission carpentry, to "stitch the ears of anyone who asked."[34] In time, "small ears," like short hair, became a Christian fashion, to be displayed with pride. At the same time it served to further differentiate and thereby isolate the Ndinguri converts from their age-mates.

This isolation intensified as elder boys approached the time of preparing for their entry into warriorhood. Tradition required them to form themselves into "councils of elder boyhood" (Kiama Kia Ndinguri), then mount challenges against the bands of true warriors in their community. Initially these contests took the form of taunting songs, which grew in insult and ferocity until the warriors were provoked to respond.

Tradition also encouraged warriors to strike back at their tormentors, imposing thankless tasks upon them as a group, then beating any boy evading the labor with the flat of their swords. Each task was sanctified by tradition. The most onerous and humiliating was the brewing of millet beer, a process involving hours of monotonous labor. It was traditionally done by women. Thus by requiring it of elder boys, warriors could both anger them and cast doubt upon their manhood.

Any warrior could demand this task of any Ndinguri. The victim would then gather age-mates to assist him in the brewing. Forbidden by custom even to taste it, Ndinguri would deliver the completed brew to warriors in their war hut. Tradition also forbade warriors to drink, however, lest they be drunk when enemies attacked. The beer, therefore, was carried onward and delivered finally to their fathers, who alone as ruling elders were allowed the luxury of drunkenness.

Unfortunately, neither the Catholic nor Protestant missionaries understood the social complexities of Meru beer drinking. Both faiths, however, refused to allow those elder boys who converted to brew beer, reasoning, not illogically, that they meant to drink it. Nor were the boys' declared intentions to "pass the beer on to the warriors" accepted by either ministers or priests, since both faiths opposed intoxication within that age-set as well. In consequence elder boys who joined a Christian mission found themselves isolated from the entire spectrum of obligations that normally would have led to their emergence into warriorhood.

This isolation intensified further as each boy reached his time of circumcision. Meru tradition exalted both male and female circumcision as the single most important event in life, signifying the abandonment of childhood and the acquisition of adult status. That abandonment was symbolized by slicing away a piece of the flesh itself: among women, the clitoris and labia minora; among men, the penile foreskin. Custom permitted no one to show pain during the cutting, because successfully bearing the "bite of the knife" marked full entry into wife- or warriorhood. The operation was universal. To avoid it would have meant acceptance of a child's status for the remainder of one's life. To call any adult an "uncircumcised child" was a deadly insult. Thus the operation was an experience for which every child in Meru yearned.

Nevertheless, both Catholic and Protestant missionaries objected violently to the operation as a direct violation of God's will. To their surprise even the most devoted among their disciples refused to abandon it. Early attempts by Catholics to preach against it resulted in a total—if temporary—withdrawal of every member of their congregations and systematic ostracism in the surrounding villages. On reflection they decided as early as 1910 to regard the operation itself as outside the sphere of religion and to concentrate their preaching against those elements of the surrounding celebrations—the drinking and dancing and so forth—that lent a "pagan atmosphere" to the entire rite.

The Methodists followed a similar, if somewhat stronger, line. Also unable to stop the actual operation, they too turned their attention against the rituals accompanying it, which they perceived as "little more than an orgy of indescribable practices affording opportunity for the unlimited exercise of gratuitous cruelty" (a reference to the cutting itself).[35] Their first solution was to Christianize the operation, allowing the actual cutting to take place within the mission but replacing the music, dancing, and "pagan" elements with Christian prayer.

Unfortunately, that decision clashed with a Meru tradition that required all newly circumcised boys to remain for one to three months in the formal isolation of a specially constructed recovery or healing hut while their wounds slowly healed. The time spent in the huts was specifically intended as a period of further trial, a final stage in their transition from boyhood to warrior status.

In theory their isolation was total. In practice it was violated continually by older warriors, allegedly intending to instruct them in the ways of their own warriorhood. In fact much instruction was in the form of beatings, as warriors took their final revenge upon the boys who would someday replace them. The beatings were intended, however, to remind the novice warriors that they were now men. Upon leaving the healing huts, they would be expected to put aside all childish ways, join their new age-mates in the war hut—and be warriors.

During this healing period, therefore, Worthington's most devoted converts would recant, abandoning their Christian training as "a thing of boyhood" in favor of a return to the ways of the tribe. The missionary's initial attempt to Christianize the operation failed when the first boys scheduled to pass through the Christian version slipped away to undergo the rite in customary fashion.

Worthington therefore shifted strategies, allowing converts the traditional operation but compelling a return to the mission immediately thereafter. In December 1916 he enforced this decision by sending a group of converts to forcibly seize two of their number on completion of their operation. Embittered protests by the two boys' fathers were ignored by the district commissioner. In June 1919 he repeated the action, seizing a larger number of converts at the moment their operation was complete.

This time, however, Worthington's action was vigorously opposed by A. E. Chamier, newly appointed to the district administration and a vocal champion of native rights. Chamier, coincidentally meeting the converts as they returned to the mission, ordered the seizures to stop. Worthington, furious at what he perceived as an attempt to dismantle his years of labor, appealed to Chamier's superiors at both the provincial and colony levels. Surprisingly, administrators at both levels supported the Methodists, contending that only through insulating their converts from the lure of pagan rituals could their educative efforts succeed in weaning them from "paganism and savagedom to a higher form of life."[36] Thus the process by which potential converts were drawn away from interaction with their age-mates was gradually intensified. But to accept it meant increasing isolation from every facet of communal life.

During the warrior years this isolation assumed sexual dimensions. Before the conquest, males entered warriorhood soon after puberty, most often between ages thirteen to sixteen. They then spent the next twelve to sixteen years at war, in an unending cycle of livestock raiding intended to allow them to acquire the livestock they would need as bridewealth. By their late twenties most men realized their warrior years were ending, and shifted their energies from cattle raids to courtship.

After the conquest, of course, cattle raiding was banned. Deprived of warfare, older warriors who had collected livestock focused on the only activity that remained. In Meru, however, the initial stage of courtship was based on mastering the intricacies of extemporaneous song and traditional dance. As in the West, both men and women used their bodies as instruments of sexual attraction. Meru tradition sanctified male nakedness, under circumstances that were both controlled and free. All dances were public and lit by blazing fires. Elders of both sexes were present. Younger men and women sang and danced only within their own age-sets. Sexual attraction was equated not only with physical grace but also with the ability to create extemporaneous songs that drew appreciative laughter from the crowds. Finally, after the dancing ended, brothers escorted their sisters home.

Unfortunately, both Methodist and Catholic missionaries were unaware of these restrictions. In consequence all Christian converts were forbidden to join, or even watch, the traditional songs and dances with which the process of courting began. Methodists and Catholics alike objected to any form of public male nudity, even if participants wore goatskin cloaks. They opposed the songmaking because the verses often elicited audience response through sexual innuendo. They associated drumming with "savagery and darkness"—the time when dances did in fact take place—and thus with their own ideas of evil. The Methodists, in addition, objected to the elders using these communal occasions to drink beer.

Faced with unrelenting mission opposition, males who had reached the age of warriorhood often initially reacted by sneaking off to dance at night, expecting to return to their studies by dawn. It proved impossible. The converts' shaven hair, lack of weapons, and Western ways all worked to turn their age-mates against them, sending them fleeing from a barrage of taunting songs in anger and humiliation. On occasion, converts who attempted to rejoin their age-mates' courting rituals were met by a hail of curses and rocks, intended to remind them that "Meru women were reserved for Meru men."[37]

Thus deprived of normal forms of courtship, converts saw no way to marry. In the first years neither Catholics nor Methodists had proved able to attract women into their congregations, and over time the problem of providing mates became crucial to the survival of the missions themselves. "In the ordinary courses of nature," Worthington wrote during these early years, "our young male Christians will want to marry. Those upon whom their choice will fall are heathen, and as such forbidden to them by the rules of the Church and the express injunction of St. Paul."[38]

The solution, of course, was to extend the web of religious isolation to as many women as there were converts. Although Christian tradition declared that no convert could wed a pagan, Meru tradition held that no woman could oppose the wishes of her prospective husband. Presumably that custom also applied to his choice of her religion.

The problem, therefore, lay in convincing the fathers of these prospective brides to permit their daughters to marry Christians. The solution, according to the prospective bridegrooms, lay in their being able to offer substantial numbers of livestock to the girls' fathers, to serve as bride-wealth in the minds of all concerned. On reflection missionaries of both faiths threw themselves enthusiastically into the proceedings, arranging for the needed livestock. Thereafter, they assumed the role traditionally assigned to each potential bridegroom's father, negotiating the customary types of livestock to be paid to the fathers of each prospective bride and participating cheerfully in the communal meat feasts intended unite the bride's and bridegroom's kin.

The women were given no voice in the decision. "We women went to the mission," one of the earliest female converts declared, "not because we liked it, but because our [future] husbands demanded it. . . . Once a girl was betrothed . . . she had to want what her husband wanted. If she refused the soap [the Christian cleansing rites], she would be beaten [by her new husband] and sent back to her father in disgrace."[39] As a result those adolescent girls who married the first generation of male converts entered the Christian faith as a matter of course, sharing both the religious conviction and social isolation of their age-mates from that point onward in their lives.

CHAPTER IX

Anti-Christian Traditions:
The War Against Converts

"When they first came, we feared them so strongly that
we used to flee into the forest and crouch in hiding as they
passed. Later they ceased to be a terror to people, and
became truly lovable friends."[1]

Daudi M'Raria
Early convert, Church of Scotland Mission
Mwimbi

GIKUYU CONVERTS

The first African converts to appear in Meru regions were Gikuyu, often barely of warrior age. Having been baptized in their own region,
they were sent on to Meru to preach the new religion until white missionaries arrived. For Gikuyu to proselytize in Meru regions in the first
years after British conquest must have required an unusual combination of religious zeal and private courage. It was a time, remember,
when the Meru considered the Gikuyu their mortal enemies. Nor were
they overawed by blacks who dressed and spoke like whites, dismissing
them as Kamuchunku, or "little whites." In that era a Gikuyu in Meru
had reason to be fearful.

The first European missionary order to rely entirely on Gikuyu converts within Meru was the Church of Scotland Presbyterian Mission
(CSM), subsequently known as the Presbyterian Church of East Africa.
The CSM first entered Kenya in 1891, initially settling at Kibwezi, an
isolated plateau one hundred miles inland from the coast. At that time
the plateau was barely inhabited, and the few Kamba tribespeople with
whom the early missionaries came in contact took no interest in the
Christian message.

The CSM was delighted, therefore, at the chance to acquire land in
the cooler, healthier, and more densely populated Gikuyu highlands.
The extension of the railway into those areas, however, triggered a frantic competition for new sites among the missionary orders. In 1902 the

British Church Missionary Society and the Church of Scotland Mission effectively divided the entire highlands, with the British acquiring the western side as its exclusive sphere and the Scots receiving the eastern. Both areas were far too vast for either order to occupy effectively. Notwithstanding, in 1903 the CSM established an initial mission station among the southern Gikuyu (Kikuyu Mission), and in 1908 a second, among the northern Gikuyu (Tumutumu Mission).

By 1912–1913 the British Church Missionary Society had become uncomfortably aware of the sheer magnitude of the region it had claimed, which comprised thousands of square miles and tens of thousands of people. In a burst of generosity it transferred "two sections of the Kikuyu tribes," known as Chuka (now Cuka) and Mwimbi, to the Church of Scotland Mission, asking only that they be occupied immediately by missionaries. The challenge was accepted within weeks. In October 1913, Rev. John W. Arthur, an evangelical and medical missionary from Glasgow, and head of the Church of Scotland mission at Tumutumu, left his Gikuyu region to inspect Cuka-Mwimbi and select a mission station site.[2]

Accompanied by W. O. Tait, the mission carpenter at Tumutumu, Arthur trekked around Mount Kenya's southern slope, entering Cuka-Mwimbi from the Embu region. On arrival he noted the "first sign of British civilization," the systematic destruction of the great forest barricade that had protected the Cuka from their enemies. The entire structure had been ordered cut down by Orde-Browne in one of his first acts as assistant district commissioner to remind every African that peace was now maintained by England.

Orde-Browne had also established a thriving government station along the Naka River, in the heart of Cuka. By 1913, Fort Naka, as it was called, consisted of a "stone house, log-cabin office, neat compound of twenty clean huts for native soldiers, a couple of broad roads, and an Indian shop."[3] Orde-Browne proved exceptionally knowledgeable about both the Cuka and Mwimbi peoples, whom he estimated at fifteen thousand and twenty-five thousand, respectively. He then provided Arthur with detailed routes and an expert guide. Over the next few days Arthur visited the villages of Kabandango, Kiambati, Gaitungi, and Mbogore M'Mwendo, whom he described as "paramount chiefs," of Cuka and lower, central, and upper Mwimbi, respectively.[4] On reflection Arthur selected sites near each of the first three as points on which to launch his mission.

In October 1914 a second CSM expedition entered Cuka-Mwimbi, essentially following the same route as the first.[5] A tentative decision was made to construct the first station at "Gaitungi's," actually the village of Mwiria ya Mburia in lower Mwimbi. The individual selected to pioneer the effect was Rev. Stanley E. Jones, a medical missionary with several years' experience in Gikuyu. In their isolation, however, the CSM had failed to reckon with the impact of World War I, which had erupted in Europe in August 1914. Within months the conflict had reached East Africa, diverting the energies of every white in Kenya colony. As a result all missionary expansion stopped, as it proved impossible to send even one European to occupy the Cuka-Mwimbi area.

The CSM then shifted strategies, reasoning that a beginning, at least, could be made of carrying on the projected expansion with the aid of Gikuyu converts. At the very least the presence of a staff of "experienced native Christians" would be sufficient to meet government requirements that the missionaries occupy their promised lands.

In October 1915, therefore, a procession of six Gikuyu Christian converts marched bravely out of the Church of Scotland's southern mission, trekking northwest to Cuka-Mwimbi. They were led by Daudi Makumi, then perhaps eighteen years old. Before the conquest he would have been a very junior warrior. Now, his spear had been replaced by a Bible. He was accompanied by Samsoni Maingi, perhaps sixteen years old. Samsoni had been trained in Tumutumu as a medical dresser and was instructed to establish a "hospital" at the new site. Daudi was also accompanied by his wife, Priscilla, her sister, and two other recent converts.[6] Two "pagan" Gikuyu served as porters to them all, in sharp contrast to the thirty to three hundred that had accompanied their European predecessors.

The trek took seven days, and it is still remembered by those who took part in it as a time of dread. No member of the group was *gichiaro* (allied) to any Cuka-Mwimbi clan, and each one feared they would be seen as enemies. On arrival, however, they were directed to Mbogore M'Mwendo. The chief informed them that they were now "under his cloak" and thus could proceed to the preselected village of Gaitungi's (Mwiria ya Mburia) and build what they wished.

The "cloak of Mborgore," however, provided them with nothing but protection. They were given just enough land to build three huts. "Not a handful was given to let women hoe their men a garden."[7] Rather the "little whites" were expected to buy daily food from local Mwimbi, paying for every bite with the money that was assumed all "whites" would have in endless quantities.

The huts were built—for cash—by Mwimbi labor. In addition Samsoni set up an English tent as a medical dispensary. That done, Daudi set out to preach the word of God. Given the insecurity of his position, Daudi's tactics were quite practical. Rather than either wandering among the villages or trying to lure people into his huts, as had his English and Italian predecessors to the north, he began each day by walking purposefully to the hut of a chief.

On arrival he asked for "readers" and expected each chief to supply them. His best reception came from Mbogore. The chief, as decisive as Daudi, initially welcomed Christianity. Always convinced that European innovations would enhance Mwimbi power, he was quick to honor the convert's request. Mbogore's first response, therefore, was to provide a wooden table, sufficient children to sit around it, and the command that they remain until they all could read. His second reaction was to compel each headman within his Mwimbi region to do the same.

Other chiefs, whether impressed or cowed by Mbogore's decisions, fell hesitantly into line, providing chairs, children, and an occasional older listener. In addition Daudi himself made special efforts to preach among those who came to Samsoni's dispensary for medicine, believing that only the afflicted would consider appeals to a new god.

Daudi's cheerful persistence produced results. He preached only in Gikuyu, a language incomprehensible to the children who had composed his earlier audiences. The language was familiar, however, to those warriors who had worked for whites within Gikuyu–speaking regions. Often, hearing him speak the language, they would stop and listen to his preaching and then return to learn more.

Several of the Ndinguri (elder boys) were also fascinated. To them, Gikuyu was the language of adventure, the door to experiences beyond the tribe. Their goal was to imitate their older brothers, who now earned praise and glory by learning how to work for the whites. "Those who came, of course, were not so much attracted to the new faith as the new learning," but for Daudi it was sufficient that they stayed.[8] As a Gikuyu, non-European, and relatively young man, he made several adaptations in preaching strategies that might have shocked his dour Scottish sponsors. One change was a decision to restrict his preaching solely to men, perhaps through fear that Mwimbi males might misunderstand his efforts with their women. His message also changed. Assuming—

perhaps unconsciously—the legitimacy and reality of African religious traditions in a way a European of that era would have found impossible, he tried constantly to recast Christian concepts into terms his listeners would understand. As his wife subsequently recalled: " 'What is the difference,' my man [Daudi] would cry, 'between the blood of Ikristo [Christ] and the blood of *ndurume* [a ram]? As the blood of a dying [sacrificial] ram serves to remove Mugiro [curse, condition of impurity], so does the blood of this white son of God serve to remove sin.' "[9]

The converts also differed from Western missionaries in their willingness to assume traditional roles within the African community in addition to their labors as the messengers of Christ. Samsoni Maingi, for example, held no illusion about his ability to preach. A quiet man, he refused to march through the villages, preferring to remain near his hospital tent and treat anyone who appeared. Nor would he evangelize as he healed, believing that his work alone would spread the Christian message. Instead, it spread his reputation as a "wonder worker and quick healer," especially after he displayed his skill in minor surgery.[10] As a result he gradually took on the duties of a circumciser, performing the traditional operation with increasing confidence and thus acquiring a traditional role within the tribe.

Daudi also assumed a traditional role. On occasion he would pass Mwimbi elders meeting in Kiama to resolve a local conflict. More rarely, spokesmen from several localities would assemble to form a council-of-councils. At such times Daudi simply joined the assembly, squatting on the fringes of the gathering with others of his age-set. There he would remain, silently listening to what the elders had to say, as both Gikuyu and Mwimbi tradition required from Meru his age. Many elders found this behavior worthy of their praise, and several chiefs, among them Mbogore, commended him as one who had not yet forgotten that wisdom only comes from listening to elders.

Daudi and Samsoni left Mwimbi after two years, in October 1917, in obedience to CSM policy that required converts to move on regularly. After their departure the demands of war kept the CSM from naming their replacements, and the mission compound was thus unoccupied for two full years. In October 1919, however, Ismaili Wangu, a second CSM convert from Gikuyu, appeared in Mwimbi to take up the work.

Wangu served in upper Mwimbi from 1919 to 1921. He found that Daudi's work had fallen into ruins. The "Wasomaji [readers] had lost their skills, those who listened to Samsoni [preach] had returned to pagan rituals and even the huts had begun to collapse due to insects and rain."[11] Nor did the local warriors intend to welcome a new Gikuyu convert. When asked to rebuild the collapsing huts into a Western-style mission compound, they demanded so much money that Wangu felt bound to refuse.

Initially, Wangu was in despair. In November 1919 the rains poured so heavily through what remained of the mission rooftops that his wife and baby "had to live under an umbrella" to survive. For the next few weeks he cajoled and threatened, always to no avail. Finally, he returned to CSM's Gikuyu station in apparent surrender, only to reappear days later with a letter—written by Arthur—for the assistant district commissioner at Cuka. Wangu recalled later: "When I showed this letter to the [assistant] District Commissioner, he read it and looked at me angrily. Then he sent for M'Muga, the oxen-beater, a blanket-policeman known for beating people like oxen. At first I thought I should be beaten, but the District Commissioner told the oxen-beater he should be sleeping in my home [mission compound] until the roofs were secure."[12] Wangu then returned with the policeman to the mission compound: "On the next day I blew the trumpet—for I had no [church] bell. When the people came, I called out to the warriors, and told them, 'You asked me to give you posho [porridge, slang for money]? Your posho is this policeman.' "[13] The rebuilding of the mission compound proceeded without further incident.

Enforced completion of the buildings, however, did not ensure they would be filled. For weeks, when Wangu blew his trumpet, no one came. Nor did visits to surrounding villages at first produce results. Wangu soon learned, for example, "never to report in advance to which place [village] I was coming, since whenever I did so, I would arrive to find nobody there."[14] He found, however, that unannounced appearances transformed him, in local eyes, from alien to guest, and thereby one deserving of traditional courtesies. His welcome was also enhanced by descriptions of his intended work. Perhaps unconsciously, he emphasized that he had come to teach young men to read. Only incidentally did he mention a second aim, which was to teach all men the word of God.

Such statements did make Wangu friends. Over time a tiny group (ten to thirty people) began to respond to his trumpet calls, straggling to the mission for chanted prayers, a little sermon, and, for those who stayed, the chance to read. As in European missions to the Meru north, Wangu's listeners were mostly younger children with a sprinkling of elder boys.

Surprisingly, Wangu also drew several girls, a development that was less a reflection of their desire to become readers than of the unsettled times in which they lived. The years 1919–1921 brought drought and famine, when the harvest of sufficient grain meant life or death. In consequence chiefs throughout Mwimbi sought more girls than ever to labor in their farmlands, a practice also imitated by their personal retainers and one that increasingly required the girls' attendance overnight. Wangu responded by offering overnight shelter from such obligations to those few girls who came to him as readers. If the girls' fathers objected in their turn and seized his pupils, Wangu went after them by force.

The test of Wangu's power to protect his pupils came in 1921. A chief from lower Mwimbi, M'Kiambati, became incensed at what he perceived as the "flight" of several youngsters working on his farmland to the safety of the CSM in upper Mwimbi. With the support of several other chiefs he lodged charges against Wangu, accusing him of shielding youths of both sexes from government-required labor and advising them not to pay their hut tax. The charges were backed by Kithamba Kirume, a lower Mwimbi government servant. If proved, they were intended to provoke Wangu's dismissal and the closing of the CSM station.

Wangu, a man capable both of great anger and considerable eloquence, argues his case with skill, carefully presenting arguments phrased in a way he believed the district commissioner would understand. His opponent based his counterarguments on Meru tradition, citing precedents in Meru oral law that the district commissioner failed entirely to comprehend. Finally, the district commissioner settled the issue.

> He stood and asked each chief in turn, if they had children in [Wangu's] school. Each assured they did not. He then asked if men could join a cow-case [a case in which the ownership of a cow came into dispute] if they themselves owned no cow. Each answered they could not. If no man joins a cow-case without a cow, then no man joins a school case without a child in school.[15]

Chief M'Kiambati was fined the then staggering sum of sixty shillings and a goat. Thereafter no chief dared raise his voice against the mission.

Despite winning such battles, however, the converts never won their war. Over time both Daudi and Wangu became part of the colonial structure. Unwelcome among the population at large, they were able to operate only through protection of the chiefs, and ultimately the colonial administration. Politically, their initial acceptance came from feelings held not only by Mbogore but also several of his comrades that the Mwimbi were being left behind by other regions, notably Embu and Imenti, because of their high number of white officials. These Mwimbi were at least partially convinced that whites of their own were required to restore the balance. They were thus understandably distressed at the decision of both Catholic and Methodist missions to expand to the north rather than into their area. To counter this trend, they sought a mission of their own and were happy to accept Gikuyu converts as long as whites would eventually appear.

In religious terms, however, the impact of these Gikuyu converts was almost nonexistent. Too few responded to their message. Though several youths learned to sing and pray, and a few began to read, no one converted. Nor were even the most avid forced to change the rhythm of their lives in ways disruptive to the community. No one intimidated the few who came to read; no one cursed, ostracized, beat, taunted, or obstructed them in any way. The Mwimbi's basic reaction to the Gikuyu converts was one of apathy. Between 1915 and 1921 they proved almost wholly indifferent to both the new faith and the new knowledge that seemed so little relevant to their communal lives.

THE SCOTSMEN

The ministers at the Church of Scotland's Gikuyu missions were only too aware that their Gikuyu converts' failure at the Mwimbi station had been matched in Cuka, where a site had been developed at Chief Kabandango's camp, two miles from the protection of Fort Naka, Orde-Browne's district headquarters. It seemed ideally placed. Nonetheless, it was abandoned after only a few months, having drawn the attention of only a single Cuka boy.

By late 1919 the successful end of war in both East Africa and Europe drew government attention to the missions once again. By 1920 the CSM received official notice that its sphere in Cuka-Mwimbi had to be occupied by at least one European missionary within the next few months, or the area would be transferred to another mission. As an inducement the colonial government offered to donate all of the existing buildings that made up Fort Naka—including Orde-Browne's well-built stone house—to the CSM for use as a base, the government having decided to move its own Cuka operation to another site. The cost to the CSM was to be £800, at that time a relatively nominal sum.

Arthur responded to the government's offer with a plea to England for funds. None proved forthcoming. The Fort Naka purchase was abandoned, and consideration was also given to abandoning the entire Cuka-Mwimbi salient as well. At this point a financial sponsor appeared—from a quite unanticipated source—offering funds sufficient for a whole new start in Mwimbi.

The sponsor was Ernest Carr, a wealthy Nairobi contractor. At the war's end his daughter had married Dr. A. Clive Irvine, a medical missionary, who had joined the CSM at Tumutumu in July 1919.[16] Irvine had grown up in Liverpool, where his father had served as a Presbyterian minister. A young man of both intelligence and energy, he had obtained degrees in both the arts and medicine at the University of Aberdeen in Scotland.

In 1917 he joined the British armed forces as a medical officer and was posted to the former German East Africa (Tanganyika), where he served for the next two years with the ammunition column service of the Camel Corps. As a medical officer his work brought him into frequent contact with African porters (karia, or carriers), men drawn from among tribes in Kenya and Uganda.

Many of the karia were from Mount Kenya's highlands, and the two years gave Irvine a solid base in what then was known as "native medicine," as well as language fluency in both Swahili and Gikuyu. As the war ended, Irvine met Arthur, who described the work of the CSM within Gikuyu and invited him to join. Irvine accepted, taking temporary charge of medical work late in 1920 at Tumutumu Mission, where he married the daughter of Ernest Carr.

Carr's subsequent financial offer electrified the entire mission. In the winter of 1921 he offered to finance the entire Cuka-Mwimbi missionary effort by guaranteeing £1,000 per year over the first five years of the station's life. The sum granted for the first few months could be used to survey and select a suitable site. Funds thereafter would be allocated for construction of a house, hospital, school, industrial (carpenter's) workshop, and whatever other buildings might be required to operate in modern style. Electricity and running water were to be provided as required. In short it was to be a missionary's dream station, and thus the envy of its Methodist and Catholic competition. In return Irvine had only to agree to occupy the site for the entire period, take charge of its activities, and tour the United Kingdom as the five years ended to raise funds to continue the work.

Irvine and his wife were in England when Carr made his offer, having completed two years' work in Tumutumu and gone on leave. They accepted within hours and made immediate plans to return. Meanwhile Carr himself joined forces with Arthur to trek into the Cuka-Mwimbi region in January 1922 to select a site. Accompanied by both the provincial commissioner of Gikuyu and the district commissioner of Embu, they followed the same route Arthur had chosen during his pioneer venture into Cuka-Mwimbi in 1915.

The chiefs of Cuka and lower and upper Mwimbi were visited in turn. Kabandango's Cuka region was rejected out of hand, as was the lower Mwimbi chiefdom of M'Kiambati. Surprisingly, Arthur also decided to abandon the upper Mwimbi mission at Gaitangi's (Mwiria ya Mburia), where both Daudi Makumi and Ismaili Wangu had labored with such diligence the previous four years. Instead the group trekked uphill toward Mbogore's headquarters near the lower edge of the black forest.

Mbogore greeted them with enthusiasm, indicating a fertile site along the Maara River and thus adjacent to his administrative camp. The party was more impressed, however, with a second, lower site along the Kamaara (Little Maara) River, downhill from Mbogore's village and thus much closer to the geographic center of Mwimbi itself. The site, now known as Chogoria, was comparatively near the Horne Road (named for E. B. Horne) that connected Mwimbi both to Meru and Embu district headquarters. More important, it possessed a striking waterfall that could provide not only irrigation but also hydroelectricity and thus assure the mission's further growth.

The whites were jubilant. Mbogore was appalled. His own plan called for the mission's location to be in or near his camp, where he could supervise and thereby benefit from its activities. He argued forcefully with Arthur for the higher site, describing with some accuracy the relative poverty of soil in the lower area, as well as the presence of malevolent spirits in the nearby forest glades. Arthur, however, fully aware of Mbogore's intentions, firmly insisted on the Chogoria site.

Work completed, Arthur and Carr left Mwimbi to return to their respective posts. Before departure, however, they left Mbogore with extensive instructions. Within a few weeks tribal policemen were sent to round up laborers from every location in Mwimbi. These were put to work constructing simple bridges across that region's racing rivers in anticipation of the coming rains.[17]

A few days after the bridges' completion a massive caravan of seventy-four carts arrived in April 1922, each hauled painfully across the rising rivers by stumbling teams of oxen. Within the carts were materials sufficient to construct a modern house, hospital, school, sheds, and whatever else the Irvines might require: "It was indeed a missionary's dream station. There was none of the struggling along with inadequate buildings and equipment. . . . Everything was planned and provided beforehand, ready for the work to go ahead."[18]

The construction was completed by September 1922. On 12 October a single ox wagon arrived containing Dr. and Mrs. Irvine and a newborn son.[19] Irvine plunged into his work with exceptional enthusiasm; the very next morning tribal police were sent around to the local villages urging "anyone who sought shillings to come and work for the new white man." The response was enormous. A large proportion of the former warriors had worked for whites in more than one capacity, either as *karia* of ammunition or on the coffee farms emerging near Nairobi. Many who were warriors at that time recall their fear that the new white man would "seize them and put them in a school."[20] Nonetheless, by 1922 the need for money had become universal, and Irvine had his pick of eager workers.

A man of unflagging zeal, Irvine worked unceasingly to earn a welcome from his hosts. The people in his immediate area were poor. Many had been forced to flee from the drought, famines, diseases, and locusts that had ravaged the area. Others had been strong-armed into the Carrier Corps and had never returned. As a result land in much of the Chogoria region had reverted to bush, often simply for lack of men to clear it. The remaining population was therefore forced to struggle not only with poor soil but also constant depredation from bands of bush pigs, which raided the farm plots each night. Irvine earned the gratitude of many Mwimbi by waging war against the pigs with strychnine, poisoning them in sufficient numbers to reduce the problem.

The missionary also made full use of Western medical knowledge. Unlike Samsoni Maingi, who preferred to heal the sick in silence, Irvine interpreted his healing mission as a major portion of his work for Christ. He was particularly fortunate to have arrived in Mwimbi when several of its more visible diseases proved amenable to new discoveries in Western medicine. One of the more striking examples was yaws, a condition in which the legs and lower body are covered with open, gaping sores.

Irvine believed that almost half of the Mwimbi population showed symptoms of the disease. In 1917, French scientists had developed a medicine known as Galyl, based on arsenic. By 1920 the treatment was available in East Africa. Irvine had previously used it to treat yaws among the Gikuyu. Drawing from that experience, he brought to Mwimbi vast quantities of the compound, which he used with conspicuous success.

Irvine wasted no chance to demonstrate the relative effectiveness of his medicines in contrast with those of the "witch doctors." When possible, he competed directly with local ritualists, contests in which the latter did indeed come off second best. As a result many of the aged who had previously enjoyed both financial security and community standing as healers became increasingly subject to verbal taunts and even physical abuse from youths influenced by Irvine. This abuse was sometimes so intense that the healers were virtually sent fleeing from the very homesteads where they had once practiced their skills.

Irvine proved equally enthusiastic in his attacks on the concept of Mugiro, or the ritual curse. As a doctor he inquired often about what the Mwimbi themselves believed to be the causes of the various illnesses that beset them. As a missionary he was both amused and angered by their continued assertions that almost every form of illness was the direct result of a curse having been ritually placed upon the sufferer, either by an ancestral spirit or a living person with whom the afflicted individual was in conflict.

Irvine lost no opportunity to convince those youths with whom he came most frequently into contact that they no longer had to fear either curses or the ancestral spirits believed to have imposed them. His central argument was that faith in Christ was like a shield, protecting Christians from the curses cast against them as they advanced against their enemies. To dramatize his point, he bid them enter with him into the spirit forests (sacred groves) in which ancestral spirits were believed to live.

These forest groves had been considered sacred to spirits for generations. No living person was allowed within one, whether by intent or accident. Those who strayed incurred an automatic curse that could be removed only by intercession of the proper ritualists, who would require sacrifice of livestock to appease the spirits involved.

The spirit forest closest to Irvine's rising mission at Chogoria was called Muriru. In it was a pond, welling up between two huge rocks, which was believed to be the opening through which the ancestors entered the grove itself. Upon hearing of it, Irvine entered the forest and blocked off the pond with stones, thereby symbolically locking the spirits into the ground. He then invited the small number of youths who had accompanied him to gather that night's firewood from within the grove itself.

This pattern was repeated in at least two other sacred areas, the groves of Gikarangu and Iiga via Mukuri.[21] Irvine may also have visited others. In each case the destruction was essentially symbolic rather than physical. In each case people from the surrounding localities waited for the ancestors' retribution against those who had desecrated their homes.

Irvine, aware of their expectations, taught those accompanying him to shield themselves against the fear of either illness or calamity by using Western rites of prayer. "The spirits [fear] could be kept at bay, he reassured them, simply by calling out to Jesus as their shield, then believing He would guard them."[22] Each day that illness or calamity failed to strike, Irvine led them in mass prayers of thanksgiving, reassuring them that continued righteous conduct would cause Jesus to shield them throughout this life and beyond it, into heaven. On those occasions when someone did fall sick, Irvine usually effected a cure with Western medicines. As belief in the new faith took root, the converts themselves began to enter the sacred groves, deliberately felling the ancient trees and, with them, a tradition that had endured for generations.

It was not the new faith that drew people to Irvine, however, but the new learning. By the early 1920s many youths had become interested in acquiring an entire range of European skills. Informants now recall with amusement the intensity of their boyhood desires to "speak through their noses like White men" or "talk the same tongue as a book."[23] More realistically, they were also aware that mastery of reading might lead to jobs within the colonial economy that could earn enough not only to pay taxes but also to purchase European goods.

In striving to acquire this new knowledge, however, these youths were exposed to the new faith, which began to attract them as well. Irvine sought to meet both needs. Those who sought work during the construction of his mission were initially required to participate in twice-daily prayers, at dawn and dusk. The evening prayer sessions were then extended to include instruction. Irvine began with stories from those sections of the Bible that he felt might most appeal to youths and warriors. His sermons, woven around the biblical selections, were in Gikuyu, the language in which he was most fluent. Inadvertently, Irvine had chosen a language unknown to Meru women, which had the effect of restricting his audiences to young males. To his listeners, however, the language was "secret," in that it spoke of things that they felt were suitable only to men. Thus, the number of listeners grew.

Eventually, the telling of biblical tales was broadened, in turn, to include an introduction to reading. At this point evening sessions were no longer of use, and special messengers were sent out to nearby villages with a school proclamation inviting anyone who wished to come and learn. Few came, but enough for Irvine to decide school could begin.

The first school teacher was Daudi Makumi, recruited from the Kikuyu Mission to take up the work he had begun with such enthusiasm back in 1915. The first group of readers fluctuated between five and ten.[24] For every youth that came, however, there were many others who wished they dared. On one hand they too were fascinated by the Europeans' knowledge and the sudden opportunities it seemed to offer in a world beyond the walls of their homeland. On the other they feared the scorn, contempt, and ridicule that would be heaped upon them by their age-mates, kin, and indirectly, every member of the tribe. One informant recalled: "One needed to be bold enough—just not care about people insulting you. I myself would have gone to school if it were not for those people who were laughing at others. Almost everyone was laughing at the Wasomaji [readers], insulting them, calling them names, and singing songs against them. In fact, at first I was among those who sang the songs."[25]

PROTESTANTS AND CATHOLICS: OPPOSING THE FAITH

Not once did the ruling elders of any Meru region act in defense of their religious traditions. Not once did the highest Kiamas, whether in Cuka-Mwimbi, Imenti, or the north, speak out against the new religions, even when the sacred groves were desecrated and their ritualists abused. In theory the regional Kiama systems could have provided a relatively centralized base from which to mount a campaign against the first intruders, or at least an appeal to colonial authority. In fact the very existence of these systems immobilized the age-set that should have been the most involved.

Since all Kiamas were ruled by tradition, they resolved conflict by applying precedents from the ancestral past. For generations, men of the mainstream had responded to deviance by publicly ostracizing deviants. By refusing to share rituals with men of the fringe, a Kiama of ruling elders could deny them all status within mainstream society. This pattern of exclusion had begun with the hunters and ironsmiths, at the time of the Meru beginnings. It had extended, successfully, through the appearance of each deviant form of Kiama. Each had remained on society's fringe.

Now, perceiving the various missionaries and their few converts as nothing more than new forms of fringemen, elders applied tradition once more. By ignoring the new religions, they could deny them status in the same way as they had the old. Better, by relegating them to insignificant positions on the Meru social fringe, they would be following tradition. This decided, the ruling elders were content.

The family heads/apprentice elders felt less secure. It was not the destruction of sacred groves that generated apprehension but the construction of schools. Their very appearance interrupted patterns of normal existence in homesteads nearby. Custom did permit children to assemble, chant, and listen to stories, but only when they lacked work. In Meru that meant at sundown, after days spent tending the family flocks. European custom, however, restricted school to daylight hours, especially when students began reading. In addition once students had begun, they were expected to remain. Absences were not allowed, even for family chores.

Under such circumstances conflict between mission youths and their families was inevitable. The issue was not one of faith but of how they spent their time. For elder boys the schools could be irresistible alternatives to the monotony of daily chores, but the loss of their labor could cause great concern if families were threatened by famine. Absence from work also suggested deviant behavior, which if not corrected could shame every member of the youngster's clan.

In many instances, therefore, the mothers of the so-called mission boys reacted first to their sons' absences. Women in certain localities became so frightened that they spread increasingly fearful rumors. In Mwimbi, Imenti, and Igembe, for example, women who had watched medical personnel perform simple surgery decided the Christians were cannibals, who caused blood to flow in order to drink it.

More often, however, the mothers turned to tears, appearing at the Catholic or Protestant mission compounds to implore their sons to give up "madness" (deviance) and return to normal, traditional lives. This pleading became particularly intense when a mission boy fell sick.

One informant recalled: "When my mother heard I was sick, she came to stand at the window near my [hospital] bed, weeping and asking, . . . 'Child, how can you wait for death in a hut of sickness [the hospital] when you can come home to a Muga [curse remover] and be made well?' "[26]

Frequently, the women's tears triggered their husbands' anger. In both Catholic and Protestant regions family heads would silently appear before a mission school hut to lead their sons away. Shortly thereafter at least some of the Ndinguri would return. Angered, the family heads would appeal to their Kiama. In several instances the ruling elders responded by sending a contingent of warriors—now armed only with the power of tradition—to seize the errant youths. The warriors would appear before a school hut, their very presence an unspoken command that every boy be off to work. Overawed, the mission boys would flee. Thereafter the warriors stood guard, "protecting" the compound against the boys' return, until ordered off by a missionary's hasty appeal to the district commissioner.

The family heads became more hostile, however, when school attendance and the consequent loss of labor became permanent. Elder boys, in particular, had specific responsibilities toward their kin, age-mates, and the existing warrior age-set. To avoid these by flight into a school hut was perceived as a return to "smaller boyhood." With few exceptions, therefore, family heads reacted to the deviance of those sons approaching warriorhood with curses, kicks, and beatings. As one early convert recalled: "He [my father] cursed me as a Mwiji [small boy: a deep insult], shouting that he had many cows that I could tend instead of lying idle like a child and hearing endless tales."[27]

Other fathers proved even less gentle, publicly expelling a son from the homestead, declaring that he "had been spoilt for manhood and had become no longer worthy of receiving cows to help him marry."[28] Converts treated in this fashion lost all contact with both age-mates and kin. The loss, traumatic within any society, was terrifying to youths raised in a communal setting, and one that sent them swiftly into the Christian embrace.

Hostility also appeared among family heads who had become chiefs. Once again the issue was the converts' obligation to labor during the time they wished to spend in school. Angry at the emergence of a group seeking to avoid communal obligations, they saw the mission youths as threatening their power. In Mwimbi, for example, the conflict centered around Chief Mbogore. Initially receptive to a mission within his district, he developed a deep respect for Irvine. He was shocked, therefore, once Irvine had established himself, to learn that the missionary had requested that every boy within the mission be freed from work on Sundays.

As always Mbogore's actions were decisive. In late 1922 and several times thereafter he appeared personally at the Church of Scotland mission compound, "arrested" every student he could find, put them to work within his camp, and subsequently freed them only on their pledge never to disobey his orders. Each time, the students marched directly back to the mission, Irvine would protest to an official, and the status quo would be restored. The pattern was similar in other districts, as chiefs from Igoji to Igembe tried to preserve their right to make the converts work. Because they always failed, they grew more hostile to the rising Christian power.

WARRIORS VERSUS ELDER BOYS:
THE WAR AGAINST CONVERSION

The warriors, however, actually spearheaded resistance against the missions. Their antagonism was communal. It erupted only when it became clear that members of the set approaching military age might join the Christians rather than themselves. To them it was once again a question of tradition. Elder boys supplied the one remaining challenge of their warriorhood: training them to assume their future duties. To permit them to evade the tasks assigned them by tradition was a threat to warriorhood itself.

Initially no force was used against potential deviants. Rather, warriors throughout Meru chose to shame the mission schoolers with bursts of song. Imenti war bands, for example, taunted Methodist and Catholic insistence on shearing the magnificent red warrior braid: "Who is the hairless animal? Who is the fearful animal? It is the mission boy."[29] In Mwimbi potential converts were taunted with the striped-mouse song: "Your little heads are shaved [in stripes], making you seem [striped] just like the mouse. You mission warriors."[30] In Igoji: "Why do you shave your heads so that you look like mission fools? Why do you dance [in Western fashion] so that you look like mission fools?"[31]

Other songs derided mission boys as "termite eaters," referring to the insect eaten only by small boys. Still others referred to "egg eaters" and "bean eaters" (women) or "wild game eaters" (A-Athi hunters).

Another type of song was sung to girls, although intended for the ears of converts. It derided girls who looked at "mission warriors," warning that those who married them would spend their lives on their knees (i.e., in prayer).

Warriors also responded to the deviants by using no song at all, or by musical ostracism. As converts approached a village or simply passed a war band, all song would die, only to start up once more after they had passed. To many converts this was worse than taunting, and several now remember wondering if they would ever sing again.

Warriors also showed their antagonism through dance. In Igoji for example, the Mujwa Catholic mission had been founded on a warriors' dancing field. Although angered, the warriors of that area took no action until several years later, when one of their potential members decided to join the church. His loss, from their perspective, meant one less participant in their dances and one less homestead from which to gather the food that made each dance into a joyous feast. All too suddenly the warriors saw the future: if one was allowed to be lost to their ranks, others would follow.

Aware of the missionaries' distaste for male nakedness, the warriors gathered to perform what priests within the mission subsequently described as "dirty dances." In fact they carried out a last magnificent Authi, or dance of the battle vows. One by one the warriors bounded across the dancing field to within inches of the mission door. Naked except for the short goatskin cloaks across their shoulders, and holding fighting sticks as substitutes for the now forbidden spears, they shouted out their battle vows as if the whites had never come. In the past they would have sworn never to return to their homesteads unless with captured herds. Under colonialism they swore never to leave the dancing field until every comrade within the mission rejoined their ranks. Then, completing their ritual, they dispersed to their homes. There was nothing more to be done.[32]

Warriors might dance their disapproval of Christian converts more directly. For example, those of the Maua region in Igembe were both scandalized and angered by the appearance of Samsoni M'Mutiga, an Imenti convert to Methodism. From their perspective M'Mutiga was clearly of warrior age, thus entitled to join their ranks. Yet be behaved like an "uncircumcised boy." Rather than come to the war hut, as tradition demanded of age-mates, he went straight to the chief's camp, demanding "children to teach."[33] The warriors responded by proclaiming a night of Authi, inviting both M'Mutiga and the chief to share in the battle vows.

Upon his arrival the young convert was horrified to learn that the entire Authi was directed against him. Warrior after warrior, clad only in skin cloak, shield, and fighting stick, bounded across the dancing field directly at the beleaguered Christian. Standing inches away, each threatened him in turn, hurling insults, obscenities, and battle oaths instead of spears: "If I scratch my ribs [draw the sword that hangs by the ribs], oh man-of-the-coast [a Swahili, or non-Meru, i.e., an insult], you would no longer like me [i.e., you would die]."[34]

Each time a warrior raised his arm to strike, the chief ordered him back. Abandoning tradition, the warriors halted, then danced and converged on the chief, their cries shifting from symbolic insults to specific complaints: "Why does man-of-the-coast [M'Mutiga] shame our warriorhood by wearing women's [Western] clothes? Why does man-of-the-coast shame our warriorhood by speaking softly to children [to whom warriors only barked orders]? Why does man-of-the-coast shame our warriorhood by giving children sugar [to lure them to school]?"[35]

As M'Mutiga now recalls it, the ordeal seemed to last forever. From the perspective of tradition each charge was true. The chief, also of warrior age, admitted the justice of their cause but was helpless. In fact, caught between his own traditions and those of colonial Kenya, he could do nothing but assure M'Mutigi of his protection. Blocked by the power of both the colonial administration and the mission, the warriors could only dance out their rage.

Warrior bands in other regions, however, proved more adept at striking back at those who chose the mission over the war hut. As early as 1912, Imenti warriors near Ka-Aga had grown particularly enraged by the appearance of aggressive bands of converts within their villages, a pattern that was repeated in localities near every other mission station within the next decade.

Initially these youths appeared in timid groups of three to five, silently accompanying their priest or minister as he preached. As they gained courage, the converts would fan out around their leader, exhorting everyone they found to come and hear his message. Inevitably, as their numbers and courage grew, certain of the converts tried to "extend the work of God" by beating the traditional Meru ritualists and destroying the goatskin bags in which they stored their magic.

Now, we church boys often used to extend the work of God by beating the Aga [ritual healers] and Aragoli [diviners]. We would find them practicing their rituals, . . . and because we feared them we beat them with long sticks. Then we seized the [antelope horns in which they kept their magic] and threw them in the Kazita [Rivers], as Kangangi [E. B. Horne] himself had done.[36]

The missionaries strongly disavowed such actions, but a single incident of what was viewed as the converts' arrogance could enrage an entire community. Fear of the missionary inevitably kept the warriors from striking back directly, but many soon developed ways to revenge themselves upon the converts by playing tricks upon them as they preached and prayed. One favored trick was to wait until the converts knelt and closed their eyes in prayer. Knowing they would be forced to complete the entire prayer before rising, a single warrior would slip forward and slash their Western clothes.

Converts also learned they could no longer return to their villages for brief periods to take up traditional pursuits. One of the early Methodists, for example, soon realized that each time he returned to his village warriors were awaiting him. He was never harmed, but when he began to herd his family's goats, the warriors would run them off and scatter them in the bush. Eventually, to preserve the animals, he was forced to give up herding them.[37]

Warriors also sometimes forgot traditional restraints and attacked individual converts outright. In 1912, for example, a single warrior, drunk and angry, began to beat three of the Ka-Aga mission converts with the shaft of a spear, calling them "Biiji," or uncircumcised boys, always a deadly insult. The three instantly abandoned their Christian training and attacked him in turn, thereby also violating the Meru tradition that permitted warriors to beat elder boys at will.[38] The violation deeply angered the warrior's age-mates, who felt the honor of their age-set had been compromised. Thereafter, they waged covert war against converted elder boys.

Unfortunately, certain types of conflict between converts and warriors were not only unavoidable but repetitive. Meru tradition required both groups to play out certain roles against each other, as the younger boys approached their time of warriorhood. Christian tradition called for other roles. Caught between the two, neither warriors nor converts proved able to give way.

One illustration of the impasse occurred each Sunday morning in front of the Methodist mission. Before each service Worthington would send his little band of converts onto a path that ran before the church. This was also the route taken by local warriors as they drove the family herds to water. Acting solely from an English perspective, Worthington asked his converts to stop the passing warriors and urge them to come to church.

The request was wholly suited for their Christian roles, yet entirely at variance with their role as elder boys. As Ndinguri they were required by tradition to display exaggerated forms of respect to warriors, thereby avoiding conflict. One of the most widely practiced of these customs called for every boy to race into the bush and crouch and hide at the sight of an approaching warrior. In war the custom cleared the paths for raiders. In peace it reinforced warrior status in the minds of those who would one day assume the role themselves.

Trapped between the demands of two conflicting cultures, the converts opted for Christianity, appearing each Sunday to coax warriors into the church, often even trying to block their way. This double violation of traditions permitted the warriors to overwhelm and beat recalcitrant Ndinguri with the flat of their spears or swords, yet they dared not display their rightful power against the converts without risking retaliation by the whites.

The converts, moreover, were not slow to exploit what they perceived to be a favorable situation. Secure within the mission's shadow, they asked permission to play at the conclusion of each service upon a field that once had been the local warrior dancing ground. Once more, when warriors raced to reclaim their field, the converts refused to flee. Once more, no warrior dared strike, yet to evade the Ndinguri challenge meant abandoning the purpose of their warriorhood.

Meeting collectively within their war hut, the Ka-Aga warriors decided to restore the proper social order. Following tradition, they felt this should be done by arranging for the circumcision of every convert, thereby transforming them into warriors whom they could welcome into their ranks. Their intent was wholly benevolent: to end the conflict once and for all. The pain of the impending circumcision was to remind the converts, finally, of whom they were, driving out the boyish foolishness that had led them into foreign ways.

As the first step in the circumcision ritual, however, the warriors collectively demanded that every convert leave his mission labors and begin to brew great quantities of millet beer. That task was long, tedious, and "shameful," in that it was usually reserved for women. Nonetheless, once completed, the product was considered the "beer of [the brewers' own] circumcision" and was delivered to the warriors with considerable pride. The warriors, forbidden by their own tradition to touch alcohol, passed the beer on to the Ndinguris' elders, who consumed it while deciding on the circumcision date.

Unfortunately, the converts refused to brew beer, following Methodist tradition that decried alcoholic consumption as sinful. Their refusal caused utter consternation among the warriors. By refusing to take the initial step, the boys were rejecting warriorhood itself, a situation utterly without precedent within Meru tradition.

Totally baffled, the warriors retired into the bush for further deliberation. By August 1913, existing evidence suggests, they had decided that the converts had become Arogi, or cursers, and thus a danger to the community. In consequence the warriors decided to invoke the punishment traditionally given only to men who have acted repeatedly and destructively to curse others with malicious intent. The converts were to be wrapped in banana leaves and burned.

Unwittingly, Worthington himself set the stage. By January 1913 the number of converts had reached eleven. By July of that year, the conflict between them and the warriors of Ka-Aga had reached such proportions that the converts were virtually isolated on the mission ground. There they lived within the "schoolers' dormitory," a pseudo–war hut composed of wooden poles, papyrus reeds, and dry banana leaves.

In early August 1913, Worthington left Meru for Nairobi, leaving Mimmack in charge of the converts' schooling. Emboldened by his absence, several warriors silently appeared outside the schoolers' hut around 4 A.M., the traditional predawn period for a raid. All eleven converts were asleep in the hut, as well as one or two of the Gikuyu who had accompanied Worthington to Meru at the mission's inception.

Survivors of that night still wonder at the anger shown by the raiders. Silently binding the door shut with a vine, they first piled wood across the opening, blocking it shut. Then, they set the pile afire. The first two youths to realize what had happened were Filipo M'Inoti and Wanjoe, the Gikuyu cook. Their shouts awakened the other converts, who rushed for the door.

The fire, of course, had been laid at the door to prevent their escape. Worse, a wind whipped up the initial blaze so that it spread instantaneously along the roof and walls, igniting the papyrus and banana leaves. Within a few seconds, or so it seemed to those inside, the entire hut was aflame.

Inside, the hut filled instantly with choking smoke. Several boys lost their direction, groping blindly for where they thought the door would be, then finding only the tightly interwoven poles, each bound with papyrus, that formed the structure's frame. Next, the poles themselves began to burn, dropping onto the screaming boys' heads and shoulders, then burning them once more as they rolled underfoot. At this point they were consumed by terror, making any unified action such as charging a single point in the wall no longer possible: "We were like frightened buffaloes charging and stumbling against one another, as each shouted out what the other should do."[39]

At some point the vine that held the door shut must have burned away, allowing an opening to appear. Seeing it, Filipo M'Inoti lunged toward it with all his strength, bursting through the entire structure to safety. The others followed, still screaming at the pain of their burns, as M'Inoti led the group at a run toward the mission cabin and the protection of Frank Mimmack.

Mimmack, deeply shaken and more than a little fearful of an attack on the mission itself, did his best to treat the boys' burns, but five of the eleven boys died. The district officers, of course, launched an immediate investigation but were met with a wall of silence, as warriors and elders alike expressed their ignorance of the deed.

Neither the local Kiama nor the Imenti Njuri were consulted by colonial officials. In fact members of either council could easily have identified the culprits simply by placing their collective curse upon anyone who had harmed the elder boys. Those involved would have then succumbed to combinations of mental anxiety and physical illness of such severity as to force them to seek the assistance of ritualists. In publicly lifting the curse, of course, they would have openly admitted their guilt. Before the conquest the incident would have been settled by the transfer of livestock from their fathers' herds to those of the victims' kin. In 1913, discovery meant imprisonment and death by hanging.

Neither of the elders' councils took this course. From their perspective the warriors had acted to preserve tradition. The behavior of the converts, through their contact with white men, had become so deviant that it endangered the very framework of a social order that had always based its sense of identity on an orderly division of its members into age-sets. For members of one set to refuse passage upward into the next was a deviation of such magnitude that it endangered the entire structure.

Tradition permitted the execution of deviants when they threatened society. In the past these had usually been Arogi, cursers who repeatedly abused their powers beyond a community's capacity to bear. In such cases the individual was cloaked in dry banana leaves and set afire. In

1913 the acts of the Christian converts had become too deviant for local warriors. They had tried to resolve the problem in the same way.
Their elders may even have agreed with the decision. In consequence
the guilty went unpunished so that warriorhood might survive.

THE CHRISTIAN ISLANDS

In the face of such overt hostility, some converts abandoned the Christian faith and returned to both ancestral tradition and their former
communal way of living. To prevent this, Catholic and Protestant missionaries alike realized that their missions must become "Christian
islands," in isolation from the surrounding tribal sea, if they were
to survive.

The concept of a Christian island was a departure from earlier vi-
sions in which Catholics and Protestants saw themselves as embracing
Africans with open arms. It was not, however, without precedent in colonial Kenya. During earlier colonial decades, pioneer colonial administrators had soon realized they would require "Western islands" of
their own to ease the strain of daily contact with an alien culture. At a
physical level they needed "health islands," within which European
standards of sanitation and hygiene could be imposed to minimize the
risk of tropical disease. At a psychological level they created "social islands," usually in the form of private clubs, where officials could relax
and act "like Englishmen."

The missionaries, beset with similar problems, were quick to follow
suit. The shift from open arms to Christian island was partially financially motivated. No Meru mission, Protestant or Catholic, proved able
to operate within a predetermined budget. Thus each appealed continually to its sponsors for more funds, often without success. To lighten
their financial burdens, most missions, particularly Catholic, urged
converts as they reached the age of marriage to settle around their respective stations, where the harvests they produced could contribute to
their Christian faith. Often, this meant estrangement and growing isolation from their kin.

The Christian island was primarily intended, however, to permit
missionaries to shield their fragile followers from both temptation and
harassment. In addition it was meant to offer solace for the often devastating loneliness that came to every convert who left the tribal world
where African religion, whether concerned with God, spirits, or human
rituals, was tightly interwoven with community life. Shared beliefs

formed the web that held communities together, binding individuals into a social whole. For single individuals to step outside that web was shattering, not only to the departed but also to those they left behind. One convert noted: "It was the greatest disobedience conceivable. Breaking such news, that you were going to join the new learning and new faith, was a blow to family, age-mates, friends, everyone. Oh, people mourned for such people. To the clan, they were gone. To their kin, they were lost. To their parents, they were dead."[40]

The converts, however, were not "dead," for they could always return. The missionaries, aware of this, tried to deter them. Drawing on Western traditions, they recreated the European boarding school and its dormitory as places of refuge wherein the converts could live in peace. Informants recalled, however, how too often in those early years the sounds of singing carried through the darkness to where they slept, and they awoke to hear songs that either mocked their manhood, or begged them to reclaim it simply by joining their age-mates in a dance that would transform them once again into comrades-at-arms.

In the years to come the Christian islands would take on new functions, becoming islands of Western agriculture as well as of the Christian faith. Faced with years of famine, the mission responded with drives toward local self-sufficiency. Deep furrows were gouged across the mountain slope, to bring fresh water to each station and with it the promise of electricity. The flow of water also led to bumper crops on mission grounds, providing enough to feed those who converted and to lure others who might.

Yet, despite the rising material wealth of all the missions, their pioneer years yielded marginal success. Between 1910 and 1924, Methodists, Presbyterians, and Catholics alike recorded fewer than three hundred conversions, a meager result for so many years of selfless labor, representing the barest fraction of the 160,000-person Meru tribe.[41] Aside from children, the few adults who joined the faith were often fringemen: half-castes, outcasts, malcontents, and even deviants. Oral evidence suggests, for instance, that several of the first adults to joint the Mwimbi mission were former men of Mwaa. In Igoji those drawn to Catholicism had once been Kagita. Perhaps, from their perspective, each mission appeared to be a new Kiama, appearing on the Meru social fringe. Certainly, they proved most attractive to the fringemen, for it was mainly those who stepped outside the sacred circle of tradition to try a wholly alien way of life.

The vast majority of Meru, however, proved utterly indifferent to the Christian message. Secure within a dynamic system of belief and ritual that fully met their spiritual, social, and physical needs, they remained relentlessly conformist to a society that praised conformity as an ideal. In the first years after conquest that religious system stood intact, unshaken and virtually untouched by Christian crusaders. Not until the 1930s, when the Meru experienced the still sharper impact of Western capitalism, would the walls of communal belief tumble, the rituals that held them up be cast aside, and the Christian islands finally drain the pagan sea.

CHAPTER X

Disaster Traditions: There Were Years When Men Ate Thorns

"The powers of the witchdoctors are enormous, and every witchdoctor is a member of a secret society."[1]

F. M. Lamb
District Commissioner, Meru

Men of Meru recall the first decade that followed British conquest (1907–1917) as the time of Kangangi, so fully was it dominated by the will of E. B. Horne. The second decade (1917–1927), however, is remembered as the time of Urogi, or "witchcraft," when growing numbers of the conquered turned to the supernatural to bring some sense of comfort to their lives. Men of Europe who lived and ruled in Meru also remember this second decade for its witchcraft. The chants of so-called witch doctors, however, were only one of what then seemed an endless sequence of disasters that struck Meru, threatening to destroy what whites and blacks alike had tried to build.

DISASTER YEARS: WHEN MEN ATE THORNS

The first of these disasters began outside Africa.[2] In 1914, England and Germany went to war. Six months thereafter the hostilities had extended to their East African colonies, where whites from both sides set out for what promised to be a glorious campaign. Their African subjects were less enthusiastic. None knew what the war was about, and few cared. The most, the command to mobilize was only one more of the incomprehensible requirements that whites had placed on them since they first appeared.

World War I reached Meru in mid-1915. The first news caused great excitement among the white population—then numbering twelve—and some bewilderment among the estimated 120,000 Africans. Their initial indifference swiftly disappeared, however, as Horne and two assistant district officers turned their energies toward mobilizing the entire district to aid England and the king.

Within weeks vast numbers of warriors were willingly recruited from every region for service in the *karia,* or carrier corps. Initially, Meru enthusiasm for the project was quite genuine, as warriors scrambled to recover long-hidden weapons and spoke with satisfaction of the restoration of raiding.

Then, startled rumors spread through every war band that only whites could fight. Those Meru already sent off to the whites' war had been stripped of their shields and spears, then told to carry head loads, the function that tradition still reserved for women.

This first rumor was followed by one still more startling. It was said that Kangangi and his two white helpers had decided to round up "all" the Meru cattle, then send them off in one great herd to feed the whites at war. Resentful, angry, and afraid, warriors on every ridgetop reacted by deciding to devour every cow they owned. Huge bonfires, across the entire region, marked the sudden reestablishment of *renta,* the bull feast.[3] For those attending, it must indeed have seemed as if the time before the conquest had returned, when whole regiments of warriors had prepared themselves for conflict by devouring bull after bull provided by their fathers' herds, symbolically drawing strength from their consumption. This time, however, the feasts proved all too brief as district officers, horrified at what was happening, galloped frantically from fire to fire denying the cattle would be taken and commanding them to stop.

The whites did not, however, deny their need for carriers. Sporadic attempts at flight and concealment were punished by collective livestock fines, imposed upon whole ridgetops, coupled with threats to shoot "shirkers" for desertion. In consequence the early recruitment of volunteers was quickly transformed into the seizure of involuntary labor, as long lines of newly disarmed warriors were roped together and marched off to war.

By 1916 they began to return, emaciated, stumbling skeletons, trickling back into their home districts in conditions ranging from exhaustion to approaching death. With them came the dysentery they had contracted while on the campaign, an illness that struck with a virulence no one in Meru had previously experienced.

Meru elders living at that time could recall the appearance of new illness only twice within the history of the tribe. Each had been directly connected with the simultaneous appearance of whites. In the 1880s, European-led coastal caravans had appeared from Tigania to Mwimbi. Each had been accompanied by the appearance of *jiga* (chiggers), tiny insects that burrowed into toes and itched until removed with iron knives. In 1913, European entry into Mwimbi had been accompanied by an outbreak of what was later diagnosed as meningitis.[4] The disease, marked by vomiting, fever, extreme lethargy, and finally seizures, proved terrifying to a population that had never experienced it, the more so since traditional forms of healing proved useless.

That outbreak, however, had been brief and limited to a single region. It had also struck primarily among small children, whom the Meru believed susceptible to illness in any case. The 1916 dysentery epidemic, however, broke out in every Meru region and among those of every age. Within three months after the first groups of *karia* returned, white administrators began to record scores, then hundreds, and finally thousands of deaths. Three thousand died that year in Igembe alone, despite its almost total isolation from the rest of Meru.[5] Every other region followed in its path.

In 1917–1918 the rising tide of illness was intensified by famine. Both years were periods of unprecedented drought. During a normal agricultural cycle, all Meru regions experienced two rainy and two dry periods each calendar year and adapted their agricultural practices accordingly. In November 1917, however, the "short rains" failed entirely. Communities nearer to the forest salvaged a portion of their crops. Those in the lowland regions of Muthambi, Mwimbi, Igoji, Imenti, and Tigania are said to have gleaned nothing at all.

The problem intensified in March–April 1918, when the now desperately awaited "long rains" came too sporadically to provide the moisture needed to ripen standing millet, the basic Meru grain crop. By June 1918 even food reserves within the highland regions were exhausted, and people everywhere began to starve. Seeds disappeared from African markets in all parts of the mountain. Work on the roads was almost totally abandoned because of lack of food supplies for those who came to work.

By October–November 1918 the approaching season of short rains was universally looked upon as bringing life or death. But when the time came for weeding many were too weakened by hunger to work. "Nor could starving children successfully sling stones at the endless flock of birds that descended on the millet, nor hurl flaming torches at the baboons and bushbucks that crept through the crops to feed each night."[6] Mission writings universally reflect the tenure of that time:

> The event which eclipsed all others at the opening of the year was the terrible famine. Three successive rains had failed and starvation spread its horrors throughout the land. People died by scores daily. Desperation drove men to crime and violence. Wives were driven away and children sold. For many months our Missionaries were grappling with death. The effect of this condition upon the Mission may be imagined. The school was depleted for want of food. The chief business was to administer what little relief could be obtained.[7]

In desperation the colonial administration moved to stave off total starvation by imparting two shiploads of yellow maize from colonies in southern Africa. They arrived without incident, only to be rejected by almost all of the elder Meru as inedible and unfit for human beings.

Under these circumstances, tax collection also became increasingly sporadic, a problem caused not only by the shortage of coins (the rupee) within the district but also by the drastic decline in livestock, particularly cattle. There were at least three reasons for this. One was a striking resurgence of cattle rustling in every region. It bore, however, little relation to the carefully regulated livestock raiding that had formed the core of precolonial warfare. Rather, many raiders were elders, because hunger forced men of all age-sets to seek food. In 1918, for example, a new district commissioner expressed his surprise at having run down and jailed a "large gang of elderly cattle thieves."[8] No doubt his surprise decreased as the pattern grew common over time.

Livestock also declined in response to the Meru tradition of seeking shelter from catastrophe with distant kin. After mid-1918 hundreds of starving Meru, particularly from lower sections of the mountain, trekked raggedly away from their communities to seek shelter among kin within neighboring tribes. With them, as required by tradition, went their wives and children and only whatever sheep, grain, and cattle were required for them to survive. The clans who sheltered them would be repaid through acquisition of the young born to livestock that the famine victims had left behind. Yet what was tradition among Meru meant constant loss in taxes to the British, who watched whole herds move off the mountain with no promise of return.

The final blow, however, was yet to fall upon those herds that still remained. An outbreak of foot-and-mouth disease in neighboring regions jarred the colonial administration into imposition of a quarantine upon all Meru cattle. This was followed by a rather too hastily organized campaign to inoculate all remaining herds. Not surprisingly, the concept of inoculation was opposed by Meru in every region, at least partially as a means of expressing a generalized resentment of the

British themselves. In Tigania, however, dissenters voted with their feet. Whole clans raced their cattle in darkness over the Meru borders and into adjoining regions, thus perhaps beyond the Meru commissioner's reach. Unfortunately, this brought at least a portion of the herds into the very areas from which the original disease had come. Once infected, they swiftly passed the sickness on to others still within Tigania. In time herds in every region felt its full effects, and the decline in livestock intensified.

The situation was further compounded by the worldwide influenza epidemic, which struck Meru in November 1918. Among a population already reeling from famine, dysentery, and drought, this final blow proved overwhelming. Colonial records suggest that more than ten percent of the population died in every region, and another ten percent fled the district seeking refuge with adjoining tribes.[9]

The British administration, for all its goodwill, could do almost nothing to stem the tide. In early 1919 the whites made an initial effort to delay what they foresaw as regionwide starvation until the coming crop of millet could be harvested. Learning, through a messenger, of a successful maize harvest in the Gikuyu region of Nyeri, on Mount Kenya's eastern slope, the Meru district commissioner sent "almost every man in Meru" to fetch a portion of the crop.[10]

Unfortunately, the influenza epidemic had already reached Nyeri. It spread immediately from the stricken Gikuyu to the arriving Meru porters, disabling them in such numbers that only a fraction of the anticipated surplus could be carried back. Some porters, of course, returned not only with maize but influenza as well, reaching Meru just before the virus struck them down. The disease therefore followed them back to their home communities, leaving many previously isolated regions worse off than before.

The whites responded with whatever resources were at hand. Over the next three years, collection of the hut tax was intermittently suspended in recognition of the Meru plight. Famine relief camps were established on the district's northern and southern boundaries, to which those in need could come for maize meal that might save their lives. Mission stations also evolved into oases for the starving, sowing land in their immediate locations to the limits allowed by their supplies.

In desperation the Meru administration began to send large contingents of the remaining able-bodied men to the European districts that by now had begun to encircle what had become the Kikuyu Native Reserve. By late 1919 no less than 10,396 former warriors and family elders had been collected and sent off to settler farms. The intent of those officials who organized the program was almost certainly benevolent, since those transferred could work for the whites in exchange for food. That meant fewer mouths to feed at home and those who left it could survive.

Unfortunately those settlers to whom the former warriors were sent proved so strongly in favor of the innovation that they decided it should be permanent. Accordingly, as the work contract of various Meru contingents expired, a growing percentage found themselves indefinitely detained. A series of increasingly angry letters from the Meru district headquarters had no effect on either the government or the settlers concerned. In consequence the practice of exporting warriors in search of sustenance ground sharply to a halt.

By the early 1920s the worst was finally past. Conditions in the highland regions returned quickly to normal. Many of the lowland areas, however, remained dangerously close to a subsistence level, and elements of the Tharaka, trapped on their almost waterless plain, were reduced to stripping bark from the trees. No homestead in Meru escaped those years unscathed, and elders still recall them as "the time when men ate thorns."

STRIFE BETWEEN AGE-SETS

The relentless drumfire of natural catastrophes took its toll upon the Meru and their conquerors alike. By the early 1920s these afflictions were intensified by a sequence of human conflicts that proved equally disruptive to both sides.

The first of these would have been apparent only to the Meru themselves. Traditionally certain types of ecological disaster led inevitably to the rise of social conflicts, usually between age-sets, that could be resolved only when environmental conditions improved.

Continued failure of the millet harvests, for example, meant different things to blacks and whites. The British thought solely of physical starvation. The Meru considered a social dimension as well. No millet harvest meant no millet beer. Without beer no Ndinguri could be circumcised, since tradition required its ceremonial consumption throughout the rituals.

Until circumcision, however, young men were still boys. Without proper ritual an entire generation was virtually forbidden entry into warriorhood and thus adulthood as well. Instead, regardless of their actual age, they remained Biiji, uncircumcised boys, locked into the status of childhood that grew less appropriate and more oppressive with each passing day.

The frustrations of youths placed in this position were fully shared by their fathers. These men had stayed for many years as family heads/ apprentice elders. As junior members of their councils they had remained at every ruling elder's beck and call. Never did their rank permit them to share—or even speak—in the deliberations. For over a decade they had been silent, civil, and subordinate, their only achievements having been to father growing sons. Now, as these sons attained warriorhood, they too should have risen in power, taking on the prerogatives of rule.

These aspirations were opposed as a matter of course by the existing set of ruling elders, who had no wish to give up their prerogatives and enter retirement. Nor did their sons, still warriors in theory if no longer in fact, wish to be pushed "upward" into family head status by a new generation of just-circumcised youth.

It was a conflict long sanctioned in Meru tradition, one that set old against new. It lasted until the emerging group of fledgling warriors grew sufficiently numerous to physically expel the established generation from its war hut. Seizing the hut by physical force, they would proclaim their age-set triumphant throughout Meru and then begin their time of warriorhood. Soon thereafter the family heads would rise to authority as well, buying the status of ruling elderhood by presenting the retiring age-set with appropriate gifts.[11]

By 1916, youths who were subsequently to form the age-set of Miriti had grown so numerous that they began to demand access to warriorhood. The demand was fiercely resisted by the men of the Murungi age-set, still proud of their status. By 1917–1918 the continued failure of each millet harvest provided warriors in every region with reasons for delay, an argument supported enthusiastically by their fathers, the ruling elders.

At this point the British unintentionally stepped forth with a decision that further delayed the impending age-set transfer. Still seeking ways to increase the district's revenue, they imposed a special poll (head) tax upon each circumcised male. The ruling elders were delighted. Logically, they argued, the fewer circumcisions, the less tax need be paid. The family heads were appalled, because the tax would draw livestock from the very herds they had so carefully preserved to use as gifts (fees) throughout their sons' impending circumcisions.

As the herds were taxed away or subsequently decimated by disease, both family heads and their grown sons were in despair. Raging at the delays put on them by nature, they turned their anger at those age-sets above them, relieving their frustrations by an endless stream of taunts and chants and petty brawls with those they felt were thwarting them. As always it was tradition that was most sharply damaged, as elder boy fought warrior and family head taunted senior; the age-set structure began to wear away.

A second source of Meru social unrest lay in the relentless rise of taxes, imposed at first by the administration during the years when every clan in the district was reeling from disaster. The concept of taxation was introduced in 1911, when Horne imposed a single tax on every hut in Meru. Initially it had been set at three rupees (later, shillings) per hut, to be acquired through labor or livestock sale. In consequence ridgetop risings had occurred in areas near the mountain's base, each of which had been broken by gunfire. Stunned, other Meru regions accepted the three-shilling tax without protest. Over time that amount had become "traditional" from a Meru perspective and was thus considered a reasonable sum for the British to demand.

This understanding, of course, existed only on the Meru side. From their perspective the arrangement they had made with Horne was unfairly and unexpectedly broken in 1919 by a British decision to raise the level of taxation throughout the entire colony. In Meru taxes were increased to five shillings in 1920, and again to eight shillings in 1921. In Nairobi the increases seemed economically justified as part of colony-wide efforts to help England's African subjects "rebuild" what war and nature had destroyed.

The Meru district commissioner knew better. He sent letter after letter of protest through appropriate colonial channels, asking that the intended increase be laid aside. His requests received some consideration, but were ultimately rejected. Dutifully, he mobilized his administrative staff, only to be faced with a windstorm of protests that seemed to come from every ridgetop in the region.

To the Meru each increase seemed particularly unjust, coming at a time when they were struggling to survive. Every single homestead in the district, without exception, simply declared themselves as livestock poor, thereby owning nothing with which the tax could possibly be paid. Many communities also claimed they had become population poor as well, whole clans having either migrated or withered away under the ravages of famine and disease. ("And yet, the huts remained and each was counted, for who could prove whether someone still lived inside.")[12]

Other protests seem to have been particularly irksome to the harassed district commissioner. Often his African staff tended to count the huts used to shelter goats or even store grain. There were also protests against counting the "huts of old women," usually widowed, of great age, and with no discernible means of support. Alternately, several of these aged women—each with her own hut—might be dependent on a single equally aged man, whose herds, flocks, and sons alike had been carried off by disease and famine.[13]

In fairness it must be noted that both the Meru and their colonial administrators had been placed under impossible conditions. The British, pressed by demands from their own superiors, found it imperative to raise district revenues simply to maintain the existing colonial structure. The Meru, however, had no means whatsoever by which to raise the required sums.

In the past individual homesteads had coped with the taxes by selling their livestock and grain, usually to members of the neighboring pastoral tribes (Maasai, Somali, Galla, and others), who had paid fair market value for that period and place. Now they found it virtually impossible to sell either commodity at anything more than a fraction of the accustomed price, their traditional buyers having suffered as deeply as they. In near desperation successive Meru district commissioners put aside their moral scruples and forced whole communities to sell livestock at whatever prices they could fetch. Thereby, they achieved at least partial collection of the required revenues but drove elders in the more afflicted areas into unprecedented depths of despair.

Their feelings were shared for different reasons by men of the younger age-sets. By 1920 many family heads and former warriors had come to accept the money economy, through either their war or work experiences with Europeans. Consequently they chose to cope with British taxes by working for rupees, then standard currency in Kenya, and saving what they received. Over time many men had saved sums that for that era seemed substantial and had even begun to use the surplus to buy goods.

The rupee had been Kenya's standard monetary unit since 1898. Its value had always been one shilling and fourpence, British sterling. Suddenly, in January 1920 it rose to two shillings and fourpence, then dropped to two shillings by March and to one shilling and fivepence in June of the same year.[14]

Normally these fluctuations would not have affected the Meru population, even those who worked wholly for wages. They did, however, affect Kenya's Indian and European communities, both of whom began enthusiastically to smuggle vast numbers of rupees into the country.

The Kenya government was thoroughly alarmed. It had also brought in large amounts of one-rupee notes, intended as belated payments to the thousands of African ex-servicemen who had returned from the great war. Worse, the payout had actually begun in mid-1920, continuing throughout Kenya for seven days, to the accompaniment of great rejoicing and enthusiastic all-night dancing by the ex-servicemen involved. On the eighth day the government clamped down on every form of smuggling in the only possible way: it withdrew all one-rupee notes from circulation. Suddenly and dramatically, the wages of war were rendered useless paper in the hands of the hundreds upon hundreds of Africans who now possessed them.[15]

In Meru the warriors and younger family heads now plunged into despair. Economic explanations proved totally useless, particularly because neither the district officers nor their sullen listeners had any grasp of the economic forces in which all were caught. What remained, among men of these younger age-sets, was a raging sense of betrayal, joined to feelings of rising despair as intense and poignant as those felt by their elders. For perhaps the first time in Meru history, neither the present nor the future offered hope.

FROM PIONEERS TO PRAGMATISTS

Times were also hard, however, for the British. The war alone had impoverished the entire colony. The subsequent sequences of medical, climatic, and economic disasters had brought the entire colonial structure to the point of collapse. British administrators responded to each individual crisis with energy and determination, mobilizing whatever resources were at hand. Unfortunately Kenya colony possessed neither the funds nor personnel to cope with disasters of such magnitude. The best that the administrators anywhere could achieve was a series of stopgap solutions, shifting existing colonial officers back and forth among the various tribal districts like small boys rushing endlessly to stick their fingers into leaking dikes.

Stopgap administration was nowhere more apparent than in Meru, remote from colonial headquarters in Nairobi and thus perhaps low in its administrative priorities. Certainly, the Meru District tradition of long-term rule by a single administrator was snapped like a twig after 1918. Horne had ruled Meru for almost the entire decade of 1907–1917. During the next ten years, he was followed by no fewer than fourteen successors. Few of these stayed in the post for more than one year. Some left after six months; one, after three. Assistant district commissioners, district officers, and cadets were assigned along the same pattern. Tours were brief; transfers were frequent. Not one officer stayed.[16]

The frequency of this turnover led to the total loss among the administrators of much that had been common knowledge about the Meru culture. Horne had been a gifted linguist who also took great pride in his increasing knowledge of the Meru social structure. He had, however, an outspoken distaste for written records, an antipathy that led him to set down as little as permitted in the required district annual reports and nothing at all outside them. The same applied, for different reasons, to other members of the pioneer administrative generation. Orde-Browne preserved his voluminous knowledge of the Cuka-Mwimbi peoples in private ledgers for publication on his return to England.[17] Others disposed of their written materials on leaving Kenya, turning their energies wholly toward learning about other tribes.

Men of that first decade were the pioneers, priding themselves on their knowledge of and empathy with the peoples they ruled. Those of the next decade might be labeled the pragmatists. Collectively they had neither the time, linguistic skills, nor personal inclination to probe deeply and searchingly into tribal societies. Their pride lay not in knowledge and empathy but in administrative efficiency, a concept they defined in terms of inducing Africans to get tasks done. Thus, during the second decade, huts were to be counted in record time, taxes collected in record amounts. Roads were to appear. Living standards were to rise. British standards of law, religion, morality, and civilized behavior were to spring up in the wilderness. Above all, in exchange for this introduction to civilization, England's subject peoples were to be taught to show a profit.

The pragmatists relied on interpreters, not merely to convey orders but also to gain information on those they ruled during the first years of British rule. Few Meru learned Swahili (the colonial lingua franca) and none learned English. Thus, the first generation of interpreters to appear in Meru were drawn initially from among Swahili and Kamba peoples and subsequently the Gikuyu.

None of these "aliens" loved Meru. The Swahili, Gikuyu, and Kamba alike felt themselves forced to live among savages. Members of all three groups identified wholly with the fortunes of England and felt themselves far above the peoples they now helped rule. The Meru fully reciprocated this hostility, having learned from their earlier experiences with the British that their interpreters were to be distrusted, hated, and feared. Several carved reputations for themselves that have become part of traditional lore. "Salimu the Small," for example, one of the Gikuyu who interpreted for Horne, distinguished himself both for his disregard of the intricacies of Meru culture and his unrelenting greed. "To see the white man [Horne]," informants recall, "Salimu demanded a goat. To argue your case in front of him [Horne], Salimu demanded a girl. He loved best eating other peoples' property and being bribed. When you complained, he asked his white man to put you into prison."[18]

Although Horne had soon learned the Meru language, a long series of Gikuyu interpreters who worked for his assistants and successors are recalled as having "left no moment undisturbed to convince their employers that Meru social institutions were both primitive and dangerous."[19] The institution of Njuri was no exception. Horne, absorbed in learning Meru ways, had actively sought out its meetings and members. His successors, lacking his linguistic and ethnological inclinations, sought information from their interpreters instead.

Tradition suggests that the interpreters often focused on those aspects of Meru life of which whites were least likely to approve. They had no need to lie, only to describe the requested customs while neglecting to explain their psychological and social context. The Meru traditions regarding execution provide an interesting example. Usually, newly appointed colonial officers were appropriately horrified to learn, from their Gikuyu interpreters, that acts of theft, adultery, and "bewitchment" (cursing) were punished in Meru by death through public stoning. In fact isolated instances of any antisocial act were usually punishable by livestock fines and then only after long deliberation by the elders.

Habitual offenders, however, whether thieves, adulterers, cursers, or other types, might indeed become more than the communities could bear. They could on order from an elders' council be put to death by stoning. An interpreter might neglect to mention, however, that such punishment was reserved for the incorrigibles. Nor did they often bother to explain that each stoning was preceded by a "prayer song" sanctified by generations of use, imploring everyone who sympathized with the offender to come forward and "buy him." Should someone stand forth, he could shield the offender from execution by placing cows between the judged and his judges, in whatever numbers they might require.

The stoning could begin only when offense had been given so often that no one in the whole community stepped forward. The first stones were always cast by kin, the missiles symbolizing the dissolution of their common bond. Thereafter, each man in the community cast a stone in turn, symbolically proclaiming his commitment to the execution as the only way in which communal harmony could be restored. The Meru procedures were cautious, deliberative, and rational, and they differed only slightly from those of the Gikuyu. By emphasizing those differences, however, or omitting the more humane aspects, interpreters could cast doubt upon the entire Meru judicial process and, beyond it, upon Meru tradition.

This sense of alienation from Meru ways was transmitted, at least in part, from the first generation of interpreters to their successors. By the 1920s the series of Gikuyu interpreters had been replaced, in part, by men of Meru. Many of these, however, had spent long years outside the district, working for Europeans. Having mastered either Swahili or English, they had also become partially detribalized, having acquired sufficient interests in Western ways to abandon some of their own.

This was particularly true for young men who had begun to make both a career and the beginnings of wealth out of working for whites. By the mid-1920s, for example, the earliest Meru interpreters had worked for the British for at least ten years. Many had originally been plucked by Horne from warriorhood to become *askari*, or tribal police. Others had served as messengers, hut counters, porters, or guides. Still others had worked over long periods with other British, whether in wartime or on settlers' lands.

All of these men shared several perceptions in common. One was the belief that their fortunes lay with the British. A second was the feeling that they were "modern" men and as such disdainful of their own "primitive" traditions. A third was based on the desire to provide whites with only that information that might best enhance themselves. Often that corresponded with precisely what white administrators wished to hear.

If, for example, a newly appointed Meru district commissioner decided that his "natives" were "sunk in superstition . . . and . . . abominable practices," as one reported in 1923, or "backward due to their belief in witchcraft and curses," as recorded by still another new appointee in 1924, his interpreters did what was required to reinforce those beliefs.[20] Small wonder, therefore, that colonial knowledge of Meru ways disappeared. What little was learned came either from aliens or the alienated, men either foreign to Meru or who had abandoned its ways.

TINKERERS AND DESTROYERS: THE ANGLICIZING YEARS

Given the distorting reports of the interpreters, it is not surprising that the new generation of administrative pragmatists turned enthusiastically to the task of anglicizing the Meru, particularly the ways they were ruled. Their approach to the Meru way of rule, as personified by the Njuri councils, was ambivalent. One group regarded the Njuri system as an ethnological curiosity, to be tinkered with and thereby anglicized in one's spare time. Others associated it with the "dark" aspects of Meru society, equating it primarily with witchcraft. The first group wished to turn Njuri meetings into replicas of English village councils and was concerned primarily with selecting Meru who had proved sufficiently anglicized to play by British rules. The second wished to replace it altogether, banning its gatherings, burning its huts, and transferring its functions to wholly British institutions, staffed by British educated youngsters.

Perhaps the most memorable of the "tinkerers" appeared in 1920. Soon after D. R. Crawford was appointed district commissioner, he proclaimed a "General Kiama" for all Meru, asking leading members of the regional Kiamas (actually, the Njuris) of Tigania-Igembe and Imenti-Igoji to meet at the Meru district headquarters. Dutifully, selected elders from the various ridgetop communities walked the many miles to appear. Having gathered, they sat down to begin deliberation while waiting for the new white man to appear.

They were initially amazed to learn that the discussions were, in fact, to be conducted by a number of younger men, handpicked by the district commissioner for their "administrative willingness and speaking skills." More disconcerting, the elders were informed that decisions were to be made in British fashion (i.e., by majority rule), with total disregard for the intricacies of Meru debating tradition, the need for consensus, and the presence of meat and beer. To no one's surprise, the elders swiftly concluded that no Kiama had in fact been convened. They quietly drifted away—to the intense satisfaction of the district commissioner—who noted subsequently that his "handpicked" group had continued to function after the tribal elders proved unsatisfactory.[21]

The "handpicked" group continued to meet as a General Kiama for the next two years. Its work was increasingly hampered, however, by the unwillingness of any other normal elders to bring any cases before it for judgment. Instead they universally continued to rely on the traditional system of Kiamas and Njuris. Starved for conflicts to resolve, the General Kiama for all Meru gradually collapsed.

The second type of administrator appeared in either 1921 or 1922 (tradition is unclear), with an alternative solution. His real name has been forgotten by informants, who refer to him only as Kivunja, "the destroyer."[22] Kivunja proved unusually outspoken against the entire system of judgment by Kiama in general and the two Njuris in particular. From a colonial perspective he had excellent reasons. In keeping with the beliefs of many British throughout the period, Kivunja saw the Njuri as not merely unprogressive but reactionary, intent on dragging its people "backward" into a stagnant and unprogressive past. Nor could Njuri gatherings be dismissed as "dogs without teeth." By using curses to support their positions, the councils still retained the power to overawe the Meru and thereby paralyze each British effort to improve and anglicize their lives. The Njuris thus stood squarely in the path of England, in a conflict in which the prize was loyalty of the entire tribe.

Kivunja came to Meru, however, during what informants remember as among the last of the famine years, thus probably 1921–1922. During his first weeks in the district he is recalled as having grown particularly angry to learn of the Njuri practice of "feasting," that is, consuming the meat of bulls provided to the Njuri members by parties to the conflict they had assembled to resolve. Meru tradition sanctified such feasting because it affirmed that the conflict had been considered by the elders and resolved.

Kivunja, uninformed about the symbolic context of the feasting, accused the elders of Tigania's Njuri Nceke of accepting bribes. Worse, he proclaimed their consumption of so much meat in time of famine as an insulting and extravagant waste. His response was to ban "the Njuri organization" throughout Meru, enforcing the decision by burning several alleged Njuri huts. The ban proved unexpectedly effective;

members of the highest elders' councils in Igoji and South Imenti sub-sequently seem to have abandoned their meetings. The Njuri ya Kiama in North Imenti initially tried to ignore the ban, but found "informers too many and police posts too near."

Tigania's Njuri Nceke, however, sent a delegation of elders to Kivunja to protest. During their meeting they informed him that "it had been [they] who had first welcomed Kangangi [Horne] to Meru, and that . . . Kivunja's failure to cooperate would force [them], if fur-ther harassed, to bring him [Horne] back to rule [them] as before."[23] Perhaps amused, the district commissioner replied by permitting the Tigania Njuri to meet "at the Boma [Meru district headquarters in Imenti] every Wednesday" to settle its affairs. He warned them, how-ever, that a chief and a clerk would always sit with them during their meetings, to record their discussions and assure that nothing was said against England.

Kivunja's reply threw the elders into consternation. Initially they meekly agreed to his terms. Thereafter selected groups of spokesmen placidly appeared for a while "on Wednesdays" to satisfy the white man, but the actual Njuri deliberations continued in traditional fashion within Tigania, shielded from administrative interference by a conspir-acy of silence. After a short time, however, the weekly delegations also ceased to appear at district headquarters, and subsequent administra-tors never realized they had come. From a British perspective the Njuri had passed into tribal history, quietly ceasing to exist.

It seemed reasonable, therefore, for subsequent district officials to follow Kivunja's path to its logical end, creating a series of wholly Brit-ish administrative institutions to fill the void left by the demise of the more "primitive" indigenous ones. The first step, taken in 1919–1920, was to reorganize the African Native Courts that had initially been es-tablished after 1911 by Horne and Platts. Now almost moribund, the courts were rechristened Local Native Tribunals and established in each of the four major regions. The number of participants within each tribunal was reduced from sixty to thirty. More important from the British perspective, the entire corps of "senior" (i.e., ruling and above) elders was gradually "weeded out," to be replaced by an energetic group of younger men, drawn almost wholly from the ranks of colonial police, thus familiar with British colonial traditions.

In the early 1920s the Local Native Tribunals were each supplied with an administrative staff, intended not only to record and regulate their decisions but also to assist in their enforcement. By 1924, for example, each tribunal had been "given" a president to guide its members, by this time reduced to twenty, in both their selection and judgment of cases. Court clerks, provided a year earlier, not only recorded evidence but also assisted in phrasing the language in which judgments were to be set down in final form, a position that gave them unusual power over the severity of sentences. Finally each tribunal was provided with five to ten process servers, chosen from the tribal police and charged to ensure swift implication of every tribunal judgment.[24]

In July 1925 the Local Native Tribunals were formally supplemented by the creation of an all-Meru Local Native Council (LNC), which was opened by the acting governor of Kenya with great solemnity in what is now known as Meru Town. It was composed of carefully chosen nominees, young, British-trained, and loyal to England. Eight of the nominees were "elected" by contending with others, equally anglicized within their respective districts. Fourteen, however, were directly nominated by the district administration, which thereby assured itself a voting majority on every issue that might arise.

Local administrators of that time described the LNC as "unmistakably popular" with the Meru, judging by the enthusiasm with which its members were elected. This popularity, they felt, was because of the opportunity offered the "more advanced and perhaps restless young men of political tendencies" to share responsibility for the ruling of their people. It seems more likely, however, that the enthusiasm of both candidates and voters was grounded in the administration's willingness to release sizable funds for the new council to spend. Armed with an initial bankroll of 2,065 shillings that had been diverted from the hut tax, the council moved enthusiastically and rapidly to spend it.[25]

Thus the era closed with the anglicizers in complete control. From the British perspective they were simply training the Meru ultimately to rule themselves in British fashion. To do so, they were following tactics used by colonizers throughout history, eliminating indigenous institutions, then filling the void with their own by training the young to assume the positions of the old. Beholden solely to the conquerors for its power, the new generation would thus forgo old ways and transform British rule into reality.

UROGI: RUMORS OF WITCHCRAFT

The commissioners' enthusiasm for their new governmental institutions, however, was short-lived. After the early 1920s almost every aspect of colonial administration fitfully halted. This decline was particularly evident in the sphere of criminal justice, where the four British-sponsored native tribunals operated only in spurts, resolving smaller numbers of disputes each year, in vague approximation of what the members of each body perceived as British law.

The same pattern was apparent at every level of the administration. The Local Native Council, after its enthusiastic start, proved increasingly reluctant to pass laws on anything at all. Those that were passed proved impossible to implement, as chiefs, headmen, process servers, and even tribal police were curiously reluctant to carry out directives, even those, such as establishing medical stations, that administrators thought were clearly to the advantage of Meru everywhere.

Initially administrators attributed this singular reluctance to a combination of sullenness, backwardness, and passive resistance. "After six months' residence here," one wrote in 1923, "I have come to the conclusion that . . . hardly a single headman (of ninety-four) can be relied on to assist government in the detection of crime, . . . arrest of criminals, . . . or in putting down abominable practices."[26]

Other Meru administrators wholly shared this view. In the 1920s the Meru became notable in colonial circles as a "backward" people, incapable of attaining either British administrative standards or the economic progress shown by their Gikuyu neighbors. This was also the era, however, when the administrators began to feel that Meru noncooperation might have another, deeper, cause. Eventually they decided the problem was witchcraft.

The British of that era were often fascinated with African witchcraft. Universal in their belief that it was based solely on deception, most administrators rather looked forward to chance encounters with the "witch doctors" of peoples whom they ruled. Never were they more pleased than when the witch doctors' magic seemed occasionally to work. Orde-Browne, within his private papers, related one such encounter with considerable glee. In the line of duty he had been forced to arrest a "little old fellow" for bewitching his workers. On arrest, the elder had "cursed him horribly." Subsequently Orde-Browne was stricken with an inflammation of his knee joints that left him incapacitated for several months. "The event," he later wrote, "was seen by every native in the district as a sign of the witchdoctor's revenge."[27]

Unfortunately the second generation of colonial administrators knew much less about Meru witchcraft than the first. A report on the Meru written in 1911, for instance, meticulously described the differences between a Murogi ("poisoner who collects . . . medicines secretly at night"), a Muga ("medicine man [who] is a power of good . . . [with] more than twenty medicines . . . of vegetable-roots and leaves"), and a Muroria ("soothsayer [who] foretells the length of famine, war, . . . as revealed . . . in dreams").[28] Ten years later, colonial administrators had lost all knowledge of their various ritualists, including their names. Reports from the 1920s tend to group all such practitioners under the title of "witch doctor," a figure to whom they attributed nothing but malice and evil. In 1924 an administrator declared: "the natives here remain backward and believe quite notably in witchcraft and curses. This is most noticeable in Tigania and Igembe, where the hold over natives by witchdoctors seems slightly on the wane."[29]

In fairness, it would have been difficult to live among the Meru of that era and remain unaware of the supernatural aspects of their daily lives. Usually, a new administrator first learned of witchcraft through his reading (or observation) of cases in court. Although conflicts brought before the native tribunals concerned crimes against people or property, the parties invariably accused one another, at some point in the process, of having bewitched (cursed) their livestock, crops, kin, or themselves.

Less frequently, victims of an alleged bewitchment might seek a private meeting with an administrative officer. Most often this happened on tour, when newly appointed officers visited the hinterlands to familiarize themselves with more remote corners of the region. Usually the officer declared a public meeting, at each stop asking all who sought justice to step forward. No one did. Then, at the meeting's conclusion, footsteps shuffled before the officer's tent as darkness fell, and low voices accused others of bewitchment.

Enthusiastic officials tended to attribute almost every Meru ritual to witchcraft, often inferring satanic overtones that had no basis in Meru life. One example of this trend occurred late in the 1920s when one of the district's first medical missionaries began to construct a Methodist mission hospital in Igembe. After the first week or so he "became aware of sorcerers around the hospital, through continuously coming across three-inch strips of red raw meat impaled on sharpened six-inch pegs and stuck around hospital grounds."[30]

In fact there were no "sorcerers," only workaday Meru, as concerned as the missionary with fighting illness and disease. One method, long sanctified by tradition, was for the community elders to gather at a single spot, slaughter a goat, slice the meat into three-inch strips, then peg them into the ground to be eaten by spirits, ideally those that caused illness. What better place could be found for such ritual than a building wherein whites themselves claimed "disease was collected and illness could always be found"? The incident illustrates the evolution of colonial administration over the first two decades. Where the first generation of colonialists had come to learn, too many of the second wave came only to teach.

Nevertheless, successive administrators throughout the 1920s began to differentiate between three different types of Meru "witchcraft." The least offensive was represented by the individual "witch doctors"—a term used to cover every type of supernatural specialist—whom the vast majority of district officers dismissed as harmless tricksters. Most administrators knew several of them and usually joked with them during their occasional meetings.

However, a second form of witchcraft began to come to official notice after 1920, a type allegedly practiced by entire bands of sorcerers. A district commissioner first wrote them into an official record in late 1920. During the last months of that year he was called into a remote corner of Igembe to suppress the practices of what he referred to as: "the Kaiita, . . . a society which consists mostly of tribal elders. It includes medicine men as its most powerful members and among other objectionable customs is responsible for the seduction of many young unmarried girls with consequent abortion of children thus conceived."[31]

Over the next four years similar "secret" societies seemed, to colonial officials, to proliferate throughout Meru. Certainly they occupied an increasingly large place in both official and private correspondence.

> They [the Kaiita] have a great influence owing to proficiency in the art of pursuing. Kaiita in Igembe had a large rough hut in each location to which they called a lot of young girls. The girls were kept there and were not allowed to return to their parents. . . . At night they held dances naked and had sexual intercourse with the girls. [11 November 1920][32]

> Aathi is the name of a secret society which exists in the middle of Meru. We know that it exists but it is impossible to find out what things they do. . . . Even members never speak of it. . . . They build large huts with long entrance corridors and stay in there . . . and eat and drink and do worse things. . . . They believe themselves invulnerable to any poisoning . . . and have great power to curse others. [November 1921][33]

> Mbujo League—this league gained considerable power and has many adherents. [Its] object is the practice of witchcraft. The high priest, Mboro [sic: M'Mburi] was sentenced to a year [imprisonment] in January, 1924.[34]

ILLEGAL TRIBUNALS AND SECRET SOCIETIES

During these years, colonial officials also became increasingly troubled by the emergence of a third type of witchcraft, which also seemed to have taken the form of a secret society. Labeled variously in official reports as "witchcraft tribunals," "illegal tribunals," "secret societies," or "witchcraft guilds," these groups were alleged to hold trials, pass judgments, and levy punishments in the form of cattle fines within remote areas of Tigania and Igembe. They were believed to enforce each decision by the threat of bewitchment through fearsome curses. District officers sent to investigate the initial rumors soon discovered that all Meru knew of them, but none was willing to divulge details. In consequence official reports over the subsequent five years suggest that the British learned little more about them than their names.

> The Natives here [1923] are sunk in superstition. No headman can be relied upon to help government . . . [in] putting down abominable practices. . . . Njuricheke Kiama [sic] is credited with supernatural power which makes . . . administration very difficult indeed.[35]

> Today [1925] the more educated [Meru] claim the Njoli [Njuri] must be abolished because it keeps the country in darkness, impeding the advancement and progress of their civilization.[36]

District officials were also troubled by rumors of a large number of allegedly "secret" societies, each dedicated to the practice of witchcraft. Although most numerous in Tigania and Igembe, reports of similar groups emerged in every region. One, the Kiama Kia A-Athi, clearly referred to a council of forest hunters. The others, the Kiamas of the Kagita, Kaundu, Makuiko, Mwaa, and several like them, remained shrouded in mystery.

Over time, nonetheless, these scattered reports began to form identifiable patterns. Each of these societies was small. Several, however, notably those of the A-Athi and the Kagita, were alleged to have branches on almost every Meru ridgetop. Their meeting places were secret, protected in the traditional Meru fashion by lethal curses that could be placed by the elders of each society on any Meru who betrayed its trust.

The activities of these two most numerous groups seemed to take two forms. One was overtly sexual, in which members of each society were said to compel women from the surrounding communities to join them for feasts of meat and beer. The rumors also suggested that the women were forced to participate in nude dancing, which continued the entire night. Male relatives who objected to a woman's participation in these practices found themselves either overawed by the threat of a society's curse or, worse, forced to join in themselves.

Such reports were extremely disturbing to British administrators only a few years removed from the Victorian age. The rumors paled, however, before subsequent allegations that added a political dimension to the problem. After 1924 at least two of the secret societies, once again the Kiama of the A-Athi and the Kagita, were reported to have taken on the roles of "illegal tribunals" and to have begun to dispense justice. Moving in small bands among villages in the more remote areas, both groups were described as having begun to resolve conflicts among local inhabitants in virtually the same manner as the other four "illegal" tribunals of the Njuri. As a result, it was said, large portions of the livestock in those areas had been transferred into the hands of these wandering judges.

Worse news, however, came in through reports that the "loyal" elders in these remote areas were immobilized by fear, daring neither to move against these societies in traditional fashion nor to appeal to colonial headmen and chiefs. Some colonial officers, although still groping for more accurate data, believed both secret societies had virtually absorbed the four "illegal" tribunals of the Njuri, "most of whose members belong [ed] to either Aathi or Kagita."[37]

More serious still, these same societies were reported to have penetrated deeply into the ranks of the Meru African Colonial Service. Indeed, in several areas, chief, headmen, tribal retainers, police, and even members of the colonial Local Native Tribunals were said to have been forcibly incorporated into one or even both societies, thereby placing them in situations that might endanger the colonial structure itself.

CHAPTER XI

Resistance Traditions:
Kiamas Underground

"There was no choice for an unmarried girl over going to
the Kagita or not. A Kagita curse remover would just point
at you with his smallest finger and say, "You, girl, come into
[the hut of] Kagita." If a girl refused, she would become ill
with their curse and perhaps die."[1]

(Mrs.) Mwakireu Gikabu
Alleged former member,
Kiama Kia Kagita, 1920s

By the mid-1920s every British administrator in Meru was concerned
with the rising power of local witchcraft. In colonial Nairobi the Meru
region was now widely considered "witch ridden and backward," thus
a particularly undesirable post at which to serve. Within the district,
however, administrators and missionaries alike strove frantically to
learn more about the forces with which they had to deal.

THE WALL OF SILENCE

The efforts of the white administrators were met with a conspiracy of
silence. No Meru wished to teach whites local customs lest the conquerors use what they learned to destroy the tribe. Certainly no Meru in
those hostile years was willing to discuss the obviously contentious topics of "illegal" tribunals, "secret" societies, and local "witchcraft." The
activities of Njuri Nceke, the traditional council-of-councils, were thus
protected by a solid wall of silence. The practices of the Kagita, Aathi,
and other deviant groups were shrouded by fear. White inquiries about
any of these associations were met by protests that to mention them
would cause the speakers' deaths.

The silence also kept whites from observing alleged "witchcraft" activity and collecting evidence to use against it: "At the mission, one
consistently heard complaints concerning terrible acts of witchcraft by
these Kiamas, but we could never actually observe [them] and thus gain
proof of their existence."[2] In 1925, for instance, a certain Catholic

father, G. Bondino, then stationed at a mission in Tigania, began to investigate complaints against what he subsequently described as the "Witchcraft Guild of Kagitha."[3] Efforts to elicit information from local elders proved useless. His own parishioners, although potentially more pliable, were mostly children, too young to have learned what he needed to know.

Father Bondino therefore decided on direct action. Kagita feasts within his area were always accompanied by the beating of great drums, which coughed and rumbled until dawn. One night, having darkened his face and hands, he dressed entirely in black. Quietly leaving the mission, he followed the drumming into the darkness.

The drum led him toward an unusually large hut, built in the beehive style of warrior barracks. He crept to its side undetected and peered through the dry banana leaves that covered it. He saw very little, because the interior was dark except for a single tiny fire. Nor, through the hum of voices, could he at first discern what was being said. Straining forward to hear, he stumbled, falling heavily against the hut. Within moments, men poured from its doorway, and he was seized.

Boldly, Bondino demanded entry, stating truthfully that he had come to learn what went on inside. He was answered by a torrent of shouts, several of which threatened him with retreat or death. Meru versions of this incident suggest that the threats referred to ancestral retribution rather than immediate physical harm. Bondino, however, interpreting them as an attack on his person, left the way he had come. The next day, the hut in question was burned to the ground—whether by the Kagita or Catholic mission converts remains unclear. No European ever repeated Bondino's attempt to unmask the society, and the mystery remained.

Colonial officials proved more successful, however, in their efforts to learn more of Meru's traditional witchcraft. Several knowledgeable elders were willing to discuss the most positive aspects to their own system. Thus, by the mid-1920s the second generation of British administrators had begun to retrieve much of the data that had been common knowledge to their predecessors. Initially, they began once again to differentiate between "good" and "bad" witch doctors, separating them into those who cursed and others who claimed to heal. In consequence several administrators grew tolerant of the curse removers (Aga), whom they perceived as "silly old fellows who could do no harm."[4] Others began to recognize parts of the witchcraft system as a means of social control, most notably the stick-and-vine concept used by the Kagita, which was clearly intended as crop protection.

Nevertheless, even the most sympathetic of the second generation British firmly disapproved of the witchcraft system as a whole and worked continuously to ensure its swift demise. By the mid-1920s the "silly old witch doctor" might indeed have been a figure of fun. His "magic bag" might well have been filled with harmless twists of grass and chalk and clay. As a healer, whites might cheerfully regard him as a joke. In political terms, however, whites perceived all "witch doctors" as powerful, potentially rebellious, and implacably opposed to British rule.

In that era it seemed logical, for example, for colonial administrators to assume that "witch doctors" had been the former leaders of the Meru peoples, fulfilling roles akin to those of high priests they had found in other corners of the British empire. It seemed equally obvious that none would take kindly to British efforts to undermine the beliefs on which their power had been based. The provision of Western substitutes for ancestral spirits and ancient forms of healing could hardly go unresented and unopposed.

From the British perspective this opposition first manifested itself through the witch doctors' insistence on adhering to obsolescent and undesirable native customs, as well as their power to collectively impose their decisions on the entire tribe. The power to compel such obedience, according to colonial observers, invariably took three forms. One was the deliberate "misreading of omens" to predict inevitable calamity for anyone adopting British ways. The second was through imposing a curse on anyone departing from ancestral ways. The third—and most important to the British—was to make sure that the calamity implicit in every act of cursing actually occurred. Since this fulfillment could not be left to chance, practitioners were believed to create their own disasters by judicious use of poisons to ensure illness, infirmity, or even death: "should an actual . . . disaster fall upon these people, the witchdoctors continue to terrorize, . . . declaiming that the same fate will befall all others who stray from tribal teachings to those of Europe. The [tribal] location can thus be worked up to such a pitch of excitement that only the removal of all witchdoctors can cure it."[5]

It seemed equally logical for British administrators to conclude that Meru witch doctors would band together in adversity, forming "witchcraft Kiamas" in the Meru manner to fight back against their conquerors. Certainly, the British themselves under the heel of invaders would have formed groups to resist as they could. Thus the witch doctors of Meru could hardly be blamed for reacting in similar fashion. The correct colonial response, therefore, was to eliminate them both individually and as groups, to clear the way for both Christianity and colonialism.

THE CASE AGAINST THE NJURI NCEKE

When the Njuri system was formally banned throughout the district in 1921–1922, the edict proved effective among every subtribe but the Tigania and Igembe. The highest elders' councils in Cuka, Muthambi, and Mwimbi had already ceased to meet. The Kiama Kia Njuri, the highest elders' council for both Igoji and Imenti, was unable to survive the ban.

In contrast the Njuri Nceke of Tigania and Igembe proved unexpectedly resilient. An initial public protest to the district commissioner had led to a government decision to allow monthly meetings of its members under supervised conditions at the Boma (Meru district headquarters). Sensibly, Njuri elders complied with this decision by sending spokesmen to meet at the times white men desired but continued to meet privately as they wished. In time, of course, these private meetings were reported to the district office. Colonial administrators responded with several well-planned raids into the two northern districts. Each time, the alleged "Njuri huts" were burned, and those within them were arrested on charges of "frightening people," "practice of witchcraft," or "extortion of cows."[6]

This pattern of punitive raiding continued sporadically through the 1920s. In 1923, for example, a newly appointed district commissioner was informed within days of his arrival in Meru of an "illegal tribunal" operating throughout Tigania. The complaint, from an anonymous informant, declared that the tribunal was "extorting cows from villagers in the [field known as] Kathaka Kai." The district commissioner responded with a police sweep of the entire area in which large numbers of alleged "Kiama huts" were destroyed and four local elders tried, convicted, and sentenced for extortion.[7] The tribunal, of course, was the Njuri Nceke. Kathaka Kai was its traditional meeting ground.

The Njuri responded to both the loss of its huts and arrest of its members with several explicit evasions. Initially the council abandoned its traditional gathering places. Instead members adopted a more flexible pattern, meeting in hidden glades at irregular times, hoping whites would not anticipate their actions. The Njuri also divested itself of all visible symbols. Before the conquest, meetings had been publicly proclaimed by junior members, who walked from village to village carrying wooden staffs to display their status. The foreheads of such messengers were daubed with bright red clay, which wordlessly proclaimed that council elders should assemble. After the ban both wooden staff and clay were quietly abandoned, and meetings were announced by word of mouth.

Changes were also made to protect the Njuri's "sacred symbols," objects allegedly brought by the Meru on their first trek from the Kenya coast. Before the conquest these had been kept within a single sacred hut at the council's primary meeting place at Nciru (Tigania), their safety guaranteed by respect for the Njuri curse. After the ban, members feared that storage in any hut might lead to their destruction by fire. As a result the sacred symbols–like the Njuri itself—began to move, passing from region to region and hand to hand among its senior members.

Beyond these changes Njuri members soon learned to rely on what might be described as "cultural invisibility." Meetings held at points other than Nciru were difficult for whites to identify. A gathering of elders might well be the Njuri but might also be nothing more than several aged men who had assembled to drink beer. Knowing nothing of the culture and little of the language, the whites could never tell.

Of course, deceptions of this type were transparent to other Meru, including those who served the British. To thus avoid exposure by native informers, the Njuri relied on the protection afforded by its collective oath. The Meru oath, it will be recalled, is not a threat to other persons, but an affirmation of one's own innocent intent. Like the judicial oaths of England, it is directed "upward" toward a higher power—in Meru, the ancestral spirits. Thus, the chanted phrase "if I break [disobey], let this oath eat [devour, kill] me" simply records a person's willingness to obey both ancestral and Njuri tradition.

During the 1920s, however, Meru administrators interpreted these oaths in terms of the British curse. In England, as in Meru, the "curse" is defined as a verbal wish to harm, hurled directly at an antagonist. Without exception whites assumed that the core of Njuri power lay in its ability to threaten every man in Meru with a "collective curse." Further, they felt Njuri elders used this power to "extort" cattle and goats from other Meru. Finally, they assumed the Njuri used this fear to threaten anyone who accepted England. Thus, one administrator wrote: "People are commended [*sic:* commanded] under penalty of being cursed . . . if they give information to government or bring their cases to be heard by government or give evidence against witchdoctors or report any extortions or injustice done by Kiamas."[8]

British officials also believed that the Njuri "curse" had also been applied, without exception, to "loyal" African members of the colonial administration, from chiefs and members of colonial tribunals down to the tribal police, clerks, hut counters, and house boys that made the British system function. The curse, administrators felt, was directed against all civil servants who enforced English law.

Njuri members, had they been asked, would have been thoroughly bewildered by the charge. They perceived the sacred oaths—not curses—as intended solely to incorporate worthy individuals into their ranks. Traditionally these oaths were directed toward leading members of the age-set just below their own, as one by one the family heads/ apprentice elders were drawn into the fellowship of those above them, eventually to become ruling elders in their turn.

By the 1920s, however, the conquest had added a new dimension to this transfer of power. At that time the ruling elders—including all members of the Njuri Nceke—came from the Kiramana (in Tigania, Kilamunya) age-set.[9] Family heads—the set below them—were men of Murungi, the group that had been warriors at the time of British conquest. Many men of Murungi had served colonialism from its inception, rising through administrative ranks from hut counters, bodyguards, and tribal police to headmen, tribunal members, and chiefs.

The British wished to pit these men—young, vigorous, and partially anglicized—against the ruling elders of the Njuri. From the colonial perspective it was simply a case of replacing the elderly with those young enough to have learned British ways, men who had been anglicized since early warriorhood and had now reached middle age. From the Meru perspective it was this same group—the family heads of Murungi age-set—whom the ruling elders of the Njuri wished to draw into their ranks. Both sides, ironically, intended the men of Murungi to assume control of tribal affairs. The question was in whose name they would rule, Meru or England.

By the mid-1920s both sides had carried out their plans. Many of the most prominent men of Murungi, now approaching the end of their period as family heads, had been incorporated into the Njuri as tradition required. Simultaneously, they had risen with the Meru colonial service to positions as headmen, chiefs, tribunal judges, and even members of the Local Native Council. Such men thus served two masters, bending to the British as required while shielding the Njuri as they could. In practice this usually meant verbal acquiescence and token compliance with British administrative orders, combined with sporadic doses of prevarication, evasion, and delay.

By 1925–1926 most (if not all) leading Meru in the colonial administration had indeed entered their period of senior (ruling) elderhood, having joined either their ridgetop Kiama of elders or—if eminent—the Njuri Nceke. Most of the senior African colonial officials, cattle rich by virtue of their administrative post, were almost certainly Njuri members. Although superficially aware of "what" was happening, district officers had no idea of the cultural context within which these changes took place, a condition of ignorance the Meru took care to maintain. As one colonial official complained: "The Murungi Mwiriga [sic: "age-set"; Mwiriga is a ridgetop community] began to take on the status of Kiama [sic: "ruling"] Elders from the Kiramana, . . . impossible to find out what is taking place."[10]

NJURI UNDERGROUND

These limits on British power allowed the Njuri Nceke to continue certain aspects of its preconquest role. Its legislative function had been largely usurped by the conquerors. The executive function had also withered, as the traditional public proclamations had been formally banned. The judicial function, however, continued "underground," as the Njuri remained the court of last resort for Meru seeking legal redress in traditional ways.

As a judicial institution the Njuri even worked together with the British in at least three ways. At one level it struck out whenever possible against the very "witchcraft bands" that so worried the administration, sending little groups of former warriors to burn the huts of the A-Athi, Kagita, Mwaa, and other fringe societies, scattering their members in the same way as before the conquest.

The Njuri members also worked to alleviate the social tensions caused by witchcraft, a point of particular irony in an era when the British were convinced they practiced it. Fulfilling their judicial functions, the Njuri elders gathered to resolve each instance of bewitchment at the moment it disturbed communal peace. Livestock fines were levied as the causes of each conflict were unraveled and resolved. The peace that was thereby restored to each community clearly dovetailed with

British expectations of a harmonious tribal society, under the guiding hand of colonialism. The British remained unaware, however, of any contribution but their own.

The Njuri finally worked with the British to preserve the Meru lands against an outside threat. During the early 1920s a small but constant trickle of partially anglicized Gikuyu appeared in Meru, hoping to buy fertile cropland. The Gikuyu system of land ownership had begun to resemble that of England, in that individuals gained full title over specific plots of ground. Many Gikuyu had grown shilling rich in British service. Now they wished to invest their surplus wealth in land, to be worked for profit by the Meru.

Before the conquest Gikuyu settlement in Meru regions would have been met by clouds of warriors. During the early 1920s, however, famine-driven Meru elders proved far more willing to exchange what they still perceived as the temporary "use" of their communal holdings for the cash (or livestock) required for survival. In theory the process could have continued until all of Meru had passed into Gikuyu ownership, with its people working as herders and sharecroppers for the wealthy outsiders.

The British, on becoming aware of the problem, promptly passed laws to forbid it. They were ignored. Alarmed, Meru district officers made frantic efforts to learn which lands had actually changed hands. This also proved impossible, because no Meru would admit such sales took place. Where Gikuyu appeared, they claimed only to be working for Meru with whom they were distant kin.

In this instance, however, the power of Njuri proved stronger than England. Equally alarmed by the appearance of traditional enemies, it proclaimed that all land exchanges must cease. The response was universal. Gikuyu wanderers were turned away, and no other Meru lands passed into outside hands for the next forty years.

The British, of course, had no idea of the extent to which the Njuri Nceke worked to further colonial goals, and thus continued sporadically to burn the council's meeting huts and arrest its members. The irony of these actions was not lost on Meru elders, who would wait until British officers were in hearing distance and then sing: "Njuri-i-i, even when doing right, Njuri-i-i, it is doing wrong."[11]

KAGITA UNDERGROUND

The 1920s was also an era of evolution for several of Meru's deviant groups. Among the most tenacious were the councils of Kagita. The

Kiama Kia Kagita had survived prior periods of famine by adopting the form of dancing societies. After 1900, Kagita bands had moved among the homesteads of every Meru region, trading song, dance, and the threat of bewitchment for porridge and beer.

By the 1920s many bands had begun to settle and take root, with at least one becoming permanent in every Meru region. Several bands, notably those along the montaine-forest fringes in Imenti and Igembe, grew relatively large. No longer willing to wander, they built huge, permanent huts modeled after the traditional war hut. These they protected in their own traditional fashion, placing three-foot tall Ndindi sticks and the customary vines around them to form their zone of safety.

Once established, each ban began to extend its influence over those homesteads nearest their own. Before the conquest they would have acquired foods for feasting through visits ("by singing") to each homestead in its turn. Now, feeling increasingly secure, several Kagita councils developed new tactics to ensure that regular supplies of beer and grain would be brought directly to them. Historically, Ndindi sticks and vines had always been set in a circle around the growing crops of those who sought protection against thieves. In the early 1920s they were placed with equal care across the public paths, especially those used by the wives and daughters of wealthy homesteads to fetch wood and water.

Women who crossed these areas and caught sight of the sticks would visibly sicken, developing the specific afflictions associated by tradition with the Kagita. Attempts to consult one of the mainstream ritualists were fruitless; they would simply "take [the victim's] goats, then 'divine' that she had been cursed by the Kagita." The women had no choice but to approach the hut of Kagita itself and ask it to alleviate the symptom ("remove the curse"). Its healers would agree to do so, once the women provided the society with foods for a feast: "Thus, Kagita would achieve its true goal, the goal of every stomach Kiama, to reach in and eat [devour] the rich man's property."[12]

Each woman, of course, was to carry the large gourds of millet porridge, beans, and beer to the Kagita assembly. Her illness was then ceremonially removed by the appropriate elders. But because the final aspect of the rituals of curse removal invoked the "kinship clause," each victim was bound in "sisterhood" to every member of the group. Thereafter, they were "invited" to remain and partake of the feast, beer, and dancing: "There was no choice for an unmarried girl over going to the Kagita [hut] or not. A Kagita curse remover would just point at you with his smallest finger and say, 'You, girl, come into [the hut of] Kagita.' If a girl refused, she would become ill with their curse and perhaps die."[13]

Colonial officials of this era made much of this element of compulsion, using it to justify their efforts to stamp out the society completely. They were particularly angered by reports that *akenye* (unmarried girls, virgins) were coerced into Kagita huts "in defiance of tribal custom in regard to sexual amusements, including all-night orgies of nude dancing. Parents were prevented from taking vengeance through their terror of a fearsome curse invoked against those who interfered."[14]

Once again colonial officials were wholly unaware of the cultural context within which these events occurred, as well as the history of the Kagita itself. Former members of the society, for example, uniformly declared that the unmarried girls most likely to be chosen for their feasts were those who had lost fathers in the years of plague and famine. Their incorporation into the Kiama, therefore, was little more than an extension of the Kagita's normal practice of offering refuge to those in distress. More hostile informants declared that the women were deliberately chosen for the wealth of their homesteads and the abundance that could thus be provided for feasts. Whatever the case, the society's primary focus was not on sex but on feasting, an emphasis wholly in keeping with its prior history.

Nonetheless, by the mid-1920s the Kagita's unprecedented inclusion of unmarried women had two unexpected consequences. One was the rising anger of family heads, whose teenage daughters were increasingly involved. A second grew from the equally unprecedented appearance of "strangers" at their feasts, for the inclusion of unmarried girls drew single men as well.

These strangers were drawn from the Miriti age-set, the group immediately below that of the family heads (Murungi) and ruling elders (Kiramana). At the time of British conquest they had been youths. Had no conquest occurred, they would have spent the decade of 1912–1922 as warriors, forbidden by tradition from contact with women. Instead they had left Meru to serve the British as plantation workers, safari porters, or members of the Carrier Corps. These experiences had steadily eroded their respect for warrior traditions, especially those that required a decade of sexual abstinence.

Thus, when the drums of the Kagita rumbled at sundown, many began to join its older members at the dancing huts, seeking relief from hunger and excitement from the dance. For over a century Kagita tradition had restricted its membership to the married of each sex. These strangers, however, were often shilling rich and came with gifts of goats and beer. By the 1920s, custom had crumbled, and no former warrior was turned away. Nor, as growing numbers of young men appeared, was compulsion needed to recruit single women. Often they simply slipped away from their parents' gaze to join the dancers.

Including the unmarried, however, caused an internal division within the Kagita itself. Many of its older men and women, especially in the southern regions, objected to the appearance of unmarried persons as a violation of ancestral ways. At some point in the 1920s these more conservative members responded in typically Meru fashion, forming a new and more select council within the old, a "higher" stage to which only the most eminent among them could belong. Appearing first in Igoji, it spread south into Mwimbi-Muthambi and then north into the other Meru regions, usually under the name of Kiama Kia Kaundu, the "council of darkness."

The Kaundu may have been ineptly named. Contemporary informants suggest that it meant nothing more than implying that the groups would meet at night. The word was picked up by the British, however, as indicative of "dark" intent:

> The Kagita is a secret society . . . said to be expert in vegetable poisons. No one can refuse to comply with a demand for food or toddy from a member. Should he do so, he is likely to be bewitched. . . . Within this society, a new order sprang up five years ago [1922], known as the Njuri a Kaundu. . . . So far as can be learnt a Kaundu [*sic:* man of Kaundu] uses . . . a poison of white powder.[15]

Once again colonial investigators lacked historical context. The term Kaundu had long been used, particularly in southern Meru, as one of several names given to the ad hoc splinter groups that formed when one of the larger councils failed to resolve a specific conflict. By tradition the smaller body would retire into the "darkness" until the issue that concerned the larger assembly had been resolved. The Kagita's selection of the term may therefore have simply reflected their adherence to that tradition.

There is no doubt that the 1920s represented an era of Kagita expansion. Existing groups grew steadily, not only by incorporating "victims" but also by offering a refuge for the hungry and the bored. New groups also hived off from existing ones, either as more select Kiamas (Njuris) or simple duplicates. The rate of increase, however, should not be overstated. British sources of the period frequently imply that all

Meru were under the sway of the witchcraft groups. The claim is exaggerated. The Kagita remained what it had been for generations, a
fringe society—composed of many tiny branches—at the geographic
and social edges of Meru communal life. Despised by the mainstream,
it survived the 1920s as it had always done, by providing a permitted
deviation from the behavioral norm.

The Kagita did, of course, incorporate African members of the colonial administration. Chiefs, headmen, police, messengers, and even
hut counters (census takers) may have entered its ranks. The British
perceived these contacts as systematic, forming part of a districtwide
effort to subvert colonial rule. Kagita elders saw the same actions as
nothing more than an extension of their normal quest for food. Before
the conquest "wealthy elders," men with the largest herds and fields,
were those whose many wives had sired warrior sons. By the 1920s,
"wealthy elders" were those who worked for Europeans. Inevitably,
these men became the favored targets of groups like the Kagita. Initially
sought out as food providers, they then entered the society itself. Having done so, they were bound by oath to conceal it from the whites.

THE EVOLUTION OF A-ATHI

The mid-1920s also proved favorable to the various bands of A-Athi
hunters who had survived the numerous restrictions imposed upon
their way of life by British conquest. Before the colonial period A-Athi
hunting bands in every Meru region had been driven gradually up
Mount Kenya's slopes, forced into retreat before the migration of
far larger numbers of the Meru mainstream—herders, cultivators, and
above all, destroyers of forest.

Until 1900 the A-Athi had sporadically delayed this uphill migration,
defending their alleged hunting zones with "automatic" curses, symbolized by the placement of the previously described Ndindi ("bones") or
Nguchua ("claws") to delineate their hunting zones. Trespass beyond
such markers triggered conditions of ritualized illness (Mugiro) that
could be removed only by petitioning the A-Athi themselves. More serious violations, such as the intrusion of entire clans into a hunting
area, were met with collective action in which whole bands of A-Athi
would march around the newcomers' homesteads, carrying the corpse
of a gazelle while chanting phrases meant to cause listeners to sicken.

Hunters armed with such supernaturally lethal weapons should have
had little difficulty in defending their terrain as long as needed, but the

A-Athi were handicapped in two ways. One was their economic dependence on the very cultivators they attempted to expel. The A-Athi boasted they lived wholly from the forest, on a diet of little more than meat and honey. In fact all hunting clans traded forest produce to people of the mainstream, exchanging surplus honey, meat, skins, and other items for grain, usually in the form of millet porridge. On festive occasions such exchanges would "turn liquid," as the A-Athi would trade *uuki,* a honey wine, for *marua,* a fermented millet beer. The A-Athi were also handicapped by their dependence on an abundance of wild game. An occasional intrusion by mainstream Meru wanderers was not disruptive. Most cultivators still held to the generations-old taboo against consumption of wild animals. Their occasional incursions, therefore, were usually meant to search out either grazing areas or firewood.

During the 1880s, however, such incursions had come often and with new intent. Responding to economic pressure from Swahili, Somali, and Kamba traders, whose caravans reached Meru from both the north and the east, individual Meru began to comb the lowest sections of the black (montaine) forest zone in search of ivory. On occasion, particularly in Mwimbi, mainstream Meru formed "partnerships" with local A-Athi to whom they were distant kin, inducing them to hunt down elephant and return with tusks to trade. Cultivators then stored the tusks beneath their huts until new caravans appeared.

Hunting of this nature gradually increased throughout the 1880s, supplemented by the first European-led caravans, which passed through portions of the lower forest from Mwimbi to Igembe, each time with unprecedented and continual slaughter of game. In response the elephants in particular began to drift away from areas in which they were most threatened, moving to higher, colder, and often impenetrable sections of the mountain and thus beyond the A-Athi reach.

The buffalo went next. The 1890s brought a series of natural catastrophes, both to the forested and cultivated sections of the mountain. The rinderpest epidemic of 1890, for example, exterminated not only most of the Meru cattle but also many of Mount Kenya's buffalo, despite the isolation of their forest. This epidemic was followed by drought and famine (1891), locust invasions (1894, 1895), a second drought (1898), a cattle (and buffalo) plague (1899), and a widespread period of semifamine that stretched over the next two years.

One consequence of these disasters was a rapid erosion of the Meru tradition that prohibited hunting and consumption of wild game. The

1890s saw ever greater numbers of mainstream Meru, driven by hunger and lack of alternatives, combing the lower forest areas in search of sustenance. As a result the various species of antelope, wild pig, mountain zebra, and even monkey also began to disappear.

Left alone, the A-Athi might have eventually succeeded in repelling the mainstream invasion, using both "automatic" and "collective" curses to strike a balance between themselves and the advancing cultivator-herders. The year 1906, however, was the time of conquest, as men of the mainstream submitted to England and the populated star-grass zone came under colonial control.

By 1907 the impact of England began to be felt in the forests as well. A series of colonial proclamations, intended to preserve wildlife, declared Mount Kenya's entire montaine forest region to be crown land and forbade both native habitation and hunting game. At one point "native inhabitants" were even forbidden to enter the lower forest fringes to cut wood. Those found violating the ban were subject to imprisonment.[16]

In 1908 the Crown Land Ordinances were supplemented by the imposition of a "native pass system," similar to that used in England's South African colonies. All natives were officially restricted to their designated tribal reserves. In Meru this meant restriction to the star-grass zone, below the montaine forest, and within that, to one's own ridgetop community. Those wishing to go elsewhere required colonial permission in the form of a *chiti* (chit, pass) from an appropriate authority. Any native found outside his reserve was subject to arrest.[17]

The pass system was enforced with increasing success during the following years. Its original intent had been to stop the movement of warrior bands as they set out on traditional raids. Subsequently, it was applied to both family heads and ruling elders, fleeing newly imposed hut tax obligations by moving their threatened flocks, herds, and often entire families into remote forest regions. Almost incidentally, it restricted the A-Athi as well, cutting them off from long-established trading patterns with their mainstream kin and thereby isolating them within the forests.

The next blows fell in 1909–1910. As the implications of hut-tax collection began to sink in, small bands of warriors decided to defend their cows. One result was the sporadic sequence of "ridgetop rebellions," in Muthambi-Mwimbi and Tigania. In each instance the colonial tax collectors were met by warriors in battle dress, shouting defiance. A volley of shots by the collectors swiftly broke their resistance, but the victorious colonial police then seized far larger numbers of livestock than were required for taxes, often leaving entire ridgetops totally impoverished.

In consequence elders throughout Meru were gripped by increasing panic. The actual loss of cattle was less important than the fact that the invader could seize them in numbers beyond those allowed by tradition, while simultaneously forbidding counterraiding in return. The thought of total and permanent destitution, predictably, sent ridgetops into action. Entire herds were shifted uphill, into the forests where whites would never find them. With them moved the warriors, intending both to guard the animals and drive them higher into the forest zone to escape detection. They were accompanied in turn by sufficient numbers of women to cook and care for the men. The impact of these migrants on the game was inevitable. Barred from water and open grazing, animals moved away.

The smallest of these refugee bands moved continually, seeking forage in the forest. Most, however, sought more permanent quarters, settling their herds and constructing new homesteads near adequate sources of grazing and water—in total disregard of the Ndindi sticks that warned of A-Athi hunting. Worse, by 1910 the colonial administration had begun responding to what it perceived as either cattle rustling or tax evasion by sending military expeditions to search the lower regions of the forest for "illegal occupants." In consequence, "whenever natives were found occupying unalienated crown land, they were compelled to move into the nearest reserve."[18]

Once more, laws aimed at mainstream Meru caught the A-Athi as well. Often their communities were totally disrupted—women and children taken into custody, food stores impounded, bee hives plundered, and huts burned to the ground. Those forced downslope into the nearest native reserve, in compliance with the British order, could always return to the forests, but the abundance of game that had sustained them depended on isolation, and that was passing away.

As a result the A-Athi way of life began to pass away as well. As Europe's wars, pandemic diseases, insect plagues, and recurrent famine took their toll upon the flocks and herds of mainstream Meru, ever greater numbers of the survivors scoured the forests for sufficient protein to survive. In consequence as wildlife nearest to the populated (star-grass) zone gradually disappeared, some A-Athi followed the game into the higher, colder regions of the forest. Others, however, unable to withstand the constant cold, began to look downhill into the populated zone for other means to keep their way of life.

PRE-1920S: MIGRATION DOWNHILL

The A-Athi way of life was centered on the meat feast, the times made joyful by collection of a surplus, when entire bands could gorge on meat and honey wine, then sing and dance through the night. Between the time of conquest and the early 1920s, band after band of A-Athi hunters abandoned the now silent montaine forest zone, drifting down-hill to resettle along the highest fringes of the star-grass regions, where meat might still be found in the remaining Meru flocks and herds.

Contemporary A-Athi informants, now among the oldest men in Meru, recall this transition as a time of terror, an era when they were forced to live among far larger numbers of mainstream Meru, deprived of the psychological protection offered by the forest. As always they fought their insecurity with magic. The first step, repeated throughout Meru, was to reestablish the traditional protective zone, within which they could continue to function as A-Athi. There were several variants. In Igembe the zone was established around a *mukiitia* tree; in Imenti, around the traditional Nkima (skull) of beeswax and antelope skin.

The outer boundaries of each zone were then delineated by Ndindi, notched, reddened, and topped with the feathers of carrion eaters, as in the days when the slender three-foot sticks protected massive hunting zones. By the 1920s, however, they often guarded little more than the area around a single shabby hut; yet for the Meru they had lost nothing of their potency. To intensify the impact of the sticks, the area between them was sprayed with liquid dung ("of an unhealthy goat"). Thereaf-ter, both sticks and dung were verbally enjoined to place a specific curse on any man of the mainstream who penetrated the protected zone.

The next step was to construct a central lodge—the normal beehive hut made of banana leaves—where the A-Athi could assemble for their rituals and feasts. On its completion each band chose a spokesman, most often the senior ritualist among them (the Muga wa A-Athi), who gathered other elders into the group's Kiama. British sources of that pe-riod believed that A-Athi elders were organized into a hierarchy of ranks and grades. In fact the only "junior" members were their male children, often gathered into small Kiamas of their own in imitation of their elders. A-Athi boys often built tiny huts of tree limbs and banana leaves. Their protective symbols were the skulls of little birds and tiny twigs daubed with red clay. Their "feasts" consisted usually of millet porridge, which they renamed "buffalo" for each occasion. Known as the "wings [messengers] of A-Athi," they would strap wooden bells upon their hips, then race pellmell through surrounding villages, their clattering passage serving to proclaim an impending A-Athi feast.

The third step, a challenge faced by A-Athi bands across Meru, was to provide meat for these intended feasts. Tradition prohibited hunters from consuming the meat of domestic livestock, just as the mainstream Meru were forbidden to devour wild game. Faced with the progressive elimination of their original meat supply, however, the A-Athi resorted to ritual. Beef, when provided for A-Athi consumption, was referred to only as *magara*, an ancient name for buffalo. Goat and mutton, once in A-Athi hands, became *nkurungu*, or bushbuck.

The acquisition of buffalo or bushbuck was referred to as "hunting." A "hunt" began with a decision by assembled A-Athi elders on which homestead would be chosen to provide the needed animals for an impending feast. Thereafter, the entire group "hunted" the flocks and herds of the selected homestead by moving openly and as a single body into the main compound.

Tradition suggests that A-Athi ritual once again evolved within this decade, now giving an expanded role to the Ndindi sticks. In the past the wooden markers had always been placed at irregular intervals in the ground as passive warnings against intrusion. Now, as the family head emerged to greet his "guests," his eyes moved first to an Ndindi, notched, reddened, and befeathered as required by custom, but held high in the hand of an A-Athi elder rather than set in the ground.

The elder, usually a ritualist, approached the homeowner with great deliberation, raised the reddened stick, then slowly passed its feathered tip around his victim's head, bringing it to rest inches from his eyes. Having thus symbolically "bound" the victim by focusing his attention, the ritualist chanted the curse by which he would be bound should he fail to heed (i.e., feed) A-Athi. After each phrase the ritualist paused as if asking a question. The assembled A-Athi would respond with one voice: "Mb-u-u-u, mbu!" (Danger!)[19]

The ritual that surrounded the A-Athi Nguchua ("claw") had also evolved. The tiny curved, clawlike sticks, used during the hunting era as final warning to those ignoring the Ndindi, served the same purpose in colonial times. In theory the mere sight of an Ndindi should have caused family heads to provide whatever livestock the A-Athi required.

In fact, many promised, later only to evade, delaying actual delivery in hope that fewer or inferior beasts would be accepted.

In such instances the Nguchua sticks once more served as final A-Athi warnings. Filled with "magic" powder and topped with the tail of a mongoose, the Nguchua had traditionally been placed before the huts of offenders who dared to cultivate in A-Athi regions. In the 1920s, although their purpose remained unchanged, the manner of use evolved along lines similar to those of the Ndindi.

A family head who evaded or delayed his promised livestock gift to the A-Athi could expect a second visit from its spokesman. Host and visitor would sit opposite one another on the ground, the hunter holding a tiny Nguchua clenched in his hand. If displeased with the subsequent discussion, he would simply open it, holding it palm up for the elder to see.

The mere sight of the little claw stick was believed sufficient to cause the host to sicken. In most instances, however, A-Athi members intensified the initial effect ("sharpened the Mugiro") by planting other Nguchua at various points within the homestead—near gates, granaries, and so forth—where their subsequent gradual discovery could steadily reinforce the initial impact and thus compel the stricken victim to comply.

MID-1920S: A-ATHI MBUJU (THE "POISONERS")

The two traditional forms of A-Athi warning were eventually supplemented by a third, drawn from outside Meru tradition. This was known among the northern A-Athi as Mbuju (or mbujuju), the "fat one." The concept of Mbuju may have appeared among the A-Athi in Tigania-Igembe as early as 1909. The original term was said to have been derived from a poison of that name, brought into Tigania by a man known as Mutiga wa Leria, a hunter from the Kamba region.[20]

Mbuju poison was believed much stronger than that used by the hunters of Meru. A-Athi poisons were vegetable based, drawn from plants found in neighboring Tharaka, where they were gathered by ritualists of that region. Once collected, they were reduced to powder, mixed with substances (e.g., bile or blood) taken from wild animals, then sold "uphill" into the Meru regions. Although the mixtures may well have been unpleasant, their toxicity almost certainly came more from the power of suggestion than from the ingredients themselves.

The Kamba poison, however, was a mineral, with the appearance and consistency of powdered salt. British administrators were unanimous in their belief that it was deadly, with ingestion leading to "vomiting, diarrhea, passage of blood . . . and death within hours."[21] Meru informants sharply disagree, declaring that the poison was never meant to kill, because the antidote was always close at hand.

If true, this assertion would have been entirely in keeping with other aspects of Meru supernatural belief, in which victims were expected to avert death by taking remedial (although ritualized) actions to resolve whatever conflicts had been engendered. Both British and Meru sources record the "antidote for Mbuju" as composed of honey, sheep's blood, and (sheep's) liver.[22] These three ingredients, however, form the basis of most of the Meru cleansing rituals, used to cast out the equally ritualized illnesses caused by traditional forms of witchcraft. In those instances the three ingredients were consumed as part of an oath through which the victim verbally cast out feelings of hostility ("If I feel anger, let this oath kill me") along with any physical symptoms. Because the antidote was entirely symbolic, it seems reasonable to assume that Mbuju "poison" was symbolic as well, deriving its alleged power from equal parts of suggestibility, faith, and fear.

By the early-1920s, therefore, practitioners of the Mbuju rituals, operating along lines entirely consistent with Meru tradition, had begun to form identifiable subgroups within several of the A-Athi Kiamas operating in Tigania, Igembe, and at least two regions of Imenti. Within these areas the most senior elders periodically withdrew from their larger associations to "buy" (learn the rituals of) Mbuju from one of their members who had traveled in distant regions. Among the A-Athi these gatherings were known as "Njuri a Mbuju" (council-of-councils to learn the rituals of Mbuju), a term eventually made known to members of the colonial administration.

By the mid-1920s, existing evidence suggests, several of these Mbuju gatherings carried A-Athi patterns of extortion to new extremes. Meru informants remember Mbuju practitioners as "carrying wooden staffs and marking lips and foreheads with red ocher," in direct imitation of the traditional Njuri Nceke. Thereafter, these bands "went around the villages demanding payments . . . or making threats to people. The songs they sang as they moved about were abusive and distasteful. At the same time, they danced, stamping their feet and thick sticks [staffs] on the ground and singing of the illness to come."[23]

Colonial reports corroborate this pattern, one in 1924 describing "Mbujo" (sic) as a "witchcraft league" of considerable power and many adherents. It was allegedly led by a certain "Mboro" (probably M'Mburu), believed by the British to be the group's "high priest," who was sentenced to prison in that year in an effort to check its growth.[24] Reports in subsequent years describe the Mbuju, with somewhat more accuracy, as a "higher grade" of the A-Athi organization, led in part by the previously mentioned Mutiga wa Leria. It was the Mbuju, one administrator declared, "who served Athi when victims evaded its demands. In such cases, two Mbuju would visit their compounds to bury pairs of Nguchua near their . . . dwelling huts and water sources."[25]

Obviously, most elders did capitulate, providing Mbuju A-Athi bands with whatever livestock was required to remove the (ritualized illness of) Mugiro, as well as other animals as "gifts" (fees) for their subsequent initiation into one of the groups themselves. Oral evidence suggests the number of livestock was subject to inflation. In 1909, for example, an elder visited by A-Athi in Igembe paid one bull and a single goat to remove his ritualized affliction, as well as a second goat to serve as his initiation fee. By the 1920s such demands had reached two bulls, two goats, one ram, seven gourds of millet beer, and (in Igembe) seven bundles of miraa (Cathulis edulis, or qhat), a mild narcotic that produced euphoria when chewed. Thereafter, as each new initiate became "kin" to all members of the group, he was required to provide one additional gift (e.g., a goat) for each subsequent A-Athi feast.

There is no doubt that incorporation into the A-Athi occurred most often through compulsion. There were, notwithstanding, several equally compelling reasons to join freely. In times of famine, of course, the A-Athi served along with other stomach Kiamas to provide society's only alternative to hunger: "Some married elders [family heads] joined just to find food. In those days the poor were the largest part of A-Athi membership. They simply sought a place where they could feed enormously on meat."[26]

MID-1920S: A-ATHI JUSTICE

By the mid-1920s, however, the A-Athi had become so powerful and widespread that many bands grew rich in surplus livestock. With one need satisfied, A-Athi tactics were extended to meet others. The most dramatic extension occurred in the judicial sphere, where A-Athi bands began to grope their way toward an alternative system of justice, different from that of either the Njuri or the crown.

Before the conquest, of course, A-Athi elders had used the Kiama to resolve conflicts among their own members, as well as those between hunters and the mainstream Meru. Cultivators and herders could not approach their own Kiamas (or Njuri) to resolve a dispute with A-Athi. In such cases elders refused their services, in keeping with their own tradition of ignoring the existence of fringe communities.

By the 1920s, however, mainstream Meru in every region had begun to appreciate the value of having A-Athi "kinsmen" resolve disputes between themselves and other cultivator-herders. A canny cattle keeper, for example, deciding to collect the livestock debts owed him by others, might actively solicit membership in an A-Athi band. Having paid the required animals as fees, he gained the right to ask his newly acquired kinsmen to assist in prompt collection of his debts, preferably by an immediate communal visit to the debtor. Such visits were always effective. Later in the decade, debts of this type were even collected en masse, with the A-Athi from a specific band passing from homestead to homestead in search of what they felt was due to any of their members.

Often the tactic used to guarantee collection was little stronger than a song. The A-Athi would assemble inside an alleged debtor's compound, then sing variations of the phrase "yai wega nokunenkerwa," which suggests that it is better to "be given." The implication, however, is that it is better to receive than to compel payment. The single song often sufficed. Because alleged victims had no recourse to their own Kiamas, they had no alternative but to submit.

Inevitably, A-Athi bands developed ways to extend their influence, in this instance over the local Kiamas themselves. When local elders had assembled to deliberate a matter of concern to local A-Athi, members of their band would slowly circle the field in which the council met, chanting variations of the phrases: "U-u-u-u, wikiri. Twengwa wikiri. Twengana wikiri. U-u-u-u-u-u-u-u." (O-h-h, woe to you. If we lose, woe to you. If we win, woe to you. O-h-h-h-h-h-h.)

The last sound, chanted with infinite menace, implied that the A-Athi would win regardless of how the conflict was resolved. In certain instances the bands left no doubt as to their wishes. If displeased with Kiama deliberations, they circled the assembled elders, chanting in the most abusive manner: "U-u-u-u, uronuka ja mai ja kuru. U-u-u-u, nyurunguru ja mai. U-u-u-u." (O-h-h, smell(s) like dog waste. O-h-h, drip(s) like feces. O-h-h-h.)

Kiama elders could scarcely fail to be influenced. Each knew that
A-Athi bands, if sufficiently displeased, could visit every one of their
homesteads, requesting "gifts" that would eventually lead to their
incorporation into the society itself. Although tradition required they
ignore the intrusions and, indeed, the fringe group's very existence,
more and more of their decisions came to conform to A-Athi expectations as larger and larger numbers of them were drawn into the
society itself.

LATE 1920S: A-ATHI VERSUS ENGLAND

By 1927 colonial administrators were thoroughly alarmed. Most agreed
that the society had become a threat to the crown itself. One district officer, having made extensive inquiries, wrote that

> membership of the [A-Athi] society has become enormous. So large have
> they become that they have become rulers of the country [i.e., Meru]. No
> member dare sue one another before the [Local Native Tribunal] Kiama. All
> disputes have to be settled by the elders of the [A-Athi] lodge. Any Mwathi
> [Mu-Athi: man of A-Athi] wishing to force anyone who is not a member to
> pay a debt, has him seized and brought to the [local branch of] Athi who
> force him to pay under penalty of being bewitched, and he has also to pay
> a "mara" [corruption of *magara*, or "buffalo"; actually, a bull] and "ngu-
> rugu" [corruption of *nkurungu*, the old term for "bushbuck"; actually, a
> goat] and become a member.[27]

This and subsequent reports argued persuasively that the ruling elders of the A-Athi, usually designated as the "Njuri a Mbuju," were at
least partially composed of Meru's leading colonial chiefs and headmen. To the British this increasing convenience suggested nothing less
than systematic subversion of the colonial African administration, with
no other goal than the eventual overthrow of British rule.

Such claims would have thoroughly surprised the elders of the
A-Athi. The gradual extension of their influence into the higher ranks of
Meru's African colonial service was unquestioned. As with both the
Njuri Nceke and the Kagita, however, A-Athi motives were much less
dramatic than the British supposed. Like other stomach Kiamas, the
A-Athi initially perceived chiefs, headmen, and other African members
of the administration simply as wealthy men. Obviously the steady
receipt of wages from their British overlords led, without exception, to
an equally steady increase in their livestock. As a result requesting
such surplus animals to atone for having wronged one of their members seemed nothing more than the continuation of a tradition that

had endured for more than two hundred years. Inviting men of power to contribute for a feast was clearly not the same as moving toward political rebellion.

Thus, by the late 1920s many chiefs, headmen, tribunal judges, and other cattle-rich members of the colonial administration had, in fact, been recruited into the A-Athi. Having entered their ranks, they were prohibited by oath from imposing government obligations on those who were now ritually kin. This was particularly apparent when they were commanded to seize livestock, particularly for such universally re-sented levies as the hut tax. In such cases government servants, from hut counters to chiefs, found themselves forced to fill their quotas by draw-ing solely from those flocks and herds owned by members of the main-stream. This use of substitutes to meet colonial obligations engendered violent opposition from the mainstream Meru. Their resentment deep-ened as A-Athi immunity extended over time from livestock levies to la-bor quotas and indefinitely beyond. To be A-Athi, in some regions, meant freedom from England.

THREE CONTENDERS FOR THE CROWN

In fact members of the African colonial service were caught between three fires. Throughout the 1920s no fewer than three coherent social forces contended for allegiance within the Meru tribal regions, and it can easily be argued that each one ruled its share. The Local Native Tri-bunals, Local Native Council, and district office were all clearly cre-ations of the alien administration, as were each of the tiny "chief's headquarters" that had emerged across the district in their image. In theory this network ruled all Meru. In fact they controlled only Afri-cans within the tiny towns, most of whom lived around the smaller re-gional headquarters and a rising number near the missions. Beyond these points colonial influence was like a radio wave, strongest and most compelling at its source, but progressively weaker as it moved into the more distant hinterlands.

Within these outlying regions, from the forest fringes to the arid plains, the traditional Kiama system continued to survive. Every ridgetop community in Meru retained its local Kiama, available for consultation on request. In Mwimbi, Muthambi, and Igoji, the Njuri system had dissolved, the regional council-of-councils having failed to survive the onslaught and repeated arrest by district officers and fervent chiefs. In the north, however, the Njuri Nceke still functioned in its decentralized, deliberative fashion, meeting to resolve the conflicts of those who sought justice in traditional fashion. Its legislative and executive functions had been usurped by the British, because neither its collective decisions nor public proclamations could be enforced. Nonetheless, its judicial power remained essentially intact, providing easily understood alternatives to those bewildered by the complexity of British justice. As such, despite its formal dissolution by the British, it retained the allegiance of the hinterlands, where "every [mainstream] man in Meru obeyed it when they dared."[28]

Not all Meru, obviously, were men of the mainstream, and it was along the upper forest edges that the authority of the Njuri Nceke was challenged in its turn by the expanding fringe societies. There was nothing supernatural about this challenge. A-Athi, Kagita, Wathua, Mwaa, and others like them may well have been "secret" to the British, but they were perfectly well known in Meru, as variants among the shifting cluster of fringe Kiamas that had formed part of Meru tradition since the original migration from Mbwaa.

Men of the fringes had shared in the major events of Meru history, including its darkest moments. The plagues and famines of the 1890s had struck at cultivator and hunter alike. Mainstream and fringe Meru had waged war together, and both had passed through the traumatic shock of British conquest, which had undone so much that gave life meaning. Both groups had been forced to adapt to the excesses of the Njama, colonial appointees who had set the precedents for mass extortion on a scale the fringe groups could never hope to match. Finally, the massive dislocations brought on by world war, global pandemics, universally imposed forced labor, and recurrent starvation had forced mainstream and fringe communities alike to adapt sharply if they intended to survive.

In retrospect it can be argued that the adaptations chosen by the fringe Kiamas proved most effective in adjusting to the reality of British rule. Faced with the demands of an outside power they could neither resist nor wholly comprehend, the men of Meru took three separate paths. With exceptions, those who were warriors (the Murungi age-set) at the moment of conquest opted gradually to join with their conquerors, whether by passive acquiescence to a labor draft or active assistance in enforcing British demands. In consequence many prospered, finding new forms of security and status as they rose within colonial ranks.

In contrast the significant minority of those who were family heads at the time of conquest (Kiramana) attempted to evade its consequences.

Abandoning mainstream tradition as inadequate against the British, men and women were drawn to the smaller, more tenuous, but nonetheless traditional points of refuge offered by the many fringe groups. Similarly, the ruling elders (Kaburia) chose to passively resist the conquerors. They gave token verbal compliance, while clinging steadily to whatever customs they could still uphold. Thus the entire Kiama system, that of Njuri (in the north), and the traditional forms of witchcraft all survived the first decades of British power, essentially through the loyalty of elders, whose steadfast use of these institutions permitted them continued life.

Interestingly, however, although the Njuri did survive as an alternative to British justice, it failed to evolve into an alternative center of command. At no time in its history did it attempt to marshal its supporters to expel, resist, or even evade the British occupiers. Rather its members proved content to take the role of "communal safety valve," indirectly supporting the colonial administration by providing an alternative to its judicial excesses. It did little else to offer refuge from the stress of alien rule.

The same cannot be said for the fringe Kiamas. Faced with identical stresses, they not only maintained tradition but also continued to evolve. The responses of each group remained firmly rooted in their individual customs, thus were largely restricted to either protecting or acquiring supplies of food. Yet each unprecedented extension of a formerly traditional ritual increased the security of its membership, thereby offering a sense of refuge from the reality of enduring foreign conquest.

Throughout Meru, as the ancient ways were legally forbidden, people turned toward ritual to relieve their rising insecurity. No ritual proved more effective than those of the fringe groups, initially in providing grain and meat, then offering beer, song, the lure of dancing, and the promise of forgetfulness through sex. Small wonder that those who joined the fringe groups came initially from men (and women) of the Kiramana age-set, the family heads deprived of their flocks and herds by plague, drought, famine, taxes, and direct extortion, thus eager to seek refuge from their insecurity. Small wonder that those who joined soon found themselves in search of status and security as well as food. Deprived of wealth in every traditional form, yet unable to lash out at England, they struck at other Meru instead, seeking both food and feelings of power. Ultimately they succeeded, for it was those of the fringes who suffered least from the demands of colonial rule.

CHAPTER XII

Persecution Traditions:
The Wars to End Witchcraft

"I have been engaged in the investigation of witchcraft
throughout this district. I have found that in addition to the
usual form of witchcraft . . . there exist in Tigania and
Igembe two secret societies in which witchcraft is used to
extort property or to enforce its orders. . . . These two . . .
are known as Aathi and Kagitha."[1]

Frank M. Lamb
District Commissioner, Meru
15 February 1928

THE CASE AGAINST WITCHCRAFT:
COMMISSIONER LAMB

By 1927, Meru's colonial administration was grinding slowly to a halt.
At headquarters, district officers felt handicapped by the system of ro-
tation that shifted them in and out of tribal regions once or twice a
year. Frank M. Lamb, for example, who became Meru district commissioner in mid-1927, found himself reading the reports of no fewer than
ten officers who had preceded him in the post during the prior decade.

Lamb had no doubt, however, as to what was happening to Meru's
administrative structure. Within Tigania, Igembe, and parts of Imenti
virtually every African colonial servant had stopped implementing
British orders unless prodded by direct command. The other regions
differed only in degree; tribunal members, chiefs, and headmen alike
showed increasing reluctance to carry out even minimal administrative routines.

The pattern seemed most evident to Lamb in the behavior of Meru's
Local Native Council. This body, launched with considerable colonial
enthusiasm in 1925, consisted of eight Meru "elected" from their communities and fourteen nominated by the British district commissioner.
In keeping with colonial ideas of vigorous administration, all members
were former warriors, selected in part for their command of Swahili
(the colonial lingua franca), success in prior posts (usually as tribal police), and pro-British attitudes. In British terms they were young, bright,

energetic, and just the men to make the legislative system come to life. In Meru terms they had been selected from among the family heads of the Murungi age-set, thus had no right to rule at all.

The Local Native Council (LNC) in fact began its work with vigor. Nominees and elected delegates found themselves in full agreement as to what they required from the government. During its opening session, for example, the LNC passed motion after motion, asking the British to provide secular rather than mission-based education, vocational rather than religious training, and the capital to begin service industries (e.g., grinding mills) to facilitate the provision of food. In 1926 and 1927, however, district officers noticed a curious passivity creep over the council, affecting nominated and elected members alike. Both groups attended regularly, yet never criticized nor even commented on any measure submitted to them by the district office. Nor, after the initial outburst of enthusiasm, did they bring forth substantive issues of their own. Indeed, British observers felt the members deliberately restricted discussions to the least significant issues they could resolve.[2]

The Local Native Tribunals displayed similar symptoms. These had originally been established in each of the major subtribes. The Tharaka tribunal was stillborn, its selected elders nodding off to sleep during meetings. The others, however, had been the focus of concentrated attention, as each administrator in turn attempted to cure what he perceived as creeping lassitude by increasingly stringent anglicization.

The Local Native Tribunal of Imenti, for example, lay closest to Meru district headquarters. Its proximity permitted interested administrators to tinker with various internal procedures in an attempt to increase judicial enthusiasm. In 1924, for example, the number of "judicial elders" was cut, an appeals system was instituted, and all "judgments were recorded in a book." In 1925 a schedule of fines was instituted, as well as a system of court fees, to be charged to both accused and plaintiff. These payments were to form the basis of regular wages for tribunal members, thus "spurring interest" in their work. In 1926 each tribunal was given a court clerk in charge of keeping the records. In 1927 most of the original elders were "retired with honor," so that younger men could be selected in their places.[3] The changes had no impact. Each move to anglicize the tribunals only drew them further from their Meru constituencies, eroding their willingness to act.

By 1927 passivity had spread across all Meru. After an initial inspection tour, Lamb found every chief in Igembe, all but one in Tigania, and all but the two nearest Imenti government headquarters either unable or unwilling to function, and at least seventy-two of the appointed headmen were afraid to carry on their work. The solution did not lie in their replacement with younger men. Subsequent experience taught the district commissioner that almost every new appointee reacted to an administrative appointment in the same way. Initially, each greeted the new responsibility with enthusiasm, touring their administrative zones to acquaint themselves with local problems in much the same way as newly appointed Europeans. Perceiving hostility, they reacted by acquiring the traditional coterie of henchmen in numbers sufficient to sustain authority. Soon, however, the new appointees also grew passive, initially about enforcing government livestock levies, then to bringing those accused of lawbreaking before the colonial tribunals. In many cases this passivity was accompanied by an increasingly obvious interest in acquiring "protective magic" in the form of talismans and charms.[4]

In other instances the new appointees resolved their inner conflicts by use of alcohol. Drunkenness had always been a problem among Meru colonial appointees, due in part to the problems of reconciling colonial requirements with their own tradition. By 1927, however, it had become endemic, and the "conflicts" were no longer solely with the British.

The relationship between colonial service and alcoholism can be most clearly illustrated by following the career of a single man, M'Mukura wa Kageta.[5] At the time of conquest he had been a warrior. He began his colonial career as a tribal policeman in Imenti. Having served in the Carrier Corps in World War I, he proved unusually adept at languages, mastering both Swahili and English. As a result he became head interpreter for Imenti in the early 1920s. Skilled, enthusiastic, and pro-British, he was selected as chief of the "largest and most unruly divisions of Imenti" in 1924.

The promotion proved his undoing. By 1925 he displayed several startling shifts in behavior. District officers described him as "increasingly obsessed with a fear of witchcraft" and uncertain that his protective talismans would protect him. In 1926 a new district officer described him as "having taken to heavy drinking," although his periods of sobriety were marked by flurries of administrative action. By 1927, Lamb perceived him as a magicphobe who had essentially stopped enforcing government authority within his district.

M'Mukura typifies the behavior of many Meru colonial servants of that era. Caught between conflicting wishes of the British, the fringe societies, and the Njuri, they grew fearful, escapist, and finally paralyzed. Lamb, not illogically, placed full blame on both the "illegal tribunals" and "secret witchcraft societies," which he perceived as having joined together through the device of potent curses "to rob the chiefs, and through them the entire machinery of British administration of all governing initiative, . . . [placing] the right of government veto directly into the hands of the most powerful and virulent of all, the Kiama of Njurincheke [sic]."[6]

THE INVESTIGATORS: HOPKINS AND LAMB

In January 1928, Lamb was joined at Meru district headquarters by J. Gerald H. Hopkins, appointed assistant district commissioner. Unlike many colonial officers of that era Hopkins had developed an intense interest in traditional African life, notably its supernatural aspects. During prior postings he had actively investigated what he referred to as "witch doctoring," generally by talking to "the cranky old fellows themselves" in regions where supernatural practitioners were not perceived as sources of resistance to British rule.[7]

Hopkins shared several of his conclusions with Lamb. He was unusual among his contemporaries in recognizing traditional forms of witchcraft as devices for social control. These controls, he felt, could take two forms: "verbal" and "visible." Visual controls among the Meru might include the vines of Kagita and the reddened sticks of A-Athi, or any other object obviously used to protect crops. Verbal controls, although taking the form of chants and curses, might also be used to scare off enemies or thieves.

Hopkins did not, however, envision the witch doctor as a positive social force. Aside from the medical merits to be derived from applying herbal remedies, he saw the entire profession as standing squarely in the path of British progress. "Surely," he argued in an earlier government report,

> such fellows looked askance upon English attempts to undermine the very superstitions upon which their powers have been based. . . . Usually this opposition takes the form of insistence upon obsolete and undesirable native customs, achieved by reading omens in such fashion as to predict [a] disastrous end for any individual who agrees to adopt a progressive innovation. Should an actual or contrived disaster fall upon these people, the witchdoctors will continue to terrorize, . . . declaiming that same fate will befall all others who stray [to] the teachings of Europe.[8]

Hopkins was initially unaware of the extent to which the A-Athi and the Kagita had spread throughout the northern Meru regions. During his first district tour, however, he was accompanied by a delegation of chiefs. Many times in Tigania and Igembe, Hopkins noted the unwillingness of his escorts to cross prominent paths that had been marked by reddened sticks or looping vines.

His requests for explanation were met with evasive responses, most chiefs simply stating that the markers denoted places where no one could pass. No wiser, Hopkins once ordered a chief to enter a forbidden area and was shocked when he refused. A second time he entered one himself and was startled to observe the faces of his entire escort become distorted with fear.

Hopkins chose to interpret both the markers and his escorts' refusal to ignore them as a restriction on British rule. No representatives of the king, he later told Lamb, could ever be restricted in their movements; nor could British authority run only into those areas where Africans approved.[9]

Lamb responded to Hopkins's argument with a decision to actively investigate the most dangerous of the societies, seeking to learn whatever might be needed to ensure their eventual destruction. He divided the labor, assigning Hopkins the Kagita and reserving the A-Athi for himself. The men chose to work together in investigation of the "illegal tribunals" (Njuri Nceke), which they perceived correctly as the most difficult task.[10]

Initially both men restricted inquiries to their own interpreters. Thereafter, they visited a considerable number of chiefs, headmen, and the most faithful of their subordinates. In addition they spoke with several converted Meru Christians, whose fear of traditional curses had been at least partially eroded by contact with English or Italian missionaries.

All of these informants were young, no elder having been willing to even discuss the topic. All proved markedly ambivalent, indicating distaste for both the fringe groups and (among Christians) the "illegal tribunals" but refusing to reveal either their whereabouts or the names of current members. Both officers found the process "quite maddening. One could spend hours patiently listening, while learning nothing at all. And yet, one was so sure that these fellows knew so much."[11]

The second stage of the investigation proved equally unsatisfying. By 1927 many thoughtful elders, including those within the Njuri Nceke, had grown increasingly concerned at the fringe groups' rising ability to distort ancestral tradition; they had even begun to cut into the prerogatives of Njuri itself. By 1927 certain of the oldest men in northern Meru—the "retired" elders, those closest to death, thus most prepared to defend ancestral ways—proved willing to denounce the fringe societies. At first such declarations were made in hushed and fearful tones. The belief that any fringe group's collective curse caused death was not lightly cast aside. Once again a solution was found within Meru tradition, in this instance, the practice of "secret" (oblique, indirect) speech.[12]

Meru tradition often alludes to the use of "secret" speech, usually during periods of crisis when men of the tribe have been captured by enemies. Under such circumstances each generation of warriors was taught to communicate indirectly ("secretly"), using proverbs, allegories, syllogisms, and even riddles to convey meaning. In such instances speakers can be certain only those who share a common oral heritage will comprehend, but outsiders—even those who learn the language—will be both subtly and suitably excluded.

The first elders to approach either Lamb or Hopkins, therefore, spoke indirectly, referring simply to the existence of certain "Kiamas of evil" and their desecration of ancestral ways. When pressed for details of the location and membership of specific branches, however, they became oblique, speaking in parables, riddles, and allegories, all intended to provide information to those familiar with the Meru way.

Such conversations proved exceptionally irritating to both Hopkins and Lamb, locked as they were into the British preference for brief, direct, and uncomplicated conversation. Still, although neither considered himself an expert on Meru culture, they were able to obtain detailed descriptions of fringe group activities in the 1920s as well as some insight into their history. Neither investigator managed to acquire accurate information on either the historical or recent activities of the Njuri Nceke, a topic that their elderly informants avoided. Instead they seem to have imposed a quasi-English judicial framework upon what they learned of the existing Meru system, crediting it with a degree of centralization and hierarchical order that no living Meru would have recognized:

> In addition to the secret societies, there are in existence four superior tribunals, most of whose members belong either to Aathi or Kagitha. Appeals have always been from the lower to the higher of these Kiamas, the names of which in order of superiority are:
> Njuri a Katha Kakai
> Njuri a Mbere
> Njuri a Mpingiri
> Njuri a Ncheke.[13]

For men of that era both Lamb and Hopkins proved skilled and dil-
igent investigators. The first of their "tribunals" (Katha Kakai) was almost certainly Kathaka Kai (the small bush), previously mentioned as a
traditional meeting point for the Njuri Nceke. The second and third
(Mbere and Mpingiri) will be remembered as two of the more select
subgroups, formed on an ad hoc basis by the Njuri Nceke to resolve
problems too hard for the larger group. The final term, of course, refers
to the Njuri Nceke itself.

The two investigators were inaccurate, however, in attributing a hierarchy to the groups. They assumed, not illogically, that the "illegal"
tribunals formed a judicial system similar to that of England, with appeals moving upward, from the "Katha Kakai" to the "Ncheke." They
also felt the core of each "court's" power lay not in native law but in
simple fear, because each of the alleged judges held the power to "lay
terrifying curses on people and things." In their view, then, native legal
proceedings were a travesty.

Hopkins claimed to have identified at least two of the tribunal's secret meeting places, at which gatherings of elders from Tigania and
Igembe had been held. He asserted that all participants in such meetings were compelled to attend. More important, he believed they had
been ordered, under penalty of being cursed, to follow policies of passive obstruction toward the colonial government. Specifically, they
were to refuse information to its officials, bring no cases of any kind
before government tribunals, give no evidence of any kind against
"witch doctors," or report any efforts at "extortion or injustice" by
the Njuri themselves.

Interestingly, Lamb and Hopkins decided the power of the Njuri
Nceke extended far beyond what could have been possible even under
favorable circumstances. To them, all chiefs, headmen, and lesser government officials were either members of these tribunals or lived in terror of their curse. And behind the tribunals lay the image of the witch
doctor: "It is essential, therefore, in order to make the work of both
government headmen and the official [i.e., colonial] tribunals possible . . . to break the power of these societies. . . . The powers of the
witchdoctors are enormous and each witchdoctor is a member of a secret society. This innovation will be checked."[14]

Lamb was unaware, of course, of the temporary, ad hoc nature of
the first three tribunals in his hierarchy. Nor did he recognize the role
all four had once played in traditional government. On the contrary he
decided the core of their power lay not within a framework of tribal law

but in the sheer terror its members could inspire through their alleged supernatural powers.

Lamb saw himself, therefore, as waging war to free his charges from a movement based entirely on fear. It is thus not surprising that both he and Hopkins placed the various levels of the Njuri squarely alongside the more overtly exploitive fringe societies, in compelling obedience from everyone in Meru: "The meetings of these tribunals are attended by the clans of Igembe and Tigania. . . . Those present are commanded under penalty of being cursed . . . if they give information to government, bring cases to be heard by government, give evidence against witchdoctors and report . . . extortions or injustice done by Kiamas."[15]

The British officials, of course, saw only the continued erosion of their own position. Having claimed a monopoly on the dispensing of justice, they could hardly allow competition from an earlier tribal institution, no matter how deeply rooted in tradition. Having established an administrative monopoly over the mainstream Meru, they could hardly make exceptions for those of the fringe. Nor, ultimately, could they permit the expansion of areas within Meru life—however neatly marked by sticks or vines—from which they or their servants were barred.

Lamb's decision to wipe out the witchcraft system was thus based on his conviction that its practitioners were centralized, hierarchical, politically malevolent, psychologically effective, and swiftly spreading. He also believed he had little choice. If colonial government was to function, its servants had to be freed from their fears. To do that, it was necessary to break the power of every supernatural society by force. Nor was the traditional witchcraft system to be spared, because both investigators believed the "witch doctors" had been more or less universally absorbed into the societies. For the sake of the British colonial system, it was clear, every facet of tribal witchcraft had to be uprooted and allowed to die.

MBOGORE'S WAR ON WITCHCRAFT

The enthusiasm of a conqueror often becomes the zeal of a convert, and none proved more zealous in their war against witchcraft than the "Kamuchunku," the Meru who were known as "little whites" through their acceptance of British ways. The most enthusiastic of these converts emerged in Meru's southern regions, where the chiefs of Mwimbi and Muthambi had proved particularly receptive to Western attitudes, particularly those that enhanced their own authority by striking at other sources of power. In upper Mwimbi, for example, the conflict between the highest Kiama of elders and Mbogore M'Mwendo, on his appointment as that region's colonial chief, led to the eventual arrest of the elders involved. Thereafter, Mbogore also launched himself against members of both the traditional witchcraft system and the fringe groups, perceiving all of them as obstacles to power.[16]

Mbogore's antipathy to tribal ritualists preceded the British conquests. As a war leader, he had raged continually at any obstacle to Mwimbi's military strength, even seeking to stop female circumcision on the military ground that it inhibited the birth of future warriors. The ritualists incurred his anger for similar reasons. He was often angered by prophecies that failed to meet his military needs or curses that temporarily struck down his strongest warriors.

After the conquest he was surprised to learn that his feelings were shared by the whites. He was particularly impressed, during the first months of British rule, with a decision by E. B. Horne (Kangangi) to chastise every man in Meru who practiced magic. The decision may have been prompted by Horne's irrepressible sense of showmanship and the conviction that British rules were best imposed by dramatic demonstrations. Meru tradition declares that during the first year of his rule Horne commanded the former warriors who now made up his personal guard to bring all known witch doctors to his camp on the edge of Imenti's Kazita River (near the present Meru Town). The ritualists were duly assembled. Horne is said to have scolded them, threatening them with dire punishment unless they ceased to practice. To enforce his orders, he confiscated all of the goatskin bags in which they kept their magic powders and tossed them into the Kazita River, declaring that no further witchcraft would be permitted where England ruled.[17]

The incident made little impact on the ritualists, who simply gathered new supplies. It did, however, make a profound impression on Mbogore. Although not present at the time, he had found powerful support for his prior conviction. Like Mbogore, Horne refused to differentiate between "good" and "bad" witchcraft, having denounced healers and cursers as one and the same. Now Mbogore could translate his earlier hostility into action.

Thus over the next two decades Mbogore, his tribal retainers, and other chiefs under his influence waged sporadic war against practitioners of the supernatural. His earliest targets were the traditional ritualists who had obstructed him in the past. During the early years of his chieftainship—to select one typical example—he was angered by reports that warriors in three clans under his jurisdiction had been bewitched by Arogi (sorcerers).[18] In fact oral informants declare that the warriors had become drunk on beer, having violated the tradition that prohibited them from drinking. Clan elders had retaliated with a collective curse upon them all, causing them to sicken.

Mbogore entered the area with an escort of tribal police. Assembling every member of the clans involved, he unexpectedly proclaimed a ban on every form of witchcraft, in exact imitation of Horne's earlier declaration years before. Several elders protested that the services of Aga (curse removers, healers) were required as protection. Mbogore answered that "all Aga are Arogi" and therefore banned. He then ordered every ritualist to appear before him within one day to surrender their goatskin bags of magic powders.

At first not a single man complied, as the gathering dispersed in total silence. That night Mbogore pitched a tent, the gift of a British official, then ordered his police escort to sleep two hundred yards away. Mwimbi informants declare that the ritualists later appeared, circling seven times around the tent and chanting to curse any man who harmed them. To intensify the ritual, they then poured blood and castor oil around the tent site, to further warn the victim by a chant that anyone who crossed it would be cursed.

The next morning Mbogore rose, crossed the circle without hesitation, and promptly ordered the arrest of every ritualist in the region. Once assembled, the elders were forced to carry water in their goatskin bags from the Maara River to Mbogore's camp. They were then compelled to cast the bags, in imitation of Horne's earlier decree, into the river itself. Having provided the chief with goats as a gesture of reconciliation, they were reprimanded and sent away.

From then on Mbogore campaigned, somewhat fitfully, against what his colonial supervisors termed "outbreaks" of traditional witchcraft. During the earlier years his struggle was conducted generally within the confines of Meru custom. Complaints against practitioners led to their arrest by his retainers. Those accused were brought forcibly to his camp. Their goatskin bags and magic powders were burned before their eyes. Each practitioner was then fined one goat for having defied the witchcraft ban. Thereafter, each provided a second goat, to form the sacrificial basis of a cleansing oath, intended to insure that they never practiced again.

This cleansing oath became the heart of Mbogore's war on witchcraft, the single means to hold a suspect to his promise to give up the practice. To carry out the oath required that the liver of each sacrificial animal be removed and sliced in eight pieces. Four strips of wood were cut from an appropriate tree (usually the *mukenia*), with two pieces of meat placed on each stick.

At the moment of oathing, suspects were surrounded by the chief's retainers, lest they break and run. Each man ate one of the two slices off each stick and tossed the other over one shoulder while chanting: "If I practice cursing [Urogi], let this meat kill me. If I practice curse removing [Uga], let this meat kill me. If I practice divining [Uraguri], let this meat kill me," and so forth.[19] Allegedly, violation of the oath led to rapid swelling of the stomach, a symptom visible to everyone in the community. Thus identified, practitioners could easily be rearrested.

MBOGORE'S WAR ON FRINGEMEN

In later years Mbogore extended the scope of his antiwitchcraft campaigns to include the ritualists of the Kagita, A-Athi, and other supernatural societies. As a wealthy cattle- and landowner he was not pleased with the continued encroachment of the stomach Kiamas into his administrative jurisdiction. Nor did he perceive that the societies might offer either entertainment or famine relief. Rather, he more or less shared the view of his colonial supervisors that all fringe groups were composed of "the idle, the hungry, and those who give shelter into which Arogi can creep."[20]

By the 1920s, however, Mbogore's earlier methods of enforcement had been sharply modified by continued contact with the whites. After World War I several of his more "tribal" administrative practices drew sharp criticism from district officers. Accepting goats from suspects was interpreted as bribery and forbidden. The use of oaths to cleanse witchcraft practitioners was labeled a repetition of the very type of activity it was meant to stamp out. Nor was the burning of goatskin bags and magic powders accepted as an adequate substitute for the more "progressive" British punishments of whipping, imprisonment, and hard labor.

Mbogore adjusted. During the 1920s, individuals accused of membership in a fringe Kiama were more and more frequently caught up in one of Mbogore's antiwitchcraft campaigns and imprisoned alongside ordinary ritualists for a one-month prison sentence at the chief's camp.

"Prison," however, meant being placed in the middle of a cleared field, under continuous guard, to do "hard labor." That labor, in turn, was redefined as collecting sufficient firewood for cookfires, bringing water from the river in the suspect's goatskin bags, and, to avoid leisure, cultivating a thorny weed known as *ngonko*.

"Prison" also meant, however, that at the end of each work day men and women alike received five strokes of a whip as their daily wages. Over a thirty-day period, denied all medical care, this requirement must have been terrifying to the captives. It was, however, far more satisfactory to Mbogore's British supervisors, several of whom lauded the progressive nature of his administration.

Interestingly, Mbogore managed to retain the most significant Meru tradition, having refused to abandon the cleansing oath. On completing the one-month sentence prisoners were still required—although now in strictest secrecy—to take the oath previously described, swearing they would never again practice any form of supernatural ritual. Afterward they left with Mbogore's promise in their ears that violation of the oath would no longer merely bring on illness but a two-month prison sentence as well.

Nevertheless, both the traditional ritualists and the fringe societies survived, no doubt because their services were still needed. The fringe groups, always more flexible in adversity, soon learned to cancel their activities and lie low when Mbogore's anger had been aroused. When his attention turned elsewhere, they would sing oblique new variants of songs he had previously banned, then "sell A-Athi" (or Mwaa, Kagita, Wathua, etc.) only to those they believed would not betray them. Gradually, the bands reassembled, gathering in areas sufficiently remote to allow them to feast in peace.

Mbogore strove erratically to prevent such reappearances, angrily goading neighboring chiefs in Muthambi as well as his own headmen. Occasionally, he tried to repeat his earlier successes against the traditional ritualists, camping without guards where the fringe societies were strong, in the hope that they would attempt to bewitch him. To his disappointment, no one ever tried. Angered, he often responded by appointing more and more tribal retainers to take action against each separate band, hoping that sheer numbers would eventually resolve the problem completely.

In one sense his efforts were successful. By the 1920s his uncompromising attitudes, reflected to some degree by certain chiefs in adjacent regions, communicated themselves to subordinates both among his personal retainers and the official tribal police. On occasion bands of these less powerful Kamuchunku would express support of their chief by launching private antiwitchcraft campaigns of their own, usually with the tacit approval of superiors. Before the 1920s these illicit expeditions took the traditional form of scattering the gatherings of fringe groups and burning their huts. After the 1920s, however, the raiders often acted as self-declared colonial police, "arresting" every suspected fringe group member they could catch. Usually, each arrest led to a minor beating, halted by promises to supply the "police" with sufficient goats to pay the "fine." Resistance, however, could mean incarceration in a chief's camp for violation of the witchcraft ordinance.[21]

However, the efforts of Meru's "little whites" ultimately failed. As chief, Mbogore and others like him could make elderly ritualists cut wood, carry water, and hoe thorns. His men could keep them under guard or even whip them. But none of the Kamuchunku could actually resolve the problem by imposing either African or British law. The former, calling ultimately for the communal execution of frequently convicted sorcerers, had been forbidden by the British. The latter, demanding long-term physical imprisonment, could be imposed only by British courts. In consequence the antiwitchcraft campaigns launched by converts to the cause seem, in retrospect, like elaborate charades. Driven by both economic and social needs, the supernatural practitioners inevitably returned to both the activities that sustained them and a community that required their services. Lacking the power to stop them, the "little whites" could only demonstrate continued zeal.

WAR AGAINST WITCHCRAFT: HOPKINS AND LAMB

By early 1928 sufficient data had been collected to allow Lamb, Hopkins, and two cadet subordinates to launch what was initially referred to as an anti–witch doctor campaign.[22] Interestingly, it was initially in no way different from those launched over past decades by the Njuri Nceke, "campaigns" of which both district officers remained completely unaware.

The British effort began with a series of public proclamations, also identical to Njuri tradition. Before the conquest Njuri messengers would run from ridgetop to ridgetop denouncing one or another of the traditional fringe societies. By 1928 this role had been taken up by the British, who rode among the chiefs' camps from Imenti to Igembe proclaiming that every known witchcraft group was henceforth to disband.

Before colonialism the regional Njuris had assembled bands of chanting warriors to march against the fringe societies. Under colonialism the enforcers mobilized bands of tribal retainers, police, and even clerks and process servers along for the excitement. To the victims, little must have seemed to change.

As the government enforcers approached a hut, they invariably halted at first sight of the A-Athi Ndindi stick or a Kagita vine. Silently, elders of the society involved appeared to face the equally silent accusers. A chief informed them of the European order to disband. As proof of compliance they were to place the symbols of their magic (Ndindi, goatskin bags, etc.) in their huts, then set them afire. None of the enforcers violated their protected zone, but neither did they leave.

The men of the fringe groups had virtually no options. Their protective magic was useless against those who remained outside its zone. Nor could they collectively curse the assembled representatives of colonial authority without guaranteeing their own arrest and imprisonment under the antiwitchcraft ordinances. Under such circumstances, compliance was universal. The drums of several Kagita groups were seized throughout Tigania and Igembe, then deposited at Meru district headquarters. Lamb himself visited certain A-Athi locations to collect some of the goatskin bags and magic powders as material evidence. The rest were left within A-Athi huts, to be consumed in flames.

For several weeks the campaign appeared to have succeeded. Thereafter, rumors once again began of dances, feasts, nighttime visits to wealthy homesteads, and subsequent "gifts" of goats and cattle. These were followed by a noticeable slackening in the performance of colonial servants in both Igembe and Tigania.

At this point a number of the "retired elders," the oldest surviving age-set, appear to have chosen to intervene once more. They may well have been spokesmen for the Njuri Nceke, reflecting that group's decision to eliminate the fringe Kiamas once and for all. Or they may have acted alone, emboldened by the whites' earlier successes, to defend tradition once again. In either case available evidence suggests that several men of extreme age sought out either Hopkins or Lamb. Although still unwilling to accuse directly, they fell once more into oblique speech patterns but managed this time to identify specific persons as fringe Kiama members.

At one point, for example, a single elder is recalled as having spoken privately with Lamb, who asked him outright to name members from his region who practiced forbidden forms of witchcraft. Perhaps to

Lamb's surprise, he did so. Thereafter, he is said to have declared that his violation of an oath of secrecy would cause him to die within three days. He proved correct. His body was subsequently examined by Dr. H. Brassington, then a Protestant medical missionary in Igembe. "Physically," Brassington later recalled, "there was no sign of death at all. His body was in good health, with no evidence of poisoning."[23]

Lamb reacted to the acquisition of this information with the decision to arrest every known practitioner of witchcraft in Meru. With total disregard for the subtleties of "good" and "bad" witch doctoring, he enlisted the aid of every European in the district to help "sweep up the lot." Missionaries, medical personnel, and agricultural officers joined in with enthusiasm. As a result sixty-two alleged practitioners were rounded up within a single day for deposit in E. B. Horne's log-cabin jail. At one point Dr. Brassington was pressed into service with his mission truck to carry suspects collected from two Igembe locations off to district headquarters. All were very old, frightened, and bewildered. The roads were rough ("shaped like nineteenth-century washboards"), and Brassington was forced to "bump the old fellows rather terribly about."[24] They were, however, deposited with other ritualists and fringe group members in the district jail.

Reports conflict as to what happened thereafter.[25] Both Meru and colonial informants agree that a considerable number of very elderly suspects were incarcerated in the district jail's single room. Informants also agree that the group contained members of the fringe societies as well as traditional ritualists. At one point a district officer, probably Hopkins, interrogated them as a single group.

The Englishman first asked who among them practiced sorcery (Urogi). All the men in the room denied it, declaring that they were nothing more than simple healers, thus innocent of causing harm. To demonstrate their innocence, the administrator then commanded each to "lick" samples of the magic powders (Mithega: medicine, magic substances) that had been collected from their goatskin bags. In theory the request was perfectly in accord with Meru tradition. For decades, supernatural practitioners had publicly tasted their Mithega before giving them to others, thereby demonstrating they were intended to heal.

Unfortunately, in collecting samples of the magic substances, colonial officials had made no effort to establish to which individual practitioners each substance belonged. The arrested elders thus unexpectedly found themselves ordered to ingest the magic of other ritualists. If this command was indeed given, it must have created feelings of utter terror within every man in the room, the cause of which would have simply bewildered the administrator.

Meru's supernatural practitioners shared traditions of their own. One was the nearly universal belief that many of their competitors, although publicly engaged in benevolent forms of ritual (e.g., healing, divination, prophecy), practiced sorcery in private. To be required to "lick" the magic substances of other practitioners, therefore, was to risk death. The demand lay so far outside normal patterns of behavior that it was horrifying to those concerned.

Their terror would have intensified, moreover, if men of the mainstream had been forced into contact with magic from men of the fringe. Here, there was no ambivalence: each group "knew" the other practiced sorcery. Their antipathy and fear reached back over generations. To be commanded to overcome it in a single moment would have been paralyzing. Cultivators had been taught that even the sight of fringe group magic led to illness; the fringemen had known for generations that only their magic held others at bay. To be suddenly stripped of those defensive symbols by exchanging them with their enemies was beyond their capacity to absorb.

Trapped by circumstances, however, every one of the prisoners complied. Within days large numbers of them fell ill, displaying increasingly severe "chest and dysentery symptoms."[26] Colonial sources suggest these were due to the dampness and cold of the jail, but the psychological impact of arrest, incarceration, and enforced ingestion of allegedly lethal substances must also have played a role. The stricken were transferred to the district hospital, where ten of them died. The cause of death was recorded as "chiefly through age, but also possibly through their own witchcraft, as after arrest they had been made to handle their fellow practitioners' symbols of office."[27]

The remaining elders were placed on trial. Under the Revised Kenya Witchcraft Ordinance of 1928, any individual "pretending" to exercise supernatural power was liable to one year's imprisonment and a fine of £50—a staggering sum from an African perspective. Any person practicing witchcraft with the "intent to cause injury, death, or misfortune," however, was subject to seven years in prison and a fine of £200, a sum that could be paid only by the sale of flocks and herds from an entire clan.[28]

By British standards the trials were unexceptional. Every one of the fifty-two assembled elders was found guilty under the 1928 ordinance and sentenced to prison terms ranging from six months to ten years.

Five of those considered ringleaders were "rusticated" as well and had to serve their sentences in an isolated prison outpost in Meru's scorching northern desert. Five more of the alleged ringleaders were deported from Meru altogether, among them one man considered by Lamb to have been the "high priest" of the A-Athi movement, perhaps partially because of his unfortunate name, M'Murogi wa Ndorobo (sorcerer, son of forest hunter).[29]

Although the sentences were implemented without incident, their impact on the Meru population was staggering. Ruling elders may have welcomed the imprisonment of fringe group leaders, but they were thunderstruck by the inclusion of widely respected healers, diviners, and foretellers. Their anxiety was briefly intensified by widespread rumors that the whites now intended to imprison everyone who "frightened people," even while removing a curse. Because inducing fear was a major component of ritualized healing, elders throughout Meru grew insecure. If no one could remove curses in the traditional manner, curse victims were certain to die.

From the traditional Meru perspective their fears were justified. Through a single show of force the British had undone, at least for the moment, the entire ritualized system of alleviating both physical illness and social conflict. For the first time in memory, informants declare, "no one dared to practice magic." Among the Meru that is the same as stating that no one practiced either medicine or law enforcement. The result was widespread insecurity, particularly among the aged. Removing the systems used to both reflect on and resolve life's calamities left them psychologically defenseless.

RITUALIZED "CLEANSING": THE SYSTEM DISSOLVES

The Meru responded to the destruction of their witchcraft system in several ways. One was an increasing willingness to accept European forms of healing. The shift was perhaps most dramatically illustrated in Igembe, where the United Methodist Mission had commissioned Dr. Brassington to construct a medical facility. Earlier reaction to the clinic had been a universal boycott, explained by those willing to discuss it as an unwillingness to enter an area where "curses [here, illnesses] are collected and people come to die." After the enforced removal of Igembe ritualists, however, much of this aversion disappeared. Nonetheless, those who did reach out for Western healing approached in desperation, and the "anxiety of the elderly over [the loss of] their former Aga [here, healers] was often pathetic to behold."[30]

Hopkins replaced Lamb as district commissioner in March 1929. The promotion gave him ample opportunity to extend his investigation of Meru tradition. After extensive consultation with chiefs and prominent elders, he decided that the custom of "ritualized cleansing" might be modified to restore the less threatening prisoners back to full fellowship with the tribe.

Cleansing rituals were clearly rooted in Meru tradition. Even before the conquest those accused of sorcery, adultery, or repetitive theft were almost always allowed to recant, taking a cleansing oath to proclaim that any return to antisocial practices would result in their death. Oaths varied from region to region, but followed a similar pattern. The most common was that used by Mbogore: accused individuals consumed the raw liver (in other areas, the heart) of a slaughtered goat while chanting oaths declaring that further practice of the supernatural would lead the oath itself to kill them.

Neither Hopkins nor his Meru advisors saw any reason why the oath could not be modified to meet a modern need. The rituals that subsequently developed adhered closely to the Meru way, deviating only rarely because because of British sensibilities. After 1929, persons accused of witchcraft, including those released from their imprisonment, would walk with a committee of elders chosen by the administration to the edge of a river. There, each slaughtered a goat, drawn from their own herds, removed the liver, then held it high for inspection by ancestral spirits. The consumption of raw meat had been eliminated from the ritual at Hopkins's order. Instead, the liver was cast into the flowing waters, accompanied by an appropriately worded sequence of oaths.

Symbolically, each man thereby cast away his capacity to practice sorcery. The oaths, however, were also modified to preserve the most respected aspects of the witchcraft system. No oath forced those recently jailed to admit prior guilt. Nor did they prevent anyone from healing. Rather the oaths were rephrased to reaffirm the elder's declaration of innocence in the past, which allowed the practice of "innocent" rites in the future: "If I practice sorcery [in the future], let this oath kill me. If I curse [someone in the future], let this oath kill me. If I harm [someone in the future], let this oath kill me," and so on.[31]

Elders throughout Meru embraced the restoration of a cleansing oath with enthusiasm. Over time these basic versions were extended to include whatever social deviations tended to reappear (e.g., "if I ask for cows, let this oath kill me"), until every action formerly associated with the fringe societies had publicly been cast away.

Thus by the early 1930s, practitioners of the more beneficial aspects of Meru magic—such as the healers, the diviners, and the foretellers—returned unobtrusively to their work, always to the relief of elders in their communities. In theory the shadowy figure of the sorcerer returned as well, for "good" ritualists of every type still proved eager to accuse their competitors of practicing "bad" magic whenever conflicts emerged or individuals fell ill. Having thus identified the cause, they felt free to combat it in traditional fashion.

The same was not true, however, for the A-Athi, the Kagita, and the smaller fringe societies. Their songs, feasts, dances, chants, and drumming, as well as the entire complex of supernatural rites that gave them meaning, were finally dissolved, remaining only in the memories of their aging former members. Hopkins, writing in 1932, could thus declare with considerable accuracy: "The campaign against both the Aathi and Kagitha secret societies was carried out by me personally . . . as Mr. Lamb's assistant in 1928. Neither society is now active. Witchcraft has ceased."[32]

Meru informants, however, add more to the story of the fringe groups' demise. "The Kagita [or, Aathi, Mwaa, Wathua, and so on] stopped," the elders declare, "because people feared whites more than they loved feasting." Members of every group were long aware that whites were not affected by their curses. They were increasingly concerned at the spreading belief among imitation whites (Kamuchunku) that working for the British or professing their religion might also render them immune.

Fringe group members were also increasingly aware of the demonstrable effectiveness of Western forms of healing. This proved particularly true in Imenti and Mwimbi (still administered from neighboring Embu), where enthusiastic and aggressive Protestant missionaries also proved highly competent medical practitioners. Perhaps the most striking example can be found in Mwimbi, where Rev. Clive Irvine, the founder of that branch of the Church of Scotland Mission in 1923, soon perceived himself as locked in battle against what he considered the quackery of local witch doctors.

Irvine began by systematically acquainting himself with the areas of healing in which ritualists specialized.[33] Discovering, for example, that the "witch doctors of Kagita" were known to cure diseases of the feet, he actively solicited people with foot and leg problems to approach him for treatment, usually with great success. Each cure shook both the medical monopoly of the Kagita healers and the collective confidence of those who had heretofore been forced to seek its aid. To them Irvine proved a welcome alternative. As his influence grew, tolerance of his fringe competitors decreased in relative proportion.

Missionaries had also struck at the fringe societies in other ways. Their Victorian morality placed them squarely alongside Meru tradition in condemning drunkenness, dancing in darkness, and, certainly, illicit copulation. To most Europeans of that era those activities were objectionable for Africans of any age. Among the Meru they were only forbidden to youths, warriors, and family heads, who were perceived as encroaching on prerogatives (such as beer drinking) explicitly reserved for ruling elders.

Thus by the 1930s, men of the former fringe societies were trapped between two fires. On one side, rising numbers of Christian converts actively opposed their restoration. On the other, Meru's traditionalists no longer sanctioned their actions as permitted deviations from an ancestral norm. Behind them both stood the government, personified in Hopkins, prepared to reach out and imprison anyone who dared restore that portion of the past.

It was thus the change in Meru's social climate that ultimately destroyed its fringes. The unprecedented sequence of physical arrests, public trials, and subsequent imprisonment was shattering, but the shift in public tolerance was the final blow. The change was partially based on fear. What had always been perceived as minor social deviation was now redefined as serious transgression. What had once been punished by the whack of a warrior's spear and the command to disburse was now cause for arrest and imprisonment. What could once be protected by wooden sticks and creeping vines was now an invitation to destruction by a mob.

Under such circumstances, permitted social deviations became private affairs. The earlier practice of assembling at dusk to feast, drink, drum, chant, and dance "in Kiama" was gone. Over time everything the fringe societies espoused was held up to public scorn. Youngsters, now enmeshed in mission schools, were taught to belittle many of their own traditions, and none more fiercely than those once tolerated as permitted deviations. Thus meat feasts, beer drinking, nocturnal dancing, traditional drumming, and "pagan" songs were increasingly associated with sorcery and held up to the rising generation to scorn as things of a "primitive" past.

Unable to refute or even reply to these charges, former members of the fringe societies retreated into silence, many denying they had ever joined such groups or even that they had existed. Today, memories of their existence have all but disappeared, remaining only in the tales—often obliquely told—of the men of the oldest living age-set. When these men die, the rites, oaths, songs, riddles, and laughter of which the fringe groups were composed will pass away as well, and with them yet another priceless portion of the Meru past.

CHAPTER XIII

Reconciliation Traditions: Meru's Golden Age

"I had come from Embu, which then included Chuka, Muthambe and Mwimbi. . . . I was told there that the local legislative bodies [the Ramare, the Kibogo, and the Ngome] had their counterparts . . . in Meru [where] the Njuri corresponded to Kibogo and Ngome. . . . [Yet] on arrival in Meru I found that the Njuri could only be mentioned in whispers and an atmosphere of secrecy."[1]

Hugo E. Lambert
District Commissioner, Meru
1933–1935, 1939–1942

THE "NATIVIST" ADMINISTRATORS

The 1929 selection of J. Gerald H. Hopkins as district commissioner marked the beginning of Meru's "Golden Age," an era in which the adherents of ancestral tradition, mission Christianity, and British colonialism reached new levels of tolerance and understanding. It was a notable shift, for the ten years prior to Hopkins's appointment had been characterized by the rule of an administrative generation of self-proclaimed pragmatists, men less concerned with native traditions than in running their districts efficiently and at a profit. In contrast the fifteen years following Hopkins's appointment were shaped by the rule of a series of self-declared "nativists", men who saw themselves as administrator-anthropologists, dedicated to the understanding and even reconstruction of native ways of life.

Meru was fortunate to have drawn no fewer than three of these men in near succession. Hopkins, having crushed the fringe societies in 1927–1929, worked tirelessly from 1929 to 1933 to restore other aspects of Meru tradition. He was followed in mid-1933 by Hugo E. Lambert, an African linguist, anthropologist, and tireless researcher, who ruled Meru until 1935 and again from 1939 to 1942. Lambert was followed—after a brief return to pragmatism—by Capt. Victor M. McKeag, who ran the district from mid-1937 to 1939 and again (following Lambert's second term) from 1942 to 1945.[2]

The three administrators were alike in several ways. All were born near the end of the 1800s and had attended English public schools. Each had had early military experience, having served with the King's African Rifles during World War I. Each then entered the colonial service, passing through a number of regional postings during the 1920s. At some point each man became fascinated with the customs, cultures, and (in Lambert's case) languages of the African peoples they ruled, a fascination that enabled all three to cast off prevailing stereotypes regarding the "savage and simplistic nature" of Kenya's tribal cultures and seek instead to understand and restore them in their full complexity.[3]

RESTORING NTUIKO: THE TRANSFER OF POWER

Hopkins had begun by restoring the traditional cleansing oath. Although the oathing ceremony had been somewhat retailored to British sensibilities, his efforts had been warmly received by the Meru. The experiment intensified his interest in Meru tradition, and he began to search out other aspects of the past that might be revived, with modifications to fit the district's current needs.

In 1929, for example, he was increasingly perplexed at the degree to which the entire Meru region had seemed to slip into lawlessness and apathy. Despite suppression of the witchcraft bands, many areas remained in an abnormal state, in which disobedience both of government and tribal authority remained widespread. Hopkins was especially alarmed about the rising passivity of many elders. Many members of the oldest age-sets, perhaps disheartened by the removal of their ritualists, now showed unprecedented apathy.[4] Many no longer helped women work the fields, even when such work was required by tradition. Others moved between sporadic brawling and a daily alcoholic stupor.

Hopkins was equally concerned with the behavior of the former warriors. All of them seemed to have taken to drinking, in universal defiance of the tradition restricting millet beer to ruling elders. Worse, many had formed themselves into the traditional war bands and taken up new forms of raiding, seizing livestock with equal determination from both family heads and ruling elders. Departing from tradition, they inflicted constant damage on homesteads, groves, granaries, and gardens. Nor did they return the captured livestock to their own fathers, as custom required. Rather, they drove entire herds into the forests or rock-strewn hills on the district's desert fringes and devoured them all.[5]

Hopkins reacted initially to both aspects of the problem by inquiring among the more prominent elders as to its probable cause. Perhaps to his surprise, several declared that at least part of the current unrest was due to a delay in Ntuiko, the ritualized transfer of administrative authority between those age-sets currently in power (ruling elders and their warrior sons) and those whose turn it was to rule (family heads and their sons approaching warriorhood).

Before the conquest this formal handing over of authority had taken place in two stages, one involving the two sets of elders; the second, their two sets of sons. The military transfer took the form of limited and stylized combat. It began at some moment when the younger age-set felt numerically strong enough to expel physically the remaining senior warriors from the war barracks and seize it for themselves. Expulsion was inevitable as the older warriors gradually abandoned warriorhood to seek wives and their juniors reached physical maturity. On reaching numerical superiority, the juniors would revolt against their seniors, with the older warriors' expulsion serving as a symbolic end to their time of warriorhood.

In practice these ritualized expulsions usually began among the clans of Tigania and Igembe, then moved southward, ridgetop by ridgetop, until every war barracks had changed hands, usually over a single season. Each expulsion was followed by a brief period of permitted anarchy within each ridgetop area as the former warriors were allowed to band together one last time. Once united, they raided at will, but this time among their own kin, despoiling groves and gardens and harrying flocks and herds. There was a social purpose in this lawlessness. It symbolized the fact that "no one" ruled, since the family heads had not yet taken power from the ruling elders. By "raiding" the gardens, flocks, and herds of both those age-sets, the former warriors symbolically prodded them into completing the transfer of power.

The expelled warriors' continued depredations probably did spur spokesmen from both age-sets to initiate Ntuiko's second stage. At some point spokesmen for the family heads in each community would approach the ruling elders bearing gifts. Assembled in a joint Kiama, they would agree to the transfer. Custom required each elder to provide a sheep and millet beer for a communal feast to symbolize the reconciliation of both age-sets with those of the ancestors and thus complete the formal transfer of administrative power.[6]

Hopkins's inquiries established that the first stage of the transfer— the military expulsion of the senior warriors—had begun a year earlier and was now virtually complete. Much of the raiding that concerned him was thus at least partially due to the tradition of interim lawlessness. But because completion of these rites had been indefinitely delayed according to the elders, the condition of permitted anarchy persisted as well.

Hopkins, unwilling to permit anarchy of any sort, demanded the reason for such delay. He was told that because the millet harvests of the last two years had been lost to locusts, too little grain remained to brew beer. Without beer no feasts of reconciliation could occur because beer alone was used to bless those assuming authority. Without the proper blessings the ancestors would disapprove. Without their approval the entire process of transfer would remain incomplete.

Meru elders found the explanation wholly logical and an ample justification for indefinite delay. Eventually new millet could be harvested, and the rituals would begin again. Hopkins sharply disagreed. Negotiating for small amounts of millet from districts outside Meru, the district commissioner moved from ridgetop to ridgetop, cajoling, explaining, and commanding that it be brewed and used symbolically to complete the rituals. Gradually, the communities complied. The feasts took place, the blessings were proclaimed, and the age-set of Murungi—warriors at the moment of British conquest—assumed authority as ruling elders of Meru.[7]

RESTORING AGAMBE: THE "SPOKESMEN" SYSTEM

Having established the authority of a single set of elders, Hopkins was gratified to see an appreciable drop in the level of illicit cattle-raiding. He then addressed the problem of the elders' passivity, feeling it was due at least partially to their lack of the administrative authority before the conquest had been used to maintain discipline within their communities. Reflecting on this, he seized on the idea of restoring the system of communal spokesmen (the Agambe system), as part of a larger goal of returning traditional authority to Meru elders as a whole. It was only owing to the frequent changes in district commissioner, he subsequently wrote, "that the system of administering clans through their own Agambe [spokesmen] has been lost sight of and has apparently fallen into disuse for many years."[8]

Hopkins began by dismantling the lowest level of the existing administrative structure, that of the tribal retainers (Njama), and replacing them with Agambe. Thereafter, he hoped to replace the colonial headmen with them as well, arguing that those considered spokesmen for their peoples should logically lead them, whereas the government-appointed headmen were disinclined to use what little authority they had.

Hopkins carried out his plan between 1929 and 1932, gradually dismissing existing tribal retainers and replacing them with men considered spokesmen for their clans. To ensure adequate selection, he informally sought out respected elders in every clan, from whom he elicited the names of individuals they wished to represent them. Once identified, he appointed these as clan Agambe (spokesmen), explaining that their role would be both to aid headmen in implementing colonial decisions and to advise them of the expectations of each clan. To stir their enthusiasm, Hopkins offered each appointee a monthly wage.

Hopkins subsequently reported that he had reinstituted the "Agambe system" throughout the district. Although several individuals did choose to serve, he made three errors. One lay in his assumption that appointees were "heads of clans," a pattern prevalent in other parts of Britain's empire. In fact, they all represented a far larger communal institution, personified initially by their local Kiamas but ultimately by their regional Njuri. Thus every appointee was spokesman for a single institution. For Hopkins to recognize them as clan leaders was not enough. For them to function as he expected, he would have had to recognize the dual Kiama and Njuri system for which they "spoke" as well.

Hopkins's second error lay in the expectation that his appointees, once recognized by government, would willingly serve two masters. They had found this impossible during the early decades of British rule and found it no easier during the 1930s. Most of the elders chosen saw Hopkins's selection as an attempt to seduce them from their rightful function as spokesmen for their own Njuris. Because the Njuris were still banned, they had no organization to represent. Most refused to serve. A few accepted. Neither group proved able to serve two masters effectively.

Hopkins's final error was his decision to offer pay. It was usually refused. Puzzled, he abandoned the idea, at least briefly, for lack of sufficient funds to pay what he feared the appointees would require. Here he misread the elders' motives. To have accepted any pay at all would have transformed them into spokesmen for the government. The qualities of spokesmanship that had originally led to their selection by their comrades were derived from serving Meru. Those would have been lost had the elders accepted wages to serve England.

Nonetheless, Hopkins persevered, gradually replacing first tribal retainers and then headmen with elders prominent in their communities.
Despite his errors, his policy marked a major turning point in relationships between colonial officials and leading Meru elders. From their
perspective he became the first administrator since E. B. Horne to see
value in the tribal past and show respect for its tradition. At the very
least, Hopkins began to inspire trust.

Hopkins saw himself simply as practical. Faced with the dual problem of lawlessness among the young and apathy among the old, it
seemed only logical to restore the authority of elders, thereby allowing
them to discipline the youth. His contribution was creating an environment wherein traditional spokesmen could speak out without fear. Its
flaw lay in his refusal to recognize the institution for which they
claimed to speak; the Njuri system was banned as a witchcraft tribunal
as long as Hopkins ruled.

LEGALIZING NJURI: THE COUNCIL SYSTEM

Legalizing the Njuri system throughout Meru was left to Hopkins's
successor, Hugo E. Lambert, who became district commissioner in
early 1933. Lambert came to Kenya just before World War I, spending
his military service in pursuit of the brilliant German East African general, Hermann von Lettow.[9]

The experience committed him completely to life in Africa, and he
eagerly accepted an opportunity to join the Kenya colonial service in
1918. During the 1920s he served in several posts from the Gikuyu regions to the Swahili Coast. During this period he demonstrated an as-
tonishing capacity to absorb African languages; he could understand all
but the most esoteric conversations within a few months after his arrival in a region.

A shy man, he proved only rarely willing to speak back or enter
into conversations. Nonetheless, his linguistic capacity opened up a
window through which he could gaze with fascination at the complexities of African life. In consequence he became the very prototype of
administrator-anthropologist, striving to understand the inner work-
ings of each tribe to which he was assigned.

In 1929, Lambert was made district commissioner of Embu, Meru's
neighbor to the south, which at that time still administered the locations of Mwimbi, Muthambi, and Cuka (formerly Chuka).[10] During
that time, he came in contact with the basic forms of the dual Kiama

and Njuri system as it operated in that region of Mount Kenya. The nature of his administrative duties, as well as his anthropological inclinations, led him to question many Embu elders about the system's structure and purposes.

He learned initially that the system operated in every region of Mount Kenya, including among the tribes (Tharaka, Mbeere, Kamba, etc.) on the adjacent plains. He was told that it always contained two levels—local Kiamas and a single higher council for each region—but that the names of both the lower and more select councils could differ from tribe to tribe and that each could have more than one name. Thus, the local Kiamas throughout Embu district—including those of Cuka, Muthambi, and Mwimbi, were known collectively as the Kibogo. The more select council-of-councils that emerged from each subtribe was known either as the Ngome (Embu, Cuka) or Nkome (Muthambi, Mwimbi).

Further inquiry led him to decide that both the lower and higher levels of this system functioned basically as units of social control, levying economic penalties in the form of livestock for violations of communal norms. To enforce their judgments, both institutions resorted to the communal curse, using the device of collective chanting to instill respect and fear. Under British law this chanting was defined as witchcraft, yet Lambert—increasingly able to comprehend the symbolic meanings of African traditions—began to realize the chanted curses were, in fact, intended to restore harmony rather than wreak destruction.

In 1933 he was transferred to Meru, assuming the post of district commissioner only one month before the transfer of Mwimbi, Muthambi, and Cuka into his jurisdiction. Having had experience with both levels of the elders' council in the three newly assigned subtribes, he felt those in Meru would prove no different.

He was only partially correct. On turning his attention to the elders council systems in Igoji-Imenti and Tigania-Igembe, he found that although the local Kiamas still functioned their more select council-of-councils had been mistakenly identified by earlier district officers with the witchcraft extortion societies that had only recently been suppressed. Lambert was convinced that no further progress could be made without cooperation from members of the three regional Njuris. The Njuri ya Kiama (Imenti-Igoji), however, existed only in the memories of its former members, having been unable to survive the government ban. The same could easily be said of the Ngome councils of

Cuka, Mwimbi, and Muthambi. Only the Njuri Nceke (Tigania-Igembe) still clung actively to life, but its members lived in an atmosphere of suspicion, hostility, and fear.

Following past practice, Lambert began by making extensive inquiries as to the nature of the two northern Njuri systems, intending to compare them to what he knew of the Ngome system in the south. He began by questioning his own interpreter, then one of the more successful chiefs. The chief revealed that most of the more important colonial appointees were members of one of the two regional Njuris, although he himself had refused to join. He spoke at length about the institution, confirming Lambert's earlier convictions that the Meru Njuri and the Mwimbi-Cuka Ngome were essentially similar and that each was a positive force within the tribe.

At this point Lambert was approached by a small number of African Christians, who offered to "teach him Njuri." The gesture was one of unusual courage. The speakers were young men of no personal standing in the tribe. As Meru they stood in awe of their Njuri. As Christians they were equally awed by their ministers, whom they had served since childhood and who disapproved strongly of Njuri members as heathen.[11]

One of these men was Filipo (later the Reverend) M'Inoti, one of the earliest Methodist converts and the first to achieve complete literacy in Swahili. In 1933 he decided to speak to the Reverends A. J. Hopkins and W. H. Laughton, then in charge of the United Methodist Mission in Imenti, about the actual functions of the Njuri Meru society.[12]

Both ministers reacted to M'Inoti's narrative with considerable interest. Hopkins then brought M'Inoti to the attention of Lambert. It was a perfect match. M'Inoti proved willing to provide detailed answers to Lambert's unending inquiries, and the district commissioner needed no further support for his decision to revoke the ban.

Among the Njuri elders, however, Lambert's initial public pronouncements were greeted with utter silence. No one came forward. No one discussed the issue. Nothing changed. Lambert's next step, therefore, was to undermine and dispel the elders' hostility and suspicion. Abandoning the device of public proclamation, he turned to intermittent mention of the Njuris—by formal name—at every public meeting he attended, publicly behaving as though the ban had never taken place.

This initial tactic was soon supplemented by repeated public appeals for assistance from the Njuri of whichever region he was visiting. The publicized requests were then continued in private conversations, when Lambert formally visited notable and respected elders, bearing gifts in traditional fashion, then calling for the "aid of their Njuri" (rather than their aid as individuals) in implementing various reforms.[13]

Over time Lambert's efforts bore fruit. Many hitherto hostile elders were unexpectedly impressed with his knowledge of their tradition, as well as with his seemingly miraculous ability—after a few months—to understand much of their language. Collectively, members of the Njuri Nceke initially responded to Lambert's coaxing with a decision to meet in daylight rather than at night as they had for over a decade. Noting Lambert's enthusiastic reaction when he learned of the meeting, they began to meet once more at Nciru, the group's traditional gathering point. Lambert reacted to this innovation by presenting them with a bull, to be consumed at a feast in his honor. Reassured as to his intentions, the Njuri Nceke reemerged, followed hesitantly by the Njuri ya Kiama of Imenti and Igoji, into public life. The ban was lifted and the Njuri system had survived.

LEGALIZING NGOME: THE NJURI OF THE SOUTH

In subsequent years Lambert turned his attention to restoring the system of elders' councils among the three southern peoples of Mwimbi, Muthambi, and Cuka. Within these regions the problems were more complex, as the three highest councils of Ngome (Cuka) and Nkome (Muthambi and Mwimbi) had all been totally suppressed by a combination of aggressive district officers, zealous chiefs, and the imposition of administrative methods from Gikuyu.[14]

Lambert's first decision was to group the three newcomers into a single administrative unit, together with Igoji and Miutini, which he christened the Nithi, or Southern, Division. The remaining peoples of Imenti, Tigania, Igembe, and Tharaka were similarly joined to make up a new Meru, or Northern, Division.

Lambert began the transformation, as always, with inquiries among respected elders in each of the three subtribes. Unfortunately, in this instance he spoke first to his personal translators, all of whom were from Imenti. These individuals told Lambert—correctly—that the concept of Njuri had begun in Tigania, thereafter spreading north into Igembe, then southward through Imenti and Igoji into Mwimbi, Muthambi, and perhaps Cuka. They then added—incorrectly—that peoples south of Igoji were not "true" Meru, thus had no real knowledge of Njuri. It seemed logical, therefore, to require them to come north, to Imenti and Tigania, where they could "buy [be taught] Njuri" at its source, then take their rightful place as younger brothers in the tribe.

Lambert, impressed by the argument, presented it to the chiefs of Mwimbi and Muthambi, essentially as it had been suggested to him. He was totally unprepared for the wave of outrage that erupted from every corner of the crowd. The formal reply was delivered a day later by a Mwimbi chief, Mburunga Ng'entu. Outraged, Ng'entu led a delegation of equally indignant Mwimbi elders, striding at the head of what became an angry pilgrimage, to protest the relegation of southern Meru peoples to junior status in the tribe:

> What kind of people would we be if Njuri had not always been among us. While it is true that the name of Njuri has changed among us, it is neither different nor below [inferior to] that of Tigania. . . . Nor will we let them declare it is so, we [Mwimbi] who have come from Mbwaa [i.e., have been Meru since its tribal beginnings].[15]

With that, the delegation departed. Nor was their anger quick to heal. For a time neither the Mwimbi, Muthambi, nor Cuka would discuss the topic of Njuri.

By the beginning of Lambert's second term, the southern peoples' indignation had ebbed away. By 1939, however, the system of elders' councils in all three locations was near extinction. The Nkome gatherings within both Mwimbi and Muthambi had long since abandoned their traditional prerogatives, having evolved into little more than social circles where elders met to curse the present and talk about the past. The situation was worse in Cuka, where the council of Ngome existed only in the memories of former members, having been systematically suppressed by the vigor of British district officers sent out from Embu. Thereafter, Cuka had been ruled by a system adapted from the Gikuyu, in which appointed chiefs and tribal retainers had become too powerful to withstand. Faced with such conditions, elders forming the indigenous institutions had retreated into apathy, abandoning even the activities that had sustained the Njuri Nceke.

Formal restoration of the Nkome system began in 1940. To Lambert's surprise the first announcement of his intention evoked such enthusiasm that the district commissioner had to dampen his own fires. His first appeal for the former members of the Nkome to step forward and be greeted was answered by what Lambert subsequently described as "the entire male population of both regions."[16] Eventually more patient inquiry yielded general agreement as to the appropriate spokesmen for each district, and the Nkome councils of both Mwimbi and Muthambi began to function.

The Cuka reaction, however, was quite different. There, Lambert's initial appeal to restore the council of Ngome was greeted with universal indifference. Nor did his subsequent inquiries among Cuka elders elicit enthusiasm for the institution's return. Initially perplexed, Lambert resorted to ritual. Selecting two of the most respected senior chiefs, as well as several widely known elders, Lambert transported them with elaborate ceremony to a specially convened meeting of the Njuri ya Kiama in Imenti. There the delegates were courteously invited to "buy Njuri," making token payments of livestock for their initiation.

Having learned the institution's "secrets" (traditions), the delegation returned to Cuka. There, as "fathers" of the new form of elders' council, they began to "sell" (teach) its secrets to other elders, who responded with gifts of livestock in return. The system expanded intermittently, requiring occasional prodding from district officers. Nonetheless, by 1940 it did begin to have an increasingly public role in district administration.[17] In so doing, however, it incurred the hostility of African members of the colonial service, the so-called little whites.

NJURI VERSUS THE "LITTLE WHITES"

Meru colonialism did not lack African defenders. By the late 1930s and early 1940s an entire age-set had grown up within the colonial service, many of its members having carved satisfying careers in the service of England. Lambert, although always attuned to the beliefs of traditional elders, was less sensitive to the feelings of Meru in colonial service. In consequence, completing his investigations of the Njuri in 1935, he began to consider ways to reintegrate the institution into colonial government.

His concern was enthusiastically reflected by his successor, Capt. Victor M. McKeag. McKeag's background was military, including several years' service in the King's African Rifles. He had neither Lambert's linguistic talent nor his anthropological inclination. He did, however, take a lively interest in the peoples he was asked to rule and spent much time studying their traditional institutions. McKeag thus found himself thoroughly caught up in the spirit of Lambert's earlier research and eager to carry out the latter's goals.

During his first months in office, however, he found that members of the Meru colonial service from Igembe to Cuka objected to the integration of the Njuri in the strongest possible terms. Chiefs, headmen, clerks, translators, and tribunal members who had served colonialism for years, occasionally decades—had become estranged from certain aspects of their tribal past. Many had spent the previous ten years working actively to suppress the Njuri system. Now they protested heatedly against integrating its operations with their own.

McKeag was therefore initially faced with what he subsequently described as a dual government.[18] During his early tours of the district he found that Lambert's administrative legacy included two sets of regional institutions, indigenous and colonial, operating continuously while scrupulously ignoring the other's existence.

Perhaps the best example of this dualism appeared in the judicial sphere, where an unspoken but identifiable competition had begun to appear between each of the regional Njuris and the colonial Local Native Councils for Imenti, Tigania, and Igembe. At one level each competed for litigants. Those who wished to seek legal judgments now weighed the comparative merit of local tradition versus English law. Simultaneously, each institution began to serve as a court of alternate appeal, as elders dissatisfied with judgments rendered by either the colonial or traditional body could try their luck once more with its competitor. In essence that meant each conflict required two decisions, a situation McKeag found both redundant and pointless.

The district commissioner moved to integrate the two systems at several points. He had least success in coordinating the work of chiefs and headmen with Njuri spokesmen. In contrast to Hopkins, McKeag began at the top, asking the appropriate higher councils to appoint as many spokesmen as were required to work with each colonial chief. He intended both sides to consult with one another while implementing colonial commands, but they refused to share authority. Chiefs insisted the spokesmen carry out their orders; spokesmen argued they were not tribal retainers. With few exceptions, McKeag's integration of the administrative structure failed to take root.

His efforts in the judicial sphere, however, were more successful. Here McKeag began to integrate Njuri spokesmen into the Local Native Tribunals. As vacancies occurred within each region, he filled them with "elected" members of the appropriate Njuri. Each "election" was preceded by conversations with Njuri elders until consensus was reached on their selection. Thereafter, McKeag proclaimed an election, requesting the regions' elders to assemble. Gravely he solicited "nominations" for each vacancy. With equal gravity one member of the regional Njuri would propose the preselected nominee. A unanimous vote followed, and both Meru and British electoral customs were thus satisfied.[19]

McKeag and Lambert were also able to restore the traditional Njuri oaths. Lambert was particularly concerned by the suppression during the previous decade of every form of oathing. His objection was ecological, based on the rapidly expanding numbers of livestock throughout every section of the Meru reserve. Before the conquest, he argued, every major moment of decision within the lives of every male Meru was marked by the sacrifice of a sheep, goat, or cow. At one level the slaughter and subsequent communal consumption of the animals were meant to symbolize contact with the ancestors, who were believed to share in the feast. Their attendance alerted them to the decisions faced by their living descendants, providing opportunity to approve or interfere with the accompanying oaths.

Both the oath and livestock sacrifice were thus central to each meeting of an elders' council. The death of an animal was the point of contact between elders and ancestors, as the slaughtered beast's spirit passed between the living and the dead. In spiritual terms, the system provided the living with a sense of steady contact with their ancestors. Ecologically, it resulted in a periodic reduction in the numbers of livestock, thereby maintaining an appropriate balance between grazers and grazing.

By abolishing every form of traditional oath, the Europeans had inadvertently cut off a major means of contact with the supernatural. More important, Lambert argued, they had simultaneously cut off the continual slaughter of livestock that had maintained a normal ecological balance. Thereafter, herds had increased at unprecedented rates until existing grazing areas were near exhaustion.[20]

Lambert's initial steps to restore the traditional forms of oathing, and accompanying animal sacrifice, were similar to those used in legalizing the Njuri itself. He followed a period of early inquiry into the social purposes of each type of oath with continual public discussion of those oaths most appropriate, both at regional mass meetings (baraza) and with selected groups of ruling elders. In so doing, Lambert symbolically proclaimed government acceptance of both the oaths themselves and the accompanying livestock sacrifices as essential elements of Njuri justice. That in turn signified an end to three decades in which district officers had regarded each cow, sheep, and goat brought to Njuri elders as living evidence of bribery, thus illegal under British law. Instead, those assembled to resolve conflicts were once again allowed their communal feasting, as symbolic evidence that harmony had been restored.

McKeag and Lambert finally tried to "give Njuri teeth" by restoring the council's power to enforce its collective decisions.[21] This proved more difficult than previous reforms, for the traditional power of enforcement conflicted sharply with British law. Before the conquest potential violators of Njuri proclamations had been deterred from noncompliance by fear of the council's collective curse. Alternatively, Njuri elders could call upon the weapons of their warrior sons to enforce their will.

Neither curses nor warriors were available to Njuri elders in the 1930s. To replace them, and thereby integrate indigenous authority into the British administration, each of the regional Njuris were "permitted" to seek enforcement of their decisions through appeal to the Local Native Tribunal of their respective regions. Each tribunal could call on the services of tribal police. If requested, it could send them out to enforce Njuri decisions as well as its own. Before doing this, however, the tribunal was required to retry the Njuri proceeding from its own perspective and essentially to find the violator guilty once again.

The decision to enforce such rulings lay solely with the tribunal, since only the colonial body could command tribal police. The method of enforcement, however, followed Meru rather than European tradition. Enforcers worked in pairs, one representing each of two adjacent age-sets. Direct proclamations to the violators were made only in the name of the appropriate Njuri. Most important, fines were levied in livestock rather than money, with a specific percentage of the animals passed on to Njuri elders to provide the basis for their subsequent feasts of reconciliation with the violators themselves.[22] From the British perspective it was a successful example of how indigenous and colonial institutions could be blended both to protect the present and preserve the past. Most Meru elders grudgingly agreed. There were younger men, however, who did not.

NJURI VERSUS THE "MISSION ELEMENT"

By 1939 senior African members of both the colonial administration and the three regional Njuris had reached a truce. Elders from both sides, however, had grown increasingly concerned about their inability to deal effectively with the Meru young. Young men who before the conquest would have submitted eagerly to the discipline of warrior-

hood, now drifted aimlessly, drinking and brawling, alienated from colonial and tribal authority alike.

Within the Nithi Division this alienation manifested itself in a rising
contempt for communal responsibilities, reflected in increasingly flagrant disregard of laws intended to protect the land, trees, and grazing
areas belonging in common to all members of the tribe.

To regain control, one of Meru's senior chiefs, M'Ngaine of Imenti,
proposed to integrate the younger generation more completely into
tribal life by initiating every member of the "warrior" age-set directly
into a regional Njuri. He argued that tribal integrity depended on the
acceptance of communal obligations, specifically those imposed on
youth through membership in their age-set, clan, local Kiama, and, ultimately, Njuri. Of these, only the Njuri had regained even a portion of
its integrative power and thus, the authority to draw young men back
under the authority of their ruling elders. To ensure that this occurred
in fact, M'Ngaine proposed establishing an "initiation school," able to
instruct the young on adherence to tradition and prepare them to assume their responsibilities as Njuri members.[23]

The administration, controlled at this time by McKeag, enthusiastically agreed. Thereafter, a number of "initiation huts" were established
at the time of harvest, first in Imenti and then elsewhere. In most areas
the innovation was well received. Whereas tradition had restricted
Njuri entry to a select few, it was now opened to every male adult who
wished to join. Hundreds responded, expanding the ranks of all regional Njuris beyond counting. On one hand it could be argued that
this dilution of the council system's selectivity diminished its authority
and prestige. On the other almost every member of a youthful Meru
age-set passed once more under the authority of schools run solely by
their elders to learn traditions of the tribe.[24]

One segment of Meru youth, however, categorically refused to join
either the initiation schools or the Njuri itself. Meru's so-called mission
element, whether Presbyterian, Methodist, or Catholic, had by this time
reached early middle age. More than two decades of teaching by their
respective mission fathers had eroded their respect for every aspect of
the Meru past. Nor did they wish to violate the wishes of the mission
heads themselves. In consequence not a single one stepped forth to join.

Their refusal irked McKeag and subsequently Lambert, who reas-
sumed administration of the district at the end of 1939. Both men
wished to continue what they regarded as the continued modernization
of the Njuri system. To ensure continuation of this process, they had

hoped to dilute the ranks of all regional councils with as many progressive, mission-taught Christians as could be induced to join.[25]

The missionaries did not agree. The Italian Catholic fathers, at least partially handicapped by their ignorance of English, proved unable to appreciate the subtleties of the issue and withdrew from all deliberations. The United Methodist Mission, under Hopkins, deliberated at length on the question, but ultimately refused to allow its members to join.

The founder of the Church of Scotland Mission, however, was more outspoken. Dr. Clive Irvine made no secret of his utter detestation of the Njuri, as well as his pronounced unwillingness to allow a single Christian convert to join its ranks: "Njuri is a secret society. It is essentially pàgan. It has traditions of cruelty, murder, intrigue. . . . No European knows what Njuri stands for or what it does. No secret society reveals it activities. . . . It is abhorrent to the British nature and the exact opposite of the open methods of Christianity."[26]

Irvine based his opposition on three points. The "pagan" nature of the Njuri, he believed, would obviously weaken Christian convictions by placing converts in situations in conflict with their religious doctrine. Its "tradition of secrecy" threatened the British administration itself, because its members would be required through their very membership to divide their loyalties. Irvine's strongest objection, however, was religious, based on differences in African and British ritual. Njuri rites of initiation, he pointed out, required the slaughter of a goat. Thereafter, new initiates were brought into physical contact with its blood. As Christians, members of his mission were permitted contact only with the "blood of Christ," and then only during periods of official church ritual. No African Christian could, therefore, be allowed to swear an oath that directly violated his religious teachings.

McKeag decided to focus his response upon Irvine's third objection, consulting initially with members of the Imenti and Tigania Njuris, then with the heads of both the Methodist and Presbyterian missions. In August 1938 he proposed a two-point compromise. He first suggested that membership in any European mission be considered the equivalent of joining a local Kiama. Thus Methodist Christians from Imenti would be excused from the preliminary obligation of "buying [membership in] Kiama Kia Nkomango." Presbyterian converts from Mwimbi would no longer need to join the corresponding Kiama system of Njuguma.

McKeag's second suggestion was to modify the Njuri oath so that mission converts could be allowed to join. To achieve this, he asked both sides to accept a dual initiation rite: traditional Njuri candidates would be oathed on a goat, whereas their Christian counterparts would swear their oaths upon a Bible. Both sides could then agree to preserve the "secrets" of the Njuri in a manner acceptable to each.

Both Irvine and Hopkins agreed to McKeag's plan, each deciding to entrust a small number of their most faithful converts to Njuri membership as an experiment. In September 1938, McKeag responded by proclaiming a regional mass meeting, initially within Imenti, but intended for Njuri members throughout Meru. More than one thousand men are said to have appeared, a far cry from the days when membership was restricted only to the selected few.

McKeag presented both aspects of his proposal. Debate is said to have continued for two full days. Thereafter, spokesmen for the "Njuri of one thousand" appeared before the commissioner to inform him that in the future Christians would be accepted into their ranks on McKeag's terms.

The United Methodist Mission put forth five candidates, among them Filipo M'Inoti and Hezikiah M'Mukiri.[27] The Church of Scotland chose two, Assistant Superintendent Erasto, from Mwimbi, and Evangelist Junius, from Muthambi. The Catholics, as before, refused to allow any form of participation.

Unfortunately, the first stage of the traditional Njuri ceremony required all candidates to remove their clothes and shoes, stepping forward "as children" to begin the rituals that would end with their acceptance into the fellowship as full adults. Initially every one of the Christian candidates refused. The impasse was resolved only after several hours' deliberation, by an Njuri decision to fine each Christian two shillings for the right to remain fully clothed during the rituals. The Christians, after impassioned deliberation of their own, submitted to this condition. They did so, however, with such obvious anger and bitterness that any feelings of unity that might have emerged from the rituals were entirely lost.[28]

FROM HALF NJURI TO FULL ACCORD

A year went by without further development on either side. Each regional Njuri continued to meet without further efforts to induct Christians or even call upon those already inducted to attend gatherings. Similarly, neither Hopkins nor Irvine urged their inductees to attend.

By early 1940, Lambert—newly reappointed as Meru district commissioner—was appalled by the lack of progress. On inquiry he decided that a misunderstanding had arisen on both sides. In fact the Njuri elders of Imenti, offended by Christian behavior during the original initiation, appear to have reinterpreted their original agreement with McKeag. They now informed Lambert they had never been willing to admit Christians into full membership, because the converts were unwilling to undergo the traditional rites—a reference to the incident of clothing and two shillings. Rather, those already accepted were allowed to attend occasional deliberations as spokesmen for topics in which they had particular interest.

Even this limited attendance, the elders declared, would be allowed only if Christian members proved willing to swear, on the Bible, secrecy regarding Njuri decisions. In exchange Christians so bound would agree never to demand further changes in the initiation process or to refuse in the future to take part. Finally, no Christian who accepted these conditions could claim to be a full Njuri member. Rather, they should consider themselves *nuthu* Njuri (half Njuri) or Njuri ya Mabuku (Njuri of the book).

Both mission heads seem initially to have accepted this reinterpretation without comment. Lambert, however, was not content to let the issue rest. Neither he nor McKeag had intended Christian participants to play restricted roles but had hoped that they could actively reintegrate themselves into the mainstream of tribal life. Deprived of Njuri membership, both men felt Christians would remain upon the Meru fringes. Worse, they might form tiny subtribes of their own, with British missionaries taking on the role of chiefs. Such a development, they felt, would both hasten the disintegration of Meru society and deprive it of the progressive leavening it needed to evolve. Once integrated into the system, however, Christians could become a catalyzing force, guiding the anglicization and Christianization of the indigenous institution and through it the communal life of the entire tribe.[29]

It was thus necessary for Lambert to begin a second series of negotiations, moving between the two Protestant ministers and members of both regional Njuris. As expected, the most explicit objections came from African converts at the Church of Scotland's "Kirk Session," a meeting of that mission's elders under the guidance of Irvine. As later summarized in mission correspondence, the elders noted that the Njuri was "pagan, . . . [with] its ceremonies based on pagan symbols, its halls littered with elements of spirit worship," and "secret, . . . [since] its secrecy is its strength. Leave its secrecy intact and there is the . . . danger of a subversive movement, unknown to government, with chiefs, headmen, government employees, and all but a few Christians sworn to secrecy." The assembled elders emphasized "the utter incompatibility of the animist following his ancient worship and customs and the African Christian," and finally proposed "that the system followed in the more advanced Kikuyu country should be adopted, [to include] Local [Native] Councils representing all services [missions] active in the country. The district officer would be chairman. This would be open, safe, acceptable to Christian and progressive opinion as well as to the less privileged."[30]

In the face of this intense opposition, Lambert was initially baffled over how to proceed. In late March 1940 he began discussions with Hopkins, whose Methodist converts, he believed, would prove most receptive to a new agreement. He also met with Irvine, seeking areas where both the Njuris and the Presbyterians could compromise.

On reflection he asked Hopkins's permission to send Filipo M'Inoti to speak personally with the Church of Scotland elders, meeting in Kirk Session, to explore their points of disagreement. M'Inoti was perfect for the task. By 1940 he had been ordained as the first Meru minister in Imenti, thereby clearly demonstrating his mastery of Christian teachings. Beyond that he had become deeply versed in Njuri tradition, so that he proved able to suggest compromises satisfactory to both sides.

M'Inoti met with the Church of Scotland elders at a Kirk Session that lasted most of a day. Sharing common language, heritage, and religion, they were able to explore the issues more fully than had proved possible when with the whites and thus agree on several compromises. At the same time, Lambert reached essentially similar agreements with Hopkins and the Methodist mission elders. Irvine, faced with such unanimity, gave way with unexpected grace, consenting to limited participation of his elders in what became known simply as "The Agreement." The first part of the agreement excused any Christian candidate wishing to enter a regional Njuri from prior membership in his local Kiama, in the same manner initially suggested by McKeag. The second required the initiation of Christians to take place in the traditional ("pagan") manner, with due allowance for their desire to remain clothed. The third dictated that whenever Christians entered an Njuri initiation hut that "pagan symbols would be covered or otherwise rendered invisible." The fourth required, as before, that every Christian oath be sworn on the Bible.[31]

The fifth requirement, however, contained the core of the entire agreement. It dealt with the transmission of Njuri teachings ("secrets") to new initiates. In essence the Njuri agreed that nothing could be taught until first approved by M'Inoti, who as both a Christian minister and Njuri "elder" reserved the right to reword the teachings to render them consistent with Christian principles.[32]

It is doubtful if any agreement would have been reached without the continuous mediation of the Reverend Filipo M'Inoti. Among the earliest of Meru's Christian converts, and the one who had climbed highest in their ranks, he held the respect of black and white, Methodist and Presbyterian, missionary and administrator alike. Rarely do agreements emerge through the conciliatory efforts of one man, yet it was M'Inoti's assurances that provided sufficient confidence to bind all sides. Soon after, Irvine sent the first of his Kirk Session elders, Jotham M'Murianki, to an Njuri for initiation. To ensure a smooth transition, the rites were led by M'Inoti himself. M'Murianki then became the recognized initiation leader for all future candidates from the Church of Scotland Mission. For Protestants the problem was resolved.

District attention then turned to the Roman Catholic Mission. By 1940 the Consolata fathers had far outstripped their Protestant competitors, having established no less than seven major mission stations and twenty-two bush schools and dispensaries in every part of the district where their presence was allowed. The Catholics operated, however, in semi-isolation, intensified by their inability to speak either English or Swahili. Their policy was to withdraw both mission fathers and their converts from contact with traditional and colonial authorities.

At Lambert's insistence, Father Guadagnini, the educational secretary for the Consolata, consented to meet with Njuri elders to explore the issue. The discussions, however, were interrupted by the outbreak of World War II and thus the beginning of hostilities between England and Italy. Within days every Italian in Meru had been imprisoned, leaving the entire Catholic mission chain bereft of European direction. The gap was partially filled by Catholic priests from allied nations, who assumed control of peoples of whose culture they knew nothing.

The results shook the confidence of Catholic elders throughout the district, briefly destroying the trust that Lambert had striven to build. The Cuka Catholic mission was taken over by two priests from Holland. Within weeks after their arrival they proclaimed a "total ban on the African religion of Njuri." All Catholics were prohibited entry into this "religion," and those who joined faced excommunication. Catholic teachers were authorized to drive out any Njuri members who appeared, while chiefs and elders were forbidden to force converts to join.

The proclamation was issued in a circular letter addressed to teachers within every Catholic school in Meru. By coincidence a copy reached Lambert as well. Enraged, the district commissioner left immediately for Cuka, to "teach this self-appointed Pope the error of his ways."[33] He arrived too late. Having issued their proclamation, the Dutch priests had moved on, completely unaware of the damage such an edict could have caused the still fragile alliance between traditional and colonial rule.

NJURI VERSUS GIKUYU: THE MERU GOLDEN AGE

For a while the alliance deepened and thrived. Lambert quickly countermanded the Dutch priests' proclamation, visiting each Catholic mission in the district to explain it had been written by mistake. He then began negotiations with Catholic missions in Imenti—now directed by an Irish priest—for admission of their converts to the Njuri. The priest posed no objection, and a small number of Catholic converts entered the Njuri in January 1941.

In later years both Lambert and McKeag took great satisfaction in the completion of their alliance. Symbolically, the entry of Meru's powerful Catholics into the "pagan" institution of Njuri marked the culmination of a dream shared by "nativist" administrators across Kenya: a colonial golden age in which indigenous and British institutions would join hands, working together to implement decisions made to benefit the entire tribe.

To a degree and for more than a decade the dream did flicker into life, as a revived and newly confident system of regional Njuris joined British administrators to protect the tribe against potential enemies. Perhaps the most striking example of the councils' vigor during this period can be found in their struggle against the threat posed to Meru by its traditional enemy, the Gikuyu.

The Gikuyu inhabit nearly seventy percent of Mount Kenya, neighboring Meru to both its west and south. Their system of land tenure, initially communal, had moved closer to that of England as individual ownership became increasingly widespread. In Meru, Gikuyu landholders were known as "tree eaters" because of their propensity to clear land of all tree cover prior to cultivation. In contrast the Meru held all trees in common, except those planted by individuals, and cutting down a tree required communal permission from an appropriate local Kiama.

British officers and Meru elders thus shared a common concern when, during the late 1930s, small bands of Gikuyu moved into the border region between the star-grass (populated) and "black" (montaine) forest zones and began to farm. Beginning in Cuka these settlements multiplied steadily, fed by a continuous trickle of new immigrants, and gradually expanded north into Muthambi and Mwimbi.

Many of the new arrivals were adopted, in traditional fashion, into existing Meru clans, accepting the use of land from local Kiama elders in exchange for gifts of livestock. Others, however, refused any type of cultural integration, creating a series of minisettlements, organized agriculturally and socially wholly along Gikuyu lines. The resulting destruction of the trees threatened to extend along the entire forest rim. Before the conquest the Meru would have responded to this devastation with warriors. During the 1930s they accepted payments of livestock and shillings from a people who seemed to have both in abundance.

In 1941 one of the more aggressive of these settlements appeared along the lower boundaries of the Ngaia forest in Igembe. Its appearance shocked district administrators and Njuri elders alike, for it was the first time Gikuyu had dared to penetrate the Meru north. Igembe elders initially approached the settlers with offers of adoption into their respective clans, a decision that would have placed them both within tradition and under control. They were contemptuously spurned.

The elder's anxiety deepened when members of the Ngaia settlement began to cultivate the very land that the Njuri Nceke had set aside as a protected zone. In Meru strips of land immediately beneath the lower forest rim had traditionally been protected, by Njuri proclamation, from cultivation, wood cutting, grazing, or any other activity that might harm trees. The result was the creation of an unmarked but universally respected buffer zone between human activities and the forest.

It was this zone, no doubt still highly fertile, that the Gikuyu chose to farm. In January 1940 a delegation of Njuri elders ordered them to leave. The Gikuyu refused. The Njuri Nceke then appealed to the district commissioner. In February 1940, Lambert personally visited the settlement, heard claims from both sides, then ordered the Gikuyu to depart within twenty days.

Initially they agreed. During the subsequent weeks, however, they worked day and night to plant every inch of the buffer zone with millet. In so doing, they followed both Gikuyu and Meru tradition, establishing the right to remain ("by their seed") on the disputed land until the harvest.

Had the incident occurred during the 1800s the Njuri Nceke would have sent warriors to expel the intruders at the moment they appeared. Had they come in the 1920s it would have done nothing, stripped of its powers and officially banned. Its decision in the fall of 1940 illustrates the degree to which the institution had recovered both its traditional authority and self-respect.

In October 1940 Njuri elders appeared in scores along the entire length of the Gikuyu fields. Singing, dancing, and waving tufts of grass as the traditional sign that they came in peace, the elders reaped the entire crop. Furious, the Gikuyu appealed en masse to the district commissioner. Completely aware of the symbolism behind the Njuri actions, Lambert dismissed their suit and expelled them from the district.[34] This became a symbolic act in itself, setting a precedent of which every elder soon became aware: if the Njuri reaped what aliens had sown, the government would support them.

For Lambert the incident must have proved a quiet triumph, a moment marking the culmination of his work, McKeag's, and perhaps Hopkins's before him: the restoration of the dignity of indigenous authority so that it could once more take up its work, then stand side by side with England to administer the tribe. The fragile alliance, colonial and Meru, had come to life. Ruling elders from the missions, regional Njuris, and district headquarters were in accord. To Lambert, it must indeed have seemed the dawn of a golden age.

If so, the new era would be brief. The sense of compromise that now joined the senior age-sets did not include the young. Even as Lambert sought to draw mission converts into the tribal mainstream, others were leaving the missions, thereby drawing beyond his reach. In the years to come, young men from Mwimbi and Muthambi, deeply influenced by the spirit of revolt among the Gikuyu, would form "independent" churches at the Meru social fringes. Their goal was less to worship than to use the pulpit as a zone of safety from which to preach against both England and the African past. Still later, they would form "independent" schools, devoid of mission teachings, where children could be taught to strive for freedom.

In time the independent churchmen, teachers, and pupils alike would find themselves increasingly involved in political actions as the oaths and promises of Gikuyu politicians drummed ever more loudly across the land. Some would respond by forming patriotic groups, such as the "Meru Helping Country Association" of 1950, which swore loyalty to England while hoping to escape it.[35] Finally, the peoples of Mount

Kenya would revolt, and the men of Meru—driven apart by what would become a Gikuyu civil war—would fight on both sides, their tribal unity destroyed.

All this, however, lay in the future. In 1940, with much of the world approaching war, the leading men of Meru—pagan and Christian, English and African, Njuri elder and colonial chief—all marched as one. For the next ten years the Njuri system would dominate much of Meru's political arena, together with an African colonial service with which it would increasingly share a loyalty to England. Most mainstream Meru would remain content. Only on the fringes, as had been the case throughout Meru history, would the new ways emerge. This time, however, the new generation of fringemen would win Meru its freedom.

Notes

INTRODUCTION

1. Gituuru wa Gikamata, MOS 27. MOS refers to the "Meru Oral Sources" section of the Bibliography, where I have provided background information on each of my informants.

2. "The usual European way of spelling this word [Gikuyu] is Kikuyu, which is incorrect. It should be Gikuyu. . . . This form refers only to the country itself. A Gikuyu person is Mu-Gikuyu, plural, A-Gikuyu. But so as not to confuse our readers, we have used one form, Gikuyu, for all purposes" (Jomo Kenyatta, *Facing Mt. Kenya*, xv). This book follows Kenyatta's guidelines. Colonial sources cited here, however, retain their original spellings.

CHAPTER ONE

1. Gaichungi Baibuatho M'Mbarui, MOS 34.

2. See Fadiman, "Early History of the Meru," for additional detail on Meru origins and subsequent migration to Mount Kenya. All sketches in this chapter are drawn from this article.

3. Lambert, *Systems of Land Tenure*, 10.

4. "How the Meru Came to Their Present Country," typed manuscript, author unknown; originally collected by E. B. Horne, first district commissioner, Meru, in 1918. Lambert Papers.

5. John Sharman, professor of African linguistics, Institute of African Studies, University of Nairobi, personal communication, July 1970.

6. N. Chittick, "Discoveries in the Lamu Archipelago," *Anzania* 2 (1967): 84, and personal communication, 1970.

7. Stigand, *The Land of Zinj*, 48.

8. R. Bunger, "Pokomo Political History and Organization," Discussion Paper, Institute of African Studies, University of Nairobi, July 1970, and personal communication, July–December 1970.

9. Monro, "Migrations of the Bantu-Speaking Peoples, 25–28.

10. Holding, "Some Preliminary Notes on Meru Age Grades," 58–65, suggests that parallel systems of councils operated among females.

11. Lambert, "Social and Political Institutions," 439–79, Lambert Papers.

12. Mahner, "The Insider and the Outsider," 1–2, and personal communication, July–December 1970.

13. Fadiman, "Mountain Witchcraft," 87–101.

14. Laughton, "An Introductory Study of the Meru People."

15. Gerrard M'Ikaria (son of a foreteller), MOS 15; M'Anyoni wa Ntangi (former curse-detector), MOS 16; M'Rinkanya M'Ringui (former curse-detector), MOS 17; M'Mwiriria M'Murungi (former bow breaker, i.e., theft detector), MOS 18; Ngaruro M'Munyiri (former oath administrator: "oath of the hot iron"), MOS 19; M'Mukira Gakoro (former curse-remover), MOS 22; all from Imenti. No practitioners of Urogi (cursing) are included: no one in all Meru admitted to having practiced the rituals of Urogi at any time, although everyone believed that others did so.

CHAPTER TWO

1. M'Ikiene M'Irimbere, MOS 40.

2. Nguruntune variants collected by H. E. Lambert and J. G. H. Hopkins, former district commissioners in Meru, who took great interest in their historical traditions. Material now in Lambert Papers.

3. Benson, ed., *Kikuyu-English Dictionary*, for example, gives three meanings of Mukuna Ruku, each of which is reflected in Meru tradition: (1) "a mythological figure . . . giving light to the sun"; (2) "one who signals by means of a gong (legendary figure, probably an ivory trader from Mombasa)"; (3) "a person of . . . authority, . . . Arab or European." In contemporary Meru children's tales Mukuna Ruku is synonymous with both a figure of authority and the sun.

4. Ogot and Kiernan, *Zamani*, 130; Oliver and Mathew, *History of East Africa*, 141; and Stigand, *The Land of Zinj*, 49–50.

5. Hobley, *Ethnology of the A-Kamba*, 158.

6. Lambert Papers. Early versions were collected by E. B. Horne (1913), J. G. H. Hopkins (1918), and C. R. Wise (1925), all district commissioners. Later versions were collected from various subtribes by Rev. W. H. Laughton and H. E. Lambert, district commissioner (all in the 1930s and early 1940s). The latest collections took place in 1967–1970 among every section of the Meru-speaking peoples and are my own.

7. E. B. Horne, private paper, 25 April 1913. Lambert Papers.

8. Ibid.

9. Mahassin, "Some Contributions of Swahili Poetry."

10. Laughton, "An Introductory Study of the Meru People."

11. Jean Brown, "Metalworking in East and Central Kenya," Discussion Paper, Institute of Development Studies, University of Nairobi, June 1970.

12. John Sharman, Professor of Linguistics, Institute of African Studies, University of Nairobi. Personal communication, October 1970.

13. The prophecy is in Ki-Igembe, a dialect of Ki-Meru (language). Kiringo M'Munyari, MOS 33.

14. Brown, Jean, "Metalworking in East and Central Kenya," 2.

15. Ibid., 5, and see L. Saggerson, "Geological Survey," in E. W. Russell, ed., *Natural Resources of East Africa* (Nairobi: East African Publishing House, 1962).

16. For this and all subsequent information about the area between the Tana River and the upland fringes of Ukambani (the area currently inhabited by the Kamba), I am indebted to Mr. Stephen Pownall, Nanyuki, Kenya, who became intimately acquainted with its topography through many years of game trapping and cattle buying in the area.

17. See note 16 above.

18. Lambert, "Social and Political Institutions," 315–17.

19. Gituuru wa Gikamata (Imenti), MOS 27; M'Thaara M'Mutani (Muthambi), MOS 28; Kiringo M'Munyari (Igembe), MOS 33; Gaichungi Baibuatho M'Mbarui (Igembe), MOS 34; these men are among the last surviving members of their Kiramana (Igembe: Kilamunya) age-set, thus the oldest living men in Meru.

20. There are many translations of the term "Mount Kenya." One of the earlier Gikuyu versions, still widely accepted, is Kirima Kia Nyaga (hill of the ostrich), currently contracted to Kirinyaga. Similarly, the earlier Meru version of Kirima Kia Maara (shining hill, referring to its ice-capped peak) has been contracted to Kirimaara. Gikuyu data provided by K. K. Sillitoe, assistant agricultural officer, Meru, 1954–1957; personal communication, May 1992.

CHAPTER THREE

1. Hezikiah M'Mukiri, MOS 26.

2. Bernardi, *Mugwe,* and personal communication, Turin, Italy, July 1969. The concept of the Mugwe as "transmitter of blessings" is my own.

3. Adamson, *Bwana Game,* 8, describes the automatic cursing system of the Ogiek in terms identical to that of Meru hunters. Corroborated in personal communication, November 1969–November 1970.

4. The complete itemized contents of an antelope-skin carrier, said to have belonged to an A-Athi "witch doctor" (i.e., curse remover) was turned in to the British Museum, circa 1920, by Lt. G. St. J. Orde-Browne, at that time assistant district commissioner of Cuka (formerly Chuka) (i.e., the Mwimbi-Muthambi-Cuka regions), and subsequent author of *The Vanishing Tribes of Kenya.*

5. Chant used in South Imenti by M'Nkanata M'Mkatemia (see MOS 46), one of that region's oldest honey hunters. Informant recalls that chants were "bought" (in exchange for millet beer) from Ogiek hunters at the time of the Michubu age-set (1750s).

6. Blackburn, "A Preliminary Report of Research on the Ogiek Tribe," and Rosen, "A Preliminary Report of Research among the Mukogodo, Laikipiak District.

7. Adamson, *A Lifetime with Lions* (American title for *Bwana Game*), 86–87, and subsequent personal communication, 1969–1970.

8. See Mathiu wa Gacece (Northeast Imenti), MOS 42; M'Mwongera wa Kabutai (Northeast Imenti), MOS 41; M'Nkanata M'Mkatemia (South Imenti), MOS 46; Daudi M'Mungaria (South Imenti), MOS 47; Majogu wa Mathiu (Northeast Imenti), MOS 44; and several others all former A-Athi or descended from A-Athi clans or both.

9. See note 8 above.

10. See note 8 above.

11. Fadiman, "The Meru Peoples," 153–73, deals with Mount Kenya's earlier occupants in greater detail.

12. Ibid.; H. S. K. Mwaniki, personal correspondence, 1970s. Fragmentary traditions collected from Tigania and Northeast Imenti also record the presence of a single Bantu-speaking people, whom they know as Michimikuru. Traditions collected by Mwaniki among the Bantu-speaking Mbeere, who live adjacent to the Embu of Mount Kenya, suggest that at least one section of their tribe was once called Michimikuru, did live on the Tigania Plain, and was driven south.

13. Alan H. Jacobs, research director, Institute of Africa Studies, University of Nairobi, 1968–1972, in a personal communication, has suggested the following sketch of the language relationships referred to in classifying Mount Kenya's earlier (pre–Bantu-speaking) occupants:

TABLE 8   LANGUAGE FAMILIES
OF MOUNT KENYA

Afro-Asiatic Language Family (Cushitic Branch)		Nilo-Saharan Language Family (Eastern Sudanic Branch)	
Southern Cushitic Speakers	*Eastern Cushitic Speakers*	*Highland Nilotic Speakers*	*Plains Nilotic Speakers*
Mokogodo	Oromo Speakers:	Kalenjin Speakers:	Maa (Maasai) Speakers:
	Galla	Ogiek (Ndorobo)	Il Tikirri
	Boran		Mumunyot
	Oromo		Il Nguisi
	Somali		
	Rendille		

14. J. G. Hopkins, assistant district commissioner, Meru, 1917–1918. Report on Mwoko (Muoko) burial customs, 25 April 1919, Meru political records, Kenya National Archives (hereinafter KNA), Nairobi, Kenya, and personal correspondence with Hopkins, Pretoria, South Africa, June–December 1970.

15. Rev. A. J. Hopkins, missionary, United Methodist Mission, Meru District, mid-1920s. Letter, 16 May 1924, to C. S. Dobbs, district commissioner, Meru, describing similarities between the alleged Muoko burials and those of the Tana River Galla with which he had grown familiar through prior postings. Lambert Papers. Copy in my possession.

16. J. G. H. Hopkins, Lambert Papers. Hopkins collected the earliest versions of the "Mwoko [Muoko] Tradition," recounted here in abbreviated form. Corroborated by contemporary oral informants, Tigania.

17. Mahner, "The Insider and the Outsider," 9, and personal discussions, 1970. Corroborated by oral informants, Tigania.

18. The following researchers, among others, have collected "Gumba" (Agumba) oral traditions among the Meru, Embu, Mbeere, Cuka, Mwimbi, and Muthambi peoples of Mount Kenya: Routledge, *With A Prehistoric People*, 4; Kenyatta, *Facing Mt. Kenya*, 23–24; Lambert, *Systems of Land Tenure*, 63–93; Leakey, *Stone Age Cultures*, 198 ff.; Orde-Browne, *The Vanishing Tribes of Kenya*, 21, 63–64 (Mwimbi-Muthambi-Cuka); Muriuki, *A History of the Kikuyu*, 23, 37–46, 54–68, 87, 111; and Mwaniki, *The Living History of Embu and Mbeere*.

19. R. D. F. Taylor, "The Gumba and Gumba Pits of Fort Hall District, Kenya," *Azania* 1 (1966): 111. Taylor describes the Gumba (Agumba) pits of Gikuyu in detail. Comparative data from Meru is based on my personal examination.

20. Blackburn, "Preliminary Report of Research on the Ogiek Tribe," 10–11 (weapons).

21. Maguire, " 'El-Torobo,' Tanganika Notes and Records," 8–13.

22. Ibid.

23. Source for Il Mosiro word list is Maguire (see note 21 above); for Kiriita, see Lambert, *Systems of Land Tenure*, 80. The Umpua word list is from Muriuki Muriithi (MOS 32), a Mwimbi elder then (1969) in his early eighties.

24. Blackburn, "A Preliminary Report of Research on the Ogiek Tribe."

25. Alan H. Jacobs, personal letter, 8 February 1987. Much of the Maasai (Ol Maa) material presented in this section was derived through extensive discussions with Professor Jacobs, research director, Institute of Africa Studies, University of Nairobi, 1968–1972, and the major Maasai scholar of this century. In 1972, Jacobs classified and estimated the number of speakers of the major Maa-speaking groups as: Il Maasai (Kenya, Tanzania), 226,000; Arusha (Tanzania), 97,000; Samburu (Kenya), 58,000; Baraguyu (Tanzania), 29,000; Ogiek (Dorobo) (Kenya, Tanzania), 22,000; Njemps (Kenya), 7,000.

26. Ibid.

27. Fadiman, *Oral History*, provides detailed information regarding Meru methods of warfare up to the conquest by Great Britain.

28. See note 25 above.

CHAPTER FOUR

1. M'Inoti, "Asili ya Wameru na tabia zao," Private Papers.

2. See Fadiman, *Oral History*, for detail on precolonial Meru warfare; idem, *The Moment of Conquest*; idem, *Mountain Warriors*.

3. See Lambert, "Social and Political Institutions," 278–79, 307–9, Lambert Papers, for territorial distribution of *gichiaro* (kinship and military alliances).

4. Ibid. Lambert suggests the pre-Cuka were split into a main body (pre-Cuka: Chabugi) and one tiny fragment (Miutini) by the advance of the Mwimbi up the mountain.

5. M'Muraa wa Kairanyi (Northeast Imenti), MOS 13; Rwito wa Ruganda (Mwimbi), MOS 30; personal observation, discussions with elders from Cuka, Muthambi, and Imenti. The Cuka, however, did hide cattle in pits to protect them from raiders.

6. M'Inoti (see note 1 above) and M'Anampiu, "Prophetic Families in Imenti," handwritten manuscript, Meru language, dealing with clan histories of North Imenti, Private Papers.

7. Throughout East Africa, Caucasians are perceived as "red" rather than white. Small children still greet Caucasians as "red men" until told by adults to call them "white." See Huxley, *Red Strangers*, a fictional account of the conquest of the Gikuyu by "red strangers," that is, the British.

8. M'Inoti, "Asili ya Wameru," chap. 4, Private Papers.

9. "Traditions and Customs of Mwimbi," undated, Saint Paul's Theological Seminary, Historical Archives (Anderson's Archives). Data on M'Agocorua corroborated by oral informants within both Mwimbi and Muthambi.

10. Information regarding the supernatural Kiamas of crop protection, food acquisition, child extortion, and supernatural dance has been supplied by former members of each group. See MOS 29, 35–36, 38, 58–59, and 61–67 as examples.

11. Mwaa: to be foolish, stupid, ignorant (Mu-Waa or Mwaa: jester, man of the fools); see Giorgis, *A Tentative Kimeru Dictionary*.

12. Sources for "deviant" Kiamas: Kairu Baimwera (Mwimbi), MOS 58; Karaya wa Njara (Muthambi), MOS 61; Kainyu Murungi (Igoji), MOS 63; Mwakireu Gikabu (Igoji), MOS 64; M'Muga M'Murithi (Miutini), MOS 74; Karema M'Ringeera (Northeast Imenti), MOS 88; and several others. Data corroborated by informants in Tigania-Igembe, with local variations. All informants were once either directly or indirectly connected with the societies.

CHAPTER FIVE

1. Mwamucheke wa Gakuru (Muthambi), MOS 23.

2. Fadiman, *Moment of Conquest*. Material for this chapter first appeared in this monograph. Revisions and additions are the result of research during 1983–1984.

3. Chanler, *Through Jungle and Desert*, 175, and "Mr. Astor Chanler's Expedition," 533–34. The incidents recounted are drawn from Chanler's narrations of "battles" with warriors in Tigania and Igembe and are confirmed by informants in both regions.

4. Peters, "Mouth of the Tana," 1.

5. Fadiman, *Mountain Warriors*, 46–48, describes the tactics used by the Tiganians against Chanler. For Chanler's version see *Through Jungle and Desert*, 175ff.

6. Chanler, *Through Jungle and Desert*, 175ff.

7. Mwaniki, "The British Impact on Embu," and *The Living History of Embu and Mbeere*. Mwaniki is Kenya's foremost authority on Embu-Mbeere oral history. I have drawn all data on the British conquest of Embu from his research and personal communication with him. For a British perspective of the conquest see Moyse-Bartlett, *The King's African Rifles;* and *Central Province Political Record, 1906*, Kenya National Archives (KNA).

8. Mwaniki, "The British Impact on Embu."

9. H. S. K. Mwaniki, personal communication, April 1970.

10. Mwamucheke wa Gakuru (Muthambi), MOS 23.

11. Marjorie R. Horne, wife of Edward Butler Horne ("Kangangi"), British conqueror and first district commissioner of Meru. Personal interview, Nairobi, Kenya, 10 October 1969. All personal data on E. B. Horne within this and subsequent chapters have been provided by his wife.

12. Orde-Brown, "Circumcision Ceremonies," 137–40.

13. Bernardi, *Mugwe*, 172. Also mentioned in *Meru District Record Book, 1908–1921*, KNA.

14. C. R. W. Lane, letter, 7 July 1908, *Embu Political Record Book*, KNA. Horne's "entourage" was the Third Battalion, King's African Rifles. He was initially assisted by Capt. Philips and Lt. Dann, neither of whom are recalled in oral tradition. This chapter, therefore, records the creation of colonialism primarily as the Meru remember it—as the work of one man, E. B. Horne (Kangangi).

15. F. C. Gamble, assistant district commissioner, Meru, 1915. Private letter, 10 October 1919, Lambert Papers.

16. Matiri wa Kirongoro, Muthambi, MOS 29. Also, "The History of Communications in Meru District," Saint Paul's Theological Seminary, Historical Archives. Corroborated by other oral sources.

17. Cuka Station, including Mwimbi and Muthambi, was administered during this period by G. St. J. Orde-Brown. He has written extensively of his experiences in *The Vanishing Tribes of Kenya*.

18. F. C. Gamble, letter, 15 December 1919, Lambert Papers.

19. H. E. Chamier, district commissioner, Meru, 1919. *Official Report*, Lambert Papers.

20. *Meru District Record Book, 1908–1921*, KNA. These contain detailed lists of early appointees to the chief and headman posts.

21. The Meru township was proclaimed 13 May 1911. The area was defined as having a radius of one square mile from the British flagstaff. W.O. 106 (Intelligence Papers), Military Operations, King's African Rifles, 1902–1914, Public Record Office, London.

22. Fadiman, "Oral History," 88–91, has a detailed description of the psychological devices used to prepare warriors for battle.

23. Orde-Brown, "Circumcision Ceremonies," 176–77.

24. See note 18 above.

25. Kenyatta, *Facing Mt. Kenya*, 155–161, describes Ngweko (Meru: Nguiko) among the neighboring Gikuyu.

26. Lambert, "Social and Political Institutions," Lambert Papers. Beginning page 432 Ngweko and its rationale are described in greater detail.

CHAPTER SIX

1. Chant of Kiama Kia Kagita, "secret witchcraft society" (*sic*), Meru District, 1908–1929. Before that, one of the supernatural dancing societies formed by deviant family heads of both sexes. Matiri (Paul) wa Kirongoro (Muthambi), MOS 29.

2. Holding, "Some Preliminary Notes," 58–65.

3. Data from former members of the Chigiira, a women's Kiama in Mwimbi and Igoji, notably Mrs. Gacaba Murungi (Igoji), MOS 65; Mrs. Mwakireu Gikabu (Igoji), MOS 64; Mrs. Kainyu Murungi (Igoji), MOS 63; and one informant (Geto village, Igoji) who withheld her name, MOS 62.

4. Lambert, "The Social and Political Institutions," 476, Lambert Papers.

5. As recounted by Meru informants who served as officials in Horne's colonial administration (usually as porter, policeman, headman, chief) from its inception. Their detestation of the dancing Kiamas remains evident to this day. M'Muraa wa Kairanyi, MOS 13, is notable.

6. Marjorie R. Horne, wife of E. B. Horne. Personal interview, Nairobi, Kenya, 1969.

7. M'Mucheke Likira (Tigania), MOS 54; and Nguluu M'Mungaine (Tigania), MOS 53. Most frequent Tigania version, 1969. Also collected in Imenti, 1950s; see Bernardi, *Mugwe*, 58.

8. Kairu Baimwera (Mwimbi), MOS 58; Matiri wa Kirongoro, (Muthambi), MOS 29; M'Thaara M'Mutani (Muthambi), MOS 28; and Mrs. Jwanina Murungi, MOS 67; Mrs. Gacaba Murungi, MOS 65; Mrs. Mwakireu Gikabu, MOS 64; and Mrs. Kainyu Murungi, MOS 63 (all women from Igoji); Data corroborated by male elders in Imenti, Tigania-Igembe. All informants were once involved with the Kagita.

9. See note 8 above.

10. See note 8 above.

11. J. Ainsworth to British East Africa Company, letter, 1898 (month illegible), marked F.O. 2/73, copy in Lambert Papers.

12. Muriuki, *A History of the Kikuyu*, 155, n. 80.

13. Involved with the Kagita: MOS 63–65, 67, 53–54, 58, 28–29.

14. See note 13 above.

15. See note 13 above.

16. See note 13 above.

17. Fadiman, *Oral History*, chap. 6, "Courtship and Marriage," 125ff. Dancing was the first of four stages of courtship. Each was strictly regulated, and conducted in public view to permit everyone in the community to appraise the match. The Kagita broke with the tradition of public dancing, holding its dances in pitch darkness and total secrecy.

CHAPTER SEVEN

1. Madeleine Laverne Platts, wife of W. A. F. Platts, first assistant district commissioner, Meru, 1912–1913. Diary, Rhodes House (see "Archival Collections" in the Bibliography).

2. *Meru District Record Book, 1911–1914,* Kenya National Archives (KNA). Platts was assisted by Hemmant, Walton, T. D. Butler, H. E. Welby, and C. M. Barton, the last three of whom remained to assist Horne on his return to Meru in June 1913.

3. *Embu [District] Political Record Book, 1914,* KNA, provides interesting examples. See, in particular, the case of Kianga, turned in by his own elders during a KAR punitive expedition against "ridgetop rebels" in upper Cuka, lower Cuka, lower Muthambi, lower Mwimbi. Note that the lower regions were farthest from centers of government control.

4. G. St. J. Orde-Browne, first assistant district commissioner, Nithi (Southern) Region (Mwimbi-Muthambi-Cuka), after its transfer from administrative jurisdiction of Meru District to Embu District in 1913. Much of the data on the three southern peoples in this and subsequent chapters are drawn from his private papers in the Rhodes House collection in Oxford, England. In addition, material has also been drawn from the following publications: *The Vanishing Tribes of Kenya;* "Circumcision Ceremonies among the Amwimbe"; "The Circumcision Ceremony in Chuka"; "Mt. Kenya and Its People"; and "The Southeast Face of Mt. Kenya." (Orde-Browne's name was spelled Orde-Brown during the early years of his career.)

5. See note 4 above.

6. Orde-Browne, untitled address, prepared in later years for delivery on BBC; Rhodes House.

7. Bernardi, *Mugwe,* 26ff.

8. Lambert, Lambert Papers. Untitled folder assembled by C. F. Adkins, district commissioner, Meru, 1938.

9. As described by former members of the Njuri ya Kiami (Imenti), notably Chief M'Muraa wa Kairanyi (Northeast Imenti), MOS 13, just prior to his death.

10. MOS 13; Lambert, untitled document, Lambert Papers.

11. *Meru District Record Book, 1911,* KNA.

12. *Meru District Record Book, 1912,* KNA. Other examples of Horne's reforms are from subsequent record books. See also Lambert, "Administrative Use of the Indigenous Institutions of the Meru," Lambert Papers, which traces the evolution of "native" administration under Horne and subsequent colonial officials.

13. M'Muraa wa Kairanyi (Imenti), MOS 13.

14. Lambert, "Administrative Use of the Indigenous Institutions of the Meru," 3, Lambert Papers.

15. *Meru District Record Book, 1915,* KNA.

16. *Meru District Record Book, 1916,* KNA.

17. *Meru District Record Book, 1917, 1919, 1920, 1921,* KNA.

18. *Meru District Record Book, 1913,* KNA.

19. Ibid.

20. Lambert, "Administrative Use of the Indigenous Institutions of the Meru," 6–8, Lambert Papers. Note that the spelling varies: Ncaama, Nchama, Njama.

21. On Kauganyama: M'Rutere M'Mbogore, Mukungu M'Mbogore, M'Iniu M'Mbogore, three brothers, all sons of Mbogore M'Mwendo, first colonial chief, upper Mwimbi, MOS 31; personal interviews, 1970.

22. See note 21 above.

23. *Meru District Record Book, 1911–1917,* KNA, comments on chiefs.

24. Orde-Browne, private papers, Rhodes House. Browne's private papers frequently mention dealings with Mbogore M'Mwendo.

25. See note 21 above.

26. See *Chuka Sub-District Political Record Book, 1914* and *Embu [District] Political Record Book, 1927* (2 August 1927) for summary and evaluation of the incidents described. Cuka (spelled Chuka in the colonial era) was a part of Embu District when this incident occurred. Both in KNA.

27. See note 21 above.

28. *Embu [District] Political Record Book, 1927,* 2nd-class criminal case #6/14, as copied from an earlier record (lost) within *Chuka Sub-District Political Record Book, 1914,* KNA.

CHAPTER EIGHT

1. A. J. Hopkins, *Trail Blazers and Road Makers,* 100. The quotation refers back to the opening of Meru District to Protestant Christianity in 1913.

2. Ibid., chaps. 1, 2.

3. "Decretum Laudis," proclamation, published by the Holy See, January 1901, *Sec. dizionario encyclopedica dei religiosi,* Societa di Sao Paulo, 1971, copy in Consolata Mission Archives, Turin.

4. Monseigneur S. Allgeyer, apostolic vicar of Zanzibar, 1901, and bishop within the Society of the Holy Ghost, a Catholic missionary order based in France. Untitled document, Consolata Mission Archives, Turin.

5. Pecomino, "Mezzo serolo di attentiva," Consolata Mission Archives, Turin. This typescript was combined with additional untitled Italian-language materials by Father P. Valentino Ghilardi, Roman Catholic, Igoji Mission, Meru, 1950. The data were made available to me by Father Ghilardi in a personal interview at the Consolata Mission Archives, in Turin in 1969.

6. Kikuyu/Gikuyu (spelling): During the colonial era *Kikuyu* was the preferred spelling. During the contemporary era, *Gikuyu* is usually preferred. I use *Gikuyu* throughout this book.

7. Hopkins, *Trail Blazers and Road Makers,* 89.

8. Ibid., 97.

9. Ibid.

10. Ibid., 98–99.

11. Father T. Gays, letter, handwritten, Italian language, undated but probably 1910; Consolata Mission Archives, Turin, made available courtesy of Fa-

ther P. V. Ghilardi, June 1969. This letter, later copied and translated into English by Father Jestero, is perhaps the earliest European description of Imenti and Igoji.

12. Embu District Miscellaneous Correspondence, 1906–1910, KNA.

13. "Brevi cenni storici," copy, Consolata Mission Archives, Turin. Combined with additional untitled mission documents written by Father P. V. Ghilardi, Igoji Mission, 1950. Made available by Father Ghilardi, June 1969.

14. As told by Albert M'Riria (MOS 90), son of the group's spokesman, who was present at the scene.

15. "Logbook" of the Mujwa (and therefore, Kiija) Roman Catholic Mission, 1911–1925, Consolata Mission Archives, Mujwa Village, Igoji; "Brevi cenni storici," Consolata Mission Archives, Turin.

16. See note 15 above.

17. Hopkins, *Trail Blazers and Road Makers*, 100, referring to the era of Griffiths and Mimmack.

18. *Kenya Mission Council Records*, undated (ca. 1913), Miscellaneous Papers, KNA.

19. As sung by Paulo M'Ituke, one of the earliest Methodist converts; see MOS 91. Many of the oldest men in Ka-Aga locality claim to have heard the song coming from the grove. However, similar variants also exist in Catholic localities regarding the "flight" of the spirits.

20. Rev. A. J. Hopkins, *United Methodist Mission Annual Report, 1911–1940*. See the 1935 annual report, in which Hopkins writes of the mission's beginnings, Laughton Papers. School of Oriental and African Studies, University of London, also has copies of the annual reports.

21. Rev. R. W. Worthington, *United Methodist Mission Annual Report, 1920* Laughton Papers (see note 20 above).

22. Filipo M'Inoti, "Asili ya wa Meru na desturi zao," (Traditions of Meru and their customs), handwritten manuscript, undated (ca. 1930), 49 pages, Swahili language, Meru United Methodist Mission Archive, North Imenti, and Laughton Private Papers. Handwritten English-language copy is in my possession. This is the earliest history of the Meru tribe, written by one of its members.

23. Father B. Airaldi, MOS 7. Father Airaldi drew extensively, in his descriptions, from the *Mikinduri Mission Logbook, 1913–1939* (Consolata Mission Archives, Mikinduri), as well as over thirty years' experience among the Meru-speaking peoples. Father Airaldi, together with the pioneer missionary Father Aimo-Boot, founded the first four Catholic mission stations in Tigania and Igembe (from personal interview, 1970).

24. See note 23 above.

25. "Logbook" (1913) of the Athuana Mission (later changed to *Mikinduri Mission Logbook*), Consolata Mission Archives, Mikinduri.

26. See note 23 above.

27. Vitalus Anicheto, MOS 92.

28. Father B. Airaldi, MOS 7.

29. Paulo M'Gaichau, MOS 93.

30. "Gli uomini venuti dal mare: Notti ethnologia sulla tribu della prefeturra apostolica di Meru" (Ethnological notes on the tribe of the apostolic prefecture of Meru). *Missioni Consolata*, 81, Consolata Mission Archives, Turin.

31. United Methodist Mission unnumbered minutes book (fragmentary), Meru District, 1923; *United Methodist Mission Annual Report, 1911–1940* ("The Meru Circuit"), Laughton Papers. The generation of female converts occurred solely as the result of arranged marriages.

32. Hopkins, *United Methodist Mission Annual Report, 1919* (see note 20 above).

33. Father B. Airaldi, MOS 7.

34. Paulo M'Ituke, MOS 91.

35. Rev. R. W. Worthington, *United Methodist Mission Annual Report, 1919* (see n. 21 above).

36. Correspondence, 24 September–7 November 1919, between Rev. R. W. Worthington, United Methodist Mission, and A. E. Chamier, district commissioner, Meru, 1919, as well as subsequent correspondence between both of them with W. Tate, provincial commissioner, Central (Gikuyu) Province, and John Ainsworth, chief, Native Administration. Miscellaneous correspondence, ref. 401/17/F/19, KNA.

37. Paulo M'Gaichau, MOS 93.

38. Rev. R. W. Worthington, *United Methodist Mission Annual Report, 1917* (see note 21 above).

39. Alice Thiriadi, MOS 94. Mrs. Thiriadi was one of the first generation of female converts as the result of an arranged marriage.

CHAPTER NINE

1. Daudi M'Raria, MOS 97.

2. Rev. J. W. Arthur, M.D., "A Journey Made in View of Extension," *Kikuyu News* no. 53 (1915): 4–15, Irvine Papers.

3. Ibid.

4. Ibid. Muthambi, in this instance was described as a branch of the Mwimbi peoples.

5. Ibid.; *Kikuyu News*, no. 58 (January–February 1916), no. 59 (April–May 1916), Irvine Papers.

6. Priscilla Makumi, MOS 95. Data from "Makumi" era are drawn primarily from personal interview.

7. See note 6 above.

8. See note 6 above.

9. See note 6 above.

10. See note 6 above.

11. Ismaili Wangu, MOS 96. Data from the "Wangu era" are drawn primarily from personal interview.

12. See note 11 above.

13. See note 11 above.

14. See note 11 above.

15. See note 11 above.

16. Rev. Dr. Clive Irvine, MOS 4. Dr. Irvine remained in Mwimbi for forty years.

17. Daudi M'Raria, MOS 97. M'Raria was among those conscripted to build the bridges at this time. Intrigued, he remained to work with Irvine on his arrival.

18. Rev. Dr. Clive Irvine, MOS 4.

19. Anthony (Tony) Irvine, son of Dr. and Mrs. Clive Irvine, and the child in the ox-wagon, MOS 9, provided many insights on his father's experiences during the mission's pioneer years.

20. Josiah M'Muntu, MOS 98; Daudi M'Raria, MOS 97; Jotham M'Muri-anki, MOS 99; early converts, Church of Scotland Mission, Mwimbi.

21. See note 20 above.

22. See note 20 above.

23. Rev. Junius Munyua, written interview transcript, 1967, Saint Paul's Theological Seminary. Munyua was an early convert, Church of Scotland Mission, Mwimbi.

24. The first group of Wasomaji (readers), Church of Scotland Mission, is said to have included the following: Daudi M'Raria, Zakayo Kinirika, Musa M'Muga, Samsoni Kanegeni, Justo Kanampiu, Arthur M'Rucha, Amos Muchara, Jason M'Aranyu, Josef M'Raiche. This list was taken from the private papers of and personal interview with Daudi M'Raria (MOS 97). It was corroborated by other informants.

25. Daudi M'Raria, MOS 97.

26. See note 25 above.

27. Jotham M'Murianki, MOS 99.

28. Germano M'Kirichio, MOS 100.

29. Hezikiah M'Mukuri, MOS 26.

30. Daudi M'Raria, MOS 97.

31. Paulo Gaichau, MOS 93.

32. Bellani, "Da Nyeri al paesi di Meru," Consolata Mission Archives, Turin. Description of Authi by M'Ruiga M'Mbatau, former warrior, Igoji, MOS 59.

33. Samsoni M'Mutiga, MOS 101. The incident described here is as perceived by M'Mutiga; details were corroborated by Igembe elders.

34. See note 33 above.

35. See note 33 above.

36. See note 33 above.

37. See note 33 above.

38. As described by Paulo M'Ituke, MOS 91. The drunken warrior was M'Mutangi of Kaaga (formerly Ka-aga), recently appointed to the tribal police and thus entitled to carry a spear.

39. As described by Samsoni M'Mutiga, MOS 101. M'Mutiga was the youngest among those inside the blazing war hut.

40. Rahab Mbiro, MOS 102.

41. *United Methodist Mission Annual Report, 1911–1924* (these reports estimated 65 converts); Dr. Clive Irvine, interviews, 1969–1970, United Church

of Scotland Mission (estimated 12 converts over 1922–1924); "Il lento movemento ascensionale nella prefettura apostolica di Meru," *Missioni Consolata,* 81, Consolata Mission Archives, Turin (estimated 194–224 converts, 1911–1924).

CHAPTER TEN

1. F. M. Lamb, *Meru District Record Book, 1927,* Kenya National Archives (KNA).

2. *Meru District Record Book, 1914–1921,* KNA.

3. See Fadiman, *Oral History,* 93ff. for *renta,* the bull feast.

4. *Meru District Record Book, 1913,* KNA.

5. *Meru District Record Book, 1916,* KNA; *United Methodist Mission Annual Report, 1917–1918,* School of Oriental and African Studies (SOAS).

6. Samsoni M'Mutiga, MOS 101.

7. *United Methodist Mission Annual Report, 1919,* SOAS. Taken from the letters of Rev. R. T. Worthington and F. Mimmack during that year.

8. *Meru District Record Book, 1918,* KNA.

9. Ibid.

10. *Meru District Record Book, 1919,* KNA.

11. Fadiman, *Oral History,* 9, 127ff., "The Transfer of Power."

12. Alice Thiriadi, MOS 94.

13. *Meru District Record Book, 1920,* KNA.

14. Temu, "British Protestant Missions in Kenya," 336.

15. Ibid.

16. *Meru District Record Book, 1918–1928,* KNA, contain lists of district officers for each year. The frequency of transfer may have been due to Meru's reputation as "witch ridden," "primitive," and so forth (see reports). It is more likely, however, that its reputation arose because of this frequency of transfer, which made knowledge of either the district or people impossible to acquire, thereby stimulating stereotypes in place of fact.

17. Orde-Browne, *Vanishing Peoples of Kenya.*

18. M'Mwongera wa Kabutai (Northeast Imenti), MOS 41. Repeated, with variations, by several informants.

19. "Native Customs," Lambert Papers, no. 9.

20. *Meru District Record Book, 1923, 1924,* KNA.

21. *Meru District Record Book, 1920,* KNA.

22. Existing evidence suggests Kivunja (the "destroyer"), was either R. Weeks, district commissioner, 1921–1922, or J. M. Silvester, acting district commissioner, Meru, 1922, and assistant district commissioner, 1923–1924.

23. M'Ikiene M'Irimbere ("M'Iniu") (North Imenti), MOS 40.

24. *Meru District Record Book, 1920–1924,* KNA.

25. *Meru District Record Book, 1925,* KNA.

26. *Meru District Record Book, 1923,* KNA.

27. Orde-Browne, untitled document, Rhodes House.

28. CP/PC/1911, Central Province File, KNA.

29. *Meru District Record Book, 1924,* KNA.

30. Dr. H. Brassington, MOS 2.

31. *Meru District Record Book, 1920,* KNA.

32. *Meru Political Record Book, 1920,* KNA.

33. Bellani, "Customi degli Bameru," Consolata Mission Archives, Turin.

34. *Meru District Record Book, 1924,* KNA.

35. *Meru District Record Book, 1923,* KNA.

36. "Note di etnologia sulla tribu Meru," typescript, undated (1925?), Consolata Mission Archives, Mujwa Mission, Igoji, Meru.

37. *Meru District Record Book, 1924–1927,* KNA.

CHAPTER ELEVEN

1. Mwakireu Gikabu, MOS 64.

2. Father B. Airaldi, MOS 7, related the story of Father Bondino. Interview (January 1970) combined with readings from the early years of *Mikinduri Mission Logbook,* Consolata Mission Archives, Mikinduri, Tigania.

3. See note 2 above.

4. J. G. H. Hopkins, MOS 11.

5. "Reports: Tribal Witchcraft," Native Affairs Division, 1926, Kenya National Archives (KNA). Corroborated by J. G. H. Hopkins, MOS 11.

6. *Meru District Record Book, 1921–1927,* KNA.

7. *Meru District Record Book, 1924,* KNA.

8. *Meru District Record Book, 1927,* KNA.

9. Age-set names vary slightly among Meru regions, both with regard to spelling and dates of transferring power (Ntuiko) to younger age-sets. For clarity, I use the age-set spellings common to Imenti (Kaburia, Kiramana, Murungi, Miriti) even when discussing adjacent regions. The same applies to periods of power transfer. When necessary, a variant is placed in parentheses. Within Imenti the age-set Murungi has two subsets: Riungu, the eldest, and Kirianki, the youngest. In Muthambi the two subsets of Murungi are Kiraithe, the eldest, and Riungu, the youngest. In Mwimbi the equivalent age-set would be Kirianki, with three subsets consisting of Riungu, Marangu, and Kirianki. All men of these sets and subsets would be in their eighties.

10. *Meru District Record Book, 1926,* KNA. The writer confuses the Meru term "Mwiriga" (ridgetop community containing one or more clans) with the Kikuyu term "Rika" (an age-set). The error suggests almost total ignorance of Meru communal life, as the writer himself attests.

11. M'Muraa wa Kairanyi, MOS 13.

12. Matiri wa Kirongoro ("Paul"), MOS 29.

13. Mwakiru Gikabu, MOS 64.

14. Rawcliffe, *The Struggle for Kenya,* 30. Similar comments appear in the *Meru District Record Book* throughout the 1920s.

15. *Meru District Record Book, 1927,* KNA. Probable author, J. G. H. Hopkins, assistant district commissioner.

16. *Chuka Sub-District Political Record Book, 1908,* KNA.

17. *Meru District Record Book, 1909,* KNA.

18. East African Ordinances, 1910, KNA.

19. Ikuciambuu Nguciala, MOS 35; M'Mutiga M'Ngaruni, MOS 36; alleged former members of the Mwaa, Igembe.

20. Special Report, "Witchcraft in Tigania and Igembe," from Frank M. Lamb, district commissioner, Meru, to senior commissioner (E. B. Horne), Nyeri Province, 15 February 1928, "Native Customs" file, Lambert Papers. Referred to hereinafter as the "Lamb Special Report." (Abbreviated version is in *Meru District Record Book, 1927*, KNA). Translation of A-Athi curse by Simon P. K. Bengi, Mwimbi, 1988.

21. Lamb Special Report.

22. Lamb Special Report; Ikuciambuu Nguciala, MOS 35.

23. Ikuciambuu Nguciala, MOS 35.

24. *Meru District Record Book, 1924*, KNA.

25. *Meru District Record Book, 1927*, KNA.

26. Gaichungi Baibuatho M'Mbarui (Igembe), MOS 34.

27. Lamb Special Report.

28. M'Muraa wa Kairanyi, MOS 13.

CHAPTER TWELVE

1. Special Report, "Witchcraft in Tigania and Igembe," from Frank M. Lamb, district commissioner, Meru, to senior commissioner (E. B. Horne), Nyeri Province, 15 February 1928, "Native Customs" file, Lambert Papers. Referred to hereinafter as the "Lamb Special Report." (Abbreviated version is in *Meru District Record Book, 1927*, Kenya National Archives, [KNA].)

2. *Meru District Record Book, 1925–1927*, KNA.

3. Ibid.

4. J. G. H. Hopkins, MOS 11. Hopkins was assistant district commissioner (under Frank M. Lamb) and aided Lamb in all stages of the witchcraft campaign.

5. The career of M'Mukura wa Kageta can be followed by perusal of the evaluations written by his colonial supervisors in the appendixes of the *Meru District Record Book, 1913–1927*, KNA.

6. *Meru District Record Book, 1927*, KNA.

7. J. G. H. Hopkins, MOS 11.

8. J. G. H. Hopkins, Native Affairs Divisional Reports, 1926, KNA.

9. J. G. H. Hopkins, MOS 11.

10. Lamb Special Report.

11. J. G. H. Hopkins, MOS 11.

12. Hezikiah M'Mukiri (Imenti), MOS 26; Kiringo M'Munyari (Igembe), MOS 33; M'Muambe M'Mbuthu (Tigania), MOS 57.

13. Lamb Special Report. Also *Meru District Record Book, 1927*, KNA.

14. See note 13 above.

15. See note 13 above.

16. Data on Mbogore M'Mwendo's "war" on witchcraft are from interviews with his sons (MOS 31); M'Icirai (last name withheld), Mbogore's cook during his early years as chief (MOS 103); and Muriuki M'Muriithi, one of Mbogore's Nchama ("chief's men" or "retainers") (MOS 32). The narrative

has become part of the Mbogore family history, and is corroborated (in less flattering terms) by other Mwimbi elders.

17. M'Ikieni ("M'Iniu") M'Irimbere, MOS 40, and others in North Imenti. The tossing of ritualists' goatskin bags into the Kazita River is widely repeated within Imenti tradition.

18. See note 16 above.

19. See note 16 above.

20. See note 16 above.

21. Muriuki M'Muriithi, MOS 32; also MOS 31, 103.

22. J. G. H. Hopkins, MOS 11, and Dr. H. Brassington, MOS 2. Both participated in the antiwitchcraft campaign.

23. Dr. H. Brassington, MOS 2.

24. See note 23 above.

25. A. T. Howell, M.D., Karta Ram, and Diwan Singh (subassistant surgeon), "Medical Report" in *Meru District Record Book, 1927,* KNA. The report describes the subsequent illnesses and deaths of the accused. Also J. G. H. Hopkins, MOS 11; Dr. H. Brassington, MOS 2; M'Muraa wa Kairanyi, MOS 13, probable translator for Hopkins and Lamb.

26. "Medical Report" (see note 25 above).

27. "Medical Report" (see note 25 above).

28. Revised Kenya Witchcraft Ordinance, 1928. The text of the ordinance is in "Witchcraft and Colonial Law," academic paper read to the Congress Internationale des Sciences Anthropologiques, 8 March 1934, by G. St. J. Orde-Browne, Rhodes House. Orde-Browne was district commissioner, Cuka subdistrict, 1909–1912.

29. *Meru District Record Book, 1928,* Appendix, KNA.

30. Dr. H. Brassington, MOS 2.

31. M'Ruiga M'Mbatau (Igoji), MOS 59; M'Muraa wa Kairanyi (Imenti), MOS 13; M'Ikieni (M'Iniu) M'Irimbere (Imenti), MOS 40. All worked for the colonial government at this time.

32. J. G. H. Hopkins, *Meru District Record Book, 1932,* KNA.

33. Rev. Dr. Clive Irvine, MOS 4.

CHAPTER THIRTEEN

1. Lambert, "Administrative Use of the Indigenous Institutions of the Meru," Lambert Papers.

2. F. G. Jennings, a "pragmatic" administrator, was district commissioner of Meru, 1935–1936; *Meru District Record Book, 1935–1936,* Kenya National Archives (KNA).

3. J. G. H. Hopkins, MOS 11; Grace Lambert, MOS 5; and Capt. Victor McKeag, MOS 10.

4. J. G. H. Hopkins, MOS 11. Also *Meru District Record Book, 1929,* KNA.

5. See note 4 above.

6. Fadiman, *Oral History,* 127–31.

7. J. G. H. Hopkins, MOS 11: *Meru District Record Book, 1929,* KNA.

8. *Meru District Record Book, 1929,* KNA.

9. Grace Lambert, MOS 5.

10. Lambert, "Administrative Use of the Indigenous Institutions of the Meru," Lambert Papers.

11. Hezikiah M'Mukiri, MOS 26, one of early Christian converts (along with M'Inoti) to approach Lambert on the Njuri.

12. W. H. Laughton, MOS 1.

13. M'Muraa wa Kairanyi, MOS 13. Kairanyi was a translator for Lambert.

14. The dual system of elders' councils that Lambert hoped to restore among the southern Meru had originally consisted of the following Kiamas:

TABLE 9   KIAMAS OF SOUTHERN MERU,
BY SUBTRIBE

Cuka (and Embu)	Muthambi	Mwimbi	Igoji (and Imenti)
Kiama Kia Kibogo	Kiama Kia Kibogo or Kiama Kia Mwendo	Kiama Kia Kibogo or Kiama Kia Njuguma	Kiama Kia Nkomango
Njuri ya Ngome	Njuri ya Nkome	Njuri ya Nkome	Njuri ya Kiama

Source: Untitled document, penciled in Lambert's handwriting, Lambert Papers.

15. Mburunga, Ng'entu, MOS 89.

16. Capt. Victor McKeag, MOS 10.

17. H. E. Lambert, "Meru Institutions and Their Place in Modern Government," original script BBC radio presentation, 1942, Lambert Papers.

18. "Meru Handing Over Report," (Capt. Victor McKeag to C. F. Adkins) in *Meru District Record Book, 1938,* KNA.

19. Capt. Victor McKeag, MOS 10.

20. H. E. Lambert, "The Place of Stock in the Native Social System," *Meru District Record Book, 1938,* Appendix 10, KNA.

21. Captain Victor McKeag, MOS 10.

22. "Notes of a Meeting of Chiefs," subtitled "Integrity of the Tribe," dated "Meru, 8/12/39," Lambert Papers.

23. See note 18 above.

24. See note 18 above.

25. See note 18 above.

26. "Correspondence Re Entry of Christians into Njuri over Opposition of Clive Irvine," *Meru District Record Book, 1940,* KNA.

27. Hezikiah M'Mukiri, MOS 26.

28. H. E. Lambert, "Njuri ya Kiama" (i.e., Kiama ya Njuri), *Meru District Record Book, 1940,* Appendix. Corroboration: Capt. Victor McKeag, MOS 10.

29. See note 25 above.

30. See note 25 above.

31. *Meru District Record Book, 1940,* Appendix, KNA.

32. See note 30 above.

33. H. E. Lambert, *Meru District Record Book, 1941,* Appendix, KNA. Corroboration: Capt. Victor McKeag, MOS 10.

34. See note 30 above.

35. Alliano M'Mwarania, MOS 14.

Bibliography

PUBLISHED BOOKS AND ARTICLES

Adamson, G. *Bwana Game: The Life Story of George Adamson.* London: Collins Press, 1968. (Published in the United States as *A Lifetime with Lions.* New York: McFadden Books, 1968.)

Adamson, J. *The Peoples of Kenya.* London: Collins Press, 1967.

Arkell-Hardwick, A. *An Ivory Trader in North Kenia.* London: Longmans, Green and Co., 1903.

Benson, T. G., ed. *Kikuyu-English Dictionary.* Oxford Press, 1964.

Bernard, F. E. *East of Mt. Kenya: Meru Agriculture in Transition.* Munich: Weltforum Verlag, 1972.

———. *Recent Agricultural Change East of Mt. Kenya.* Africa Series. Athens: Ohio University Press, 1973.

———. "Recent Agricultural Change among the Meru of Mt. Kenya." In *Readings on Spacial Structure in Kenya,* eds. R. Obduho and F. Taylor. Boulder: Westview Press, 1980.

Bernardi, B. *The Mugwe: A Failing Prophet.* London: Oxford Press, 1959.

Broun, W. H. "A Journey to the Lorian Swamp, British East Africa." *Geographical Journal* 27 (1906): 533–34.

Champion, A. H. "The Atharaka." *Journal of the Royal Anthropological Institute* 42 (1912): 68–90.

Chanler, W. A. "Mr. Astor Chanler's Expedition to East Africa." *Geographical Journal* 1 (1893): 533–34.

———. *Through Jungle and Desert: Travels in Eastern Africa.* New York: Macmillan, 1896.

Dundas, C. "The History of Kitui." *Journal of the Royal Anthropological Institute* 43 (1913): 480ff.

Dutton, E. A. T. *Kenya Mountain.* London: Jonathan Cape, 1929.

367

Fadiman, J. A. "Early History of the Meru of Mt. Kenya." *Journal of African History* 14, no. 1 (1973): 9–27.

———. *Mountain Warriors: The Pre-Colonial Meru of Mt. Kenya.* Africa Series, no. 29. Athens: Ohio University Press, 1975.

———. "The Meru Peoples." In *Kenya before 1900: Eight Regional Studies,* ed. B. A. Ogot, 153–73. Nairobi: East Africa Publishing House, 1976.

———. "Mountain Witchcraft: Supernatural Practices and Practitioners among the Meru of Mt. Kenya." *African Studies Review* 20, no. 1 (April 1977): 87–101.

———. *The Moment of Conquest: Meru, Kenya, 1907.* Africa Series, no. 36. Athens: Ohio University Press, 1979.

———. *An Oral History of Tribal Warfare: The Meru of Mt. Kenya.* Athens: Ohio University Press, 1982.

First, R. *Power in Africa: Political Power and the Coup d'Etat.* Penguin: New York, 1971.

Freeman-Grenville, G. S. P. "The Coast, 1498–1840." In *History of East Africa,* eds. R. Oliver and G. Mathew, vol. 1, 128–68. Oxford: Clarendon Press, 1963.

Gedge, E. "A Recent Exploration under Captain F. G. Dundas, R.N., up the River Tana to Mt. Kenya." *Proceedings of the Royal Geographical Society* 14 (1892): 513–33.

Giorgis, B. *A Tentative Kimeru Dictionary.* Meru, Kenya: Catholic Bookshop (Consolata Mission Society), 1964.

Gurney, H. L. G. "The Mwimbi." In *Kenya Mountain,* E. A. T. Dutton, appendix 6, 203–7. London: Jonathan Cape, 1929.

Henderson, I., and P. Goodheart. *The Hunt for Kimathi.* London: Pan Books, 1958.

Hobley, C. W. *Ethnology of the A-Kamba and Other East African Tribes.* Cambridge: Cambridge University Press, 1910.

Holding, E. M. "Some Preliminary Notes on Meru Age Grades." *Man* 42 (1942): 58–65.

Hopkins, A. J. *Trail Blazers and Road Makers: A Brief History of the East African Mission of the United Methodist Church.* London: Henry Hooks United Methodist Publishing House, 1928.

Huxley, E. *White Man's Country: Lord Delamere and the Making of Kenya.* Vol. 1, *1870–1914.* London: Chatto and Windus, 1953.

———. *Red Strangers.* London: Chatto and Windus, 1964.

———. *A New Earth: An Experiment in Colonialism.* London: Chatto and Windus, 1969.

Jacobs, A. H. "The Chronology of the Pastoral Maasai." *Hadithi,* vol. 1. University of Nairobi, Department of History, 1968.

———. "Maasai Pastoralism in Historical Perspective." In *Pastoralism in Tropical Africa,* ed. T. Monod. London: International African Institute, 1975.

———. "Maasai Inter-Tribal Relations: Belligerent Herdsmen or Peaceful Pastoralists?" In *Warfare among East African Herders,* eds. K. Fukui and D. Turton, Senri Ethnological Studies, no. 3. Senri, Osaka: National Museum of Ethnology, 1979.

Kenyatta, Jomo. *Facing Mt. Kenya: The Tribal Life of the Gikuyu.* London: Secker and Warburg, 1938.

Kolb, G. "Vom Mombasa Durch Ukambani Zum Kenia." *Petermanns Mitteilungen* 42 (1896): 221–31.

Lambert, Hugo E. *History of the Tribal Occupation of the Land.* Part 1 of *The Systems of Land Tenure in the Kikuyu Land Unit.* Communication of the School of African Studies, no. 22. Cape Town: Cape Town University, 1950.

———. *The Use of Indigenous Authorities in Tribal Administration: Studies of the Meru in Kenya Colony.* Communication of the School of African Studies, no. 16. Cape Town: Cape Town University, 1947.

———. *Kikuyu Social and Political Institutions.* London: Oxford University Press for the International African Institute, 1956.

Laughton, W. H. "A Meru Text." *Man* 64, no. 9 (1964): 17–18.

———. *The Meru.* Peoples of Kenya Series, no. 10. Nairobi: Ndia Kuu Press, 1944.

Leakey, L. S. B. *The Stone Age Cultures of Kenya Colony.* Cambridge: Cambridge University Press, 1931.

Maguire, R. A. J. " 'El-Torobo,' Tanganyika Notes and Records." *The Journal of the Tanganyika Society* (1948): 8–13.

Mahner, J. "Outsider-Insider in Tigania-Meru." *Africa* 45, no. 54 (1975): 400–409.

Mathew, G. "The East African Coast until the Coming of the Portuguese." In *History of East Africa,* eds. R. Oliver and G. Mathew, 34–129. Oxford: Clarendon Press, 1963.

Middleton, J., and G. Kershaw. *The Central Tribes of the Northeastern Bantu.* Part 5 of *Ethnographic Survey of Africa: East Central Africa,* ed. D. Ford. London: International African Institute, 1965.

Moyse-Bartlett, H. *The King's African Rifles: A Study of the Military History of East and Central Africa.* Aldershot, U.K.: Gale and Polden, 1956.

Mungeam, G. H. *British Rule in Kenya, 1895–1912: The Establishment of Administration in the East African Protectorate.* Oxford: Clarendon Press, 1966.

Munro, J. F. "Migrations of the Bantu-Speaking Peoples of the Eastern Kenya Highlands: A Reappraisal." *Journal of African History* 7, no. 1 (1967): 25–28.

Muriuki, G. "Kikuyu Reaction to Traders and British Administration, 1850–1904." *Hadithi,* vol. 1, 101. University of Nairobi, Department of History, 1968.

———. *A History of the Kikuyu, 1500–1900,* London: Oxford University Press, 1974.

Mwaniki, H. S. K. *The Living History of Embu and Mbeere.* Nairobi: East African Literature Bureau, 1973.

Needham, R. "The Left Hand of the Mugwe: An Analytical Note on the Structure of Meru Symbolism." *Africa* 30, no. 1 (1960): 20–33.

Neumann, A. H. *Elephant Hunting in East Equatorial Africa.* London: Rowland Ward, 1898.

Ogot, B. A., and J. A. Kiernan. *Zamani: A Survey of East African History.* Nairobi: East African Publishing House; Longmans, Green; London, 1968.

Ogot, B. A., ed. *War and Society in Africa.* Nairobi: East African Publishing House, 1972.

————, ed. *Kenya before 1900: Eight Regional Studies.* Nairobi: East African Publishing House, 1976.

Oliver, R., and G. Mathew. *History of East Africa.* Vol. 1. Oxford: Clarendon Press, 1963.

Orde-Brown, G. St. J. *The Vanishing Tribes of Kenya.* London: Seeley, Service and Co., 1925.

————. "Circumcision Ceremonies among the Amwimbe." *Man* 13, no. 79 (1913): 137–40.

————. "The Circumcision Ceremony in Chuka." *Man* 15, no. 5 (1915): 65–68.

————. "Mount Kenya and Its People: Some Notes on the Chuka Tribe." *Journal of the African Society* 15 (1916): 225–33.

————. "The Southeast Face of Mt. Kenya." *Geographical Journal* 51 (1918): 389–92.

Peters, K. "From the Mouth of the Tana to the Source Region of the Nile." *Scottish Geographical Magazine* 7 (1891): 113–23.

Piggot, J. R. W. "Journey to the Upper Tana." *Proceedings of the Royal Geographic Society* 12 (1890): 129–36.

Prins, A. J. H. "The Coastal Tribes of the Northeast Bantu." In *Ethnographic Survey of Africa: East Central Africa,* part 3. London: International African Institute, 1952.

Rawcliffe, D. H. *The Struggle for Kenya.* London: V. Gollanez, 1954.

Routledge, W. S. *With a Prehistoric People: The Akikuyu of British East Africa.* London: E. Arnold, 1910.

Russell, E. W., ed. *Natural Resources of East Africa.* Nairobi: East African Publishing House, 1962.

Shackleton, E. R. "The Njuwe." *Man* 30, no. 143 (1930): 201–2.

Sorrenson, M. P. K. *Origins of European Settlement in Kenya.* Nairobi: Oxford University Press, 1968.

Stigand, C. H. *The Land of Zinj, Being an Account of British East Africa, Its Ancient History and Present Inhabitants.* London: Constable, 1913.

Tate, H. R. "Journey to the Rendile Country, British East Africa." *Geographical Journal* 23 (1904): 220–28.

Taylor, R. D. F. "The Gumba and Gumba Pits of Fort Hall District, Kenya." *Azania* 1 (1966): 111.

Thompson, J. *Through Masailand: A Journey of Exploration among the Snow-clad Volcano Mountains and Strange Tribes of Eastern Equatorial Africa.* Boston: Houghton-Mifflin, 1885.

Tignor, R. L. *The Colonial Transformation of Kenya: The Kamba, Kikuyu, and Maasai from 1900–1934.* Princeton, N.J.: Princeton University Press, 1976.

Vansina, J. *Oral Tradition: A Study in Historical Methodology.* Trans. H. M. Wright. Chicago: Aldine Publishing, 1965.

Wisner, B., and P. O'Keefe. *Land Use and Development*. London: International African Institute, 1977.

UNPUBLISHED RESEARCH

Almy, S. W. "Rural Development in Meru, Kenya: Economic and Social Factors in Accelerating Change." Ph.D. diss., Stanford University, 1974.

Blackburn, R. "A Preliminary Report of Research on the Ogiek Tribe of Kenya." Research paper, no. 89. Institute of Development Studies, Cultural Division, University of Nairobi, January 1970.

Jacobs, A. H. "The Traditional Political Organization of the Pastoral Maasai." Ph.D. diss., Oxford University, 1965.

Kamunchululu, J. S. T. "Meru Participation in Mau-Mau." University of Nairobi, 1975. Typescript.

Laughton, W. H. "An Introductory Study of the Meru People." M.A. thesis, Cambridge University, 1938.

Lowenthal, R. A. "Tharaka Age-Organization and the Theory of Age-Set Systems." Ph.D. diss., University of Illinois at Urbana-Champaign, 1973.

Mahassin, A. Gh. El-Safi. "Some Contributions of Swahili Poetry to the Understanding of the History of the Northern Coast of Kenya." Institute of Development Studies, Cultural Division, University of Nairobi, 1970. Typescript.

Mahner, J. "The Insider and the Outsider in Tigania, Meru." Institute of Development Studies, Cultural Division, University of Nairobi, May, 1970. Typescript. (Published as "Outsider-Insider in Tigania-Meru," *Africa* 45, no. 54, 1975.)

McKim, W. L. "The Role of Interaction in Spacial Economic Development Planning: A Case Study from Kenya." University of Nairobi, 1975. Typescript.

Mwaniki, H. S. K. "The British Impact on Embu, 1906–1919." Department of History, University of Nairobi, 1969. Typescript.

Rosen, D. M. "A Preliminary Report of Research among the Mukogodo, Laikipiak District." Discussion paper, Institute of Development Studies, Cultural Division, University of Nairobi, January 1968.

Temu, A. J. "British Protestant Missions in Kenya, 1873–1929." Ph.D. diss., University of Alberta, 1967.

ARCHIVAL COLLECTIONS

Consolata Mission Archives. Consolata Roman Catholic Mission Order. Turin, Italy.

The archives contain several diaries written by the first Roman Catholic priests to enter Meru after 1912–1913. There are several detailed descriptions of Meru customs as observed up to the 1920s. All diaries are in Italian. The most significant are the following:

Balbo, Father R. P. Diary. 1914–1926.

Bellani, Father P. A. "Costumi degli Bameru" (Customs of the Meru peo-
    ple). Notebook, handwritten. Dated 1920 but continuous over several
    years.
————. "Da Nyeri al paese di Meru" (From Nyeri to the country of Meru).
    Travel diary, handwritten. February, 1915.
————. "Ntuara ya Egoji" (The bell of Igoji). Diary. 1923–1926.
Pecomino, Brother Gerinte (probable author). "Mezzo serolo di attentiva
    dei missionari della Consolata nell' Africa Orientale, Inglese visto a volo
    d'uccello" (Half a century of activities of missionaries of the Consolata
    of British East Africa seen from a bird's-eye view.) Typescript. Undated
    but probably written in the mid-1920s.
Consolata Mission Archives. Mikinduri Roman Catholic Mission. Mikinduri,
Tigania, Meru, Kenya.
Mikinduri Mission Logbook, 1913–1939. In Italian.
Consolata Mission Archives. Mujwa Village, Igoji, Meru, Kenya.
"Brevi cenni storici sulla prefettura apostolica di Meru" (Brief historical ac-
    count of the apostolic prefecture of Meru). Typescript, 15 pages. Un-
    signed, undated copy.
"Logbook" of the Mujwa [and therefore Kiija]. Roman Catholic Mission,
    1911–1925. Typescript. Unsigned, undated (1925?).
"Note di etnologia sulla tribu Meru" (Ethnological notes on the Meru
    tribe). Typescript. Unsigned, undated.
Kenya National Archives (KNA). Nairobi, Kenya.
The Kenya National Archives contain voluminous records of the colonial
period, the earliest years of which are relevant to this study. It should be noted
that Mwimbi and Muthambi were originally designated as part of the Cuka
subdistrict, which in turn was administered from Embu. Insight as to the initial
British impact on Meru-Mwimbi social institutions can be gained from exam-
ination of the following:
Chuka Sub-District Political Record Book, 1907–1918. See "Early History
    of Chuka and Mwimbi," unsigned typescript.
Central Province Political Record, 1906.
Marsabit [District] Political Record Book, 1908–1914. See Appendix D
    (Meru), "Safari Record," by Capt. J. Bois, which is one of the earliest
    European accounts of conditions in Meru at the time of its submission
    to Britain.
Meru District Record Book, 1911–1926.
Meru Political Record Book, 1908–1921.
Embu [District] Political Record Book, 1907–1928.
Rhodes House. Oxford, England.
The collections at Rhodes House hold the private papers of those working in
British Africa during the colonial period. Investigators dealing with the history
of Meru will find the following of interest:
Orde-Browne, G. St. J. District commissioner, Cuka subdistrict, 1913.
Platts, Mrs. Madeleine Laverne. Diary. November 1912 through May 1913.
    She resided in Meru as wife of W. F. Platts, acting district commissioner.

Saint Paul's Theological Seminary. Historical Archives (Anderson's Archives).
Limuru, Kenya.

Rev. William B. Anderson, Master of History, has supervised the collection
of oral history by students of the seminary since 1961. The emphasis is on precolonial customs and initial experiences with European missionaries. The data
were not always systematically collected and should be considered reliable only
if corroborated by additional oral testimony. The collection has, however,
proven valuable in identifying historically reliable informants and as corrobo-
rative material.

> "Customs and Traditions of the Meru People of Thaichu, Tigania." Hand-
> written manuscript. Collected by Festus Ringeera, 1961.

> "The History of Communications in Meru District." Handwritten manu-
> script in English. Deals with precolonial obligations for communal labor
> with regard to construction and maintenance of paths, bridges, and so
> on. Collected by Justus Thambu, Imenti, 1962.

> "Traditions and Customs of Meru Long Ago." Handwritten manuscript.
> Unsigned, undated.

> "Traditions and Customs of Mwimbi." Handwritten manuscript. Unsigned,
> undated.

> "Traditions and Customs of Nyambeni Division, Igembe." Handwritten
> manuscript from Igembe, North Meru. Unsigned, undated.

School of Oriental and African Studies (SOAS). University of London. London,
England.
United Methodist Mission Annual Report, 1911–1940.

PRIVATE PAPERS

Irvine, Rev. Dr. Clive. (Irvine Papers.)

> Founder, Church of Scotland Mission, Chogoria, Mwimbi, 1923. Now res-
> ident of Nairobi, Kenya. Private papers on founding of the mission include
> early issues (1915–1916) of the *Kikuyu News,* which carry articles detailing
> Church of Scotland Mission efforts prior to the actual founding of the
> Mwimbi Mission. Among the most useful are issues nos. 53 (January ?
> 1915), 58 (January–February 1916), and 59 (April–May 1916).

Kirera, Rufus.

> Farmer and storekeeper, Nkubu, South Imenti. "Murembere jwa tene jwa
> Imenti: Murembere jwa ntire" (Imenti prayers of long ago: Prayers of sac-
> rifice). Manuscript. Meru language.

Lambert, Hugo E. (Lambert Papers.)

> Lambert was district commissioner of Meru in 1933–1935, and 1939–
> 1941. During these periods he spent considerable time investigating Meru
> history and social structure. After his death in the late 1960s his pri-
> vate papers were donated by his widow to the University of Nairobi.
> As of this writing they have not been catalogued but are accessible to
> scholars. Only a small portion of Lambert's writings were devoted to the
> Meru, chiefly a series of essays appended to Meru District's annual reports.

In addition he had begun to organize a number of larger manuscripts, including one of almost five hundred pages, for eventual publication. A partial listing of the documents most relevant to the study of the Meru appears below:

"Administrative Use of the Indigenous Institutions of the Meru." Typescript, 18 pages, 8 October 1939. A revised version of this appears as: *The Use of Indigenous Authorities in Tribal Administration: Studies of the Meru in Kenya Colony* (Communication of the School of African Studies, no. 16. Cape Town: Cape Town University, 1947).

"The Constitution and Personnel of Statutory Institutions in the Meru Native Reserve." Typescript, 47 pages, 6 December 1939.

"Disintegration and Reintegration in the Meru Tribe." Typescript, 22 pages, 9 January 1940.

"Female Circumcision and Early Initiation." Typescript, 13 pages, 3 November 1934.

"Meru District: Notes for Chiefs." Typescript, 14 pages, 11 January 1941.

"The Meru Yet to Come." Typescript, 38 pages, Christmas 1941.

"Native Customs." Long, bound notebook, filled with handwritten notations.

"Native Customs." Short, thick, bound notebook, filled with handwritten notations.

"The Place of Stock in the Native Social System." Typescript, 16 pages, 1938.

"The Social and Political Institutions of the Tribes of the Kikuyu Land Unit." Part 2 of *The Systems of Land Tenure in the Kikuyu Land Unit.* Typescript, 479 pages, used as the basis of his book *Kikuyu Social and Political Institutions.*

Laughton, W. H. (Laughton Papers.)

These papers are in the owner's possession in Hull, England, and are as yet uncatalogued. Laughton was an educational missionary for the United Methodist Mission in Meru between 1931 and 1957. His papers deal primarily with his work for the mission during the 1930s and 1940s, as well as with anthropological research conducted in Imenti.

M'Anampiu, Stephan.

Master of History and vice principal, Meru Teacher Training College, Meru Town, Imenti. Several handwritten manuscripts, in English or Meru, dealing with the origins and precolonial history of selected clans of North Imenti. (See also MOS 79.)

Mbabu, Ephantus.

Chief, Igoji subdivision, Meru. Handwritten manuscript, untitled, Meru language. Deals with the origins and precolonial methods of war among the Mwimbi, Muthambi, and Cuka.

Mbogore, Mukungu wa.

Chogoria, Mwimbi. Handwritten notebook, Meru language, untitled. Deals with family affairs, genealogy, and property of his father, M'Mbogore M'Mwendo, first chief of upper Mwimbi under the colonial regime (see also Meru Oral Sources).

M'Inoti, Rev. Filipo.
  Ex-chief, Miiriga Mieru, North Imenti, Meru; among the first wave of con-
  verts and later the first African missionary. Became the first Meru minister
  of the United Methodist Mission, Imenti, in 1934.
  "Asili ya Wameru na tabia zao" (The origin of the Meru and their customs).
    Typescript, 49 pages, Swahili language. Meru United Methodist Mission
    Archive, Imenti. Copy, Swahili language, Laughton Papers. English
    translation (handwritten) by Fabian Njage, Muthambi. Both Swahili and
    English language copies are in my possession.
M'Mwarania, Alliano.
  Housepainter, South Imenti. Several handwritten manuscripts, Meru language, dealing with precolonial law, military training, spirit worship, and
  cursing (ironsmiths). Written data subsequently corroborated by oral interviews with original informants.

MERU ORAL SOURCES

The following is a partial list of individuals interviewed during the fieldwork
period of this study. Interviews with Europeans were in English. Interviews
with Africans were in Swahili or Meru, with subsequent translation into English. All interviews were tape-recorded and subsequently transcribed. Copies
of these manuscripts have been deposited with the department of history, University of Nairobi, where they currently available to scholars.

Informants, including Meru sources, whose names have been transliterated,
have been assigned a number based on the order in which I interviewed them.
These numbers are referred to in the notes as MOS (Meru Oral Source) numbers. I have provided information on each informant in the following order:
full name; place and date interviewed; name of Meru age-set (e.g., Murungi)
and estimated age in 1969; occupation or status within Meru or colonial structure (e.g., warrior, farmer); additional relevant data; main interview topics
(e.g., duties of warriorhood).

  1. Laughton, William Henry. Six interviews, May 1969, Hull, England. Educational missionary, Methodist Mission Society (later, United Methodist Mission), 1931–1957. Carried out anthropological research in North Imenti, Tigania, 1930s. Topics: identification of potential informants, anthropological and
historical orientation.

  2. Brassington, Howard, M.D. One interview, May 1969, Bristol, England.
Medical missionary, United Methodist Mission, late 1920s to late 1930s.
Founded Maua Methodist Mission Hospital, Igembe, Meru. Topic: supernatural forms of resistance ("witchcraft") used by local population to stop construction of hospital, 1930–1931.

  3. Bernardi, Bernard. One interview, June 1969, Consolata Roman Catholic Mission Headquarters, Turin, Italy. Missionary in Meru, 1950s, author of
The Mugwe: A Failing Prophet. Topics: traditional position of Mugwe; impact
of colonial occupation upon the institution.

  4. Irvine, Rev. Dr. Clive. Four interviews, August 1969, April 1970,
Nairobi, Kenya. Medical missionary, Church of Scotland Mission (later, Pres-

byterian Church of East Africa), Mwimbi, 1923–1963. Founded Chogoria Mission, Mwimbi, 1923. Forty years of mission work in Mwimbi area. Topics: reaction of Mwimbi to early mission contact; supernatural forms of resistance.

5. Lambert, Grace. One interview, August 1969, Nairobi, Kenya. Widow of H. E. Lambert, former district commissioner, Meru. Residence in Meru 1935–1937, 1940–1941. Topics: location of husband's private papers; identification of potential informants; discussion of husband's methods of oral research.

6. Horne, Marjorie R. One interview, October 1969, Nairobi, Kenya. Widow of Edward Butler Horne ("Kangangi"), British conqueror and first district commissioner of Meru. Topics: location of husband's private papers; identification of potential informants; discussion of husband's methods of oral research; early responses to pacification.

7. Airaldi, Father B. Three interviews, December 1969, Mikinduri Village, Mission chief, Mikinduri Roman Catholic Mission, Consolata Mission Order, Mikinduri, Tigania, Meru. Topic: Initial Catholic (missionary) penetration into Meru.

8. Ghilardi, Father P. V., M.D. One interview, Turin, Italy, July 1967. Archivist, Consolata Roman Catholic Mission, Turin, Italy. Topic: Initial Catholic (missionary) penetration into Meru.

9. Irvine, Anthony (Tony). Two interviews, June 1969, December 1969, April 1970, Nairobi, Kenya. Son of Dr. and Mrs. Clive Irvine, and the child in the ox wagon (see chapter 9). Provides significant insights on his father's experiences during the mission pioneer years.

10. McKeag, Capt. Victor Malcolm. One interview, May 1969, Armagh, Northern Ireland. District commissioner, Meru, 1937–1939, 1943–1945. Topic: Reconciliation of Njuri Nceke with colonial administration, 1930s–mid-1940s.

11. Hopkins, J. Gerald H. One interview, December 1970, Stellenbosch, South Africa, by J. Hewson. Former assistant district commissioner, 1917–1918, district commissioner, Meru District, 1927–1932. Instrumental in breaking the influence of two supernatural societies (A-Athi, Kagita) over large sections of Meru District. Topics: supernatural societies in Meru; impact on nonmembers; stages of elimination.

12. Pownall, Stephen. Two interviews, August and September, 1969, Nanyuki, Kenya. Former trapper and cattle buyer, Ukambani region, Central Kenya. Topics: Meru migration route through Ukambani (Kamba Country) with particular reference to their passage by the "four white peaks" referred to in Meru oral tradition.

13. Kairanyi, M'Muraa wa. Six interviews, September and October 1969, Kirua Village, North Imenti. Murungi age-set; estimated age, 85 years. Status: warrior (claims to have been a war leader); translator for H. E. Lambert; chief; senior chief; member and later chairman of the Njuri Nceke (highest elders' council) for northern Meru. Considered by community as expert on historical subjects, especially those related to military affairs. Topics: traditional war; history and functions of councils of elders; warriors. Frequently corroborated data from other areas.

14. M'Mwarania, Alliano. Five interviews, September and October 1969, Nkubu, South Imenti. Kiruja age-set; estimated age, 50 years. Member of Omo clan (clan of Mugwe), thus unusually interested in retention of precolonial customs; former member, Meru Helping Country Association, 1950–1953. Has spent leisure time in learning from elders of Imenti, Igoji. Topics: identification of potential informants (his original sources); Kiamas of boyhood; spirit worship; traditional curses; ironsmiths.

15. M'Ikaria, Gerrard. Two interviews, September and October 1969, Nkubu, South Imenti. Kiruja age-set; estimated age, fifties. Status: farmer, housepainter. Member of Omo clan; father a prophet (Muroria); claims also to have dealt with spirits (Nkoma) in childhood. Unusual interest in singing of traditional (precolonial) songs, particularly those concerned with male circumcision, warriorhood. Topics: traditional spirit worship; relations between spirits and men.

16. Ntangi, M'Anyoni wa. Four interviews, October 1969, Nkubu, South Imenti. Murungi age-set; estimated age, late seventies. Status: Muroria (prophet); also functions as curse detector (Muringia). Topics: functions of Muroria and related ritual specialists; types of contact between ancestral spirits (Nkoma) and man.

17. M'Ringui, M'Rinkanya. Two interviews, October 1969, Nkubu, South Imenti. Kiruja age-set; estimated age, late fifties. Status: curse detector (Muringia) and son of a curse detector. Allegedly circumcised by ancestral spirits (Nkoma) as a child. Topics: work of the Muringia and related ritual specialists; types of contact; relationships between ancestral spirits and man.

18. M'Murungi, M'Mwiriria. One interview, October 1969, Kirea Village, South Imenti. Murungi age-set; estimated age, eighties. Status: curse detector (Muni wa Uta: breaker of the bow). Topics: functions of the Muni wa Uta and related ritual specialists.

19. M'Munyiri, Ngaruro. One interview, October 1969, Kirea Village, South Imenti. Murungi (Kirianki) age-set; estimated age, early eighties. Status: truth seeker (Mugwatithania Gikama: administrator of the oath of the "hot" iron). Topics: functions of Mugwatithania and related ritual specialists.

20. Kinugu, M'Mukwea. One interview, October 1969, near Kirea Village, South Imenti. Murungi age-set; estimated age, eighties. Status: curse detector (Muringia); allegedly circumcised by ancestral spirits (Nkoma) as a child; still practicing today. Topics: functions of Muringia and related ritual specialists.

21. Kiringuri, Mwembu wa. Two interviews, December 1969 and January 1970, upper Chure Village, South Imenti. Murungi age-set; estimated age, eighties. Status: curse remover (Muga) and son of a curse remover (Muraguri). Topics: functions of Muga and related ritual specialists; traditional spirit worship; persecution of ritual specialists by the colonial regime.

22. Gacoro, M'Mukira. One interview, December 1969, Miiriga Mieru, North Imenti. Murungi age-set; estimated age, eighties. Status: curse remover (Muga). Topics: work of a Muga and related ritual specialists; traditional spirit worship; persecution of ritual specialists by colonial regime; supernatural societies (Mwaa, Wathua) in North Imenti.

23. Gakuru, Mwamucheke wa. Twelve interviews, December 1969 to June 1970, Gaichau Village, Muthambi. She refused to reveal name of age-set; estimated age, eighties. Nearly blind, thus took unusual pleasure in recounting events of the past. Topics: traditional death and afterlife; traditional religion (spirit worship); supernatural societies, with particular focus on the role of women therein; traditional courtship and marriage in Muthambi. Frequently corroborated data gathered from or about women in other areas.

24. Muiri, M'Muthanya M'Kieberia. Two interviews, April 1970, Kirirwa Village, South Imenti. Murungi (Riungu) age-set; estimated age, eighties. Member of Omo clan (clan of Mugwe). Status: farmer. Topics: traditional functions of the Mugwe and related ritual specialists; initial reactions to colonialism; decline and disappearance of the Mugwe institution (Ugwe).

25. M'Imotho, M'Munyugi. Two interviews, April 1970, near Kirirwa Village, South Imenti. Murungi (Riungu) age-set; estimated age, eighties. Member of Omo clan. Status: farmer. Topics: traditional functions of the Mugwe and related ritual specialists; initial reactions to colonialism.

26. M'Mukiri, Hezikiah. Nine interviews, December 1969 to July 1970, Katheri Village, North Imenti. Murungi (Riungu) age-set; estimated age, eighties. Status: former member of the Njuri Nceke; present member of Kiama Kia Mbiti (council of oldest living age-set). Early convert, United Methodist Mission, Imenti. Highly intelligent, deeply aware of the Meru past and his own role in transmitting it to the young. When younger, actively sought out knowledgeable elders to learn historical traditions; one of the first Methodist Christians to join the Njuri. Now considered by contemporaries as the most historically learned man of his area (North Imenti). Topics: origins of Imenti people; migration onto Mount Kenya; relations with Maasai; Tigania-Katheri wars; history of the Njuri Nceke, witchcraft societies (A-Athi); traditional warfare. Frequently corroborated data from other areas.

27. Gikamata, Gituuru wa. Five interviews, December 1969 to June 1970, Kionyo Village, South Imenti. Kiramana (Kiriambobua) age-set; estimated age, mid-nineties. Status: war leader (Ncamba). Topics: origins of Meru; pre-Meru occupants of Mount Kenya; traditional military tactics, training; persecution of ritual specialists under colonialism. Considered by contemporaries as most historically reliable man in his area (South Imenti). Consistently refused to deviate from original wording of traditions, even when logically flawed. Frequently corroborated data gathered from other areas.

28. M'Mutani, M'Thaara. Fifteen interviews, December 1969 to July 1970, Kauuni Village, Muthambi. Murungi (Riungu) age-set; estimated age, early eighties. Status: warrior; later, chief of warriors, upper Muthambi, under early colonial administration. Extraordinary command of the past. Topics: traditional warfare; impact of colonialism on (Muthambi) warriorhood; origins of Muthambi; supernatural societies; elders' council of Muthambi (Kiama Kya Kibogo).

29. Kirongoro, Matiri wa (Paul). Twelve interviews, December 1969 to July 1970, Muthambi Chief's Camp, Muthambi. Miriti, age-set; estimated age, seventies. Status: farmer, former member, supernatural societies. Unusual interest

in Meru past, specifically traditional forms of war and religion. Topics: traditional spirit worship; cursing; supernatural societies; traditional warfare.

30. Ruganda, Rwito wa. Eight interviews, January to March 1970, Thigaa Village, Mwimbi. Kiramana (Kabaya) age-set (only one remaining in Mwimbi-Muthambi); estimated age, nineties. Status: warrior, farmer. Considered most knowledgeable in area. Topics: origins of Mwimbi; migration to Mount Kenya; earlier occupants; traditional war; cursing; supernatural societies in Mwimbi.

31. M'Mbogore, M'Rutere, Mukungu M'Mbogore, and M'Iniu M'Mbogore. Three brothers, all sons of Mbogore M'Mwendo, former war leader (Ncamba wa Mbui ya Mugongo) for Mwimbi and the first chief of upper Mwimbi under colonial administration. Three interviews, January to March 1970, Chogoria, upper Mwimbi. Miriti and Kiruja age-sets. M'Rutere served as spokesman for all three, the others commenting as required. Topics: traditions of their family, which go back to the initial occupation of Mwimbi area; struggle between Mbogore M'Mwendo and ritual specialists before and after the coming of Europeans; military exploits of Mbogore M'Mwendo.

32. M'Muriithi, Muriuki. Seven interviews, January to April 1970, Kyeni Village, Mwimbi. Murungi (Riungu) age-set; estimated age, early eighties. Status: warrior; thereafter, subordinate of Mbogore M'Mwendo; respected by contemporaries as knowledgeable of the past. Topics: origins of Mwimbi; earlier occupants of Mwimbi region; traditional warfare; Mwimbi council of elders; military role of Mbogore M'Mwendo; expulsion of Cuka.

33. M'Munyari, Kiringo. Five interviews, April 1970, Itura Village, Igembe. Gichunge age-set (Igembe equivalent of Kiramana), only one remaining in Igembe; estimated age, nineties. Considered most knowledgeable in area. Status: warrior. Topics: origin of people of Igembe (Mbe); migration to Mount Kenya; earlier occupants; traditional warfare; origins of warrior councils (Kiama Kia Ramare); supernatural societies.

34. M'Mbarui, Gaichungi Baibuatho. Five interviews, April 1970, Kithetu Village, Igembe. Kilamunya age-set (equivalent of Murungi); estimated age, eighties. Status: warrior. Topics: traditional war; origins of Igembe; supernatural societies.

35. Nguciala, Ikuciambuu. Three interviews, April 1970, Luluma Village, Igembe. Kilamunya age-set (equivalent to Murungi); estimated age, eighties. Status: warrior; farmer alleged former member of Mwaa Igembe. Topics: supernatural societies in Igembe; origins of warriors' council (Kiama Kia Lamale) in Igembe.

36. M'Mutiga, M'Ngaruni. One interview, April 1970, near Luluma Village, Igembe. Kilamunya age-set (equivalent to Murungi); estimated age, eighties. Status: farmer; allegedly former member of the Mwaa supernatural society. Topic: the Mwaa society in Igembe.

37. Gichoro, M'Ikirima wa. One interview, January 1970, Kigane Village, South Imenti. Murungi (Riungu) age-set; estimated age, late eighties. Respected by contemporaries as knowledgeable of past. Status: warrior. Topics: traditional war; council of elders for South Imenti (Njuri ya Kiama).

38. M'Mungania M'Mwongera. One interview, January 1970, Menwe Village, South Imenti. Murungi (Riungu) age-set; estimated age, eighties. Status:

allegedly a member of a supernatural society. Topics: secret societies; ritual and magic.

39. Nkurunge, M'Mukindia wa. One interview, January 1970, Menwe Village, South Imenti. Murungi (Riungu) age-set; estimated age, early eighties. Status: warrior; herder; farmer. Allegedly knowledgeable of "magic" used by ironsmiths. Topics: ironsmiths; relations with agricultural community.

40. M'Irimbere, M'Ikiene (M'Iniu). Two interviews, February 1970, Thimangari Market (Thuura), North Imenti. Murungi (Riungu) age-set; estimated age, eighties. Status: warrior (allegedly war leader); farmer. Topics: traditional warfare; origins of peoples of North Imenti; previous occupants of Imenti area; impact of Europeans on warriors of Thuura.

41. Kabutai, M'Mwongera wa. Two interviews, February 1970, Kibirichia Market and Ntugi Village, Northeast Imenti. Miriti age-set; estimated age, seventies. Status: warrior, farmer. Allegedly connected with A-Athi (hunters). Topics: "magic" of A-Athi ("bite" and "blow"); traditional warfare against Maasai.

42. Gacece, Mathiu wa. Two interviews, February 1970, Kiamogo Village (Kibirichia), Northeast Imenti. Miriti age-set; estimated age, early eighties. Status: forest hunter; farmer. Former member of the Kiama Kia A-Athi. Topics: functions of Kiama Kia A-Athi; protective magic ("bite" and "blow"); cursing; relations of A-Athi to agricultural Meru.

43. Kairanya, Thangara wa. Two interviews, near Kibirichia Market, Northeast Imenti. Miriti age-set; estimated age, seventies. Status: cattle herder. Reputed by contemporaries to be knowledgeable of past. Topics: traditional warfare, weaponry; Meru and Maasai postraid rituals.

44. Mathiu, Majogu wa. One interview, February 1970, Kitheruni Village, Northeast Imenti. Miriti age-set; estimated age, seventies. Status: cattle herder. Alleged to be knowledgeable of the A-Athi. Topics: occupation of Northeast Imenti by present inhabitants; warfare with Maasai, Umpua (Ogiek); hunter, herder groups (A-Athi?) within Northeast Imenti.

45. Mbagine, Kibere wa. Two interviews, February 1970, Kiamogo Village, Northeast Imenti. Miriti age-set; estimated age, seventies. Status: cattle herder. Topic: cattle raiding by Maasai (defensive tactics).

46. M'Mkatemia, M'Nkanata (Kibunja, the "destroyer"). Three interviews, February 1970, near Menwe Village, South Imenti. Miriti age-set; estimated age, seventies. Status: honey hunter. Topics: council of the A-Athi (Kiama Kia A-Athi); magic, rituals of the A-Athi.

47. M'Mungaria, Daudi. Two interviews, February 1970, upper Chure area (near forest edge), South Imenti. Miriti age-set; estimated age, seventies. Status: honey hunter. Topics: work of honey hunters; council of the A-Athi; rituals of the A-Athi; cursing (Urogi).

48. Kathugu, M'Thaara wa. Two interviews, February 1970, Ruguta Village, Muthambi. Murungi (Riungu) age-set; estimated age, eighties. Status: warrior; farmer. Topics: traditional warfare; origins of Muthambi.

49. Kiithithira, M'Ndegwa. Two interviews, February 1970, Iriene Village, Kibirichia, Northeast Imenti. Miriti age-set, estimated age, early eighties. Eldest living member of Ncuunca clan, a Maasai group that was assimilated into

Northeast Meru during the 1870s to 1880s. Status: warrior; farmer. Topics: clan history; Maasai-Meru nonmilitary relationships.

50. Kirenga, M'Kiambati wa. One interview, February 1970, Katheri Village, North Imenti. Murungi age-set; estimated age, eighties. Status: warrior; farmer. Topics: history of Katheri area; the Maasai of Katheri-Tigania wars.

51. Kainyuru, M'Murithi. One interview, February 1970, near Katheri Village, North Imenti. Murungi age-set; estimated age, eighties. Status: warrior; farmer; herder. Topics: Maasai of Katheri; Katheri-Tigania wars.

52. M'Rinyiru, M'Kirera. One interview, February 1970, Mpuri Village (Katheri location), North Imenti. Murungi (Riungu) age-set; estimated age, eighties. Status: warrior; herder. Allegedly descended from the Maasai. Topics: Maasai assimilation into Katheri (rituals of mutual adoption); Tigania-Katheri wars.

53. M'Mungaine, Nguluu. Two interviews, March to June 1970, Kanjalu Village (Kianjai), Tigania. Kiramunya age-set (equivalent to Murungi in Central Meru); estimated age, eighties. Status: herder; farmer. Topics: history of Kianjai area; assimilation of Maasai; Tigania-Katheri (Kianjai) wars.

54. Likira, M'Mucheke. Two interviews, March to June 1970, Nkui Village (Akithii), Tigania, North Meru. Kiramunya age-set; estimated age, eighties. Status: warrior; herder. Topics: history of Akithii area; assimilation of Maasai; Tigania (Akithii)-Katheri wars; raiding tactics against Northeast Imenti.

55. M'Amuru, M'Arusha. Two interviews, April to June 1970, Amatu Village (Mikinduri), Tigania, North Meru. Kiramunya age-set; estimated age, eighties. Status: warrior; herder; farmer. Topics: history of Mikinduri area; assimilation of Maasai; Tigania (Mikinduri) raids against Katheri, Northeast Imenti, Igembe.

56. Kabuthu, M'Nourai wa. One interview, May 1970, near Tigania Mission station (Muthara area), Tigania, North Meru. Kiramunya age-set; estimated age, late eighties. Status: warrior; herder; farmer. Topics: history of Muthara area; assimilation of Maasai; raid against North and Northeast Imenti; elders' council of Tigania-Igembe (the Njuri Nceke).

57. M'Mbuthu, M'Muambe. One interview, May 1970, Muthara, Tigania. Kilamunya age-set; estimated age, eighties. Status: warrior, policeman for colonial administration; farmer. Topics: impact of colonialism on military and judicial councils of Muthara; history of elders' council of Tigania-Igembe.

58. Baimwera, Kairu. Two interviews, March 1970, Mugaani Village, Mwimbi. Miriti age-set; estimated age, early seventies. Status: farmer. Alleged former member of supernatural society. Topic: supernatural societies of Mwimbi.

59. M'Mbatau, M'Ruiga. Three interviews, March 1970, Igoji Township, Igoji. Murungi age-set; estimated age, eighties. Status: warrior; farmer. Former member of supernatural society. Topics: supernatural societies of Igoji; traditional raiding; military resistance to colonial rule by Miutini; persecution of supernatural specialists, societies, under colonialism.

60. Baikare, M'Mungori wa. Two interviews, April 1970, Magundu Village, Muthambi (near Cuka boundary). Murungi (Riungu) age-set; estimated

age, eighties. Status: warrior; farmer. Topics: origins and migration route of Muthambi; military expulsion of Cuka, 1880s.

61. Njara, Karaya wa (Benjamin). Two interviews, April 1970, Kauri Village, Muthambi. Kabuuru age-set (equivalent of Kiruja); estimated age, 60 years. Status: farmer. Former member of supernatural society. Topic: the Mwaa society (Kiama Kia Nkoma) in Muthambi.

62. Informant withheld name. One interview, May 1970, Geto Village, Igoji. Regeria age-set (married Murungi); estimated age, early seventies. Status: alleged member of supernatural society. Topics: supernatural societies in Igoji; role of women within the Kagita; Chigiira, a supernatural society (A-Athi) of unmarried females.

63. Murungi, Kainyu. One interview, May 1970, Mureru Village, Igoji. Regeria age-set (married Murungi); estimated age, late sixties. Status: alleged member of the Kagita, A-Athi. Topic: women's roles in supernatural societies.

64. Gikabu, Mwakireu. One interview, May 1970, Karia Village, Igoji. Regeria age-set (married Murungi); estimated age, late sixties. Status: alleged member of the Kiama Kia Kagita, 1920s. Topics: women's roles in supernatural societies; cursing and curse removal by supernatural societies.

65. Murungi, Gacaba. One interview, May 1970, near Mureru Village, Igoji. She refused to reveal age-set; estimated age, late sixties. Status: allegedly a member of the Kagita (refused to "break oath" on this topic). Topics: women's role within supernatural societies; Chigiira, supernatural society (A-Athi) for unmarried females.

66. M'Muguongo, Mburunga. One interview, May 1970, Mureru Village, Igoji. Murungi age-set; estimated age, early eighties. Status: alleged member of the Kagita. Topics: roles of men, women, within supernatural societies; cursing and curse removal by supernatural societies.

67. Murungi, Jwanina. One interview, May 1970, Mwira jwa Ngondu Village, Igoji. She refused to reveal age-set (married to Murungi). Status: allegedly member of supernatural society. Topic: Chigiira, supernatural society (A-Athi) for unmarried females.

68. M'Ngentu, Neiru. One interview, March 1970, Mugaami Village, Mwimbi. Riungu age-set; estimated age, eighties. Status: warrior; farmer. Topics: origins of Mwimbi; secret societies in upper Mwimbi.

69. M'Mugambe, M'Raria. One interview, June 1970, Mathagwe Village, Igoji. Murungi age-set; estimated age, eighties. Status: warrior; farmer. Topic: origins of Igoji.

70. M'Muga, M'Muga. One interview, June 1970, Kathigiri Village, Igoji. Miriti age-set; estimated age, late seventies. Status: farmer. Topics: origins of Igoji; curse removal in Igoji.

71. Kiruguru, M'Matiri. One interview, June 1970, Rugomo Village, Miutini. Murungi (Riungu) age-set; estimated age, early eighties. Status: warrior; farmer. Topics: origins of Miutini; military resistance to colonialism.

72. Nkarami, Kibuja. One interview, June 1970, Kiamwere Village, Miutini. Murungi (Riungu) age-set; estimated age, early eighties. Status: warrior; farmer. Topics: origins of Miutini; initial resistance to colonialism.

73. Njogu, Matiiri wa. One interview, June 1970, Kioni Village, Miutini. Murungi age-set; estimated age, late eighties. Status: warrior; farmer. Topics: origins of Miutini; resistance of Miutini to people of Kangangi (E. B. Horne, first British administrator).

74. M'Murithi, M'Muga. One interview, June 1970, Ithitu Village, Igoji. Murungi age-set; estimated age, eighties. Status: warrior; cattle herder. Accepted by contemporaries as most knowledgeable of the past. Topics: origins of Miutini, Igoji; military resistance of Miutini to colonialism; supernatural societies (A-Athi) in Miutini, Igoji.

75. M'Mcomba, Muthongomia, and Kirumu Muthongomia. One interview, June 1970, Geto village, Igoji. Mr. M'Mcomba is in Murungi age-set; estimated age, nineties; his spouse, Kirumu, in late seventies. Man's memory is failing; when prodded by wife, he recalls. Status of man: warrior; farmer; allegedly member of supernatural society. Status of woman: allegedly member of supernatural society. Topics: men's and women's roles within the Kagita, A-Athi; cursing and curse removal by secret societies; Chigiira, supernatural society for unmarried females.

76. M'Mwebia, M'Muthara. One interview, June 1970, Kuiri Village, Igoji. Murungi age-set; estimated age, early eighties. Status: warrior; farmer. Parents were A-Athi, thus, he was a member of an A-Athi boys Kiama. Topics: organization, activities, dynamics of supernatural (boys) societies.

77. M'Njage, Mukangu, and Miemba wa Njeru. One interview, June 1970, Muthambi Chief's Camp, Muthambi. Miriti age-set; estimated age, seventies. Mukangu is older, thus served as spokesman for both. Miemba commented and corrected. Status: farmers. Topics: A-Athi in Muthambi; traditional courtship; "cow-in-lawship" (*uthoni wa ngombe*); "girl-in-lawship" (*uthoni wa nkenye*).

78. Rwito, Karuke. One interview, June 1970, Kianjage Village, lower Mwimbi. Murungi (Riungu) age-set; estimated age, early nineties. Status: warrior; farmer. Topics: traditional raiding; resistance of Kanyoro's village (lower Mwimbi) to British control.

79. M'Anampiu, Stephan. Five interviews, December 1969 to April 1970, Meru Teaching Training College, North Imenti. Age-set not given. Status: Master of History and vice-principal, Meru Teacher Training College, North Imenti. Topics: research into origins, history of major clans of North Imenti.

80. M'Mburu, M'Mugambe. One interview, December 1969, Katheri Village, North Imenti. Murungi age-set; estimated age, eighties. Status: warrior; farmer. Topic: Meru traditional religion.

81. M'Mangania, Mwoga. One interview, June 1970, near Kiamwere Village, Miutini. Murungi age-set; estimated age, eighties. Status: warrior; farmer. Topics: origins of Miutini; Miutini raiding patterns; military alliance.

82. M'Irogi, M'Rimberia (Henry). Two interviews, April to June 1970, near Katheri Village, North Imenti. Murungi age-set; estimated age, late seventies. Status: warrior; farmer. Topics: traditional warfare; relations of Katheri (*gaaru*) with Maasai.

83. M'Ringeera, Muchena. Four interviews, April to June 1970, Ruiga Village, North Imenti. Murungi age-set; estimated age, late eighties. Status: war-

rior; farmer. Topics: history of clan (claims ability to trace ancestry back to Mbwaa); origins of Meru; relations with Maasai; obligations of ritual alliance (*gichiaro*).

84. M'Iteria, Gikabu, and Kiagia Njeru. One interview, April 1970, Ithambare Village, Miutini. Both Miriti age-set; estimated age, seventies. Gikabu, the eldest, acted as spokesman. Status: farmers. Topic: training for warriorhood.

85. Thariaba, Baigumba. One interview, June 1970, Kambi ya Kairanya, North Igembe. Kilamunya age-set (Murungi in Imenti); estimated age, eighties. Status: warrior; herder. Topics: earlier occupants of Igembe; invaders of Igembe; tactics of defense.

86. Irembi, M'Mukira wa (Joseph). One interview, March 1970, near Ithambari Primary School, Nkubu, South Imenti. Miriti age-set; estimated age, late seventies. Status: warrior; farmer; former teacher. Intelligent, interested in recording Meru past. Topics: traditional structure of Njuri ya Kiama, South Imenti; Njuri history before colonial era; traditional war; warrior courtship and marriage.

87. Nkuruaru, Kirimi. One interview, March 1970, Karaa Market (near Chogoria), Mwimbi. Kiruji age-set; estimated age, fifties. Father and uncles were Ogiek who made *gichiaro* (ritual alliance) with *miiriga* (ridgetop communities) in upper Mwimbi; subsequently served as "scout." Clan: Rukuruku (Mokogodo?) in Ki-Ogiek; Rukinga in Ki-Mwimbi. Topics: relations of Ogiek with *miiriga* of Mwimbi, in peace (intermarriage, etc.) and war.

88. M'Ringeera, Karema. One interview, February 1970, Ncoore Village, Northeast Imenti. Murungi age-set; estimated age, early eighties. Status: warrior; herder. Alleged to have been visited by ancestral spirits (Nkoma); contact with A-Athi. Topics: traditional spirit worship; Nkoma; relations with A-Athi; Kiama Kia A-Athi.

89. Ng'entu, Mburunga. One interview, January 1970, Chogoria Village, Mwimbi. Murungi age-set; estimated age, early eighties. Status: warrior; farmer; ex-chief of upper Mwimbi, 1930s. Reliable on aspects of precolonial history, unreliable where his own role is concerned. Topics: origins of Mwimbi; early (*gichiaro*) relationship to Tigania, Embu; entry of Mwimbi people onto Mount Kenya.

90. M'Riria, Albert. One interview, June 1970, Kiuni Village, Muitini. Kiruja age set; estimated age, seventies. Witness (as a child) to resistance of Miutini warriors (among them, his father) to E. B. Horne's conquest of their region. Topics: Miutini rebellion, mission intrusion into Igoji.

91. M'Ituke, Paulo. One interview, March 1970, United Methodist Mission, Imenti. Early convert, Methodist Mission Society. Topics: origin of Christianity in Imenti, initial responses to missionaries.

92. Anicheto, Vitalus. One interview, March 1970, Igoji Roman Catholic Mission, Igoji. Early convert, Consolata Roman Catholic Mission. Topics: Initial Meru responses to Catholicism; initial warrior, elder response to first Christian converts.

93. M'Gaichau, Paulo. One interview, March 1970, Mujwa Roman Catholic Mission, Igoji. First Christian convert, (1915?), Mujwa Mission, Consolata Mission Society. Topic: origin of Catholicism in Igoji.

94. Thiriadi, Alice. One interview, March 1970, United Methodist Mission, Imenti. Wife of Isak M'Muga, early convert, Methodist Mission Society. Topic: origins of first generation of female Christians.

95. Makumi, Priscilla. One interview, April 1970, Gikuyu Presbyterian Mission, Gikuyu Township, Kenya. Widow of Daudi Makumi, member of the first party of Gikuyu (Protestant) converts to enter Mwimbi as lay evangelists. Topic: Meru Christianity during the "Makumi era."

96. Wangu, Ismaili. One interview, April 1970, Gikuyu Presbyterian Mission, Gikuyu Township, Kenya. Early Church of Scotland Mission convert, Gikuyu tribe. Second Church of Scotland Evangelist (after Daudi Makumi) to work in the Mwimbi-Cuka region, based at "Gaitungi's mission" (Mwiria ya Mburia Village), October 1920–October 1921. Topic: Meru Christianity during the "Wangu era."

97. M'Raria, Daudi. One interview, January 1970, Chogoria Presbyterian Mission, Chogoria Township, Mwimbi. Early convert, Church of Scotland Mission. Topic: origins of Christianity in Mwimbi.

98. M'Muntu, Josiah. One interview, January 1970, Chogoria Presbyterian Mission, Chogoria Township, Mwimbi. Early convert, Church of Scotland Mission. Topic: origins of Christianity in Mwimbi.

99. M'Murianki, Jotham. One interview, February 1970, Chogoria Township, Mwimbi. Early convert, Church of Scotland Mission. Topic: origins of Christianity in Mwimbi.

100. M'Kirichio, Germano. One interview, February 1970, Mikinduri Roman Catholic Mission, Tigania. Early convert, Athuana (now Mikinduri) Mission. Topic: origins of Christianity in Tigania.

101. M'Mutiga, Samsoni. One interview, February 1970, United Methodist Mission, Imenti. Early convert, Methodist Mission Society, and first Methodist convert to "penetrate" Maua region of Igembe as lay evangelist. Topics: origins of Christianity in Igembe; warrior resistance to Christianity in Maua region.

102. Mbiro, Rahab. One interview, February 1970, Chogoria Township, Mwimbi. Early convert and wife of an early convert, Church of Scotland Mission, Mwimbi, 1920s. Topic: origins of Christianity among Meru women.

103. M'Icirai (last name withheld). One interview, March 1970, Chogoria Township, Mwimbi. Chief cook for Mbogore M'Mwendo during that man's early years as district chief, upper Mwimbi. Topic: resistance by elders to Mbogore's efforts at reform.

Glossary-Index

A- Plural prefix for words referring to human beings. Thus, Ameru means more than one Meru, A-Athi means more than one hunter, and so on.

A-Athi [or *Aathi*] Forest hunters, who formed fringe groups increasingly distinct from mainstream Meru (agriculturalists, herders) while on migration. Each band of A-Athi formed a fringe Kiama or council. Over time, these bands evolved into food-seeking societies that used mild forms of supernaturally based extortion. Perceived by colonial administrators as witchcraft guilds, these groups were destroyed in the late 1920s (56, 57, 313–22).

Achunku "Red men"; Europeans (121).

Acomba [or *Achomba*] Meru term for (Kenya) coast dwellers (121).

African Native Courts (ANC) Originally established by E. B. Horne in 1911, these were revived and nurtured across Meru after 1919 in attempts by the colonial administration to gradually replace Meru tradition with English law. Also known as Local Native Tribunals (270).

Agambe See *Mugambe*

Age-sets Meru social groupings based on age. Membership in age-sets was fixed and permanent. Each age-set was given a name, and historical events were dated by the age-set whose members were warriors at that time. For example, the British conquest took place while Murungi were warriors (11–14).

Akenye Virgins, unmarried girls (286).

All-Meru Local Native Council (LNC) Created in 1925 in an attempt by the colonial administration to gradually replace Meru tradition with English forms of administration (271).

Aruau Junior elders; the heads of families. Apprenticed to senior elders until their sons had reached the age of warriorhood (8).

Askari ya Kanga   "Blanket police": Meru warriors picked by colonial administrators to enforce British authority. Each was given a blanket to symbolize his position. *Askari* means "guard" or "police" in Ki-Swahili (136).

Aturi   Ironsmiths; the earliest Meru fringe group (55).

Authi   Battle vow; a public declaration by each warrior on the eve of battle of what he intended to achieve. Warriors danced out their vows, naked and fully armed, before the entire ridgetop community (144).

Balbo, Giovanni   One of the first Catholic priests to undertake mission work in Meru (Igoji) 1911 (210).

Baraza   Ki-Swahili word for "public meeting" (208).

Battle of Embu   War between Embu and England, 1906, after which the Meru surrendered without resistance (125).

Boma   Ki-Swahili word for "homestead." Adopted by colonial administrators to mean government headquarters, the administrative center. The Meru Boma formed the heart of Meru Town (189).

Bondino, G.   A Catholic priest, stationed in Tigania Mission in the 1920s, who attempted to enter the hut of a branch of Kagita to uncover the secrets of their alleged witchcraft. He was discovered and driven away (278).

Brassington, H.   Doctor and Protestant missionary at Igembe in the late 1920s; a participant in the war against witchcraft from a medical perspective (316).

Butler, R. A. B.   Assistant district commissioner under E. B. Horne (211).

Chanler, William Astor   American explorer who reached Meru in 1892, waging war with both Tigania and Igembe (122).

Chigiira, Kiama of   "Seashell Kiama": a society of women, active in Igoji and Mwimbi before British conquest. Its activities were kept secret from Meru men (and subsequently from the colonial administration); it taught girls correct adult behavior (155).

Chogoria   Site of the first Church of Scotland Mission, Upper Mwimbi (229).

Church of Scotland Presbyterian Mission (CSM)   First Christian mission to enter Mwimbi, 1921. Now known as Presbyterian Church of East Africa (229).

Circumcision, female   Meru ritual in which the female clitoris and major and minor labia were partially removed at puberty, to mark the onset of adulthood and consequent availability for courtship (133).

Crawford, D. R.   District commissioner, 1920. Created a General Kiama for all Meru to replace existing Meru institutions. Ignored by all Meru outside the colonial administration, it collapsed for lack of issues to resolve (268).

Crop Protection, Kiamas of   Groups of land owners who adapted A-Athi magic for the protection of their growing crops, e.g., Kiama Kia Wathua (104–8).

Cucu   Old Meru word for a mainland tribe near the island of Mbwaa, probably Somali (20).

Cuka [or *Chuka*]   Southern Meru subtribe, often considered separate from the other Meru regions because of its hostility toward all other groups. Allied only to Tharaka and Miutini (4).

Cushitic-speaking peoples   Members of Galla, Boran, and Oromo tribes, known to the Meru as Mukuguru, Ukara, and Muoko. Driven from Mount Kenya by Meru subtribes, 1730s–1750s (81).

Dominuki   See *M'Minyuki*

Embu   A people living immediately south of Meru, on the southeast slope of Mount Kenya (125).

Gaaru   A huge hut that served as military barracks to warriors (142).

Gichiaro   A ritual alliance between two groups, based on a mutual agreement to become kin (91, 95).

Gikuyu [or *Kikuyu*]   A people who live on the southeastern, southern, and western slopes of Mount Kenya (5, 125–26).

Githangaria   Meru age-set; warriors around 1787 (13).

Githarie   Meru age-set; warriors around 1748 (13).

Hopkins, J. Gerald H.   Assistant district commissioner under Frank M. Lamb, 1928; district commissioner, 1929. Continued Lamb's "anti-witchdoctor campaign," completing the destruction of the Meru fringe societies: Kagita, A-Athi, Mwaa, etc. He then began reviving elements of the Njuri system, hoping to integrate it into the Local Native Tribunals and other units at the lower levels of colonial administration (305ff., 323 ff.).

Horne, Edward Butler   British conqueror of Meru, 1907, then its first colonial administrator, 1907–17. Known to the Meru as "Kangangi" (little walker) because of his diminutive stature and energetic marches throughout the region (131, 134ff.).

Hut tax   Tax imposed on Meru after British conquest; initially set at one coin per hut. Since the Meru had no money, hut owners had to seek work from the British to pay it (176).

Igembe   Northern Meru subtribe; the most remote social grouping (4).

Igoji [or *Igosi*]   Central Meru subtribe (4).

Imenti   Central and largest Meru subtribe (4).

Irea itune   The Tana River; the "red sea" allegedly crossed by the pre-Meru on their journey across the mainland (52).

Irvine, Arthur Clive   Doctor and founder of the Chogoria Mission Station, Upper Mwimbi, 1921 (237–38).

Ka-Aga   "Little place of the curse removers"; a sacred grove used only by gatherings of Aga for their rituals. Selected as site of the first United Methodist Mission in Meru, 1912 (208).

Kaburia   Meru age-set. Warriors around 1880; apprentice elders and household heads in 1907, the year of Meru's subjection by Britain (13, 152).

Kagairo   Fragmentation; the era (ca. 1730s) when the pre-Meru people divided into subtribes (61).

Kagita, Kiama of   Supernatural society of both men and women in the age-set of apprentice elders and household heads. From its beginning as a society of crop protectors, it evolved into an association of dancers and sexual exhibitionists who used both magic and mild forms of extortion to obtain food. Perceived by the colonial administration as a witchcraft society (151ff.).

Kalenjin-speaking peoples   Ogiek tribal groups, known to the Meru as Umpua and Agumba. Driven off Mount Kenya by Meru subtribes, 1730–1750 (84).

Kallai "Gazelle"; a type of A-Athi magic used to impose a curse (Mugiro) on whole communities of mainstream Meru (79).

Kamuchunku "Little whites"; a pejorative term applied by Meru to other Meru who helped the British conquerors (141).

KAR King's African Rifles, a military force composed of British officers and African mercenaries, which took part in the subjugation of Meru and neighboring Embu, 1906–1907 (128).

Karia "Carriers"; members of the East Africa Carrier Corps during World War I. Thousands died from exhaustion, hunger, and disease. The diseases they brought home also spread through Meru, killing thousands more (237, 256).

Kauganyama, Kiama Kya "Council of Meat Chewers"; an exploitative Kiama selected by Mwimbi chief M'Mbogore wa Mwendo to enforce his personal authority in the name of British colonialists, 1910–1920 (198).

Kaundu, Kiama Kia "Council of Darkness"; daughter-unit of a larger council (whether Nkome or Njuri), which would meet separately from the parent body to resolve an issue. Perceived by colonial administration in the 1920s as a secret witchcraft society (183).

Keiea Parasitic vine that grows on a tree held sacred to A-Athi; a major component in their magic (79).

Ki- Prefix meaning "the language of." Thus, Ki-Meru is the Meru language, Ki-Americani the American language (15).

Kiama Council or association of Meru males within a single age-set; these gatherings formed the governing bodies of Meru (15, 23). Other Kiamas, including all-female groups and mixed groups, formed in response to various pressures.

Kiariga North Imenti prophet, one of several who prophesied the coming of the Europeans between the 1860s and the 1890s (94).

Kidnappers, Kiamas of Food-gathering Kiamas that kidnapped children during times of famine and ransomed them for food, e.g., Kiama Kia Kirima, 1890s (110–11).

Kiramana The oldest living Meru age-set in 1969–1970, in their early nineties (13).

Kirima Kia Maara [or *Kirimaara*] "Shining Mountain"; Mount Kenya (65).

Kiruja Meru age-set; warriors around 1826 (13).

Kivunja "The destroyer"; Meru district commissioner in the early 1920s (identity unknown) who banned the Meru Njuri system, sending it underground (269).

Koome Njoe Meru curse-remover during the Meru enslavement by the Nguo Ntuni, who led the subsequent flight to freedom (48).

Kubai Meru age-set; warriors around 1868 (13).

Lamb, Frank M. Meru District Commissioner, 1927–1928. Began the "anti-witchdoctor campaign" that destroyed Meru's supernatural fringe societies, notably Kagita and A-Athi (255).

Lambert, H. E. Meru district commissioner, 1933–1935 and 1939–1942; anthropologist, historian, and linguist who wrote extensively about the Meru past. Successfully revived elements of the traditional Njuri system, integrating them into the lower levels of colonial administration (323ff.).

Lamu archipelago   Original home of the pre-Meru people (23, 24).

Local Native Tribunal (LNT)   Law-making body developed by colonial administrators in 1913 to replace the Njuri Nceke and similar councils throughout Meru (193).

Maa, ol Maa   Maasai language and those who speak it: Il Maasai (pastoral groups) or Il Oikop (agricultural groups). Both the language and the people are known to the Meru as "Uru" (89–90).

Maasai   Cattle-owning people who roamed the plains adjacent to Mount Kenya's northeastern slope. Frequent raiders of Meru herds and flocks (5).

McKeag, Victor M.   Meru district commissioner, 1937–1939 and 1942–1945. Successfully revived elements of the traditional Njuri system, integrating them into the lower levels of colonial administration (323ff.).

Maingi, Simon   First Gikuyu Christian to practice western medicine in Meru, 1915 (231).

Makumi, Daudi   First Gikuyu Christian to evangelize in Meru, 1915 (231).

Marua   Fermented millet beer, a prerequisite for all Meru rituals; exchanged with forest hunters for uuki, a fermented honey wine (289).

Mbaringu   Meru age-set, warriors around 1800 (13).

Mbeere [or *Emberre*]   A people living to the southeast of Meru, adjacent to the southeast slope of Mount Kenya (60, 126).

Mbogore M'Mwendo   War leader in upper Mwimbi, sent to negotiate that region's surrender to E. B. Horne. Subsequently a chief within the colonial administration, known for the zeal with which he tried to supplant African customs with those of Britain (130ff.).

Mbujo [or *Mbuju*]   Poisonous substance imported from the Kamba region, allegedly to intensify the effect of a curse. In the mid-1920s, colonial administrators believed that a league of such cursers (the Mbujo league) was operating against the British government (274, 294).

Mb-u-u-u!   Danger! A warning cry (293).

Mbwaa [or *Mbwa, Mbwara*]   Meru island of origin, today known as Manda Island, within the Lamu archipelago (19).

Meiru   Maasai term for "black forest"; the Meru may have adopted this name as their own (92).

Michubu   Meru age-set; warriors when pre-Meru subtribes migrated up the slopes of Mount Kenya, ca. 1740s, 1760s (13, 66).

Miraa   *Cathus edulis;* a twig that induces a state of mild euphoria when chewed. More commonly known as *quat.* Chewing it was one of the privileges of Meru elderhood (181).

Miriti   Meru age-set. Men in their mid-sixties to mid-seventies in 1969–1970. Youths during the British conquest, 1906–1907 (2, 13).

Miutini   Smallest Meru subtribe, located between Igoji and Imenti (4).

Mkanda Channel   Channel between Mbwaa and the mainland, across which the pre-Meru fled to escape enslavement (22).

M'Minyuki   Tiganian war leader who befriended (and was misnamed by) W. A. Chanler, one of the first whites to reach Meru in 1892. Subsequently appointed headman, then chief, under the British administration (124, 219).

M'Mutiga, Samsoni   First Gikuyu Christian to enter Igembi to evangelize for Church of Scotland Mission, 1919 (246).

MOS   Meru Oral Source; a listing in the bibliography that describes each informant (16).

Mount Kenya   Long-dormant volcano, over 17,000 feet, in central Kenya. The Meru-speaking peoples live on and adjacent to its northeast slope (65).

Mpaatha   First, prophetic leader of the pre-Meru, who "rolled back the waters" to lead them to freedom (99).

Mu-   Singular prefix for words referring to human beings. Thus, Mu-Meru means one Meru, Mu-Athi one hunter, and so on (14).

Muga   Curse-remover; one who ritually removes a curse (Mugiro) imposed by a Murogi (15, 35).

Mugambe   Spokesman of a Kiama, who represented the group in dealings with outsiders (132).

Mugiro   1. Verbal curse; a wish to inflict harm. 2. Ritually created condition of impurity inflicted by a verbal curse. If not ritually removed, the condition brings calamity upon the victim (30, 31).

Mugwe   1. Prophet for an entire segment of the Meru-speaking peoples (e.g., Tigania). 2. Transmitter of a blessing from Ngai, the Meru high god (3, 32, 72).

Mukuna Ruku   "Wood beater"; a mythological trader, allegedly an Arab from the Kenya coast, who appears at several points in Meru mythology as a merchant who exchanged goods without speaking a word (46–47).

Mukuruma   Meru age-set; warriors around the 1730s, when pre-Meru subtribes crossed the Tana River and entered a desert to reach the base of Mount Kenya (13, 66).

Munene ya Kanga   "Blanket chief"; a war leader designated as a ridgetop chief by British administrators, who gave each chief a black blanket to symbolize his authority (131).

Muringia   Curse detector; his task was to identify the individual who originally "cursed" another through the agency of a Murogi (36).

Murogi   Professional curser; one who places a verbal curse upon another Meru, often for a fee (15, 33).

Muroria   Prophet who examines the immediate future of a single individual (32).

Murungi   Meru age-set in their late seventies to mid-eighties in 1969–1970. Warriors during the British conquest, 1906–1907 (2).

Muthaka (pl: *Nthaka*)   Warrior (10).

Muthambi   Southern Meru subtribe (4).

Mwaa, Kiama of   "Kiama of Fools"; an association of transsexual men who banded together to sing and dance in exchange for food. Perceived by both mainstream Meru and the colonial administration as a witchcraft society (113ff., 157).

Mwiji   Small boy, not yet circumcised. A grave insult to an adult (244).

Mwimbi   Southern Meru subtribe (4).

Mwiriga   Long, narrow ridgetop, inhabited by one or more Meru clans, running up Mount Kenya (15, 70).

Mzee   Elder; one whose sons have been circumcised. Also a title of respect (8, 10).

Ncaama, Ncaama Zha Anene   Servants, chiefs' men. Former Meru warriors picked by chiefs to enforce their orders after British conquest; they subsequently degenerated into bands of semi-legalized plunderers, extorting meat, labor, and sexual services (195–97).

Ndindi   "Bones"; sticks from a sacred A-Athi tree, representing a type of A-Athi magic that automatically cursed anyone who passed them (77).

Ndinguri   Elder boys, usually aged between eleven and fifteen, not yet circumcised. The Kiama Kia Ndinguri would be a "Council of Eldest Boys." This group was the first to be drawn to the Christian missions (10, 216).

Ngaa   An early name for the pre-Meru peoples, ca. 1700–1730 (53).

Ngaaruni   Arid place; a semi-desert region the pre-Meru crossed on their migration, from which they took their name (53).

Ngome, Kiama Kia   Council of Councils for Mwimbi and Muthambe combined; equivalent to the Njuri ya Kiama of Imente and Njuri Nceke of Tigania-Igembe (182).

Nguchua   "Claws"; small branches, heated on one side to curl into claws, representing a type of A-Athi magic that automatically cursed anyone who passed them. Placed before the huts of mainstream Meru by A-Athi. (78, 293).

Nguo Ntuni   "Red clothes"; the Meru name for invaders of their island (Mbwaa) who subsequently enslaved them (ca. 1700). Probably East African coastal Arabs (45).

Nguthugua   Meru age-set; warriors around 1813 (13).

Ngweko   "Bundling"; a sexual practice in which courting couples lay together, partially clothed, and caressed one another, without full sexual intercourse (147, 148).

Njage wa Kathiore   War leader of Muthambe during British conquest. Subsequently appointed first "blanket chief" of Muthambe under colonial administration (133).

Njeru   The color white (50).

Njiru   The color black (50).

Njuguma, Kiama Kya   "Council of the Throwing Club"; the highest elders' council within Mwimbi and Muthambi (182).

Njuri, Njuri Nceke   A Kiama of Kiamas; the highest council in northern Meru, and subsequently in all Meru (73, 180).

Njuri Mpingiri, Njuri Mpere   "Daughter councils"; from Njuri Nceke. These were smaller groups that would break off from the main body and go into seclusion to resolve specific issues. Labeled by the colonial administration as secret witchcraft societies (181, 287).

Nkima   "Skull"; an animal skull, or a ball of wax wrapped in animal-skin strips, representing a type of A-Athi magic used to protect stationary sites (76).

Nkireba   Secret sessions. When deadlocked, a Kiama or Njuri sent a daughter body into Nkireba to resolve the problem (182).

Nkoma   Spirits; e.g., ancestral spirits (16).

Nkomango, Kiama Kia   "Council of the Throwing Stone"; the highest elders' council within each of the three regions that made up today's Imenti. In times of crisis, spokesmen from each group would meet to form a single body, known as Njuri ya Biama (182).

Nkuthuku   Meru age-set; warriors during the Meru migration, ca. 1720s (13, 59).

Ntaane [sing: *Mutaani*]   Just-circumcised boys, those who had not yet joined the warriors and thus reached full adulthood (10).

Ntangi   Meru age-set; warriors when the pre-Meru fled Mbwaa, ca. 1700 (13).

Nthaka ya Kristo [or *Ikristo*]   "Warriors for Christ"; i.e., Christian converts (212).

Ntuiko   Ritualized transfer of administrative authority between two Meru age-sets (325).

Ntuni   The color red (50).

Nturutimi   Meru age-set; warriors around 1856 (13).

Nyambeni Mountains   Low range of hills to the northeast of Mount Kenya, home to the Igembe subtribe (66).

Ogiek   A forest-dwelling people whose economy was based on hunting for meat and gathering honey. Some segments had shifted to a cattle-herding economy on the plains. Because they adopted many of the languages and cultures of neighboring tribes, their own traditions have largely disappeared (5).

Orde-Browne, E. G. St. J.   First district officer of Meru's southern (Nithi) division, including Mwimbi, Cuka, and Muthambi. Known by the Meru as "Kiraune." Wrote extensively on Nithi customs (178).

Platts, W. A. F.   First assistant district commissioner, under E. B. Horne. His wife, Madeleine Platts, wrote a memoir of her life as the first European woman (175).

Ratanya [or *Latanya*]   Meru age-set; warriors around 1774 (13).

Ridgetop rebellions   A series of ridgetop (Mwiriga) revolts against British colonial authority in the first years after British conquest. Suppressed by gunfire, 1909–1911 (176).

Secret speech   One of the "secrets of Kiama," and one component of elders' wisdom. Oblique speech, using proverbs, allegories, syllogisms, and riddles that have meaning only to other members of one's age-set, which therefore allows conversation in the presence of enemies (307).

Star grass zone   A narrow, fertile ecological zone at 4,000–5,000 feet on Mount Kenya; the major population zone for the Meru peoples (67).

Stomach Kiamas   Food-gathering Kiamas that used magic and ritual to extort food during periods of famine from the 1880s until the 1930s, e.g., Kiama Kia Wathi (108, 161).

Tharaka [or *Thaaka*]   An eastern Meru subtribe, often considered separate from the other Meru groups, because of its history of warfare with almost all of the other groups. Allied only to Cuka and Miutini (5, 22).

Tigania   A northern Meru subtribe (5).

Ua   "Blow"; a type of A-Athi magic (75, 159). *See also* Uma

Uga   Curse-removal; removal of the condition of Mugiro through ritual. Thus, a cleansing oath (34, 324ff.).

Ugambe Spokesmanship, leadership; leaders (Agambe) were selected by each age-set for such qualities as wisdom and oratorical skills (142–44).

Ugwe 1. Prophecy. 2. Transmission of a blessing from Ngai, the Meru high god (32).

Uma "Bite"; a type of A-Athi magic. Subsequently both Uma and Ua evolved into war magic, then magic to protect crops, and then magic to extort food from crop growers (75, 159).

Uringia Curse-detection through ritual (36).

Urogi A system of cursing another person, using verbal incantations, rituals, and herbal, mineral, or animal compounds. Used to invoke supernatural intervention (ancestral curses) to bring illness or physical calamity upon a chosen victim. Mistranslated as "witchcraft." In fact, it is a form of social control using rituals to generate economic penalties for violations of communal norms (3, 15).

Uroria Prophecy of the immediate future of a single individual (32).

Uuki Fermented honey-wine; produced by forest hunters as a prerequisite to every ritual and for exchange with mainstream Meru for millet beer (Marua) and millet porridge (289).

Wangu, Ismaili Third Gikuyu Christian convert to enter Meru as a Church of Scotland missionary, 1919 (233).

War on witchcraft Campaign carried on 1927–1929 by colonial administrators and those of their Meru followers (including Mbogore wa Mwendo) who by now shared their ideas (309ff.).

Wathua A Kiama of crop protection, late 1800s–1930s (104).

Worthington, R. T. First Methodist missionary to enter Imenti, 1912. Founder, United Methodist Mission (UMM) (207–8).

Compositor: BookMasters, Inc.
Text: 10/13 Sabon
Display: Sabon
Printer: Braun-Brumfield, Inc.
Binder: Braun-Brumfield, Inc.